ML for the Working Programmer

D0506705

ML for the Working Programmer

Lawrence C. Paulson
Computer Laboratory and Clare College, University of Cambridge

CAMBRIDGE
UNIVERSITY PRESS

Published by the Press Syndicate of the University of Cambridge
The Pitt Building, Trumpington Street, Cambridge CB2 1RP
40 West 20th Street, New York, NY 10011–4211, USA
10 Stamford Road, Oakleigh, Melbourne 3166, Australia

© Cambridge University Press 1991

First published 1991
First paperback edition (with corrections) 1992
Reprinted 1993

Printed in Great Britain at the University Press, Cambridge

Library of Congress cataloguing in publication data available

British Library cataloguing in publication data available

ISBN 0 521 39022 2 hardback
ISBN 0 521 42225 6 paperback

The cover illustration is taken from *Work* by Ford Madox Brown
© Manchester City Art Galleries, and is reproduced with their
permission.

Trademarks. Miranda is a trademark of Research Software Limited. Sun is a trademark of Sun Microsystems. Unix is a trade mark of AT&T Bell Laboratories. Poplog is a trademark of the University of Sussex. MLWorks is a trademark of Harlequin Limited.

Dedication. For Sue and Nathaniel.

DISCLAIMER OF WARRANTY

The programs listed in this book are provided 'as is' without warranty of any kind. We make no warranties, express or implied, that the programs are free of error, or are consistent with any particular standard of merchantability, or that they will meet your requirements for any particular application. They should not be relied upon for solving a problem whose incorrect solution could result in injury to a person or loss of property. If you do use the programs or procedures in such a manner, it is at your own risk. The author and publisher disclaim all liability for direct, incidental or consequential damages resulting from your use of the programs, modules or functions in this book.

CONTENTS

A sequent calculus for first-order logic. Processing terms and formulae in ML. Tactics and the proof state. Searching for proofs.

PREFACE

This book originated in lectures on Standard ML and functional programming. It can still be regarded as a text on functional programming — one with a pragmatic orientation, in contrast to the rather idealistic books that are the norm — but it is primarily a guide to the effective use of ML. It even discusses ML's imperative features.

Readers are expected to have written programs in languages such as Pascal or C, and to know basic concepts such as stacks, queues and sorting. Some of the material requires an understanding of discrete mathematics, namely sets and elementary logic.

The organization reflects my experience with teaching. Higher-order functions appear late, in Chapter 5. They are usually introduced at the very beginning with some contrived example that only confuses students. Higher-order functions are conceptually difficult and require thorough preparation. This book begins with basic types, lists and trees. When higher-order functions are reached, a host of motivating examples is at hand.

The exercises vary greatly in difficulty. They are not intended for assessing students, but for providing practice, broadening the material and provoking discussion.

Because Standard ML is fairly new on the scene, many institutions will not have a compiler. The following is a partial list of existing Standard ML compilers, with contact addresses. The examples in this book were developed under Poly/ML and Standard ML of New Jersey. I have not tried the other compilers.

To obtain **Poly/ML**, contact Abstract Hardware Ltd, The Howell Building, Brunel University, Uxbridge UB8 3PH, England.

To obtain **Standard ML of New Jersey**, contact David Mac-Queen, AT&T Bell Laboratories, 600 Mountain Avenue, Murray Hill, NJ 07974, USA. This compiler is available by FTP. Connect to `research.att.com`; login as `anonymous` with your name as password; set binary mode; transfer files from the directory `dist/ml`.

To obtain **Poplog Standard ML**, contact Integral Solutions Ltd, Unit 3, Campbell Court, Bramley, Basingstoke RG26 5EG, England.

To obtain **MLWorks**, contact Harlequin Limited, Barrington Hall, Barrington, Cambridge CB2 5RG, England.

The programs in this book will be circulated by electronic mail. Send requests to me, `lcp@cl.cam.ac.uk` — but, please, only after checking that they are not already available at your site.

Acknowledgements. The editor, David Tranah, assisted with all stages of the writing and suggested the title. Graham Birtwistle, Glenn Bruns and David Wolfram read the text carefully. Dave Berry, Simon Finn, Mike Fourman, Kent Karlsson, Robin Milner, Richard O'Keefe, Keith van Rijsbergen, Nick Rothwell, Mads Tofte, David N. Turner and the staff of Harlequin also commented on the text. A. Appel, G. Bierman, P. Brabbin, R. Brooksby G. Cousineau, L. George, M. Gordon, M. Hansen, D. Kindred, K. Mughal, T. Nipkow, K. Olender, R. Thomas, R. Toal and H. Wilson found errors in previous printings. Piete Brooks, John Carroll and Graham Titmus helped with the computers. I wish to thank Dave Matthews for developing Poly/ML, which was for many years the only efficient implementation of Standard ML.

Of the many works in the bibliography, Abelson & Sussman (1985), Bird & Wadler (1988) and Burge (1975) have been especially helpful. Reade (1989) contains useful ideas for implementing lazy lists in ML.

The Science and Engineering Research Council has supported LCF and ML in numerous research grants over the past 15 years.

I wrote most of this book while on leave from the University of Cambridge. I am grateful to the Computer Laboratory and Clare College for granting leave, and to the University of Edinburgh for accommodating me for six months.

Finally, I would like to thank Sue for all she did to help, and for tolerating my daily accounts of the progress of every chapter.

1

Introduction

The first ML compiler was built in 1977. Recently the language has grown in popularity, attracting users in many countries. Various dialects have appeared, but as happened with Lisp, the programming community has got together to develop and promote a common language. This language is called Standard ML — sometimes sml, or just ML. Efficient and reliable Standard ML compilers are available. Standard ML resembles Lisp in certain respects, but has a number of advantages.

ML's syntax for function definitions is highly readable. **Pattern-matching** eliminates the need for 'destructor' functions like Lisp's CAR and CDR. ML also does away with Lisp's many parentheses.

ML's **polymorphic types** prevent run-time type errors, while retaining much of the flexibility of typeless languages. For each function definition, ML infers a type that is as general as possible.

ML's **modules** may be the most advanced of any language. The ML **functor** extends the usual notion of generic module.

Like Lisp, ML supports procedural programming with assignments, references and input/output commands. But ordinary variables cannot be updated, and the procedural constructs have been kept to a minimum. ML is mainly for **functional programming**.

Programmers experienced with C, Pascal, etc., will need to learn about functional programming in order to use Standard ML effectively. This book is for them. It is a programming manual, not a reference manual; it covers the major aspects of ML without getting bogged down with every detail. It devotes some time to theoretical principles, but is mainly concerned with efficient algorithms and practical programs.

Functional Programming

Fortran, the first high-level programming language, gave programmers the arithmetic expression. No longer did they have to code sequences of additions, loads and stores on registers: the FORmula TRANslator did this for them. Why are expressions so important? Not because they are familiar: the Fortran syntax for

$$\sqrt{\frac{\sin^2 \theta}{1 + |\cos \phi|}}$$

has but a passing resemblance to that formula. Let us consider the advantages of expressions in detail. Expressions in Fortran can have side-effects, but let us restrict attention to pure expressions.

Expressions have a recursive structure. A typical expression like

$$f(E_1 + E_2) - g(E_3)$$

is built out of other expressions E_1, E_2 and E_3, and may itself form part of a larger expression.

The value of an expression is given recursively in terms of the values of its subexpressions. The subexpressions can be evaluated in any order, or even in parallel.

Expressions can be transformed using mathematical laws. For instance, replacing $E_1 + E_2$ by $E_2 + E_1$ does not affect the value of the expression above, thanks to the commutative law of addition. This ability to substitute equals for equals is called **referential transparency**. In particular, an expression may safely be replaced by its value.

Commands share most of these advantages. In structured programming languages like Pascal, commands have a recursive structure. The meaning of a command like

> while B_1 do (if B_2 then C_1 else C_2)

can be given in terms of the meanings of its parts. Commands even enjoy referential transparency: laws like

> (if B then C_1 else C_2); $C \equiv$
> if B then $(C_1; C)$ else $(C_2; C)$

can be proved and applied as substitutions.

However, the meaning of an expression is simply the result of evaluating it, which is why subexpressions can be evaluated independently of each other. The meaning of an expression can be extremely simple, like the number 3. The meaning of a command is a state transformation or something equally complicated. Therefore, commands satisfy few interesting laws. To understand a command, you have to understand its effect on an entire program state, and that can be too much to grasp at once.

1.1 *Expressions in procedural programming languages*

How far have programming languages advanced since Fortran? Consider Euclid's Algorithm, which is defined by recursion, for computing the Greatest Common Divisor (GCD) of two natural numbers:

$$gcd(0, n) = n$$

$$gcd(m, n) = gcd(n \bmod m, m) \qquad \text{for } m > 0$$

In Pascal, a procedural language, most people would code the GCD as an imperative program:

```
function gcd(m,n: integer): integer;
  var prevm: integer;
begin
  while m<>0 do
      begin prevm := m;  m := n mod m;  n := prevm  end;
  gcd := n
end;
```

Here it is in Standard ML as a functional program:

```
fun gcd(m,n) =
        if m=0 then n
             else gcd(n mod m, m);
```

The imperative program, though coded in a 'high-level' language, is hardly clearer or shorter than a machine language program. It repeatedly updates three quantities, one of which is just a temporary storage cell. Proving that it correctly implements Euclid's algorithm requires Floyd-Hoare proof rules — a tedious enterprise. In contrast, the functional version obviously implements Euclid's Algorithm.

A recursive program in Pascal would be only a slight improvement. Recursive procedure calls are seldom implemented efficiently. Thirty years after its introduction to programming languages, recursion is still regarded as something to eliminate from programs. Correctness proofs for recursive procedures have a sad history of complexity and errors.

Expressions in procedural languages have progressed little beyond Fortran; they have not kept up with developments in data structures. A Pascal record can represent a date, but there are no record-valued expressions. To express a date in Pascal we must declare a record variable and assign into its fields; a function cannot return a date as its result. Similarly, Pascal has no notation for the value of an array. If something happens to be represented by an array then it cannot be returned by a function.

Nor do Pascal expressions satisfy the usual mathematical laws. An optimizing compiler might transform $f(z)+u/2$ into $u/2+f(z)$. However, these expressions may not compute the same value if the 'function' f changes the value of u. The meaning of an expression in Pascal involves states as well as values. For all practical purposes, referential transparency has been lost.

In a purely functional language there is no state. Expressions satisfy the usual mathematical laws (excluding real arithmetic, which is approximate). Purely functional programs can also be written in Standard ML. However, ML is not pure because of its assignments and input/output commands. The ML programmer whose style is 'almost' functional had better not be lulled into a false sense of referential transparency.

1.2   *What are functional programs like?*

Functional programs work with values, not states. Their tools are expressions, not commands. How can assignments, arrays and loops be dispensed with? Does not the outside world have state? These questions pose real challenges, but the functional programmer can exploit a wide range of data structures and techniques to solve problems.

Functions. Expressions consist mainly of function applications. To increase the power of expressions, functions must be freed from arbitrary restrictions. Functions must be allowed to take any type of arguments and return any type of result. As we shall see, 'any type' includes functions themselves, which can be treated like other data. The terms **functional programming** and **applicative programming** (which mean the same thing) refer to those function applications.

Recursion. Variables in a functional program get their values from outside (when a function is called) or by definition. They cannot be updated, but recursive calls can produce a changing series of argument values. Recursion is easier to understand than iteration — if you do not believe this, recall our two GCD programs. Recursion eliminates the baroque looping constructs of procedural languages.

Lists and trees. Collections of data are processed as lists or trees. Lists suffice for most purposes, such as sorting and even matrix operations. Balanced trees permit random access with the same theoretical efficiency as arrays, although arrays are faster in real time. Trees play key roles in symbolic computation, representing logical terms and formulae in theorem provers.

Higher-order functions. Functions themselves are computational values. Even Fortran lets a function be passed as an argument to another function, but few procedural languages let function values play a full role in data structures.

A **higher-order** function (or **functional**) is a function that operates on other functions. The functional *map*, when applied to a function f, returns another function; that function takes

$$[x_1, \ldots, x_n] \quad \text{to} \quad [f(x_1), \ldots, f(x_n)].$$

Another higher-order function, when applied to a function f and value e, returns

$$f(\ldots f(f(e, x_1), x_2), \ldots, x_n).$$

If $e = 0$ and $f = +$ (yes, the addition operator is a function) then we get the sum of $x_1, \ldots, x_n$, computed by

$$(\cdots ((0 + x_1) + x_2) + \cdots) + x_n.$$

If $e = 1$ and $f = \times$ then we get their product, computed by

$$(\cdots ((1 \times x_1) \times x_2) \times \cdots) \times x_n.$$

Other computations are expressed by suitable choices for f and e.

Infinite data structures. Infinite lists like $[1, 2, 3, \ldots]$ can be given a computational meaning. Adding them to our language can be of great help when tackling sophisticated problems. Infinite lists are processed using **lazy evaluation**, which ensures that no value — or part of a value — is computed until it is actually needed to obtain the final result. An infinite list never exists in full; it is rather a process for computing successive elements upon demand.

The search space in a theorem prover may form an infinite tree, whose success nodes form an infinite list. Different search strategies, like depth-first and breadth-first, produce different lists of success nodes. The list can be given to another part of the program, which need not know how it was produced.

Infinite lists can also represent sequences of inputs and outputs. Many of us have encountered this concept in the **pipes** of the Unix operating system. A chain of processes linked by pipes forms a single process. Each process consumes its input when available and passes its output along a pipe to the next process. Thus a large file can undergo several transformations without storing the result of each intermediate stage. Mathematically, every process is a function from inputs to outputs, and the chain of processes is their composition.

Input and output. Communication with the outside world, which has state, is hard to reconcile with functional programming. Infinite lists handle sequential input and output (as mentioned above), but interactive programming and process communication are thorny issues. One idea is that a function could compute a sequence of commands to the imperative world. But when can a function see the result of a communication? Researchers are investigating these questions.

1.3   *Languages for Functional Programming*

Purely functional languages are mainly vehicles for research into functional programming. Countless such languages exist; here are a few major ones. John Backus (1978) introduced the language FP in his Turing Award Lecture, which attracted much attention; FP provides many higher-order functions (called 'combining forms'), but the programmer may not define new ones. Miranda is an elegant language by David Turner (1986); it adopts lazy evaluation and ML-style polymorphic types. Lazy ML is a dialect of ML with lazy evaluation; its compiler generates efficient code (Augustsson & Johnsson, 1989). Haskell was designed by a committee of researchers as a common language (Hudak & Wadler, 1990).

The term 'functional language' can be misleading. Many programming languages permit some functional techniques, while pure functions can express a style that is patently imperative. Most working functional code is embedded in imperative systems, and these are written in impure languages such as Lisp and ML.

Lisp introduced recursive functions over lists and trees (McCarthy et al., 1962). Many compiling techniques for functional programming, such as garbage collection (a method of reclaiming storage), originated with Lisp. The language includes low-level features that can be misused to disastrous effect. Only a few dialects, including Scheme and Common Lisp, provide true higher-order functions. Although many Lisp programs are entirely imperative, the first functional programs were written in Lisp.

Standard ML, of course, is the subject of this book. Most ML dialects, while cleaner than Lisp, include imperative features. Only Lazy ML is purely functional.

Functional programming techniques are used in artificial intelligence (AI), formal methods, computer aided design, and other tasks involving symbolic computation. They have also been investigated for numerical processing, especially on dataflow computers and other highly parallel machines.

1.4 *The efficiency of functional programming*

A functional program typically carries a large run-time system with a resident compiler. It may not use arrays, which are highly efficient in space and time. String and bit-vector operations are seldom available. Despite all this, most functional programs should run nearly as fast as their procedural counterparts — perhaps five times slower in the worst case.

Efficiency is regarded with suspicion by many researchers, doubtless because many programs have been ruined in its pursuit. Functional programmers have sometimes chosen inefficient algorithms for the sake of clarity, or have sought to enrich their languages rather than implement them better. This attitude, more than technical reasons, has given functional programming a reputation for inefficiency.

We must now redress the balance. Functional programs must be efficient, or nobody will use them. Algorithms, after all, are designed to be efficient. The Greatest Common Divisor of two numbers can be found by searching through all possible candidates. This exhaustive search algorithm is clear, but useless. Euclid's Algorithm is fast and simple, having sacrificed clarity.

The **transformational** approach to program design might begin with the exhaustive search algorithm, viewed as an **executable specification** of the GCD. This would be transformed into mathematically equivalent but faster versions, eventually arriving at Euclid's Algorithm. Program transformation can indeed improve efficiency, but we should regard executable specifications with caution. The Greatest Common Divisor of two integers is, by definition, the largest integer that exactly divides both; the specification does not mention search at all. The exhaustive search algorithm is too complicated to be a good specification.

Functional programming and logic programming are instances of **declarative programming**. The ideal of declarative programming is to free us from writing programs — just state the requirements and the computer will do the rest. Hoare (1987) has explored this ideal in the case of the Greatest Common Divisor, demonstrating that it is still a dream. A more realistic aim for declarative programming is to make programs easier to understand through mathematical methods. Declarative programming is still programming; we still have to code efficiently.

This book gives concrete advice about performance and tries to help you decide where efficiency matters. Some ML compilers offer **execution profiling**, which measures the time spent by each function. The function that spends the most time (never the one you would expect) becomes a prime candidate for improvement. Such bottom-up optimization can produce dramatic results, although it may not reveal global causes of waste. These general considerations hold for all programming methodologies — functional, procedural, object-oriented, ...

Correctness must come first. Clarity must usually come second, and efficiency third. Whenever you sacrifice clarity for efficiency, be sure to measure the improvement in performance and decide whether the sacrifice is worth it. A judicious mixture of realism and principle, with plenty of patience, makes for efficient programs.

Standard ML

Every successful language was designed for some specific purpose: Lisp for AI, Fortran for numerical computation, Prolog for natural language processing. Conversely, languages designed to be general purpose — particularly the 'algorithmic languages' Algol 60 and Algol 68 — have succeeded more as sources of ideas than as practical tools.

ML was designed for theorem proving. This is not a broad field, and ML was intended for the programming of one particular theorem prover — a specific purpose indeed! This theorem prover, called Edinburgh LCF (Logic for Computable Functions) spawned a host of successors, all of which were coded in ML. And just as Lisp, Fortran and Prolog have applications far removed from their origins, ML is being used in diverse problem areas.

1.5   *The evolution of Standard ML*

ML was the Meta Language for the programming of proof strategies in Edinburgh LCF (Gordon, Milner & Wadsworth 1977). Borrowing ideas from the language ISWIM (Landin, 1966), ML's designers added the facilities that their theorem proving method demanded:

> The inference rules and proof methods were to be represented as functions, so ML was given the full power of higher-order functional programming.
>
> The inference rules were to define an abstract type: the type of theorems. Strong type checking (as in Pascal) would have been too restrictive, so ML was given polymorphic type checking.
>
> Proof methods could be combined in complex ways, through higher-order functions. Failure at any point had to be detected — so that another proof method could be tried. So ML was allowed to raise and trap exceptions.
>
> For communication with the outside world, ML was given imperative features. Pragmatism took precedence over the ideal of programming with pure functions.
>
> Since a theorem prover would be useless if there were any loopholes, ML was designed to be completely secure, with no way of defeating the type system or corrupting the

environment.

The ML system of Edinburgh LCF was slow. Programs were translated into Lisp and then interpreted. Luca Cardelli wrote an efficient compiler for his version of ML, which included a rich set of declaration and type structures. At Cambridge University and INRIA, the ML system of LCF was extended and its performance improved. ML also influenced HOPE, a purely functional language with polymorphism, recursive type definitions and pattern-matching in functions.

Milner led a standardization effort to consolidate the dialects into Standard ML. Many people contributed. The modules system — the language's most complex and innovative feature — was designed by David MacQueen and refined by Mads Tofte. In 1987, Milner won the British Computer Society Award for Technical Excellence for his work on Standard ML. The first compilers were developed at the Universities of Cambridge and Edinburgh.* The formal language definition recently appeared in print (Milner, Tofte & Harper 1990), with a separate commentary (Milner & Tofte, 1991).

Standard ML has not displaced all other dialects. The French, typically, have gone their own way. Their language CAML provides broadly similar features with the traditional ISWIM syntax (Cousineau & Huet, 1990). Extensions over Standard ML include lazy data structures and dynamic types. The intermediate language for code generation is the Categorical Abstract Machine, which is based on category theory. Lazy dialects of ML also exist, as mentioned previously.

Several universities adopt Standard ML as a teaching language. It is the first language taught to Computer Science students at Cambridge. Many students arrive knowing nothing but Basic, a primitive language where programs consist of assignments and jumps. ML provides a fresh start, breaking the bad habits learned in Basic. ML demonstrates the importance of mathematics in programming, and is powerful enough to tackle interesting problems. The type checker detects common errors, which is especially important for beginners. ML is also more fun than Basic.

In research, Standard ML is being applied to formal methods,

---

* The Preface of this book lists some addresses for obtaining compilers.

artificial intelligence, the construction of ML compilers, and many other areas. Theorem provers written in ML are described next.

1.6   *The ML tradition of theorem proving*

Automated theorem proving and functional programming go hand in hand. One of the first functional programs ever written appears in the *Lisp 1.5 Programmer's Manual* (McCarthy et al., 1962); it is a theorem prover for propositional logic. Back in the 1970s, when some researchers were wondering what functional programming was good for, Edinburgh LCF was putting it to work.

Theorem proving originated as a task for artificial intelligence; it requires intelligence and the problem can easily be set up on a computer. Later AI programs included theorem provers as a reasoning component. Theorem provers have investigated problems in mathematics. Program verification aims to prove the correctness of software. Hardware verification, although less well known, has been more successful (Birtwistle & Subrahmanyam, 1988).

Fully automatic theorem proving is usually impossible: most logics are undecidable. The resolution method is powerful for first-order logic (Wos et al., 1984), but for other important logics, no good proof methods are known. The obvious alternative to automatic theorem proving is interactive proof checking. You can get the feel of a logic by proof checking, but it soon becomes intolerable; most proofs involve long, repetitive combinations of rules.

Edinburgh LCF represented a new kind of theorem prover, where the level of automation was entirely up to the user. It was basically a programmable proof checker. Users could write proof procedures in ML — the Meta Language — rather than typing repetitive commands. The Object Language was Scott's Logic of Computable Functions, which was a logic based on the λ-calculus and domain theory. ML programs could operate on expressions of this logic.

Edinburgh LCF introduced the idea of representing a logic as an abstract type of theorems. Each axiom was a primitive theorem while each inference rule was a function from theorems to theorems. Type checking ensured that theorems could be made only by axioms and rules. Applying inference rules to already known theorems constructed proofs, rule by rule, in the forwards direction.

Tactics permitted a more natural style, backwards proof. A tactic was a function from goals to subgoals, justified by the existence of an inference rule going the other way. The tactic actually returned this inference rule (as a function) in its result: tactics were higher-order functions.

Tacticals provided control structures for combining simple tactics into complex ones. For instance, the tactical *THEN* applied two tactics in sequence, *ORELSE* chose one of two tactics, and *REPEAT* applied a tactic repeatedly. The resulting tactics could be combined to form still more complex tactics, which in a single step could perform hundreds of primitive inferences.

Tacticals were even more 'higher-order' than tactics. Other applications of higher-order functions turned up in rewriting and elsewhere. These ideas were not planned, but discovered by users.

Offshoots of Edinburgh LCF include Cambridge LCF, which is a re-engineered version of Edinburgh LCF (Paulson, 1987); the HOL system, which verifies hardware using higher-order logic; Nuprl, which supports constructive reasoning (Constable et al., 1986); there are many others.

Other recent systems adopt Standard ML. My system, called Isabelle, is a generic theorem prover. It works in many different formal systems and has its own notions of inference rule, tactic, and tactical.

1.7 *Overview of the book*

Most chapters are devoted to aspects of ML. Chapters 2–5 cover the **core language**, which consists of everything except modules. Basic types, lists, trees and higher-order functions are presented. The fundamentals of functional programming are covered alongside ML.

Chapter 6 presents formal methods for reasoning about functional programs. If this seems to be a mere distraction from the main business of programming, consider that a program is worth little unless it is correct. Ease of formal reasoning is a major argument in favour of functional programming.

Chapter 7 covers modules; Chapter 8 covers ML's imperative features. The remainder of the book consists of extended examples. Chapter 9 presents a functional parser and a λ-calculus interpreter. Chapter 10 presents a theorem prover, demonstrating the techniques of LCF and Isabelle.

The book is full of examples. Some of these serve only to demonstrate some aspect of ML, but most are intended to be useful in themselves — sorting, functional arrays, priority queues, search algorithms, pretty printing, ... Please note: although I have tested these programs, they undoubtedly contain some errors.

ML is not perfect. Certain pitfalls can allow a simple coding error to waste hours of a programmer's time. Warnings of possible hazards appear throughout the book. They look like this:

! *Beware the Duke of Gloucester.* O Buckingham! take heed of yonder dog. Look, when he fawns, he bites; and when he bites, his venom tooth will rankle to the death. Have not to do with him, beware of him; Sin, Death, and Hell have set their marks on him, and all their ministers attend on him.

I hasten to add that nothing in ML can have consequences quite this dire. ML is more secure than most other languages; no fault in a program can corrupt the ML system itself. On the other hand, we programmers must remember that even correct programs can do harm in the outside world.

2

Names, Functions and Types

Most functional languages are interactive. If you enter an expression, the computer immediately evaluates it and displays the result. Interaction is fun; it gives immediate feedback; it lets you write functions in easily managed pieces.

We can enter an expression followed by a semicolon ...

```
2+2;
```

... and ML responds

```
> 4 : int
```

Here we see some conventions that will be followed throughout the book. Most ML systems print a prompt character when waiting for input; here, the input is shown in **typewriter characters**. The response is shown, in slanted characters,

```
> on a line like this.
```

At its simplest, ML is just a calculator. It has integers, as shown above, and real numbers. ML can do simple arithmetic ...

```
3.2 - 2.3;
> 0.9 : real
```

... and square roots:

```
sqrt 2.0;
> 1.414213562 : real
```

Again, anything typed to ML must end with a semi-colon (;). ML has printed the value and type. Note that *real* is the type of real numbers, while *int* is the type of integers.

Interactive program development is more difficult with imperative languages because they are too verbose. A self-contained program is too long to type as a single input.

Chapter outline

This chapter introduces Standard ML and functional programming. The basic concepts include declarations, simple data types, record types, recursive functions and polymorphism. Although this material is presented using Standard ML, it illustrates general principles.

The chapter contains the following sections:

Value declarations. Value and function declarations are presented using elementary examples.

Numbers, character strings, truth values. The types *int*, *real*, *string* and *bool* are described, along with predefined functions such as the arithmetic operations.

Pairs, tuples and records. Ordered pairs and tuples are presented. These serve both as a data structure and to allow functions to have multiple arguments and results.

The evaluation of expressions. The difference between strict evaluation and lazy evaluation is explained. The evaluation method is not just a matter of efficiency, but concerns the very meaning of expressions.

Writing recursive functions. Several worked examples illustrate the use of recursion.

Local declarations. The Standard ML syntax for local declarations is presented, with examples.

Polymorphic type checking. The principles of polymorphism, including type inference and polymorphic functions, are introduced.

Value declarations

A **declaration** gives something a name. ML has many classes of things that can be named: values, types, signatures, structures and functors. (The last three pertain to modules and are discussed in Chapter 7.) Most names in a program stand for values, like numbers, strings — and functions. Although functions are values in ML, they have a special declaration syntax.

2.1 *Naming constants*

Any value of importance can be named, whether its importance is universal (like the constant π) or transient (the result of a previous computation). As a trivial example, suppose we want to compute the number of seconds in an hour. We begin by letting the name *seconds* stand for 60.

```
val seconds = 60;
```

The value declaration begins with ML keyword **val** and ends with a semi-colon. Names in this book usually appear in *italics*. ML repeats the name, with its value and type:

```
> val seconds = 60 : int
```

Let us declare constants for minutes per hour and hours per day:

```
val minutes = 60;
> val minutes = 60 : int
val hours = 24;
> val hours = 24 : int
```

These names are now valid in expressions:

```
seconds*minutes*hours;
> 86400 : int
```

If you enter an expression at top level like this, ML stores the value under the name *it*. By referring to *it* you can use the value in a further calculation:

```
it div 24;
> 3600 : int
```

The name *it* always has the value of the last expression typed at top level. Any previous value of *it* is lost. To save the value of *it*, declare a permanent name:

```
val secsinhour = it;
> val secsinhour = 3600 : int
```

Incidentally, names may contain underscores to make them easier to read:

```
val secs_in_hour = seconds*minutes;
> val secs_in_hour = 3600 : int
```

To demonstrate real numbers, we compute the area of a circle of radius r by the formula $area = \pi r^2$:

```
val pi = 3.14159;
> val pi = 3.14159 : real
val r = 2.0;
> val r = 2.0 : real
val area = pi * r * r;
> val area = 12.56636 : real
```

2.2   *Defining functions*

The formula for the area of a circle can be made into an ML function like this:

```
fun area (r) = pi*r*r;
```

The keyword **fun** starts the function declaration, while *area* is the function name, r is the **formal parameter**, and *pi*r*r* is the **body**. The body refers to r and to the constant *pi* declared above.

Because functions are values in ML, a function declaration is a form of value declaration, and so ML prints the value and type:

```
> val area = fn : real -> real
```

The type, which in standard mathematical notation is $real \rightarrow real$, says that *area* takes a real number as argument and returns another real number. The value of a function is printed as **fn**. In ML, as in most functional languages except Lisp, functions are abstract values that may not be examined.

Let us call the function, repeating the area calculation performed above:

```
area(2.0);
> 12.56636 : real
```

Let us try a different argument. Observe that the parentheses around the argument are optional:

```
area 1.0;
> 3.14159 : real
```

The parentheses are also optional in function definitions. This definition of *area* is equivalent to the former one.

```
fun area r = pi*r*r;
```

The evaluation of function applications is discussed in more detail below.

Comments. Programmers often imagine that their creations are too transparent to require further description. This logical clarity will not be evident to others unless the program is properly commented. A comment can describe the purpose of a declaration, give a literature reference, or explain an obscure matter. Needless to say, comments must be correct and up-to-date.

A comment in Standard ML begins with (* and ends with *), and may extend over several lines. It can be inserted almost anywhere:

```
fun area r =    (*area of circle with radius r*)
        pi*r*r;
```

Functional programmers should not feel absolved from writing comments. People once claimed that Pascal was self-documenting.

Redefining a name. Value names are called **variables**. Unlike variables in imperative languages, they cannot be updated. A name can be reused for another purpose. If a name is declared again then the new meaning is adopted afterwards, but does not affect existing uses of the name. Let us redefine the constant pi:

```
val pi = 0.0;
> val pi = 0.0 : real
```

Clearly, *area* still takes the original value of pi:

```
area(1.0);
> 3.14159 : real
```

Thanks to the permanence of names (called **static binding**), redefining a function cannot damage the system or your program.

!   *Debugging.* Static binding means that redefining a function called by your program may have no visible effect. When modifying a program, be sure to recompile the entire file.

Large programs should be divided into modules (Chapter 7). After the modified module has been recompiled, the program merely has to be relinked.

2.3   *Identifiers in Standard ML*

An **alphabetic name** must begin with a letter, which may be followed by any number of letters, digits, underscores (_), or primes ('), usually called single quotes. For instance:

```
x    UB40   Hamlet_Prince_of_Denmark   h''3_H
names_can_be_as_LONG_AS_YOU_WANT_unlike_some_other_languages
```

The case of letters matters, so q differs from Q. Prime characters are allowed because ML was designed by mathematicians, who like variables called x, x', x''. When choosing names, be certain to avoid ML's keywords:

```
abstype and andalso as case datatype do else end eqtype
exception fn fun functor handle if in include infix infixr
let local nonfix of op open orelse raise rec sharing sig
signature struct structure then type val while with withtype
```

Watch especially for the short ones: `as`, `fn`, `if`, `in`, `of`, `op`.

ML also permits **symbolic names**. These consist of the characters

$$! \quad \% \quad \& \quad \$ \quad \# \quad + \quad - \quad * \quad / \quad : \quad < \quad = \quad > \quad ? \quad @ \quad \backslash \quad \sim \quad ` \quad ^\wedge \quad |$$

Names made up of these characters can be as long as you like:

```
---->      $^$^$^$      !!?@**??!!      :-|==>->#
```

Certain strings of special characters are reserved for ML's syntax and should not be used as symbolic names:

```
:  |  =  =>  ->  #
```

A symbolic name is allowed wherever an alphabetic name is:

```
val +-+-+ = 1415;
> val +-+-+ = 1415 : int
```

Names are more formally known as **identifiers**. An identifier can simultaneously denote a value, a type, a module and a record field.

Exercise 2.1   On your computer, learn how to start an ML session and how to terminate it. Then learn how to make the ML compiler read declarations from a file — a typical command is *use*`"myfile"`.

Numbers, character strings, truth values

The simplest ML values are integer and real numbers, character strings, and the booleans or truth values. This section introduces these types with their constants and principal operations.

2.4   *Arithmetic*

ML distinguishes between integers (type *int*) and real numbers (type *real*). Integer arithmetic is exact (with unlimited precision in some ML systems) while real arithmetic is only as accurate as the computer's floating-point hardware.

Calling *real*(i) converts the integer i to the equivalent real number. Calling *floor*(r) converts the real number r to the greatest integer not exceeding r. These conversion functions are necessary whenever integers and reals are used in the same expression. The absolute value of x, whether integer or real, is written $abs(x)$.

Integers. An integer constant is a sequence of digits, possibly beginning with a minus sign ($\sim$). For instance:

    0    $\sim$23   01234 $\sim$85601435654678

Integer operations include addition (+), subtraction (-), multiplication (*), division (*div*) and remainder (*mod*). These are infix operators with conventional precedences: thus in

    $(((m*n)*k) - (m\ div\ j)) + j$

all the parentheses can be omitted without harm.

Real numbers. A real constant contains a decimal point or E notation, or both. For instance:

    0.01   2.718281828 $\sim$1.2E12   7E$\sim$5

The ending En means 'times the nth power of 10'. A negative exponent begins with the unary minus sign ($\sim$). Thus 123.4E$\sim$2 denotes 1.234.

Negative real numbers begin with unary minus ($\sim$). Infix operators for real numbers include addition (+), subtraction (-), multiplication (*) and division (/).

Other functions on real numbers are square root (*sqrt*), sine (*sin*), cosine (*cos*), arctangent (*arctan*), exponential (*exp*) and natural logarithm (*ln*). Each takes one real argument and returns a real result. Function application binds more tightly than infix operators. For instance, *exp a* + *b* is equivalent to (*exp a*) + *b*, not *exp* (*a* + *b*).

!   *Unary plus and minus.* The unary minus sign is a tilde ($\sim$). Do not
·   confuse it with the subtraction sign (-)! ML has no unary plus sign.
Neither + nor - may appear in the exponent of a real number.

Type constraints. ML can deduce the types in most expressions from the types of the functions and constants in it. But certain built-in functions are **overloaded**, having more than one meaning. For example, + and * are defined for both integers and reals. The type of an overloaded function must be determined from the context; occasionally types must be stated explicitly.

For instance, ML cannot tell whether this squaring function is intended for integers or reals, and therefore rejects it.

```
fun square x = x*x;
> Error- Unable to resolve overloading for *
```

Suppose the function is intended for real numbers. We can insert the type **real** in a number of places.

We can specify the type of the argument:

```
fun square(x : real) = x*x;
> val square = fn : real -> real
```

We can specify the type of the result:

```
fun square x : real = x*x;
> val square = fn : real -> real
```

Equivalently, we can specify the type of the body:

```
fun square x = x*x : real;
> val square = fn : real -> real
```

Type constraints can also appear within the body, indeed almost anywhere.

2.5   *Character strings*

Character strings represent messages and other text. They have type *string*. String constants are written in double quotes:

```
"How now! a rat? Dead, for a ducat, dead!";
> "How now! a rat? Dead, for a ducat, dead!" : string
```

Escape sequences, which begin with a backslash (\), insert certain special characters into a string:

\n inserts a newline character (line break)

\t inserts a tabulation character

\" inserts a double quote

\\ inserts a backslash

\ followed by a newline followed by another \ inserts nothing, but continues a string across the line break.

Here is a string containing newline characters:

```
"This above all:\nto thine own self be true\n";
```

The concatenation operator (^) joins two strings end-to-end:

```
"Fair " ^ "Ophelia";
> "Fair Ophelia" : string
```

The function *size* returns the number of characters in a string. Here *it* refers to "Fair Ophelia":

```
size (it);
> 12 : int
```

The space character counts, of course. The empty string contains no characters; *size* ("") is 0.

Here is a function that makes noble titles:

```
fun title(name) = "The Duke of " ^ name;
> val title = fn : string -> string
title "York";
> "The Duke of York" : string
```

The functions *ord* and *chr* convert between strings and ASCII character codes. If k is in the range $0 \leq k \leq 255$ then $chr(k)$ returns the string consisting of the character with code k. Conversely, if s is a non-empty string then $ord(s)$ is the integer code of its first character. For instance, here is a function to convert a number between 0 and 9 to a string between "0" and "9":

```
fun digit i = chr(i + ord"0");
> val digit = fn : int -> string
```

2.6   *Truth values and conditional expressions*

To define a function by cases — where the result depends on the outcome of a test — we employ a conditional expression.* The test is an expression E of type *bool*, whose values are *true* and *false*. The outcome of the test chooses one of two expressions E_1 or E_2. The value of the conditional expression

if E **then** E_1 **else** E_2

is that of E_1 if E equals *true*, and that of E_2 if E equals *false*. The **else** part may never be omitted.

The simplest tests are the relations:

less than (<)
greater than (>)
less than or equals (<=)
greater than or equals (>=)

---

* Because a Standard ML expression can update the state, conditional expressions can also act like the **if** commands of procedural languages.

These are defined on integers and reals. They also test alphabetical ordering on strings (with some compilers — this usage is not given in the language definition). Thus the relations are overloaded and may require type constraints. Equality (=) and its negation (<>) can be tested for most types.

For example, the function *sign* computes the sign (1, 0, or −1) of an integer. It has two conditional expressions and a comment.

```
fun sign(n) =
        if n>0 then 1
    else if n=0 then 0
    else ~1;      (*in this case n<0*)
> val sign = fn : int ->int
```

Tests are combined by ML's boolean operations:

> logical or (called **orelse**)
> logical and (called **andalso**)
> logical negation (the function *not*)

Functions that return a boolean value are known as **predicates**. Here is a predicate to test whether its argument, a string, consists of one lower-case letter:

```
fun is_letter s =
        "a"<=s andalso s<="z" andalso size s = 1;
> val is_letter = fn : string -> bool
```

When a conditional expression is evaluated, either the **then** or the **else** expression is evaluated, never both. The boolean operators **andalso** and **orelse** behave differently from ordinary functions: the second operand is evaluated only if necessary. Their names reflect this sequential behaviour.

Exercise 2.2 A Lisp hacker says: 'Since the integers are a subset of the real numbers, the distinction between them is wholly artificial — foisted on us by hardware designers. ML should simply provide numbers, as Lisp does, and automatically use integers or reals as appropriate.' Do you agree? What considerations are there?

Exercise 2.3 Which of these function definitions requires type constraints?

```
fun double(n) = 2*n;
fun f u = sin(u)/u;
fun g k = k - abs k;
```

Exercise 2.4 Let d be an integer and m a string. Write an ML boolean expression that is true just when d and m form a valid date: say 25 and `"October"`. Assume it is not a leap year.

Pairs, tuples and records

In mathematics, a collection of values is often viewed as a single value. A vector in two dimensions is an ordered pair of real numbers. A statement about two vectors $\vec{v}_1$ and $\vec{v}_2$ can be taken as a statement about four real numbers, and those real numbers can themselves be broken down into smaller pieces, but thinking at a high level is easier. Writing $\vec{v}_1 + \vec{v}_2$ for their vector sum saves us from writing $(x_1 + x_2, y_1 + y_2)$.

Dates are a more commonplace example. A date like 25 October 1415 consists of three values. Taken as a unit, it is a triple of the form $(day, month, year)$. This elementary concept has taken remarkably long to appear in programming languages, and only a few handle it properly.

Standard ML provides ordered pairs, triples, quadruples and so forth. For $n \geq 2$, the ordered collection of n values is called an n-tuple, or just a **tuple**. The tuple whose components are x_1, x_2, $\ldots$, x_n is written $(x_1, x_2, \ldots, x_n)$ and is created by an expression of the form $(E_1, E_2, \ldots, E_n)$. With functions, tuples give the effect of multiple arguments and results.

The components of an ML tuple may themselves be tuples or any other value. For example, a period of time can be represented by a pair of dates, regardless of how dates are represented. It also follows that pairs can represent n-tuples. The values x_1, x_2, $\ldots$, x_n can be packaged as $((\ldots(x_1, x_2), \ldots), x_n)$.

An ML record has components identified by name, not by position. A record with 20 components occupies a lot of space on the printed page, but is easier to manage than a 20-tuple.

2.7 *Vectors: an example of pairing*

Let us develop the example of vectors. To try the syntax for pairs, enter the vector $(2.5, -1.2)$:

```
(2.5, ~1.2);
> (2.5, ~1.2) : real * real
```

The vector's type, which in mathematical notation is *real* × *real*, is the type of a pair of real numbers.

Vectors are ML values and can be given names. We declare the zero vector and two others, called *a* and *b*.

```
val zerovec = (0.0, 0.0);
> val zerovec = (0.0, 0.0) : real * real
val a = (1.5, 6.8);
> val a = (1.5, 6.8) : real * real
val b = (3.6, 0.9);
> val b = (3.6, 0.9) : real * real
```

Many functions on vectors operate on the components. The length of (x, y) is $\sqrt{x^2 + y^2}$, while the negation of (x, y) is $(-x, -y)$. To code these functions in ML, simply write the argument as a pattern:

```
fun lengthvec (x,y) = sqrt(x*x + y*y);
> val lengthvec = fn : real * real -> real
```

The function *lengthvec* takes the pair of values of x and y. It has type *real* × *real* → *real*: its argument is a pair of real numbers and its result is another real number.* Here, *a* is a pair of real numbers.

```
lengthvec a;
> 6.963476143 : real
lengthvec (1.0, 1.0);
> 1.414213562 : real
```

Function *negvec* negates a vector with respect to the point $(0, 0)$.

```
fun negvec (x,y) : real*real = (~x, ~y);
> val negvec = fn : real * real -> real * real
```

This function has type *real* × *real* → *real* × *real*: given a pair of real numbers it returns another pair. The type constraint *real* × *real* is necessary because minus (~) is overloaded.

We negate some vectors, giving a name to the negation of *b*:

```
negvec (1.0, 1.0);
> (~1.0, ~1.0) : real * real
val bn = negvec(b);
> val bn = (~3.6, ~0.9) : real * real
```

Vectors can be arguments and results of functions and can be given names. In short, they have all the rights of ML's built-in values,

---

* The overloaded operators are constrained to type *real* by the function *sqrt*, which is defined only for real numbers.

like the integers. We can even declare a type of vectors:

```
type vec = real*real;
> type vec
```

Now *vec* abbreviates *real* × *real*. It is only an abbreviation, though: every pair of real numbers has type *vec*, regardless of whether it is intended to represent a vector. We shall employ *vec* in type constraints.

2.8   *Functions with multiple arguments and results*

Here is a function that computes the average of a pair of real numbers.

```
fun average(x,y) = (x+y)/2.0;
> val average = fn : (real * real) -> real
```

This would be an odd thing to do to a vector, but *average* works for any two numbers:

```
average(3.1,3.3);
> 3.2 : real
```

A function on pairs is a function of two arguments: $lengthvec(x, y)$ and $average(x, y)$ operate on the real numbers x and y. Whether we view (x, y) as a vector is up to us. Similarly *negvec* takes a pair of arguments — and returns a pair of results.

Strictly speaking, every ML function has one argument and one result. With tuples, functions can effectively have any number of arguments and results. Currying, discussed in Chapter 5, also gives the effect of multiple arguments.

Since the components of a tuple can themselves be tuples, two vectors can be paired:

```
((2.0, 3.5), zerovec);
> ((2.0, 3.5), (0.0, 0.0)) : (real * real) * (real * real)
```

The sum of vectors (x_1, y_1) and (x_2, y_2) is $(x_1 + x_2, y_1 + y_2)$. In ML, this function takes a pair of vectors. Its argument pattern is a pair of pairs:

```
fun addvec ((x1,y1), (x2,y2)) : vec = (x1+x2, y1+y2);
> val addvec = fn : (real * real) * (real * real) -> vec
```

Type *vec* appears for the first time, constraining addition to operate on real numbers. ML gives *addvec* the type

$$((real \times real) \times (real \times real)) \rightarrow vec$$

which is equivalent to the more concise $(vec \times vec) \rightarrow vec$. The ML system may not abbreviate every *real* × *real* as *vec*.

Look again at the argument pattern of *addvec*. We may equivalently view this function as taking

one argument: a pair of pairs of real numbers

two arguments: each a pair of real numbers

four arguments: all real numbers, oddly grouped

Here we add the vectors (8.9,4.4) and *b*, then add the result to another vector. Note that *vec* is the result type of the function.

```
addvec((8.9, 4.4), b);
> (12.5, 5.3) : vec
addvec(it, (0.1, 0.2));
> (12.6, 5.5) : vec
```

Vector subtraction involves subtraction of the components, but can be expressed by vector operations:

```
fun subvec(v1,v2) = addvec(v1, negvec v2);
> val subvec = fn : (real * real) * (real * real) -> vec
```

The variables *v*1 and *v*2 range over pairs of reals.

```
subvec(a,b);
> (~2.1, 5.9) : vec
```

The distance between two vectors is the length of the difference:

```
fun distance(v1,v2) = lengthvec(subvec(v1,v2));
> val distance = fn : (real * real) * (real * real) -> real
```

Since *distance* never refers separately to *v*1 or *v*2, it can be simplified:

```
fun distance pairv = lengthvec(subvec pairv);
```

The variable *pairv* is a pair of vectors. This version may look odd, but is equivalent to its predecessor. How far is it from *a* to *b*?

```
distance(a,b);
> 6.262587325 : real
```

A final example will show that the components of a pair can have different types: here, a real number and a vector. Scaling a vector means multiplying both components by a constant.

```
fun scalevec (r, (x,y)) : vec = (r*x, r*y);
> val scalevec = fn : real * (real * real) -> vec
```

The type constraint *vec* ensures that the multiplications apply to reals. The function *scalevec* takes a real number and a vector, and returns a vector.

```
scalevec(2.0, a);
> (3.0, 13.6) : vec
scalevec(2.0, it);
> (6.0, 27.2) : vec
```

Selecting the components of a tuple. A function defined on a pattern, say (x,y), refers to the components of its argument through the pattern variables x and y. A **val** declaration may also match a value against a pattern: each variable in the pattern refers to the corresponding component.

Here we treat *scalevec* as a function returning two results, which we name *xc* and *yc*.

```
val (xc,yc) = scalevec(4.0, a);
> val xc = 6.0 : real
> val yc = 27.2 : real
```

The pattern in a **val** declaration can be as complicated as the argument pattern of a function definition. In this contrived example, a pair of pairs is split into four parts, which are all given names.

```
val ((x1,y1), (x2,y2)) = (addvec(a,b), subvec(a,b));
> val x1 = 5.1 : real
> val y1 = 7.7 : real
> val x2 = ~2.1 : real
> val y2 = 5.9 : real
```

The 0-tuple and the type unit. Previously we have considered n-tuples for $n \geq 2$. There is also a 0-tuple, written () and pronounced 'unity', which has no components. It serves as a placeholder in situations where no data needs to be conveyed. The 0-tuple is the sole value of type *unit*.

Type *unit* is used with imperative programming in ML. A procedure is typically a 'function' whose result type is *unit*. The procedure is called for its effect — not for its value, which is always (). For instance, some ML systems provide a function *use* of type *string* $\rightarrow$ *unit*. Calling *use*"myfile" has the effect of reading the definitions on the file "myfile" into ML.

A function whose argument type is *unit* passes no information to its body when called. Calling the function simply causes its body to be evaluated. In Chapter 5, such functions are used to delay evaluation for programming with infinite lists.

Exercise 2.5 Write a function to test whether one time of day, in the form $(hours, minutes, AM/PM)$, comes before another. Thus (11,59,"AM") comes before (1,15,"PM").

Exercise 2.6 The old English money had 12 pence in a shilling

and 20 shillings in a pound. Write functions to add and subtract
two amounts, working with triples (*pounds, shillings, pence*).

2.9   *Records*

A record is a tuple whose components — called **fields** —
have labels. While each component of an *n*-tuple is identified
by its position from 1 to *n*, the fields of a record may appear
in any order. Transposing the components of a tuple is a common error. If employees are taken as triples (*name, age, salary*)
then there is a big difference between ("Jones",25,15300) and
("Jones",15300,25). But the records

> {*name*="Jones", *age*=25, *salary*=15300}

and

> {*name*="Jones", *salary*=15300, *age*=25}

are equal. Observe ML's syntax for a record. It is enclosed in braces
{...}; each field has the form *label* = *expression*.

Records are appropriate when there are many components. Let
us record five fundamental facts about some Kings of England, and
note ML's response:

```
val henryV =
    {name    = "Henry V",
     born    = 1387,
     crowned = 1413,
     died    = 1422,
     quote   = "Bid them achieve me and then sell my bones"};
> val henryV =
>    {born = 1387,
>     died = 1422,
>     name = "Henry V",
>     quote = "Bid them achieve me and then sell my bones",
>     crowned = 1413}
> : {born: int,
>     died: int,
>     name: string,
>     quote: string,
>     crowned: int}
```

ML has rearranged the fields into a standard order, ignoring the
order in which they were given. The record type lists each field as

label : *type*, within braces. Here are two more Kings:

```
val henryVI =
  {name    = "Henry VI",
   born     = 1421,
   crowned = 1422,
   died     = 1471,
   quote    = "Weep, wretched man,\
\ I'll aid thee tear for tear"};
```

```
val richardIII =
  {name    = "Richard III",
   born     = 1452,
   crowned = 1483,
   died     = 1485,
   quote    = "Plots have I laid..."};
```

The *quote* of *henryVI* extends across two lines, using the backslash, newline, backslash escape sequence.

Record field selections. The selection #*label* gets the value of the given *label* from a record.

```
#quote richardIII ;
> "Plots have I laid..." : string
#died henryV - #born henryV ;
> 35 : int
```

Different record types can have labels in common. Both employees and Kings have a *name*, whether "Jones" or "Henry V". The three Kings given above have the same record type because they have the same number of fields with the same labels and types.

Here is another example of different record types with some labels in common: the *n*-tuple $(x_1, x_2, \ldots, x_n)$ is just an abbreviation for a record with numbered fields:

$$\{1 = x_1, 2 = x_2, \ldots, n = x_n\}$$

Yes, a label can be a positive integer! This obscure fact about Standard ML is worth knowing for one reason: the selector #*k* gets the value of component *k* of an *n*-tuple. So #1 selects the first component and #2 selects the second. If there is a third component then #3 selects it, and so forth:

```
#2 ("a","b",3,false);
> "b" : string
```

Record patterns. A record pattern with fields *label* = *variable* gives each variable the value of the corresponding label. If we do not require all the fields, we can write three dots (...) in place of the others. Here we get two fields from Henry V's famous record, calling them *nameV* and *bornV*:

```
val {name=nameV, born=bornV, ...} = henryV;
> val nameV = "Henry V" : string
> val bornV = 1387 : int
```

Often we want to open up a record, making its fields directly visible. We can specify each field in the pattern as *label* = *label*, making the variable and the label identical. Such a specification can be shortened to simply *label*. We open up Richard III:

```
val {name,born,died,quote,crowned} = richardIII;
> val name = "Richard III" : string
> val born = 1452 : int
> val died = 1485 : int
> val quote = "Plots have I laid..." : string
> val crowned = 1483 : int
```

To omit some fields, write (...) as before. Now *quote* stands for the quote of Richard III. Obviously this makes sense for only one King at a time.

! *Partial record specifications.* A field selection that omits some of the fields does not completely specify the record type; a function may only be defined over a complete record type. For instance, a function cannot be defined for all records that have fields *born* and *died*, without specifying the full set of field names (typically with a type constraint). This restriction makes ML records efficient but inflexible.

Let us declare the record type of Kings. This abbreviation will be useful for type constraints in functions.

```
type king = {name    : string,
             born     : int,
             crowned  : int,
             died     : int,
             quote    : string};
> type king
```

We now can define a function on type *king* to return the King's lifetime:

```
fun lifetime(k: king) = #died k - #born k;
> val lifetime = fn : king -> int
```

Using a pattern, *lifetime* can be defined like this:

```
fun lifetime({born,died,...}: king) = died - born;
```

Either way the type constraint is mandatory. Otherwise ML will print a message like 'A fixed record type is needed here'.

> *lifetime henryV*;
> `> 35 : int`
> *lifetime richardIII*;
> `> 33 : int`

Exercise 2.7 Does the following function definition require a type constraint? What is its type?

> **fun** *lifetime* ({*name*, *born*, *crowned*, *died*, *quote*}) = *died* - *born*;

Exercise 2.8 Discuss the differences, if any, between the selector #*born* and the function

> **fun** *born_at* ({*born*}) = *born*;

2.10 *Infix operators*

An **infix operator** is a function that is written between its two arguments. We take infix notation for granted in mathematics. Imagine doing without it. Instead of 2+2=4 we would have to write =(+(2,2),4). Most functional languages let programmers define their own infix operators.

Let us define an infix operator *xor* for 'exclusive or'. First we issue an ML **infix** directive:

> `infix` *xor*;

We now must write *p xor q* rather than *xor*(p, q):

> **fun** *p* xor *q* = (*p* **orelse** *q*) **andalso** *not* (*p* **andalso** *q*);
> `> val xor = fn : (bool * bool) -> bool`

The function *xor* takes a pair of booleans and returns a boolean.

> *true xor false xor true*;
> `> false : bool`

The infix status of a name concerns only its syntax, not its value, if any. Usually a name is made infix before it has any value at all.

Precedence of infixes. Most people take $m \times n + i/j$ to mean $(m \times n) + (i/j)$, giving $\times$ and $/$ higher precedence than $+$. Similarly $i - j - k$ means $(i - j) - k$, since the operator $-$ associates to the left. An ML infix directive may state a precedence from 0 to 9. The default precedence is 0, which is the lowest. The directive **infix** causes association to the left, while **infixr** causes association to the right.

To demonstrate infixes, the following functions construct strings enclosed in parentheses. Operator *plus* has precedence 6 (the precedence of + in ML) and constructs a string containing a + sign.

```
infix 6 plus;
fun a plus b = "(" ^ a ^ "+" ^ b ^ ")";
> val plus = fn : string * string -> string
```

Observe that *plus* associates to the left:

```
"1" plus "2" plus "3";
> "((1+2)+3)" : string
```

Similarly, *times* has precedence 7 (like * in ML) and constructs a string containing a * sign.

```
infix 7 times;
fun a times b = "(" ^ a ^ "*" ^ b ^ ")";
> val times = fn : string * string -> string
"m" times "n" times "3" plus "i" plus "j" times "k";
> "((((m*n)*3)+i)+(j*k))" : string
```

The operator *power* has higher precedence than times and associates to the right, which is traditional for raising to a power. It produces a $ sign. (ML has no operator for powers.)

```
infixr 8 pow;
fun a pow b = "(" ^ a ^ "$" ^ b ^ ")";
> val pow = fn : string * string -> string
"m" times "i" pow "j" pow "2" times "n";
> "((m*(i$(j$2)))*n)" : string
```

Many infix operators have symbolic names. Let ++ be the operator for vector addition:

```
infix ++;
fun (x1,y1) ++ (x2,y2) : vec = (x1+x2, y1+y2);
> val ++ = fn : (real * real) * (real * real) -> vec
```

It works exactly like *addvec*, but with infix notation:

```
b ++ (0.1,0.2) ++ (20.0, 30.0);
> (23.7, 31.1) : vec
```

! *Keep symbolic names separate.* Symbolic names can cause confusion if you run them together. Below, ML reads the characters +~ as one symbolic name, then complains that this name has no value:

```
1+~3;
> Unknown name +~
```

Symbolic names must be separated by spaces or other characters:

```
1+ ~3;
> ~2 : int
```

Taking infixes as functions. Occasionally an infix has to be treated like an ordinary function. In ML the keyword **op** overrides infix status: if $\oplus$ is an infix operator then **op**$\oplus$ is the corresponding function, which can be applied to a pair in the usual way.

```
> op++ ((2.5,0.0), (0.1,2.5));
(2.6, 2.5) : real * real
op^ ("Mont","joy");
> "Montjoy" : string
```

Infix status can be revoked. If $\oplus$ is an infix operator then the directive **nonfix**$\oplus$ makes it revert to ordinary function notation. A subsequent infix directive can make $\oplus$ an infix operator again.

Here we deprive ML's multiplication operator of its infix status. The attempt to use it produces an error message, since we may not apply 3 as a function. But * can be applied as a function:

```
nonfix *;
3*2;
> Error: Invalid types...
*(3,2);
> 6 : int
```

The **nonfix** directive is intended for interactive development of syntax, for trying different precedences and association. Changing the infix status of established operators leads to madness.

The evaluation of expressions

An imperative program contains a definition of its state — the variables, files and communication channels — as well as commands to update the state. During execution the state changes millions of times per second. Its structure changes too: local variables are created and destroyed. Even if the program has a mathematical meaning independent of hardware details, that meaning is beyond the comprehension of the programmer. Axiomatic and denotational semantic definitions make sense only to a handful of experts. Programmers trying to correct their programs rely on debugging tools and intuition.

Functional programming aims to give each program a simple mathematical meaning. This meaning should be independent of execution details and intelligible to people who have not written a PhD in the subject. Functional programming also simplifies our mental picture of execution, for there are no state changes. Execution is the reduction of an expression to its value, replacing equals by equals. Most function definitions can be understood within elementary mathematics.

When a function is applied, as in $f(E)$, the argument E must be supplied to the body of f. If there are several function calls, one must be chosen according to some evaluation rule. The evaluation rule in ML is **call-by-value** (or **strict** evaluation), while most purely functional languages adopt **call-by-need** (or **lazy** evaluation).

Each evaluation rule has its partisans. To compare the rules we shall consider two trivial functions. The squaring function *sqr* uses its argument twice:

```
fun sqr(x) : int = x*x;
> val sqr = fn : int -> int
```

The constant function *zero* ignores its argument and returns 0:

```
fun zero(x : int) = 0;
> val zero = fn : int -> int
```

When a function is called, the argument is substituted for the function's formal parameter in the body. The evaluation rules differ over when the argument is evaluated: before the substitution or after. The formal parameter indicates where in the body to substitute the argument. The name of the formal parameter has no other significance, and no significance outside of the function definition. This treatment of the formal parameter, called **static binding**, is adopted by virtually all functional languages except certain dialects of Lisp.

The meaning of recursion in functional languages depends on the evaluation rule, but requires no further elaboration. The evaluation of a recursive function is certainly easier to comprehend than the execution of a recursive procedure. That is fortunate, for the functional programmer writes recursive functions all the time. Although functional languages have no iterative commands like `while`, certain forms of recursion correspond to iteration.

2.11 *Evaluation in ML: call-by-value*

Let us assume that expressions consist of constants, variables, function calls and conditional expressions (`if-then-else`). Constants have an explicit value and variables should have some value, so evaluation has only to deal with function calls and conditionals. ML's evaluation rule is based on an obvious idea.

> To compute the value of $f(E)$, first compute the value of the expression E.

This value is substituted into the body of f, which then can be evaluated. Pattern-matching is a minor complication. If f is defined by, say

```
fun f (x,y,z) = body
```

then substitute the corresponding parts of E's value for the pattern variables x, y and z.

Let us examine how ML evaluates $sqr(sqr(sqr(2)))$. Of the three function calls, only the innermost call has a value for the argument. So $sqr(sqr(sqr(2)))$ reduces to $sqr(sqr(2 \times 2))$. The multiplication must now be evaluated, yielding $sqr(sqr(4))$. Evaluating the inner call yields $sqr(4 \times 4)$, and so forth. Reductions are written $sqr(sqr(4)) \Rightarrow sqr(4 \times 4)$. The full evaluation looks like this:

$$sqr(sqr(sqr(2))) \Rightarrow sqr(sqr(2 \times 2))$$
$$\Rightarrow sqr(sqr(4))$$
$$\Rightarrow sqr(4 \times 4)$$
$$\Rightarrow sqr(16)$$
$$\Rightarrow 16 \times 16$$
$$\Rightarrow 256$$

Now consider $zero(sqr(sqr(sqr(2))))$. The argument of $zero$ is the expression evaluated above. It is evaluated but the value is ignored:

$$zero(sqr(sqr(sqr(2)))) \Rightarrow zero(sqr(sqr(2 \times 2)))$$
$$\vdots$$
$$\Rightarrow zero(256)$$
$$\Rightarrow 0$$

Such waste! Functions like $zero$ are uncommon, but frequently a function's result does not depend on all of its arguments.

ML's evaluation rule is known as **call-by-value** because a function is always given its argument's value. It is not hard to see that call-by-value corresponds to the usual way we would perform a calculation on paper. Almost all programming languages adopt it. But perhaps we should look for an evaluation rule that reduces $zero(sqr(sqr(sqr(2))))$ to 0 in one step. Before such issues can be examined, we must have a look at recursion.

2.12   *Recursive functions under call-by-value*

The factorial function is a standard example of recursion. It includes a base case, $n = 0$, where evaluation stops.

```
fun fact n =
        if  n=0   then   1   else   n * fact(n-1);
> val fact = fn : int -> int
fact 7;
> 5040 : int
fact 35;
> 10333147966386144929666651337523200000000  : int
```

ML evaluates $fact(4)$ as follows. The argument, 4, is substituted for n in the body, yielding

$$\textsf{if } 4 = 0 \textsf{ then } 1 \textsf{ else } 4 \times fact(4-1)$$

Since $4 = 0$ is false, the conditional reduces to $4 \times fact(4-1)$. Then $4 - 1$ is selected, and the entire expression reduces to $4 \times fact(3)$. Figure 2.1 summarizes the evaluation. The conditionals are not shown: they behave similarly apart from $n = 0$, when the conditional returns 1.

The evaluation of $fact(4)$ exactly follows the mathematical definition of factorial: $0! = 1$, and $n! = n \times (n-1)!$ if $n > 0$. Could the execution of a recursive procedure be shown as succinctly?

Iterative functions. Something is odd about the computation of $fact(4)$. As the recursion progresses, more and more numbers are waiting to be multiplied. The multiplications cannot take place until the recursion terminates with $fact(0)$. At that point $4 \times (3 \times (2 \times (1 \times 1)))$ must be evaluated. This paper calculation shows that $fact$ is wasting space.

A more efficient version can be found by thinking about how we would compute factorials. By the associative law, each multiplica-

Figure 2.1 *Evaluation of fact*(4)

$$fact(4) \Rightarrow 4 \times fact(4 - 1)$$
$$\Rightarrow 4 \times fact(3)$$
$$\Rightarrow 4 \times (3 \times fact(3 - 1))$$
$$\Rightarrow 4 \times (3 \times fact(2))$$
$$\Rightarrow 4 \times (3 \times (2 \times fact(2 - 1)))$$
$$\Rightarrow 4 \times (3 \times (2 \times fact(1)))$$
$$\Rightarrow 4 \times (3 \times (2 \times (1 \times fact(1 - 1))))$$
$$\Rightarrow 4 \times (3 \times (2 \times (1 \times fact(0))))$$
$$\Rightarrow 4 \times (3 \times (2 \times (1 \times 1)))$$
$$\Rightarrow 4 \times (3 \times (2 \times 1))$$
$$\Rightarrow 4 \times (3 \times 2)$$
$$\Rightarrow 4 \times 6$$
$$\Rightarrow 24$$

---

tion can be done at once:

$$4 \times (3 \times fact(2)) = (4 \times 3) \times fact(2) = 12 \times fact(2)$$

The computer will not apply such laws unless we force it to. The function *facti* keeps a running product in p, which initially should be 1:

```
fun facti (n,p) =
        if n=0 then p  else  facti(n-1, n*p);
> val facti = fn : int * int -> int
```

Compare the evaluation for $facti(4, 1)$, shown in Figure 2.2, with that of $fact(4)$. The intermediate expressions stay small; each multiplication can be done at once; storage requirements remain constant. The evaluation is **iterative** — also termed **tail recursive** or **terminal recursive**.

Good compilers detect iterative forms of recursion and execute them efficiently. The result of the recursive call $facti(n - 1, n \times p)$ undergoes no further computation, but is immediately returned as the value of $facti(n, p)$. Such a **terminal call** can be executed by assigning the arguments n and p their new values and then jumping back into the function, avoiding the cost of a proper function

Figure 2.2 *Evaluation of facti*$(4, 1)$

$$facti(4, 1) \Rightarrow facti(4 - 1, 4 \times 1)$$
$$\Rightarrow facti(3, 4)$$
$$\Rightarrow facti(3 - 1, 3 \times 4)$$
$$\Rightarrow facti(2, 12)$$
$$\Rightarrow facti(2 - 1, 2 \times 12)$$
$$\Rightarrow facti(1, 24)$$
$$\Rightarrow facti(1 - 1, 1 \times 24)$$
$$\Rightarrow facti(0, 24)$$
$$\Rightarrow 24$$

---

invocation. The recursive call in *fact* is not terminal because its value undergoes further computation, namely multiplication by n.

Many functions can be made iterative by adding an argument, like p in *facti*. With some compilers the iterative function may run much faster; with others, slower. Sometimes, making a function iterative is the only way to avoid running out of store. In the absence of such compelling reasons, recursive functions should be expressed in their most natural form. Although *facti* may be more efficient than *fact*, it is less readable. Factorials of large numbers are seldom computed, so little space will be saved. Therefore *fact* is to be preferred.

The special role of conditional expressions. The conditional expression permits definition by cases. Recall how the factorial function is defined:

$$0! = 1$$
$$n! = n \times (n - 1)! \qquad \text{for } n > 0$$

These equations determine $n!$ for all integers $n \geq 0$. Omitting the condition $n > 0$ from the second equation would lead to absurdity:

$$1 = 0! = 0 \times (-1)! = 0$$

Similarly, in the conditional expression

```
if E then E₁ else E₂,
```

ML evaluates E_1 only if $E = true$, and evaluates E_2 only if $E = false$.

Owing to call-by-value, there is no ML function *cond* such that $cond(E, E_1, E_2)$ is evaluated like a conditional expression. Let us try to define one and use it to code the factorial function:

```
fun cond(p,x,y) : int = if p then x else y;
> val cond = fn : bool * int * int -> int
fun badf n = cond(n=0, 1, n*badf(n-1));
> val badf = fn : int -> int
```

This may look plausible, but every call to *badf* runs forever. Observe the evaluation of $badf(0)$:

$$badf(0) \Rightarrow cond(true, 1, 0 \times badf(-1))$$
$$\Rightarrow cond(true, 1, 0 \times cond(false, 1, -1 \times badf(-2)))$$
$$\vdots \ \cdot$$

Although *cond* never requires the values of all three of its arguments, the call-by-value rule evaluates them all. The recursion cannot terminate.

Conditional and/or. ML's boolean operators **andalso**/**orelse** are not functions, but stand for conditional expressions.

The expression E_1 **andalso** E_2 abbreviates

> if E_1 then E_2 else *false*.

The expression E_1 **orelse** E_2 abbreviates

> if E_1 then *true* else E_2.

These operators compute the boolean and/or but evaluate E_2 only if necessary. If they were functions, the call-by-value rule would evaluate both arguments. All other ML infixes are really functions.

The sequential evaluation of **andalso** and **orelse** makes them ideal for recursive predicates (boolean-valued functions). The function *powoftwo* tests whether a number is a power of two:

```
fun even n  = (n mod 2 = 0);
> val even = fn : int -> bool
fun powoftwo n = (n=1) orelse
                (even(n) andalso powoftwo(n div 2));
> val powoftwo = fn : int -> bool
```

You might expect *powoftwo* to be defined by conditional expressions, and so it is, through `orelse` and `andalso`. Evaluation terminates once the outcome is decided:

$$powoftwo(6) \Rightarrow (6 = 1) \ \texttt{orelse} \ (even(6) \ \texttt{andalso} \ \cdots)$$
$$\Rightarrow even(6) \ \texttt{andalso} \ powoftwo(6 \ div \ 2)$$
$$\Rightarrow powoftwo(3)$$
$$\Rightarrow (3 = 1) \ \texttt{orelse} \ (even(3) \ \texttt{andalso} \ \cdots)$$
$$\Rightarrow even(3) \ \texttt{andalso} \ powoftwo(3 \ div \ 2)$$
$$\Rightarrow false$$

Exercise 2.9   Write the reduction steps for *powoftwo*(8).

Exercise 2.10   Is *powoftwo* an iterative function?

2.13   *Call-by-need, or lazy evaluation*

The call-by-value rule has accumulated a catalogue of complaints. It evaluates E needlessly in *zero*(E). It evaluates $E1$ or $E2$ needlessly in *cond*($E, E1, E2$). Conditional expressions and similar operations cannot be functions. ML provides `andalso` and `orelse`, but we have no means of defining similar things.

Shall we give functions their arguments as expressions, not as values? We must take care to ensure that functions retain some mathematical meaning. The general idea is this:

> To compute the value of $f(E)$, substitute E immediately into the body of f. Then compute the value of the resulting expression.

This is the **call-by-name** rule. It reduces $zero(sqr(sqr(sqr(2))))$ at once to 0.

Certain built-in functions, like multiplication ($\times$), need special treatment. Multiplication must be applied to values, not expressions: it is an example of a **strict** function. To evaluate $E_1 \times E_2$, the expressions E_1 and E_2 must be evaluated first.

Call-by-name does badly by $sqr(sqr(sqr(2)))$. It duplicates the argument, $sqr(sqr(2))$. The result of this 'reduction' is

$$sqr(sqr(2)) \times sqr(sqr(2)).$$

This happens because $sqr(x) = x \times x$.

Now the outermost function is $\times$, which is strict, so the rule selects the leftmost call to *sqr*. Its argument is also duplicated:

$$(sqr(2) \times sqr(2)) \times sqr(sqr(2))$$

A full evaluation goes something like this.

$$
\begin{aligned}
sqr(sqr(sqr(2))) &\Rightarrow sqr(sqr(2)) \times sqr(sqr(2)) \\
&\Rightarrow (sqr(2) \times sqr(2)) \times sqr(sqr(2)) \\
&\Rightarrow ((2 \times 2) \times sqr(2)) \times sqr(sqr(2)) \\
&\Rightarrow (4 \times sqr(2)) \times sqr(sqr(2)) \\
&\Rightarrow (4 \times (2 \times 2)) \times sqr(sqr(2)) \\
&\quad\vdots
\end{aligned}
$$

Does it ever reach the answer? Eventually. But call-by-name cannot be the evaluation rule we want.

The **call-by-need** rule (lazy evaluation) is like call-by-name, but ensures that each argument is evaluated at most once. Rather than substituting an expression into the function's body, the occurrences of the argument are linked by pointers. If the argument is ever evaluated, the value will be shared with its other occurrences. The pointer structure forms a directed graph of functions and arguments. As a part of the graph is evaluated, it is updated by the resulting value.

To avoid drawing graphs, let $[x = E]$ indicate that all occurrences of x share the value of E. Let us lazily evaluate $sqr(sqr(sqr(2)))$:

$$
\begin{aligned}
sqr(sqr(sqr(2))) &\Rightarrow x \times x \; [x = sqr(sqr(2))] \\
&\Rightarrow x \times x \; [x = y \times y] \; [y = sqr(2)] \\
&\Rightarrow x \times x \; [x = y \times y] \; [y = 2 \times 2] \\
&\Rightarrow x \times x \; [x = 4 \times 4] \\
&\Rightarrow 16 \times 16 \\
&\Rightarrow 256
\end{aligned}
$$

We seem to have the best of both worlds: no wasteful duplication, yet $zero(E)$ reduces immediately to 0.

Lazy evaluation of $cond(E, E_1, E_2)$ behaves like a conditional expression provided that its argument, the tuple (E, E_1, E_2), is itself evaluated lazily. The details of this are quite subtle: tuple formation must be viewed as a function. The idea that a data structure like (E, E_1, E_2) can be partially evaluated — either E_1 or E_2 but not both — leads to infinite lists.

A comparison of strict and lazy evaluation. Call-by-need, by doing
the least possible evaluation, may seem like the route to efficiency.
But it requires much bookkeeping. Realistic implementations became possible only after David Turner's application of **graph reduction** to **combinators**. Turner (1979) exploited obscure facts
about the λ-calculus and combinatory logic to develop compilation
techniques, which researchers are continuing to improve. Every
new technology has its evangelists: some people are claiming that
lazy evaluation is the way, the truth and the light. Why does Standard ML not adopt it?

Lazy evaluation says that $zero(E) = 0$ even if E fails to terminate. This flies in the face of mathematical tradition: an expression
is meaningful only if all its parts are. Alonzo Church, the inven-
tor of the λ-calculus, preferred a variant (the λI-calculus) banning
constant functions like *zero*.

Infinite data structures complicate mathematical reasoning. To
fully understand lazy evaluation, it is necessary to know some domain theory, as well as the theory of the λ-calculus. The output
of a program is not simply a value, but a partially evaluated expression. These concepts are not easy to learn, and many of them
are mechanistic. If we can only think in terms of the evaluation
mechanism, we are no better off than the imperative programmers.

Efficiency is problematical too. Sometimes lazy evaluation saves
vast amounts of space; sometimes it wastes space. Recall that *facti*
is more efficient than *fact* under strict evaluation, performing each
multiplication at once. Lazy evaluation of $facti(n, p)$ evaluates n
immediately (for the test $n = 0$), but not p. The multiplications
accumulate, taking considerable space:

$$
\begin{aligned}
facti(4, 1) &\Rightarrow facti(4 - 1, 4 \times 1) \\
&\Rightarrow facti(3 - 1, 3 \times (4 \times 1)) \\
&\Rightarrow facti(2 - 1, 2 \times (3 \times (4 \times 1))) \\
&\Rightarrow facti(1 - 1, 1 \times (2 \times (3 \times (4 \times 1)))) \\
&\Rightarrow 1 \times (2 \times (3 \times (4 \times 1))) \\
&\quad\vdots \\
&\Rightarrow 24
\end{aligned}
$$

Lazy evaluation is important in research, but it has not yet made
a serious impact on practical programming.

Writing recursive functions

Since recursion is so fundamental to functional programming, let us take the time to examine a few recursive functions. There is no magic formula for program design, but perhaps it is possible to learn by example. One recursive function we have already seen implements Euclid's Algorithm:

```
fun gcd(m,n) =
      if m=0 then n
             else gcd(n mod m, m);
> val gcd = fn : int * int -> int
```

The Greatest Common Divisor of two integers is by definition the greatest integer that divides both. Euclid's Algorithm is correct because the divisors of m and n are the same as those of m and $n - m$, and, by repeated subtraction, the same as the divisors of m and n mod m. Regarding its efficiency, consider

$$gcd(5499, 6812) \Rightarrow gcd(1313, 5499) \Rightarrow gcd(247, 1313)$$
$$\Rightarrow gcd(78, 247) \Rightarrow gcd(13, 78) \Rightarrow gcd(0, 13) \Rightarrow 13$$

Euclid's Algorithm dates from antiquity. We seldom can draw on 2000 years of expertise, but we should aim for equally elegant and efficient solutions.

Recursion involves reducing a problem to smaller subproblems. The key to efficiency is to select the right subproblems. There must not be too many of them, and the rest of the computation should be reasonably simple.

2.14   *Raising to an integer power*
Integer exponentiation is a practical demonstration of recursion, for ML has no exponentiation operator. The obvious way to compute x^k is repeated multiplication by x. Using recursion, the problem x^k is reduced to the subproblem x^{k-1}

But x^{10} need not involve 10 multiplications. We can compute x^5 and then square it. Since $x^5 = x \times x^4$, we can compute x^4 by squaring also:

$$x^{10} = (x^5)^2 = (x \times x^4)^2 = (x \times (x^2)^2)^2$$

By exploiting the law $x^{2n} = (x^n)^2$ we have improved vastly over repeated multiplication. But the computation is still messy; using instead $x^{2n} = (x^2)^n$ eliminates the nested squaring:

$$2^{10} = 4^5 = 4 \times 16^2 = 4 \times 256^1 = 1024$$

By this approach, *power* computes x^k for real x and integer $k > 0$:

```
fun power(x,k) : real =
    if k=1 then x
    else if k mod 2 = 0 then      power(x*x, k div 2)
                         else x * power(x*x, k div 2);
> val power = fn : real * int -> real
```

Note how *mod* tests whether the exponent is even. Integer division (*div*) truncates its result to an integer if k is odd. The function *power* embodies the equations (for $n > 0$)

$$x^1 = x$$
$$x^{2n} = (x^2)^n$$
$$x^{2n+1} = x \times (x^2)^n.$$

We can test *power* using the built-in exponential and logarithm functions:

```
power(2.0,10);
> 1024.0 : real
power(1.01, 925);
> 9937.353723 : real
exp(925.0 * ln 1.01);
> 9937.353723 : real
```

Reducing x^{2n} to $(x^2)^n$ instead of $(x^n)^2$ makes *power* iterative in its first recursive call. The second call (for odd exponents) can be made iterative only by introducing an argument to hold the result, which is a needless complication.

Exercise 2.11   Write the computation steps for $power(2.0, 29)$.

Exercise 2.12   How many multiplications does $power(x, k)$ perform in the worst case?

Exercise 2.13   Why not take $k = 0$ for the base case instead of $k = 1$?

2.15   *Fibonacci numbers*

The Fibonacci sequence 0, 1, 1, 2, 3, 5, 8, 13, 21, 34, 55, ..., is popular with mathematical hobbyists because it enjoys many fascinating properties. The sequence (F_n) is defined by

$$F_0 = 0$$
$$F_1 = 1$$
$$F_n = F_{n-2} + F_{n-1} \qquad\qquad \text{for } n \geq 2.$$

The corresponding recursive function is a standard benchmark for measuring the efficiency of compiled code! It is far too slow for any other use because it computes subproblems repeatedly. Since

$$F_8 = F_6 + F_7 = F_6 + (F_5 + F_6)$$

it computes F_6 twice.

Each Fibonacci number is the sum of the previous two:

$$0 + 1 = 1 \quad 1 + 1 = 2 \quad 1 + 2 = 3 \quad 2 + 3 = 5 \quad 3 + 5 = 8 \cdots$$

So we should compute with pairs of numbers. The function *nextfib* takes (F_{n-1}, F_n) and returns the next pair (F_n, F_{n+1}).

```
fun nextfib(prev, curr :int) = (curr, prev+curr);
> val nextfib = fn : int * int -> int * int
```

The special name *it*, by referring to the previous pair, helps to demonstrate *nextfib*:

```
nextfib (0,1);
> (1, 1) : int * int
nextfib it;
> (1, 2) : int * int
nextfib it;
> (2, 3) : int * int
nextfib it;
> (3, 5) : int * int
```

Recursion applies *nextfib* the requisite number of times:

```
fun fibpair (n) =
        if n=1 then  (0,1)  else  nextfib(fibpair(n-1));
> val fibpair = fn : int -> int * int
```

It quickly computes (F_{19}, F_{20}), which previously would have required over a million function calls:

```
fibpair 20;
> (4181, 6765) : int * int
```

This illustrates computing with pairs, but is clumsy: *fibpair* builds the nest of calls

$$nextfib(nextfib(\cdots nextfib(0, 1) \cdots)).$$

Let us turn the computation inside out:

```
fun itfib (n, prev, curr) : int =
        if n=1 then curr        (*does not work for n=0*)
        else itfib (n-1, curr, prev+curr);
> val itfib = fn : int * int * int -> int
```

The function *fib* calls *itfib* with correct initial arguments:

```
fun fib (n) = itfib(n,0,1);
> val fib = fn : int -> int
fib 20;
> 6765 : int
fib 100;
> 354224848179261915075 : int
```

For Fibonacci numbers, iteration is clearer than recursion:

$$itfib(7, 0, 1) \Rightarrow itfib(6, 1, 1) \Rightarrow \cdots itfib(0, 8, 13) \Rightarrow 13$$

Exercise 2.14   How is the repeated computation in the recursive definition of F_n related to the call-by-name rule? Could lazy evaluation execute this definition efficiently?

Exercise 2.15   Show that the number of steps needed to compute F_n by its recursive definition is exponential in n. How many steps does *fib* perform? Assume that call-by-value is used.

Exercise 2.16   What is the value of $itfib(n, F_{k-1}, F_k)$?

2.16   *Integer square roots*

The integer square root of n is the integer k such that

$$k^2 \leq n < (k + 1)^2.$$

To compute this by recursion, we must choose a subproblem: some integer smaller than n. Division by 2 is often helpful, but how can we obtain $\sqrt{2x}$ from $\sqrt{x}$? Observe that $\sqrt{4x} = 2\sqrt{x}$ (for real x); division by 4 may lead to a simple algorithm.

Suppose $n > 0$. Since n may not be exactly divisible by 4, write $n = 4m + r$, where $r = 0$, 1, 2, or 3. Since $m < n$ we can recursively find the integer square root of m:

$$i^2 \leq m < (i + 1)^2.$$

Since m and i are integers, $m + 1 \leq (i + 1)^2$. Multiplication by 4 implies $4i^2 \leq 4m$ and $4(m + 1) \leq 4(i + 1)^2$. Therefore

$$(2i)^2 \leq 4m \leq n < 4m + 4 \leq (2i + 2)^2.$$

The square root of n is $2i$ or $2i + 1$. There is only to test whether $(2i + 1)^2 \leq n$, determining whether a 1 should be added.

```
fun increase(k,n) = if (k+1)*(k+1) > n  then  k  else  k+1;
> val increase = fn : int * int -> int
```

The recursion terminates when $n = 0$. Repeated integer division
will reduce any number to 0 eventually:

```
fun introot n =
        if n=0 then  0  else  increase(2 * introot(n div 4), n);
> val introot = fn : int -> int
```

There are faster methods of computing square roots, but ours is
respectably fast and is a simple demonstration of recursion.

```
introot 123456789;
> 11111 : int
it*it;
> 123454321 : int
introot 2000000000000000000000000000000000;
> 1414213562373095 : int
it*it;
> 1999999999999999861967979879025 : int
```

Exercise 2.17   Code this integer square root algorithm using iteration in a procedural programming language.

Exercise 2.18   Define an ML function for computing the Greatest
Common Divisor, based on these equations (m and n range over
positive integers):

$$GCD(2m, 2n) = 2 \times GCD(m, n)$$
$$GCD(2m, 2n + 1) = GCD(m, 2n + 1)$$
$$GCD(2m + 1, 2n + 1) = GCD(n - m, 2m + 1) \qquad m < n$$
$$GCD(m, m) = m.$$

How does this compare with Euclid's Algorithm?

Local declarations

Reducing the fraction n/d to least terms, where n and d
have no common factor, involves dividing both numbers by their
GCD.

```
fun fraction (n,d) = (n div gcd(n,d), d div gcd(n,d));
```

The wasteful re-computation of $gcd(n, d)$ can be prevented by first
defining an auxiliary function:

```
fun divideboth (n,d,com) = (n div com, d div com);
fun fraction (n,d) = divideboth (n,d,gcd(n,d));
```

But this is a contorted way of giving $gcd(n, d)$ the name *com*. ML allows the declaration of names within an expression:

```
fun fraction (n,d) =
    let val com = gcd(n,d)
    in  (n div com, d div com)  end;
> val fraction = fn : int * int -> int * int
```

We have used a **let** expression, which has the general form

> **let** D **in** E **end**

During evaluation, the declaration D is evaluated first: expressions within the declaration are evaluated, and the results given names. Then the expression E is evaluated, and the value returned. The declaration is visible only inside the **let** expression.

Typically D is a compound declaration, which consists of a list of declarations:

> $D_1; D_2; \ldots; D_n$

The effect of each declaration is visible in subsequent ones. The semicolons are optional and many programmers omit them.

2.17 *Example: real square roots*

The Newton-Raphson method of finding roots of a function, given a good initial approximation, converges rapidly. It is highly effective for computing square roots. To compute $\sqrt{a}$, choose any positive x_0, say 1, as the first approximation. If x is the current approximation then the next approximation is $(a/x + x)/2$. Stop as soon as the difference becomes small enough.

The function *findroot* performs this computation, where x approximates the square root of a and *acc* is the desired accuracy (relative to x). Since the next approximation is used several times, it is given the name *nextx*.

```
fun findroot (a, x, acc) =
    let val nextx = (a/x + x) / 2.0
    in  if abs (x-nextx) < acc*x
        then  nextx  else  findroot (a, nextx, acc)
    end;
> val findroot = fn : (real * real * real) -> real
```

The function *sqroot* calls *findroot* with suitable starting values.

```
fun sqroot a = findroot (a, 1.0, 1.0E~10);
> val sqroot = fn : real -> real
sqroot 2.0;
> 1.414213562 : real
it*it;
> 2.0 : real
```

Nested function definitions. Our square root function is still not ideal. The arguments *a* and *acc* are passed unchanged in every recursive call of *findroot*. They can be made global to *findroot* for efficiency and clarity.

A further **let** declaration nests *findroot* within *sqroot*. The accuracy *acc* is declared first, to be visible in *findroot*; the argument *a* is also visible.

```
fun sqroot a =
      let val acc = 1.0E~10
          fun findroot x =
                  let val nextx = (a/x + x) / 2.0
                  in  if abs (x-nextx) < acc*x
                         then   nextx  else   findroot nextx
                  end
      in   findroot 1.0   end;
> val sqroot = fn : real -> real
```

As we see from ML's response, *findroot* is not visible outside *sqroot*.

Most kinds of declaration are permitted within **let**. Values, functions, types and exceptions may be declared.

When not to use **let**. Consider taking the minimum of sin *x* and cos *x*. You could name these quantities using **let**:

```
let val a = sin x
    val b = cos x
in  if a<b then a else b   end
```

Instead, define a function for the minimum of two real numbers:

```
fun min(a,b) : real =  if a<b then a else b;
```

Now *min*(*sin x, cos x*) is clear because *min* computes something familiar. Take every opportunity to define meaningful functions, even if they are only needed once.

2.18   *Hiding declarations using* `local`

A `local` declaration resembles a `let` expression:

`local` D_1 `in` D_2 `end`

This declaration behaves like the list of declarations D_1; D_2 except that D_1 is visible only within D_2, not outside. Since a list of declarations is regarded as one declaration, both D_1 and D_2 can declare any number of names.

While `let` is frequently used, `local` is not. Its sole purpose is to hide a declaration. Recall *itfib* and *fib*, which compute Fibonacci numbers. The function *itfib* should be called only from *fib*:

```
local
    fun itfib (n, prev, curr) : int =
            if n=1
            then curr
            else itfib (n-1, curr, prev+curr)
in
    fun fib (n) = itfib(n,0,1)
end;
> val fib = fn : int -> int
```

Here the `local` declaration makes *itfib* private to *fib*.

Exercise 2.19   Above we have used `local` to hide the function *itfib*. Why not simply nest the declaration of *itfib* within *fib*? Compare with the treatment of *findroot* and *sqroot*.

2.19   *Simultaneous declarations*

A simultaneous declaration defines several names at once. Normally the declarations are independent. But `fun` declarations allow recursion, so a simultaneous declaration can introduce mutually recursive functions.

A `val` declaration of the form

`val` Id_1 `=` E_1 `and` $\cdots$ `and` Id_n `=` E_n

evaluates the expressions E_1, ..., E_n and then declares the identifiers Id_1, ..., Id_n to have the corresponding values. Since the declarations do not take effect until all the expressions are evaluated, their order is immaterial.

Here we define names for π, e and the logarithm of 2.

```
val pi   = 4.0 * arctan 1.0
and e    = exp 1.0
and log2 = ln 2.0;
> pi = 3.141592654 : real
> e = 2.718281828 : real
> log2 = 0.693147806 : real
```

A single input declares three names. The simultaneous declaration emphasizes that they are independent.

Now let us define the chimes of Big Ben:

```
val one = "BONG ";
> val one = "BONG " : string
val three = one^one^one;
> val three = "BONG BONG BONG " : string
val six = three^three;
> val six = "BONG BONG BONG BONG BONG BONG " : string
```

There must be three separate declarations, and in this order.

A simultaneous declaration can also swap the values of names:

```
val one = three and three = one;
> val one = "BONG BONG BONG " : string
> val three = "BONG " : string
```

Mutually recursive functions. Several functions are **mutually recursive** if they are defined recursively in terms of each other. A recursive descent parser is a typical case. This sort of parser has one function for each element of the grammar, and most grammars are mutually recursive: an ML declaration can contain expressions, while an expression can contain declarations. Functions to traverse the resulting parse tree will also be mutually recursive.

Parsing and trees are discussed later in this book. For a simpler example, consider summing the series

$$\frac{\pi}{4} = 1 - \frac{1}{3} + \frac{1}{5} - \frac{1}{7} \cdots + \frac{1}{4k+1} - \frac{1}{4k+3} \cdots$$

By mutual recursion, the final term of the summation can be either positive or negative:

```
fun pos d = neg(d-2.0) + 1.0/d
and neg d = if d>0.0  then  pos(d-2.0) - 1.0/d  else  0.0;
> val pos = fn : real -> real
> val neg = fn : real -> real
```

Two functions are declared. The series converges glacially:

```
4.0 * pos(201.0);
> 3.151493401
4.0 * neg(8003.0);
> 3.141342779
```

Mutually recursive functions can often be combined into one function with the help of an additional argument:

```
fun sum(d,one) =
        if d>0.0  then  sum(d-2.0, ~one) + one/d  else  0.0;
```

The value of $sum(d,1.0)$ equals that of $pos(d)$, and $sum(d,~1.0)$ equals $neg(d)$.

Emulating goto *statements.* Functional programming and imperative programming are more alike than you may imagine. Any combination of goto and assignment statements — the worst of imperative code — can be translated into a set of mutually recursive functions. Here is a simple case:

```
var x := 0;   y := 0;   z := 0;
F:   x := x+1; goto G
G:   if y<z then goto F   else   (y := x+y;   goto H)
H:   if z>0 then (z := z-x;   goto F)  else   stop
```

For each of the labels, F, G and H, define mutually recursive functions. The argument of each function is a tuple holding all of the variables.

```
fun F(x,y,z) = G(x+1,y,z)
and G(x,y,z) = if y<z then F(x,y,z)  else  H(x,x+y,z)
and H(x,y,z) = if z>0 then F(x,y,z-x)  else  (x,y,z);
> val F = fn : int * int * int -> int * int * int
> val G = fn : int * int * int -> int * int * int
> val H = fn : int * int * int -> int * int * int
```

Calling $f(0,0,0)$ gives x, y and z their initial values for execution, and returns the result of the imperative code.

```
f(0,0,0);
> (1,1,0) : int * int * int
```

Functional programs are referentially transparent, yet can be totally opaque. If your code starts to look like this, beware!

Exercise 2.20   What is the effect of this declaration?

```
val (pi,log2) = (log2,pi);
```

Exercise 2.21 Consider the sequence (P_n) defined for $n \geq 1$ by

$$P_n = 1 + \sum_{k=1}^{n-1} P_k.$$

(In particular, $P_1 = 1$.) Express this computation as an ML function. How efficient is it? Is there a faster way of computing P_n?

Polymorphic type checking

Until recently, the debate on type checking has been deadlocked, with two rigid positions:

> Weakly typed languages like Lisp and Prolog give programmers the freedom they need when writing large programs.
> Strongly typed languages like Pascal give programmers security by restricting their freedom to make mistakes.

Polymorphic type checking offers a new position: the security of strong type checking, as well as great flexibility. Programs are not cluttered with type specifications since most type information is deduced automatically.

A type denotes a collection of values. A function's argument type specifies which values are acceptable as arguments. The result type specifies which values could be returned as results. Thus, *div* demands a pair of integers as argument; its result can only be an integer. If the divisor is zero then there will be no result at all: an error will be signalled instead. Even in this exceptional situation, the function *div* is faithful to its type.

ML can also assign a type to the identity function, which returns its argument unchanged. Because the identity function can be applied to an argument of any type, it is **polymorphic**. Generally speaking, an object is polymorphic if it can be regarded as having multiple types. There are several approaches to polymorphism (Cardelli & Wegner, 1985). ML polymorphism is based on **type schemes**, which are like patterns or templates for types. For instance, the identity function has the type scheme $\alpha \to \alpha$.

2.20   *Type inference*

Given little or no explicit type information, ML can infer all the types involved with a function definition. Type inference follows a natural but rigorous procedure. ML notes the types of any constants, and applies type checking rules for each form of expression. Each variable must have the same type everywhere in the definition. The type of each overloaded operator (like +) must be determined from the context.

Here is the type checking rule for the conditional expression. If E has type *bool* and E_1 and E_2 have the same type, say τ, then

$$\text{if } E \text{ then } E_1 \text{ else } E_2$$

also has type τ. Otherwise, the expression is ill-typed.

Let us examine, step by step, the type checking of *facti*:

```
fun facti (n,p) =
        if n=0 then p   else   facti(n-1, n*p);
```

The constants 0 and 1 have type *int*. Therefore $n=0$ and $n-1$ involve integers, so n has type *int*. Now $n*p$ must be integer multiplication, so p has type *int*. Since p is returned as the result of *facti*, its result type is *int* and its argument type is $int \times int$. This fits with the recursive call. Having made all these checks, ML can respond

```
> val facti = fn : int * int -> int
```

If the types are not consistent, the compiler rejects the definition.

Exercise 2.22   Describe the steps in the type checking of *itfib*.

Exercise 2.23   Type check the following function definition:

```
fun f (k,m) = if k=0 then 1 else f(k-1);
```

2.21   *Polymorphic function definitions*

If type inference leaves some types completely unconstrained then the definition is polymorphic — literally, 'having many forms.' Most polymorphic functions involve pairs, lists and other data structures. They usually do something simple, like pairing a value with itself:

```
fun pairself x = (x,x);
> val pairself = fn : 'a -> 'a * 'a
```

This type is polymorphic because it contains a **type variable**, namely 'a. In ML, type variables begin with a prime (single quote) character.

     'b   'c   'we_band_of_brothers   '3

Let us write α, β, γ for the ML type variables 'a, 'b, 'c, because type variables are traditionally Greek letters. Write $x : \tau$ to mean 'x has type τ', for instance *pairself* $: \alpha \to (\alpha \times \alpha)$. Incidentally, $\times$ has higher precedence than $\to$; the type of *pairself* can be written $\alpha \to \alpha \times \alpha$.

A polymorphic type is a type scheme. Substituting types for type variables forms an **instance** of the scheme. The collection of values denoted by a type scheme is essentially the intersection of all of its instances. An object having a polymorphic type has infinitely many types. When *pairself* is applied to a real number, it effectively has type $real \to real \times real$.

> *pairself* 4.0;
> *> (4.0, 4.0) : real * real*

Applied to an integer, *pairself* effectively has type $int \to int \times int$.

> *pairself* 7;
> *> (7, 7) : int * int*

Here *pairself* is applied to a pair; the result is called *pp*.

> val *pp* = *pairself* ("Help!",999);
> *> val pp = (("Help!", 999), ("Help!", 999))*
> *> : (string * int) * (string * int)*

Projection functions return a component of a pair. The function *fst* returns the first component; *snd* returns the second:

> fun *fst* (*x*,*y*) = *x*;
> *> val fst = fn : 'a * 'b -> 'a*
> fun *snd* (*x*,*y*) = *y*;
> *> val snd = fn : 'a * 'b -> 'b*

Before considering their polymorphic types, we apply them to *pp*:

> *fst pp*;
> *> ("Help!", 999) : string * int*
> *snd*(*fst pp*);
> *> 999 : int*

The type of *fst* is $\alpha \times \beta \to \alpha$, with two type variables. The argument pair may involve any two types (not necessarily different); the result has the former type.

Polymorphic functions can express other functions. The function that takes $((x, y), w)$ to x could be coded directly, but two applications of *fst* also work:

```
fun fstfst z = fst(fst z);
> val fstfst = fn : ('a * 'b) * 'c -> 'a
fstfst pp;
> "Help!" : string
```

A polymorphic function can have different types within the same expression. The inner *fst* has type $(\alpha \times \beta) \times \gamma \rightarrow \alpha \times \beta$. This instance is itself polymorphic. The outer *fst* has type $\alpha \times \beta \rightarrow \alpha$. The type $(\alpha \times \beta) \times \gamma \rightarrow \alpha$ is natural for *fstfst*.

Now for something obscure. What does this function do?

```
fun silly x = fstfst(pairself(pairself x));
> val silly = fn : 'a -> 'a
```

Not very much:

```
silly "Just let me be!";
> "Just let me be!" : string
```

Its type, $\alpha \rightarrow \alpha$, suggests that *silly* is the identity function. This function can be expressed rather more directly:

```
fun I x = x;
> val I = fn : 'a -> 'a
```

Exercise 2.24   What is the type of this function?

```
fun swap (x,y) = (y,x);
```

2.22   *Further issues*

Milner (1978) presented an algorithm for polymorphic type checking and proved that a type-correct program could not suffer a run-time type error. Damas and Milner (1982) proved that the types inferred by this algorithm are principal: as polymorphic as possible. These results hold for an ideal functional language. For Standard ML, things are much more complicated.

Equality. The function that tests equality is polymorphic in a limited sense: it is defined for most, not all, types. Standard ML provides a class of **equality type variables** to range over this restricted collection of types. Equality type variables begin with two prime characters: ''a, ''b, ''c and so forth. Equality polymorphism is discussed in the next chapter.

Overloading. Recall that certain built-in functions are overloaded, standing for several different functions at once. Addition (+) is defined for integers and reals, for instance. Overloading sits uneasily with polymorphism. It complicates the type checking algorithm and frequently forces programmers to write type constraints. Fortunately there are only a few overloaded functions, and programmers cannot introduce further overloading.

Reference types and assignments. ML's reference values denote store locations that can be updated. The basic type checking algorithm does not cope with assignments to polymorphic references. ML provides yet another class of type variables, called **weak type variables**, which offer a limited degree of polymorphism in such cases. Chapter 8 describes these matters; for now, let us remain with purely functional programming.

Summary of main points

A variable stands for a value and cannot be updated.

A declaration gives a meaning to a name without affecting existing uses of that name.

The type of an expression can be determined without computing its value.

A function can take a tuple of arguments and return a tuple of results.

An iterative function employs recursion in a limited fashion, where recursive calls are essentially jumps.

A polymorphic type is a scheme containing type variables.

3

Lists

In a public lecture, C. A. R. Hoare (1971) described his algorithm for finding the ith smallest integer in a collection. This algorithm is subtle, but Hoare described it with admirable clarity as a game of solitaire. Each playing card carried an integer. Moving cards from pile to pile by simple rules, the required integer could quickly be found.

Then Hoare changed the rules of the game. Each card occupied a fixed position, and could only be moved if exchanged with another card. This described the algorithm in terms of arrays. Arrays have great efficiency, but they also have a cost. They probably defeated much of the audience, as they defeat experienced programmers. Harlan Mills and Richard Linger (1986) claim that programmers become more productive when arrays are restricted to stacks, queues, etc., without subscripting.

Functional programmers process collections of items using lists. Like Hoare's stacks of cards, lists allow items to be dealt with one at a time, with great clarity. Lists are easy to understand mathematically, and turn out to be more efficient than commonly thought.

Chapter outline

This chapter describes how to program with lists in Standard ML. It presents several examples that would normally involve arrays, such as sorting 10,000 random numbers.

The chapter contains the following sections:

Introduction to lists. The notion of list is introduced. Standard ML operates on lists using pattern-matching.

Some fundamental list functions. A library of functions is presented. These are instructive examples of list programming, and are indispensable when tackling harder problems.

Applications of lists. Some complicated examples demonstrate the kinds of problems that can be solved using lists.

The equality test in polymorphic functions. Equality polymorphism is introduced and illustrated with many examples. These include a useful library of functions on finite sets.

Sorting: A case study. Procedural programming and functional programming are compared in efficiency. On a particular machine, a procedural program sorts 10,000 real numbers about three times faster than a functional program. Functional sorting programs, however, are concise and clear.

Introduction to lists

A **list** is a finite sequence of elements. Typical lists are [3,5,9] and ["fair","Ophelia"]. The empty list, [], has no elements. The order of elements is significant, and elements may appear more than once. For instance, the following lists are all different:

> [3,4]   [4,3]   [3,4,3]   [3,3,4]

The elements of a list may have any type, including tuples and even other lists. Every element of a list must have the same type. Suppose this type is τ; the type of the list is then τ *list*. Thus

```
[(1,"One"), (2,"Two"), (3,"Three")]    :   (int*string) list
[ [3.1], [], [5.7, ~0.6] ]             :   (real list) list
```

The empty list, [], has the polymorphic type α *list*. It can be regarded as having any type of elements.

Observe that the type operator *list* has a postfix syntax. It binds more tightly than $\times$ and $\rightarrow$. So *int* $\times$ *string list* is the same type as *int* $\times$ (*string list*), not (*int* $\times$ *string*)*list*. Also, *int list list* is the same type as (*int list*)*list*.

3.1   *Building a list*

Every list is constructed by just two primitives: the constant *nil* and the infix operator :: , pronounced 'cons' for 'construct'.

> *nil* is a synonym for the empty list, [].
>
> The operator :: makes a list by putting an element in front of an existing list.

Every list is either *nil*, if empty, or has the form $x :: l$ where x is its **head** and l its **tail**. The tail is itself a list. The list operations are not symmetric: the first element of a list is much more easily reached than the last.

If l is the list $[x_1, \ldots, x_n]$ and x is a value of correct type then $x :: l$ is the list $[x, x_1, \ldots, x_n]$. Making the new list does not affect the value of l. The list $[3, 5, 9]$ is constructed as follows:

$$
\begin{aligned}
nil &= [] \\
9 :: [] &= [9] \\
5 :: [9] &= [5, 9] \\
3 :: [5, 9] &= [3, 5, 9]
\end{aligned}
$$

Observe that the elements are taken in reverse order.*

The list $[3, 5, 9]$ can be written in many ways, such as $3 :: (5 :: (9 :: nil))$, or $3 :: (5 :: [9])$, or $3 :: [5, 9]$. To save writing parentheses, the infix operator 'cons' groups to the right. The notation $[x_1, x_2, \ldots, x_n]$ stands for $x_1 :: x_2 :: \cdots :: x_n :: nil$. The elements may be given by expressions, not just constants. A list of the values of various real expressions is

```
[ sin 0.5, cos 0.5, exp 0.5 ];
> [0.4794255386, 0.8775825619, 1.648721271] : real list
```

List notation makes a list with a fixed number of elements. Consider how to build the list of integers from m to n:

$$[m, m + 1, \ldots, n]$$

First compare m and n. If $m > n$ then there are no numbers between m and n; the list is empty. Otherwise the head of the list is m and the tail is $[m+1, \ldots, n]$. Constructing the tail recursively,

---

* ML's syntax for lists differs subtly from Prolog's. In Prolog, [5|[6]] is the same list as [5,6]. In ML, [5::[6]] is the same list as [[5,6]].

the result is obtained by

$$m :: [m + 1, \ldots, n].$$

This process corresponds to a simple ML function:

```
fun upto (m,n) =
    if m>n then [] else  m :: upto(m+1,n);
> val upto = fn : int * int -> int list
upto(2,5);
> [2,3,4,5] : int list
```

The only difference between the list $x::l$ and the pair (x, l) is the type. Weakly typed languages like Lisp represent lists by pairing:

```
(3, (5, (9, "nil")))
```

Here `"nil"` is some end marker and the list is $[3, 5, 9]$. This representation of lists does not work in ML because the type of a 'list' depends on the number of elements. What type could *upto* have?

3.2   *Operating on a list*

Lists, like tuples, are structured values. In ML, a function on tuples can be written with a pattern for its argument, showing its structure and naming the components. Functions over lists can be written similarly. For example,

```
fun prodof3 [i,j,k] : int = i*j*k;
```

defines a function to take the product of a list of numbers — but only if there are exactly three of them!

List operations are usually defined by recursion, treating several cases. What is the product of a list of integers?

> If the list is empty, the product is 1 (by convention).
> If the list is non-empty, the product is the head times the product of the tail.

It can be expressed in ML like this:

```
fun prod []       = 1
  | prod (n::ns) = n * (prod ns);
> val prod = fn : int list -> int
```

The function consists of two clauses separated by a vertical bar (I). Each clause treats one argument pattern. There may be several clauses and complex patterns, provided the types agree. Since the patterns involve lists, and the result can be the integer 1, ML infers that *prod* maps a list of integers to an integer.

```
prod[2,3,5];
> 30 : int
```

Empty versus non-empty is the commonest sort of case analysis for lists. Finding the maximum of a list of integers requires something different, for the empty list is awkward. (Is its maximum infinity?) The two cases are

> The maximum of the one-element list $[m]$ is m.
>
> To find the maximum of a list with two or more elements $[m, n, \ldots]$, remove the smaller of m or n and find the maximum of the remaining numbers.

This gives the ML function

```
fun maxl[m] : int   = m
  | maxl(m::n::ns) = if m>n  then maxl(m::ns)
                            else maxl(n::ns);
> ***Warning:  Patterns not exhaustive
> val maxl = fn : int list -> int
```

Note the warning message: ML detects that *maxl* is undefined for the empty list. Also, observe how the pattern $m :: n :: ns$ describes a list of the form $[m, n, \ldots]$. The smaller element is dropped in the recursive call.

It works — except for the empty list.

```
maxl [ ~4, 0, ~12];
> 0 : int
maxl [];
> Exception: Match
```

An **exception**, for the time being, can be regarded as a run-time error. The function *maxl* has been applied to an argument for which it is undefined. Normally exceptions abort execution. They can be trapped, as we shall see in the next chapter.

Intermediate lists. Lists are sometimes generated and consumed within a computation. For instance, the factorial function has a clever definition using *prod* and *upto*:

```
fun factl (n) = prod (upto (1,n));
> val factl = fn : int -> int
factl 7;
> 5040 : int
```

This definition is concise and clear, avoiding explicit recursion. The cost of building the list $[1, 2, \ldots, n]$ may not matter. On the other hand, functional programming should facilitate reasoning about programs. This does not happen here. The trivial law

$$factl(m + 1) = (m + 1) \times factl(m)$$

has no obvious proof. Opening up its definition, we get

$$factl(m + 1) = prod(upto(1, m + 1)) = ?$$

The next step is unclear because the recursion in *upto* follows its first argument, not the second. The honest recursive definition of factorial seems better.

Strings and lists. Lists are important in string processing. Most functional languages provide a type of single characters, regarding strings as lists of characters. In Standard ML, *string* is a primitive type and a character is simply a string whose *size* equals 1. The built-in function *explode* converts a string to a list of characters. The built-in function *implode* performs the inverse operation, concatenating a list of strings.

```
explode "Macbeth";
> ["M", "a", "c", "b", "e", "t", "h"] : string list
implode it;
> "Macbeth" : string
```

Some fundamental list functions

Given a list we can find its length, select the nth element, take a prefix or suffix, or reverse the order of its elements. Given two lists we can append one to the other, or, if they have equal length, pair corresponding elements. The functions defined in this section are indispensable, and will be taken for granted in the rest of the book. Most Standard ML systems provide these functions; **append** (the infix @) and **reverse** (*rev*) are part of the language itself. All of these functions are polymorphic.

Efficiency becomes a central concern here. For some functions, a naïve recursive definition is less efficient than an iterative version. For others, an iterative style impairs both readability and efficiency. Many functions can be made more efficient by eliminating their calls to append.

3.3   *Testing lists and taking them apart*
The three basic functions on lists are *null*, *hd* and *tl*.

The function null. This function tests whether a list is empty:

```
fun null    []    = true
  | null (_::_) = false;
> val null = fn : 'a list -> bool
```

The function is polymorphic: testing whether a list is empty does not examine its elements. The underscores (_) in the second pattern take the place of components whose values are not needed in the clause. These underscores, called **wildcard** patterns, save us from inventing names for such components.

The function hd. This function returns the head (the first element) of a non-empty list:

```
fun hd (x::_) = x;
> ***Warning:  Patterns not exhaustive
> val hd = fn : 'a list -> 'a
```

This pattern has a wildcard for the tail, while the head is called x. Since there is no pattern for the empty list, ML prints a warning. It is a partial function like *maxl*.

Here we have a list of lists. Its head is a list and the head of that is an integer. Each use of *hd* removes one level of brackets.

```
hd[[[1,2], [3]], [[4]]];
> [[1,2],[3]] : (int list) list
hd it;
> [1,2] : int list
hd it;
> 1 : int
```

What if we type *hd it*; once more?

The function tl. This returns the tail of a non-empty list. The tail, remember, is the list consisting of the all elements but the first.

```
fun tl (_::xs) = xs;
> ***Warning:  Patterns not exhaustive
> val tl = fn : 'a list -> 'a list
```

Like *hd*, this is a partial function. Its result is always another list:

```
tl ["Out","damned","spot!"];
> ["damned","spot!"] : string list
tl it;
> ["spot!"] : string list
tl it;
> [] : string list
tl it;
> Exception: Match
```

Attempting to take the tail of the empty list is an error.

Through *null*, *hd* and *tl*, all other list functions can be written without pattern-matching. The product of a list of integers can be computed like this:

```
fun prod ns = if null ns then 1
                         else (hd ns) * (prod (tl ns));
```

If you prefer this version of *prod*, you might as well give up ML for Lisp. For added clarity, Lisp primitives have names like CAR and CDR. Normal people find pattern-matching more readable than *hd* and *tl*. A good ML compiler analyses the set of patterns to generate the best code for the function. More importantly, the compiler prints a warning if the patterns do not cover all possible arguments of the function.

Exercise 3.1 Write a version of *maxl* using *null*, *hd* and *tl*, instead of pattern-matching.

Exercise 3.2 Write a function to return the last element of a list.

3.4   *List processing by numbers*

We now define the functions *length*, *take* and *drop*, which behave as follows:

$$l = [\underbrace{x_0, \ldots, x_{i-1}}_{take(i, l)}, \underbrace{x_i, \ldots, x_{n-1}}_{drop(i, l)}] \qquad length(l) = n$$

The function length. The length of a list can be computed by a naïve recursion:

```
fun nlength []       = 0
  | nlength (x::xs) = 1 + nlength xs;
> val nlength = fn : 'a list -> int
```

Its type, $\alpha\ list \rightarrow int$, permits *nlength* to be applied to a list regardless of the type of its elements. Let us try it on a list of lists:

> *nlength* [[1,2,3], [4,5,6]];
> > *2 : int*

Did you think the answer would be 6?

Although correct, *nlength* is intolerably wasteful for long lists:

$$nlength[1, 2, 3, \ldots, 10000] \Rightarrow 1 + nlength[2, 3, \ldots, 10000]$$
$$\Rightarrow 1 + (1 + nlength[3, \ldots, 10000])$$
$$\vdots$$
$$\Rightarrow 1 + (1 + 9998)$$
$$\Rightarrow 1 + 9999 \Rightarrow 10000$$

The ones pile up, wasting space proportional to the length of the list, and could easily cause execution to abort. Much better is an iterative version of the function that accumulates the count in another argument:

```
local
    fun addlen (n, [])   = n
      | addlen (n, x::l) = addlen (n+1, l)
in
    fun length l = addlen (0,l)
end;
> val length = fn : 'a list -> int
length (explode"Throw physic to the dogs!");
> 25 : int
```

The function *addlen* adds the length of a list to another number, initially 0. Since *addlen* has no other purpose, it is declared **local** to *length*. It executes as follows:

$$addlen(0, [1, 2, 3, \ldots, 10000]) \Rightarrow addlen(1, [2, 3, \ldots, 10000])$$
$$\Rightarrow addlen(2, [3, \ldots, 10000])$$
$$\vdots$$
$$\Rightarrow addlen(10000, []) \Rightarrow 10000$$

The new length function is more efficient but less readable. If it is better, then should other recursive functions also be made iterative? Probably not. The length function is a basic utility, likely to be placed in a library. Library functions must be efficient and robust, even if they are not beautiful. Specialized functions like *prod* can be left in their natural form provided they perform adequately.

The function take. Calling $take(i,l)$ returns the list of the first i elements of l:

```
fun take (i, [])    = []
  | take (i, x::xs) = if i>0 then x::take(i-1,xs)
                             else [];
> val take = fn : int * 'a list -> 'a list
take (5, explode"Throw physic to the dogs!");
> ["T", "h", "r", "o", "w"] : string list
```

Here is a sample computation:

$$take(3, [9, 8, 7, 6]) \Rightarrow 9 :: take(2, [8, 7, 6])$$
$$\Rightarrow 9 :: (8 :: take(1, [7, 6]))$$
$$\Rightarrow 9 :: (8 :: (7 :: take(0, [6])))$$
$$\Rightarrow 9 :: (8 :: (7 :: []))$$
$$\Rightarrow 9 :: (8 :: [7])$$
$$\Rightarrow 9 :: [8, 7]$$
$$\Rightarrow [9, 8, 7]$$

Observe that $9 :: (8 :: (7 :: []))$ above is an expression, not a value. Evaluating it to the list $[9, 8, 7]$ performs work: it allocates store, which can be time-consuming. This point is obscured because our notation does not distinguish list expressions from list values.

The recursive calls to *take* get deeper and deeper, like *nlength*, which we have recently deplored. Let us try to make an iterative version of *take* by accumulating the result in an argument:

```
fun rtake (_, [], taken)    = taken
  | rtake (i, x::xs, taken) =
        if i>0  then  rtake(i-1, xs, x::taken) else  taken;
> val rtake = fn : int * 'a list * 'a list -> 'a list
```

The recursion is nice and shallow ...

$$rtake(3, [9, 8, 7, 6], []) \Rightarrow rtake(2, [8, 7, 6], [9])$$
$$\Rightarrow rtake(1, [7, 6], [8, 9])$$
$$\Rightarrow rtake(0, [6], [7, 8, 9])$$
$$\Rightarrow [7, 8, 9]$$

... but the output is reversed!

If a reversed output is acceptable, *rtake* is worth considering. However, the size of the recursion in *take* is reasonable compared with the size of the result. While *nlength* returns an integer, *take* returns a list. Building a list is slow, which is usually more important than the space temporarily consumed by deep recursion. Efficiency is a matter of getting the costs into proportion.

The function drop. The list $drop(i,l)$ contains all but the first i elements of l:

```
fun drop (_, [])    = []
  | drop (i, x::xs) = if i>0 then drop (i-1, xs)
                              else x::xs;
> val drop = fn : int * 'a list -> 'a list
```

Luckily, the obvious recursion is iterative.

```
take (3, ["Never","shall","sun","that","morrow","see!"]);
> ["Never","shall","sun"] : string list
drop (3, ["Never","shall","sun","that","morrow","see!"]);
> ["that","morrow","see!"] : string list
```

Exercise 3.3 What results do $take(i,l)$ and $drop(i,l)$ return when $i > length(l)$? When $i < 0$?

Exercise 3.4 Write a function $nth(l,n)$ to return the nth element of l (where the head is element 0).

3.5   *Append and reverse*
    The infix operator @, which appends one list to another, and *rev*, which reverses a list, are built-in functions. Their definitions deserve close attention.

The append operation. Append puts the elements of one list after those of another list:

$$[x_1,\ldots,x_m] \,@\, [y_1,\ldots y_n] = [x_1,\ldots,x_m,y_1,\ldots y_n]$$

What sort of recursion accomplishes this? The traditional name **append** suggests that the action takes place at the end of a list, but lists are always built from the front. The following definition, in its essentials, dates to the early days of Lisp:

```
infix @;
fun []      @ ys = ys
  | (x::xs) @ ys = x :: (xs@ys);
> val @ = fn : 'a list * 'a list -> 'a list
```

Its type, $\alpha\ list \times \alpha\ list \to \alpha\ list$, accepts any two lists with the same element type — say, lists of strings and lists of lists:

```
["Why", "sinks"] @ ["that", "cauldron?"];
> ["Why", "sinks", "that", "cauldron?"] : string list
[[2,4,6,8], [3,9]] @ [[5], [7]];
> [[2, 4, 6, 8], [3, 9], [5], [7]] : int list list
```

The computation of $[2, 4, 6]$ @ $[8, 10]$ goes like this:

$$[2, 4, 6] \text{ @ } [8, 10] \Rightarrow 2 :: ([4, 6] \text{ @ } [8, 10])$$
$$\Rightarrow 2 :: (4 :: ([6] \text{ @ } [8, 10]))$$
$$\Rightarrow 2 :: (4 :: (6 :: ([] \text{ @ } [8, 10])))$$
$$\Rightarrow 2 :: (4 :: (6 :: [8, 10]))$$
$$\Rightarrow 2 :: (4 :: [6, 8, 10])$$
$$\Rightarrow 2 :: [4, 6, 8, 10]$$
$$\Rightarrow [2, 4, 6, 8, 10]$$

The last three steps put the elements from the first list on to the second. As with *take*, the cost of building the result exceeds that of the deep recursion; an iterative version is not needed. The cost of evaluating xs @ ys is proportional to the length of xs and is completely independent of ys. Even xs @ $[]$ makes a copy of xs.

In Pascal you can implement lists using pointer types, and join them by updating the last pointer of one list to point towards another. Destructive updating is faster than copying, but if you are careless your lists could end up in knots. What happens if the two lists happen to be the same pointer? ML lists involve internal pointers used safely. If you like living dangerously, ML has explicit pointer types — see Chapter 8.

The function rev. List reversal can be defined using append. The head of the list becomes the last element of the reversed list:

```
fun nrev []      = []
  | nrev (x::xs) = (nrev xs) @ [x];
> val nrev = fn : 'a list -> 'a list
```

This is grossly inefficient. If *nrev* is given a list of length $n > 0$, then append calls cons $(::)$ exactly $n-1$ times to copy the reversed tail. Constructing the list $[x]$ calls cons again, for a total of n calls. Reversing the tail requires $n - 1$ more conses, and so forth. The total number of conses is

$$0 + 1 + 2 + \cdots + n = \frac{n(n + 1)}{2}.$$

This cost is quadratic: proportional to n^2.

We have already seen, in *rtake*, another way of reversing a list: repeatedly move elements from one list to another.

```
fun revto ([],    ys) = ys
  | revto (x::xs,ys) = revto (xs, x::ys);
> val revto = fn : 'a list * 'a list -> 'a list
```

Append is never called. The number of steps is proportional to the length of the list being reversed. The function resembles append but reverses its first argument:

```
revto (["Macbeth","and","Banquo"], ["all", "hail!"]);
> ["Banquo","and","Macbeth","all","hail!"] : string list
```

The efficient reversal function calls *revto* with an empty list:

```
fun rev xs = revto(xs,[]);
> val rev = fn : 'a list -> 'a list
```

Here a slightly longer definition pays dramatically. Reversing a 1000-element list, *rev* calls :: exactly 1000 times, *nrev* 505,000 times. Furthermore, the recursion in *revto* is iterative. Its key idea — of accumulating list elements in an extra argument rather than appending — applies to many other functions.

Exercise 3.5   Write an append function, intended for a library, that handles *xs* @ [] efficiently.

Exercise 3.6   What would happen if we changed [*x*] to *x* in the definition of *nrev*?

Exercise 3.7   Show the computation steps to reverse the list $[1, 2, 3, 4]$ using *nrev* and then *rev*.

3.6   *Lists of lists, lists of pairs*

Pattern-matching and polymorphism cope nicely with combinations of data structures. Observe the types of these functions.

The function flat. This function makes a list consisting of all the elements of a list of lists:

```
fun flat []     = []
  | flat(l::ls) = l @ flat ls;
> val flat = fn : 'a list list -> 'a list
flat [["When","shall"], ["we","three"], ["meet","again"]];
> ["When","shall","we","three","meet","again"]: string list
```

The copying in *l* @ *flat ls* is reasonably fast because *l* is usually much shorter than *flat ls*.

The function combine. This function pairs corresponding members of two lists:

$$combine([x_1, \ldots, x_n], [y_1, \ldots, y_n]) = [(x_1, y_1), \ldots, (x_n, y_n)]$$

Although the definition contains complex patterns, it should be self-explanatory:

```
fun combine ([], [])     = []
  | combine(x::xs,y::ys) = (x,y) :: combine(xs,ys);
> ***Warning:  Patterns not exhaustive
> val combine = fn : 'a list * 'b list -> ('a*'b) list
```

The function split. The inverse of *combine*, called *split*, takes a list of pairs to a pair of lists:

$$split[(x_1, y_1), \ldots, (x_n, y_n)] = ([x_1, \ldots, x_n], [y_1, \ldots, y_n])$$

Building two lists simultaneously can be tricky in functional languages. One approach uses an extra function:

```
fun conspair ((x,y), (xs,ys)) = (x::xs, y::ys);

fun split []             = ([],[])
  | split(pair::pairs) = conspair(pair, split pairs);
```

A `let` declaration, where pattern-matching takes apart the result of the recursive call, eliminates the function *conspair*:

```
fun split []              = ([],[])
  | split((x,y)::pairs) =
          let val (xs,ys) = split pairs
          in  (x::xs, y::ys)  end;
> val split = fn : ('a*'b) list -> 'a list * 'b list
```

An iterative function can construct several results in its arguments. This is the simplest way to split a list, but the resulting lists are reversed.

```
fun revsplit([], xs, ys)          = (xs,ys)
  | revsplit((x,y)::pairs, xs, ys) =
          revsplit(pairs, x::xs, y::ys);
```

Exercise 3.8 Compare the following function with *flat*, considering its effect and efficiency:

```
fun f []          = []
  | f([]::ls)     = f(ls)
  | f((x::l)::ls) = x :: f(l::ls);
```

Exercise 3.9 Explain the warning for *combine*. Generalize the function to eliminate the warning.

Exercise 3.10 Discuss whether *rev*(*rtake*(*i*,*l*,[])) is more efficient than *take*(*i*,*l*), considering all the costs involved.

Applications of lists

This section demonstrates how lists can perform sophisticated tasks, like binary arithmetic and matrix operations. Two examples from the classic book *A Discipline of Programming* (Dijkstra, 1976) are also solved. Dijkstra presents programs in all their 'compelling and deep logical beauty'. His programs use arrays; do lists possess greater beauty?

3.7   *Binary arithmetic*

Functional programming may seem far removed from hardware, but lists are good for simulating digital circuits. Binary addition and multiplication are defined here for lists of zeros and ones.

Addition. If you have forgotten the rules for binary sums, have a look at the binary version of $11 + 30 = 41$:

$$
\begin{array}{r}
11110 \\
+ \quad 1011 \\
\hline
101001
\end{array}
$$

Addition works from right to left. The two bits plus any carry (from the right) give a sum bit for this position and a carry to the left. Right to left is the wrong direction for lists; the head of a list is its leftmost element. So the bits will be kept in reverse order.

The two binary numbers may have unequal lengths. If one bit list terminates then the carry must be propagated along the other bit list.

```
fun bincarry (0, ps)    = ps
  | bincarry (1, [])    = [1]
  | bincarry (1, p::ps) = (1-p) :: bincarry(p, ps);
> ***Warning:  Patterns not exhaustive
> val bincarry = fn : int * int list -> int list
```

Yes, patterns may contain constants: integers, reals, booleans and strings. Function *bincarry* can propagate a carry of 0 or 1, the only sensible values. It is undefined for others.

The binary sum is defined for two bit lists and a carry. When either list terminates, *bincarry* deals with the other. If there are two bits to add, their sum and carry are computed:

```
fun binsum (c, [], qs)        = bincarry (c,qs)
  | binsum (c, ps, [])        = bincarry (c,ps)
  | binsum (c, p::ps, q::qs) =
       ((c+p+q) mod 2)   ::   binsum((c+p+q) div 2, ps, qs);
> val binsum = 'fn : int * int list * int list -> int list
```

Let us try $11 + 30 = 41$, remembering to reverse the lists:

```
binsum(0, [1,1,0,1], [0,1,1,1,1]);
> [1, 0, 0, 1, 0, 1] : int list
```

Multiplication. The binary product is computed by shifting and adding. For instance, $11 \times 30 = 330$:

$$
\begin{array}{r}
11110 \\
\times \quad 1011 \\
\hline
11110 \\
11110 \\
+ \quad 11110 \\
\hline
101001010
\end{array}
$$

Here, shifting is performed by inserting a 0:

```
fun binprod ([], _)      = []
  | binprod (0::ps, qs) = 0::binprod(ps,qs)
  | binprod (1::ps, qs) = binsum(0, qs, 0::binprod(ps,qs));
> ***Warning: Patterns not exhaustive
> val binprod = fn : int list * int list -> int list
```

Let us evaluate $11 \times 30 = 330$:

```
binprod([1,1,0,1], [0,1,1,1,1]);
> [0, 1, 0, 1, 0, 0, 1, 0, 1] : int list
```

Exercise 3.11 Write functions to compute the binary sum and product of a list of boolean values, using no built-in arithmetic.

Exercise 3.12 Write a function to divide one binary number by another.

Exercise 3.13 Decimal numbers can be held as lists of integers from 0 to 9. Write functions to convert between binary and decimal: both directions. Compute the factorial of 100.

3.8   *Matrix transpose*

A matrix can be viewed as a list of rows, each row a list of matrix elements. The matrix

$$\begin{pmatrix} a & b & c \\ d & e & f \end{pmatrix},$$

for instance, can be declared in ML by

```
val matrix = [ ["a","b","c"],
               ["d","e","f"] ];
> val matrix = [["a","b","c"], ["d","e","f"]]
> : string list list
```

Matrix transpose works well with this list representation because it goes sequentially along rows and columns, with no jumping. The transpose function changes the list of rows

$$A \quad = \quad \begin{matrix} [[x_{11}, & x_{12}, & \ldots, & x_{1m}], \\ \vdots & \vdots & & \vdots \\ [x_{n1}, & x_{n2}, & \ldots, & x_{nm}]] \end{matrix}$$

to the list of the columns of A:

$$A^T \quad = \quad \begin{matrix} [[x_{11}, & \ldots, & x_{n1}], \\ [x_{12}, & \ldots, & x_{n2}], \\ \vdots & & \vdots \\ [x_{1m}, & \ldots, & x_{nm}]] \end{matrix}$$

One way to transpose a matrix is by repeatedly taking columns from it. The heads of the rows form the first column of the matrix:

```
fun headcol []                   = []
  | headcol ((x::_) :: rows) = x :: headcol rows;
> ***Warning:  Patterns not exhaustive
> val headcol = fn :  'a list list -> 'a list
```

The tails of the rows form a matrix of the remaining columns:

```
fun tailcols []                    = []
  | tailcols ((_::xs) :: rows)  = xs :: tailcols rows;
> ***Warning:  Patterns not exhaustive
> val tailcols = fn :  'a list list -> 'a list list
```

Consider their effect on our small matrix:

```
headcol matrix;
> ["a","d"]  : string list
tailcols matrix;
> [["b","c"],["e","f"]]  : string list list
```

Calling *headcol* and *tailcols* chops the matrix like this:

$$\begin{pmatrix} a & | & b & c \\ d & | & e & f \end{pmatrix}$$

These functions lead to an unusual recursion: *tailcols* takes a list of n lists and returns a list of n shorter lists. This terminates with n empty lists.

```
fun transp ([]::rows) = []
  | transp rows        = headcol rows :: transp (tailcols rows);
> val transp = fn : 'a list list -> 'a list list
transp matrix;
> [["a","d"],["b","e"],["c","f"]] : string list list
```

The transposed matrix is

$$\begin{pmatrix} a & d \\ b & e \\ c & f \end{pmatrix}.$$

Exercise 3.14 What input pattern do *headcol* and *tailcols* not handle? What does *transp* return if the rows of the 'matrix' do not have the same length?

Exercise 3.15 Write an alternative transpose function. Instead of turning columns into rows, it should turn rows into columns.

3.9   *Matrix multiplication*

We begin with a quick review of matrix multiplication. The **dot product** (or inner product) of two vectors is

$$(a_1, \ldots, a_k) \cdot (b_1, \ldots, b_k) = a_1 b_1 + \cdots + a_k b_k.$$

If A is an $m \times k$ matrix and B is a $k \times n$ matrix then their **product** $A \times B$ is an $m \times n$ matrix. For each i and j, the (i, j) element of $A \times B$ is the dot product of row i of A with column j of B. Example:

$$\begin{pmatrix} 2 & 0 \\ 3 & -1 \\ 0 & 1 \\ 1 & 1 \end{pmatrix} \times \begin{pmatrix} 1 & 0 & 2 \\ 4 & -1 & 0 \end{pmatrix} = \begin{pmatrix} 2 & 0 & 4 \\ -1 & 1 & 6 \\ 4 & -1 & 0 \\ 5 & -1 & 2 \end{pmatrix}$$

The (1,1) element of the product above is computed by

$$(2, 0) \cdot (1, 4) = 2 \times 1 + 0 \times 4 = 2.$$

In the dot product function, the two vectors must have the same length; ML prints a warning that some cases are not covered. Henceforth these warnings will usually be omitted.

```
fun dotprod([], [])      = 0.0
  | dotprod(x::xs,y::ys)  = x*y + dotprod(xs,ys);
> ***Warning: Patterns not exhaustive
> val dotprod = fn : real list * real list -> real
```

If A has just one row, so does $A \times B$. Function *rowprod* computes
the product of a row with B. The matrix B must be given as its
transpose: a list of columns, not a list of rows.

```
fun rowprod(row, [])      = []
  | rowprod(row, col::cols) =
        dotprod(row,col)  ::  rowprod(row,cols);
> val rowprod =
>    fn : real list * real list list -> real list
```

Each row of $A \times B$ is obtained by multiplying a row of A by the
columns of B:

```
fun rowlistprod([], cols)        = []
  | rowlistprod(row::rows, cols) =
        rowprod(row,cols)  ::  rowlistprod(rows,cols);
> val rowlistprod =
>    fn : real list list * real list list -> real list list
```

The matrix product function makes *transp* construct a list of the
columns of B:

```
fun matprod(Arows,Brows) = rowlistprod(Arows, transp Brows);
> val matprod =
>    fn : real list list * real list list -> real list list
```

Here are the declarations of the sample matrices, omitting ML's
response:

```
val Arows = [ [2.0,   0.0],
              [3.0,  ~1.0],
              [0.0,   1.0],
              [1.0,   1.0] ]
and Brows = [ [1.0,   0.0,   2.0],
              [4.0,  ~1.0,   0.0] ];
```

Here is their product:

```
matprod(Arows,Brows);
> [[2.0,   0.0,   4.0],
>  [~1.0,  1.0,   6.0],
>  [4.0,  ~1.0,   0.0],
>  [5.0,  ~1.0,   2.0]] : real list list
```

3.10   *Gaussian elimination*

One of the classic matrix algorithms, Gaussian elimination
may seem an unlikely candidate for functional programming. This
algorithm (Sedgewick, 1988) can compute the determinant or inverse of a matrix, or solve systems of independent linear equations

such as the following:

$$\begin{array}{rrrrrrr} x & + & 2y & + & 7z & = & 7 \\ - \quad 4w & & + & 3y & - & 5z & = & -2 \\ 4w & - & x & - & 2y & - & 3z & = & 9 \\ - \quad 2w & + & x & + & 2y & + & 8z & = & 2 \end{array} \quad (*)$$

Gaussian elimination works by isolating each of the variables in turn. Equation (*), properly scaled and added to another equation, eliminates w from it. Repeating this operation, which is called **pivoting**, eventually reduces the system to a triangular form.

$$\begin{array}{rrrrrr} - \quad 4w & & + & 3y & - & 5z & = & -2 \\ x & + & 2y & + & 7z & = & 7 \\ & & 3y & - & z & = & 14 \\ & & & & 3z & = & 3 \end{array}$$

Now the solutions come out, beginning with $z = 1$.

Equation (*) is a good choice for eliminating w because the absolute value (4) of its coefficient is maximal. Scaling divides the equation by this value; a small divisor (not to mention zero!) could cause numerical errors. Function *pivotrow*, given a list of rows, returns one whose head is greatest in absolute value.

```
fun pivotrow [row]           = row : real list
  | pivotrow (row1::row2::rows) =
      if abs(hd row1) >= abs(hd row2)
      then pivotrow(row1::rows)
      else pivotrow(row2::rows);
> val pivotrow = fn : real list list -> real list
```

If the selected row has head p, then $delrow(p, rows)$ removes it from the list of rows.

```
fun delrow (p, [])        = []
  | delrow (p, row::rows) =  if p = hd row  then rows
                             else row :: delrow(p, rows);
> val delrow = fn : ''a * ''a list list -> ''a list list
```

Function *scalarprod* multiplies a row or vector by a constant k:

```
fun scalarprod(k, [])     = [] : real list
  | scalarprod(k, x::xs) = k*x :: scalarprod(k,xs);
> val scalarprod = fn : real * real list -> real list
```

Function *vectorsum* adds two rows or vectors:

```
fun vectorsum ([], [])       = [] : real list
  | vectorsum (x::xs,y::ys)  = x+y :: vectorsum(xs,ys);
> val vectorsum = fn : real list * real list -> real list
```

Function *elimcol*, declared inside *gausselim*, refers to the current pivot row by its head p (the leading coefficient) and tail *prow*.

Given a list of rows, *elimcol* replaces each by its sum with *prow*, properly scaled. The first element of each sum is zero, but these zeroes are never computed; the first column simply disappears.

```
fun gausselim [row] = [row]
  | gausselim rows  =
      let val p::prow = pivotrow rows
          fun elimcol []                    = []
            | elimcol ((x::xs)::rows) =
                  vectorsum(xs, scalarprod(~x/p, prow))
                  :: elimcol rows
      in  (p::prow) :: gausselim(elimcol(delrow(p,rows)))
      end;
> val gausselim = fn : real list list -> real list list
```

Function *gausselim* removes the pivot row, eliminates a column, and calls itself recursively on the reduced matrix. It returns a list of pivot rows, decreasing in length, forming an upper triangular matrix.

A system of n equations is solved by Gaussian elimination on an $n \times (n+1)$ matrix, where the extra column contains the right-side values. The solutions are generated recursively from the triangular matrix. Known solutions are multiplied by their coefficients and added — this is a vector dot product — and divided by the leading coefficient. To subtract the right-side value we employ a trick: a spurious solution of -1.

```
fun solutions []               = [~1.0]
  | solutions((x::xs)::rows) =
      let val solns = solutions rows
      in ~(dotprod(solns,xs)/x) :: solns   end;
> val solutions = fn : real list list -> real list
```

Now we come to the example. We compute the triangular matrix:

```
gausselim [[ 0.0,   1.0,   2.0,   7.0,   7.0],
           [~4.0,   0.0,   3.0,  ~5.0,  ~2.0],
           [ 4.0,  ~1.0,  ~2.0,  ~3.0,   9.0],
           [~2.0,   1.0,   2.0,   8.0,   2.0]];
> [[~4.0,   0.0,   3.0,  ~5.0,  ~2.0],
>  [ 1.0,   2.0,   7.0,   7.0],
>  [ 3.0,  ~1.0,  14.0],
>  [ 3.0,   3.0]] : real list list
```

Ignoring the final -1, the solutions are $w = 3$, $x = -10$, $y = 5$ and $z = 1$.

```
solutions it;
> [3.0, ~10.0, 5.0, 1.0, ~1.0] : real list
```

Exercise 3.16   Show that if the input equations are linearly in-dependent, then division by zero cannot occur within *gausselim*.

Exercise 3.17   Do *pivotrow* and *delrow* work correctly if the heads of several rows have the same absolute value?

Exercise 3.18   Write a function to compute the determinant of a matrix.

Exercise 3.19   Write a function to invert a matrix.

3.11   *Writing a number as the sum of two squares*

Dijkstra (1976) presents a program that, given an integer r, finds all integer solutions of $x^2 + y^2 = r$. (Assume $x \geq y \geq 0$ to suppress symmetries.) For instance, $25 = 4^2 + 3^2 = 5^2 + 0^2$, while 48,612,265 has 32 solutions.

Brute force search over all (x, y) pairs is impractical for large numbers, but fortunately the solutions have some structure: if $x^2 + y^2 = r = u^2 + v^2$ and $x > u$ then $y < v$. If x sweeps downwards from $\sqrt{r}$ as y sweeps upwards from 0, then all solutions can be found in a single pass.

Let $Bet(x, y)$ stand for the set of all solutions between x and y:

$$Bet(x, y) = \{(u, v) \mid u^2 + v^2 = r \wedge x \geq u \geq v \geq y\}$$

The search for suitable x and y is guided by four observations:

  1 If $x^2 + y^2 < r$ then $Bet(x, y) = Bet(x, y + 1)$. There are no solutions of the form (u, y) with $x \geq u$, for then $u^2 + y^2 < r$.

  2 If $x^2 + y^2 = r$ then $Bet(x, y) = \{(x, y)\} \cup Bet(x - 1, y + 1)$. A solution! There can be no other for the same x or y.

  3 If $x^2 + y^2 > r > x^2 + (y - 1)^2$ then $Bet(x, y) = Bet(x - 1, y)$. There can be no solutions of the form (x, v).

  4 Finally, $Bet(x, y) = \emptyset$ if $x < y$.

These suggest a recursive — indeed iterative — search method. Case 3 requires special care if it is to be used efficiently. At the start, make sure $x^2 + y^2 < r$ holds. Increase y until $x^2 + y^2 \geq r$. If $x^2 + y^2 > r$ then y must be the least such, and so Case 3 applies. Decreasing x by one re-establishes $x^2 + y^2 < r$.

Initially $y = 0$ and $x = \sqrt{r}$ (the integer square root of r), so the starting condition holds. Since $x > y$, we know that y will be increased several times when x is decreased. As a further concession to efficiency, therefore, the program takes the computation of x^2 outside the inner recursion:

```
fun squares r =
    let fun between (x,y) =   (*all pairs between x and y*)
            let val diff = r - x*x
                fun above y =   (*all pairs above y*)
                        if y>x then []
                        else if y*y<diff then above (y+1)
                        else if y*y=diff then (x,y)::between(x-1,y+1)
                        else (* y*y>diff *)  between(x-1,y)
                in above y  end;
            val firstx = floor(sqrt(real r))
    in between (firstx, 0) end;
> val squares = fn : int -> (int * int) list
```

Execution is fast, even for large r:

```
squares 50;
> [(7, 1), (5, 5)] : (int * int) list
squares 1105;
> [(33, 4), (32, 9), (31, 12), (24, 23)] : (int * int) list
squares 48612265;
> [(6972, 59), (6971, 132), (6952, 531), (6948, 581),
>   (6944, 627), (6917, 876), (6899, 1008), (6853, 1284),
>   (6789, 1588), (6772, 1659), ...] : (int * int) list
```

Dijkstra's program has a different search method: x and y start with equal values, then sweep apart. Our method could well be the one he rejected because 'the demonstration that no solutions had been omitted always required a drawing.'

Number theorists have characterized all numbers of the form $x^2 + y^2$ in terms of prime factors. A program exploiting this theory would pay off only for huge numbers. It might be fun though — this is a toy problem in the best sense!

3.12   *The problem of the next permutation*

Given a list of integers, we are asked to rearrange the elements to produce the permutation that is next greater under lexicographic ordering. The new permutation should be greater than the one given, with no other permutation in between.

Let us modify the problem slightly. Lexicographic order means the head of the list has the most significance. The next greater permutation will probably differ in the least significant elements. Since the head of a list is the easiest element to reach, let us make it least significant. Fighting the natural order of lists would be foolish. We therefore compute the next permutation under reverse lexicographic ordering.

The problem is hard to visualize — even Dijkstra gives an example. The next eight permutations after 4 3 2 1 (the initial permutation) are

$$
\begin{array}{cccc}
\underline{3}\ \underline{4}\ 2\ 1 \\
\underline{4}\ \underline{2}\ \underline{3}\ 1 \\
\underline{2}\ \underline{4}\ \underline{3}\ 1 \\
\underline{3}\ \underline{2}\ \underline{4}\ 1 \\
\underline{2}\ \underline{3}\ \underline{4}\ 1 \\
\underline{4}\ \underline{3}\ \underline{1}\ 2 \\
\underline{3}\ \underline{4}\ 1\ 2 \\
\underline{4}\ \underline{1}\ \underline{3}\ 2 \\
\end{array}
$$

The affected part of each is underlined. The sequence of permutations terminates at 1 2 3 4, which has no successor.

To make a greater permutation, some element of the list must be replaced by a larger element to its left. To make the very next permutation, this replacement must happen as far to the left — the least significant position — as possible. The replacement value must be as small as possible, and the elements to the left of the replacement must be arranged in descending order. All this can be done in two steps:

1 Find the leftmost element y that has a greater element to its left. The elements to its left will therefore be an increasing sequence $x_1 \leq \cdots \leq x_n$. (We are really speaking of positions rather than elements, but this only matters if the elements are not distinct.)

2 Replace y by the smallest x_i, with $1 \leq i \leq n$, such that $y < x_i$, and arrange $x_1, \ldots, x_{i-1}, y, x_{i+1}, \ldots, x_n$ in descending order. This can be accomplished by scanning $x_n, x_{n-1}, \ldots, x_1$ until the correct value is found for x_i, placing larger elements in front of the final result.

Calling $next(xlist, ys)$ finds the y in ys to replace, while $xlist$ accumulates the elements passed over. When $xlist$ holds the reversed list $[x_n, \ldots, x_1]$, the function *swap* performs the replacement and rearrangement. The list manipulations are delicate.

```
fun next(xlist, y::ys) : int list =
    if hd xlist <= y then   next(y::xlist, ys)
    else   (*swap y with greatest xk such that x>=xk>y *)
        let fun swap [x]            = y::x::ys
              | swap (x::xk::xs) = (*x >= xk *)
                    if xk>y then x::swap(xk::xs)
                            else (y::xk::xs)@(x::ys)
                            (* x > y >= xk >= xs *)
        in swap(xlist) end;
> val next = fn : int list * int list -> int list
```

Function *nextperm* starts the scan.

```
fun nextperm (y::ys) = next([y], ys);
> val nextperm = fn : int list -> int list
nextperm [1,2,4,3];
> [3, 2, 1, 4] : int list
 nextperm it;
> [2, 3, 1, 4] : int list
 nextperm it;
> [3, 1, 2, 4] : int list
```

It also works when the elements are not distinct:

```
nextperm [3,2,2,1];
> [2, 3, 2, 1] : int list
 nextperm it;
> [2, 2, 3, 1] : int list
  nextperm it;
> [3, 2, 1, 2] : int list
```

Exercise 3.20 Write the steps to compute *nextperm*[2, 3, 1, 4].

Exercise 3.21 My first version of this program worked only for lists of distinct elements. It differed from the current version in a single comparison. What was this faulty program?

Exercise 3.22 What does *nextperm*(*ys*) return if there is no next permutation of *ys*? Modify the program so that it returns the initial permutation in that case.

The equality test in polymorphic functions

Polymorphic functions like *length* and *rev* accept lists having elements of any type because they do not perform any operations on those elements. Now consider a function to test whether a value *e* is a member of a list *l*. Is this function polymorphic? Each member of *l* must be tested for equality with *e*. Equality testing is possible for most types, but not for function types and abstract types:

> The equality test on functions is not computable because *f* and *g* are equal just when $f(x)$ equals $g(x)$ for every possible argument *x*. There are other ways of defining equality of functions, but there is no escaping the problem.
>
> An abstract type provides only those operations specified in its definition. Although a full discussion of abstract types must wait until Chapter 7, we shall see how finite sets can be represented by lists.

The equality test is defined for values constructed of integers, reals, strings, booleans, tuples, lists and datatypes (introduced in the next chapter). It is not defined for values containing functions or elements of abstract types. Equality is polymorphic in a restricted sense. It should not be extended to all types in an arbitrary way.

Standard ML has **equality type variables** $\alpha^=, \beta^=, \gamma^=, \ldots$ ranging over the **equality types**, which are the types that admit equality testing. Equality types contain no type variables except equality type variables. For example, *int*, *bool* × *string* and (*int list*) × $\beta^=$ are equality types, while *int* → *bool* and *bool* × β are not.

Here is the type of the equality test itself, the infix operator (=):

```
op= ;
> fn : (''a * ''a) -> bool
```

In mathematical notation this type is $\alpha^= \times \alpha^= \rightarrow bool$. In ML, an equality type variable begins with two ' characters.

Now let us define the membership testing function:

```
infix mem;
fun x mem []     =   false
  | x mem (y::l)  =   (x=y) orelse (x mem l);
> val mem = fn : ''a * ''a list -> bool
```

The type $\alpha^= \times (\alpha^= list) \rightarrow bool$ means that *mem* may be applied to any list whose elements permit equality testing.

```
"Sally" mem ["Regan","Goneril","Cordelia"];
> false : bool
```

3.13   *Polymorphic set operations*

A function's type contains equality type variables if it per-forms polymorphic equality testing, even indirectly, for instance via *mem*. The function *newmem* adds a new element to a list, provided it is really new:

```
fun newmem(x,xs) = if x mem xs then  xs    else  x::xs;
> val newmem = fn : ''a * ''a list -> ''a list
```

Lists constructed by *newmem* can be regarded as finite sets. Let us define some set operations and note their types. If equality type variables appear, then equality tests are involved.

The function *setof* converts a list to a 'set' by eliminating re-peated elements:

```
fun setof []     = []
  | setof(x::xs) = newmem(x, setof xs);
> val setof = fn : ''a list -> ''a list
setof [true,false,false,true,false];
> [true, false] : bool list
```

Observe that *setof* may perform a large number of equality tests. To minimize the use of *setof*, the following functions must be ap-plied to 'sets' — lists of distinct elements — if their result is to be a 'set'.

Union. The list *union*(*xs, ys*) includes all elements of *xs* not already in *ys*, which is assumed to consist of distinct elements:

```
fun union([],ys)     = ys
  | union(x::xs, ys) = newmem(x, union(xs, ys));
> val union = fn : ''a list * ''a list -> ''a list
```

The type variable ''a indicates equality testing, here via *newmem*.

```
union([1,2,3], [0,2,4]);
> [1, 3, 0, 2, 4] : int list
```

Intersection. Similarly, *inter*(*xs, ys*) includes all elements of *xs* that also belong to *ys*:

```
fun inter([],ys)     = []
  | inter(x::xs, ys) = if x mem ys then x::inter(xs, ys)
                                   else    inter(xs, ys);
> val inter = fn : ''a list * ''a list -> ''a list
```

A baby's name can be chosen by intersecting the preferences of both parents ...

```
inter(["John","James","Mark"], ["Nebuchadnezzar","Bede"]);
> [] : string list
```

... although this seldom works.

The subset relation. Set T is a **subset** of S if all elements of T are also elements of S:

```
infix subs;
fun  []       subs ys = true
  | (x::xs) subs ys = (x mem ys) andalso (xs subs ys);
> val subs = fn : ''a list * ''a list -> bool
```

Recall that equality types may involve tuples, lists and so forth:

```
[("May",5), ("June",6)] subs [("July",7)];
> false : bool
```

Equality of sets. The built-in list equality test is not valid for sets. The lists $[3, 4]$ and $[4, 3, 4]$ are not equal, yet they denote the same set, $\{3, 4\}$. Set equality ignores the order and repetition of elements. It can be defined in terms of subsets:

```
infix seq;
fun xs seq ys = (xs subs ys) andalso (ys subs xs);
> val seq = fn : ''a list * ''a list -> bool
[3,1,3,5,3,4] seq [1,3,4,5];
> true : bool
```

Many abstract types require a special equality test.

Powerset. The **powerset** of a set S is the set consisting of all the subsets of S, including the empty set and S itself. It can be computed by removing some element x from S and recursively computing the powerset of $S - \{x\}$. If T is a subset of $S - \{x\}$ then both T and $T \cup \{x\}$ are subsets of S and elements of the powerset. The argument *base* accumulates items (like x) that must be included in each element of the result. In the initial call, *base* should be empty.

```
fun powset ([], base)    = [base]
  | powset (x::xs, base) =
        powset(xs, base) @ powset(xs, x::base);
> val powset = fn : 'a list * 'a list -> 'a list list
```

The ordinary type variables indicate that *powset* does not perform equality tests.

```
powset (rev ["the","weird","sisters"], []);
> [[], ["the"], ["weird"], ["the", "weird"], ["sisters"],
>  ["the", "sisters"], ["weird", "sisters"],
>  ["the", "weird", "sisters"]]  :  string list list
```

Using set notation, the result of *powset* can be described as follows, ignoring the order of list elements:

$$powset(S, B) = \{T \cup B \mid T \subseteq S\}$$

Cartesian product. The **Cartesian product** of S and T is the set of all pairs (x, y) with $x \in S$ and $y \in T$. In set notation,

$$S \times T = \{(x, y) \mid x \in S, \, y \in T\}.$$

Several functional languages adopt set notation, following David Turner; see Bird & Wadler (1988) for examples. Since ML does not adopt this notation, we have to use recursion over lists. The function to compute Cartesian products is surprisingly complex.

```
fun cartprod ([],    ys) = []
  | cartprod (x::xs, ys) =
        let val xsprod = cartprod(xs,ys)
            fun pairx []        = xsprod
              | pairx(y::ytail) = (x,y) :: (pairx ytail)
        in  pairx ys   end;
> val cartprod = fn : 'a list * 'b list -> ('a * 'b) list
```

The function *cartprod* does not perform equality tests.

```
cartprod([2,5], ["moons","stars","planets"]);
> [(2,"moons"), (2,"stars"), (2,"planets"), (5,"moons"),
>  (5,"stars"), (5,"planets")] : (int * string) list
```

Chapter 5 demonstrates how higher-order functions can express this function. For now, let us continue with simple methods.

Exercise 3.23   How many equality tests does ML perform when evaluating the following expressions?

```
1 mem upto(1,500)
setof(upto(1,500))
```

Exercise 3.24   Compare *union* with the function *itunion* defined below. Which function is more efficient?

```
fun itunion([],ys)      = ys
  | itunion(x::xs, ys) = itunion(xs, newmem(x, ys));
```

Exercise 3.25   Write a function *choose* such that *choose*(k, xs) generates the set of all k-element subsets of xs. For instance, *choose*$(29, upto(1, 30))$ should return a list containing 30 subsets.

Exercise 3.26 The following function is simpler than *cartprod*.
Is it better for computing Cartesian products?

```
fun cprod ([],    ys) = []
  | cprod (x::xs, ys) =
       let fun pairx  []       = cprod(xs,ys)
             | pairx(y::ytail) = (x,y) :: (pairx ytail)
       in  pairx ys  end;
```

3.14   *Association lists; Graph algorithms*
A dictionary or table can be represented by a list of pairs.
Functions to search such tables involve equality polymorphism. To
store the dates of history's greatest battles we could write

```
val battles =
  [("Crecy",1346),  ("Poitiers",1356),  ("Agincourt",1415),
   ("Trafalgar",1805),  ("Waterloo",1815)];
```

A list of (key, value) pairs is called an **association list**. The
function *assoc* finds the value associated with a key by sequential
search:

```
fun assoc ([], a)          = []
  | assoc ((x,y)::pairs, a) = if a=x then  [y]
                                     else  assoc(pairs, a);
> val assoc = fn : (''a * 'b) list * ''a -> 'b list
```

Its type, $(\alpha^= \times \beta)\,list \times \alpha^= \to \beta\;list$, indicates that keys must have
some equality type $\alpha^=$, while values may have any type β at all.
Calling *assoc*(*pairs*,*x*) returns [] if the key x is not found, and
returns [y] if y is found paired with x. Returning a list of results
is a simple method of distinguishing success from failure.

```
assoc(battles, "Agincourt");
> [1415] : int list
assoc(battles, "Austerlitz");
> [] : int list
```

Searching can be slow, but updating is trivial: put a new pair in
front. Since *assoc* returns the first value it finds, existing associ-
ations can be overridden. Pairing names with types in a block-
structured language is a typical application. A name will be paired
with several types in the association list if it is declared in nested
blocks.

Directed graphs. A list of pairs can also represent a directed graph.

Each pair (x, y) stands for the edge $x \longrightarrow y$. Thus the list

```
val graph1 = [("a","b"), ("a","c"), ("a","d"),
              ("b","e"), ("c","f"), ("d","e"),
              ("e","f"), ("e","g")];
```

represents the graph

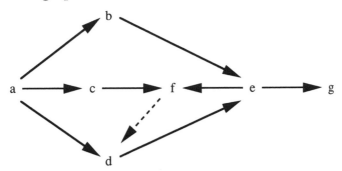

(The dashed line from f to d will be added to the graph in some examples later.)

The function *nexts* finds all successors of a node a — the destinations of all edges leading from a — in the graph:

```
fun nexts (a, [])            = []
  | nexts (a, (x,y)::pairs)  =
        if a=x then   y :: nexts(a,pairs)
               else          nexts(a,pairs);
> val nexts = fn : ''a * (''a * 'b) list -> 'b list
```

This function differs from *assoc* by returning all values that are paired with a, not just the first:

```
nexts("e", graph1);
> ["f", "g"] : string list
```

Depth-first search is the basis of many graph algorithms that work by visiting the nodes.

```
fun depthfirst ([],      graph, visited) = visited
  | depthfirst (x::xs, graph, visited) =
        if x mem visited then depthfirst (xs, graph, visited)
        else depthfirst (nexts(x,graph)@xs, graph, x::visited);
> val depthfirst =
>    fn : ''a list * (''a * ''a) list * ''a list -> ''a list
```

The nodes of the graph may have any equality type. Here is a depth-first search of *graph1* starting at a:

```
depthfirst(["a"], graph1, []);
> ["d", "c", "g", "f", "e", "b", "a"] : string list
```

Adding an edge from f to d makes the graph cyclic. Let us search
that graph starting at b:

```
depthfirst(["b"], ("f","d")::graph1, []);
> ["g", "d", "f", "e", "b"] : string list
```

After visiting a node x that has not been visited before, depth-first
search recursively visits each successor of x. In the list computed by
nexts(x, *graph*)@*xs*, the successors of x precede the other nodes xs
that are awaiting visits. This list behaves as a stack. **Breadth-
first search** results if the list of nodes to visit behaves as a queue.

Depth-first search can also be coded as follows:

```
fun depth ([],     graph, visited) = visited
  | depth (x::xs, graph, visited) =
      depth (xs, graph,
             if x mem visited then   visited
             else depth (nexts(x,graph), graph, x::visited));
```

A nested recursive call visits the successors of x, then another call
visits the other nodes, xs. The functions *depthfirst* and *depth* are
equivalent, although the proof is subtle. By omitting a call to
append (@), *depth* is a bit faster. More importantly, since one call
is devoted to visiting x, it is easily modified to detect cycles in
graphs and perform topological sorting.

Topological sorting. Constraints on the order of events form a directed graph. Each edge $x \longrightarrow y$ means 'x must happen before y.'
The graph

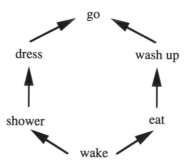

says everything about getting to work. Here it is as a list:

```
val grwork = [("wake","shower"),   ("shower","dress"),
              ("dress","go"),       ("wake", "eat"),
              ("eat","washup"),     ("washup","go")];
```

Finding a linear sequence of events from such a graph is called

topological sorting. Sedgewick (1988) points out that depth-first search can do this if the visit to node x is recorded after its successors have been searched. Thus x comes after every node reachable from x: a topological sort in reverse.

This means a simple change to *depth*: put x on the result of the recursive call instead of the argument. The list forms in reverse so no other reversal is necessary.

```
fun topsort graph =
  let fun sort ([],     visited) = visited
        | sort (x::xs, visited) =
              sort(xs, if x mem visited then   visited
                         else x :: sort(nexts(x,graph), visited))
      val (starts,_) = split graph
  in
    sort(starts, [])
  end;
> val topsort = fn : (''a * ''a) list -> ''a list
```

The **let** declaration of *sort* allows this function to refer to *graph*. It also declares *starts*, the list of all starting nodes of edges, to ensure that every node in the graph is reached.

So how do we get to work?

```
topsort grwork;
> ["wake", "eat", "washup", "shower", "dress", "go"]
>    : string list
```

Reversing the list of edges gives a different answer for the graph:

```
topsort(rev grwork);
> ["wake", "shower", "dress", "eat", "washup", "go"]
>    : string list
```

Cycle detection. Now consider a further constraint: we must go before we eat. The resulting graph contains a cycle and admits no solution. The function call runs forever:

```
topsort(("go","eat")::grwork);
```

Looping is not acceptable; the function should somehow report that no solution exists. Cycles can be detected by maintaining a list of all nodes being searched. This list of nodes, called *path*, traces the edges from the start of the search.

```
fun pathsort graph =
  let fun sort ([],      path, visited) = visited
       | sort (x::xs, path, visited) =
           if x mem path then hd[]    (*abort!!*)
           else sort(xs, path,
                      if x mem visited  then  visited  else
                        x::sort(nexts(x,graph),x::path,visited))
        val (starts,_) = split graph
  in sort(starts, [], []) end;
> val pathsort = fn : (''a * ''a) list -> ''a list
```

It works on our original graph. Given a cycle it causes an error:

```
pathsort graph1;
> ["a", "d", "c", "b", "e", "g", "f"] : string list
pathsort(("go","eat")::grwork);
> Exception: Match
```

An error message is better than looping, but *pathsort* aborts by making an erroneous function call (namely *hd* []), an ugly trick. The next chapter explains how to define an **exception** for such errors.

Exceptions are not the only way to report cycles. The following function returns two results: a list of visits, as before, and a list of nodes found in cycles. Maintaining two results, let us define a function to add a visit:

```
fun newvisit (x, (visited,cys)) = (x::visited, cys);
> val newvisit = fn : 'a * ('a list * 'b) -> 'a list * 'b
```

With the help of this function, topological sorting is easily expressed:

```
fun cyclesort graph =
  let fun sort ([],      path, (visited,cys)) = (visited, cys)
       | sort (x::xs, path, (visited,cys)) =
           sort(xs, path,
                 if x mem path          then (visited, x::cys)
                 else if x mem visited then (visited, cys)
                 else newvisit(x, sort(nexts(x,graph),
                                        x::path, (visited,cys)))))
        val (starts,_) = split graph
  in sort(starts, [], ([],[])) end;
> val cyclesort = fn: (''a *''a)list -> ''a list * ''a list
```

If there is a cycle, then *cyclesort* says where it is:

```
cyclesort (("go","eat")::grwork);
> (["wake", "shower", "dress", "go", "eat", "washup"],
>  ["go"])  :  string list * string list
```

And if not, then *cyclesort* sorts the graph:

```
cyclesort(rev graph1);
> (["a", "b", "c", "d", "e", "f", "g"], [])
>  : string list * string list
```

These polymorphic graph functions are too slow for large graphs because of the list searches. Restricting the nodes to integers, more efficient functions can be written using the functional arrays of the next chapter.

Exercise 3.27 Modify *pathsort* to return [] if the graph has a cycle and the singleton list [*visited*] otherwise.

Exercise 3.28 Let (*visited*, *cys*) be the result of *cyclesort*. If the graph contains many cycles, will *cys* contain a node belonging to each? What can be said about *visited* if the graph contains cycles?

Sorting: A case study

Sorting is one of the most studied topics in the theory of computing. Several sorting algorithms are widely known. To sort n items, **insertion sort** takes order n^2 time; **merge sort** takes order $n \log n$ time; **quick sort** takes order $n \log n$ on average, n^2 in the worst case.

These algorithms usually sort an array. Apart from **heap sort**, where the array encodes a binary tree, they are easily coded as functions on lists. Their time complexity remains unchanged: not that a list sort will win a race against an array sort! A complexity estimate such as 'order n^2 time' means the execution time is proportional to n^2. The list sort will have a higher constant of proportionality.

This section compares several sorting functions, giving the time taken to sort a list of 10,000 random numbers. These timings are informal but illustrate the practical performance of each algorithm.*

---

* Timings were conducted on a Sun 3/80 workstation running Standard ML of New Jersey, version 0.33.

The Pascal version of quick sort by Sedgewick (1988) can sort the 10,000 numbers in under two seconds. The best time for functional sorting in ML is five seconds. This is a small price to pay for the clarity and simplicity of functional programming. The overheads of lists would matter less for sorting, say, a bibliography, where the cost of comparisons would dominate.

3.15   *Random numbers*

First, we must produce 10,000 random numbers. Park and Miller (1988), complaining that good random number generators are hard to find, recommend the following.

```
local val a = 16807.0  and  m = 2147483647.0
in  fun nextrand seed =
           let val t = a*seed
           in  t - m * real(floor(t/m))  end
     end;
> val nextrand = fn : real -> real
```

Calling *nextrand* with any *seed* between 1 and 2,147,483,646 yields another number in this range, performing the integer calculation

$$(a \times seed) \bmod m.$$

Real arithmetic is used to avoid integer overflow. The function works provided mantissae are accurate to 46 bits. When trying this on your machine, check that the random numbers are exact integers.

Calling *randlist*(n, *seed*, []) generates a random list of length n starting from *seed*. Because the list accumulates in *tail*, its order is reversed:

```
fun randlist (n,seed,tail) =
       if n=0 then  (seed,tail)
       else   randlist(n-1, nextrand seed, seed::tail);
> val randlist =
>    fn : int * real * real list -> real * real list
```

The list of 10,000 random numbers is called *rs*. Here are the first 15.

```
val (seed,rs) = randlist(10000, 1.0, []);
> val seed = 1043618065.0 : real
> val rs =
> [1484786315.0, 925166085.0, 1614852353.0, 721631166.0,
>  173942219.0, 1229443779.0, 789328014.0, 570809709.0,
>  1760109362.0, 270600523.0, 2108528931.0, 16480421.0,
>  519782231.0, 162430624.0, 372212905.0, ...] : real list
```

3.16   *Insertion sort*

Insertion sort works by inserting the items, one at a time, into a sorted list. It is slow but simple. Here is the insertion function:

```
fun ins (x, []): real list = [x]
  | ins (x, y::ys)         =
      if x<=y then x::y::ys    (*it belongs here*)
              else y::ins(x,ys);
> val ins = fn : real * real list -> real list
```

The type constraint *real list* resolves overloading of the comparison operator. All the sorting functions have a type constraint.

We insert some numbers into [6.0], which is trivially sorted:

```
ins(4.0, [6.0]);
> [4.0, 6.0] : real list
ins(8.0,it);
> [4.0, 6.0, 8.0] : real list
ins(5.0,it);
> [4.0, 5.0, 6.0, 8.0] : real list
```

Insertion sort calls *ins* on every element of the input:

```
fun insort []        = []
  | insort (x::xs)   = ins(x, insort xs);
> val insort = fn : real list -> real list
```

These functions require deep recursion. But this inefficiency is insignificant. Insertion, functional or imperative, does a lot of copying. The execution time of the sort is order n^2. For our 10,000 integers it takes over 11 minutes. Insertion sort can be considered only for short lists or those that are nearly sorted.

3.17   *Quick sort*

Quick sort, invented by C. A. R. Hoare, was among the first efficient sorting algorithms. It works by divide and conquer:

Choose some value *a*, called the **pivot**, from the input.

Partition the remaining items into two parts: the items less than or equal to *a*, and the items greater than *a*.

Sort each part recursively, then put the smaller part before the greater.

Quick sort is ideal for arrays — the partition step is extremely fast, moving few items. For lists, it copies all the items; *partition* is a good example of an iterative function that builds two results.

```
fun quick []      = []
  | quick [x]     = [x]
  | quick (a::bs) = (*the head "a" is the pivot*)
       let fun partition (left,right,[]) : real list =
                  (quick left) @ (a :: quick right)
             | partition (left,right, x::xs)        =
                  if x<=a then partition (x::left, right, xs)
                          else partition (left, x::right, xs)
       in  partition([],[],bs)  end;
> val quick = fn : real list -> real list
```

This function sorts our 10,000 numbers in about 6 seconds:

```
quick rs;
> [1.0, 8383.0, 13456.0, 16807.0, 84083.0, 86383.0,
>  198011.0, 198864.0, 456291.0, 466696.0, 524209.0,
>  591308.0, 838913.0,866720.0, 1237296.0, ...] : real list
```

The append (@) can be eliminated by accumulating the sorted result in a second argument. This version of quick sort, which is left as an exercise, takes only about 5 seconds.

Like its imperative counterpart, *quick* takes order $n \log n$ time in the average case. If the input is already in increasing or decreasing order, then quick sort takes order n^2 time.

3.18   *Merge sorting*

Several algorithms work by merging sorted lists. The merging function repeatedly takes the smaller of the heads of two lists:

```
fun merge([],ys)         = ys : real list
  | merge(xs,[])         = xs
  | merge(x::xs, y::ys) =
       if x<=y then x::merge(xs,  y::ys)
               else y::merge(x::xs,  ys);
> val merge = fn : real list * real list -> real list
```

When sorting 10,000 items, the recursion in *merge* may be too deep for some ML systems. The fault lies with those ML systems, not with *merge*. As with *take* and *append*, the dominant cost is that of constructing the resulting list. An iterative merging function, although avoiding the deep recursion, would probably have to perform costly list reversals.

Merge sort can be **top-down** or **bottom-up**. Either way, merging is efficient only if the two lists have similar lengths.

Top-down merge sort. In the top-down approach, the input list is divided into two roughly equal parts using *take* and *drop*. These are sorted recursively and the results merged.

```
fun tmergesort []    = []
  | tmergesort [x]   = [x]
  | tmergesort xs    =
        let val k = length xs div 2
        in  merge(tmergesort (take(k,xs)),
                  tmergesort (drop(k,xs)))
        end;
> val tmergesort = fn : real list -> real list
```

This function takes 7 seconds to sort the 10,000 numbers. Unlike quick sort, its worst case execution time is order $n \log n$. It can be recommended as a simple and reasonably fast method.

Bottom-up merge sort. The basic bottom-up approach divides the input into lists of length 1. Adjacent pairs of lists are then merged, obtaining sorted lists of length 2, then 4, then 8 and so on. Finally one sorted list remains. This approach is easy to code but wasteful. Why should the 10,000 numbers be copied into a list of 10,000 singleton lists?

Richard O'Keefe (1982) has found a beautiful way to simultaneously merge the lists of various lengths, never storing these lists in full.

$$\underline{\underline{A\ B}}\ \underline{\underline{C\ D}}\ \underline{\underline{E\ F}}\ \underline{\underline{G\ H}}\ \underline{I\ J}\ K$$

The underlining shows how adjacent lists are merged. First A with B, then C with D, and now AB and CD have equal length and can be merged. O'Keefe accumulates the merges at all levels in one list. Rather than comparing the sizes of lists, he lets the count k of members determine how to add the next member. If k is even then there are two members of equal size s to merge. The resulting list is treated as member $k/2$ of size $2s$, which may cause further merging.

```
fun mergepairs([l],         k) = [l]
  | mergepairs(l1::l2::ls, k) =
        if k mod 2 = 1 then l1::l2::ls
        else mergepairs(merge(l1,l2)::ls, k div 2);
> val mergepairs =
>     fn : real list list * int -> real list list
```

For $k = 0$, *mergepairs* merges the entire list of lists into one list. Calling *sorting*(xs, [],0) sorts the list xs (which must be nonempty). It takes 6 seconds to sort the 10,000 numbers.

```
fun sorting([],     ls, k) = hd(mergepairs(ls,0))
  | sorting(x::xs, ls, k) =
            sorting(xs, mergepairs([x]::ls, k+1), k+1);
> val sorting =
>   fn : real list * real list list * int -> real list
```

A **smooth** sort has a linear execution time (order n) if its input is nearly sorted, degenerating to $n \log n$ in the worst case. O'Keefe has developed a 'smooth applicative merge sort' by exploiting order in the input. Rather than dividing it into singleton lists, he divides the input into increasing runs. If the number of runs is independent of n (and so 'nearly sorted') then the execution time is linear.

The function *nextrun* returns the next increasing run from a list, paired with the list of unread items. (An imperative program would delete items as they were processed.) The run grows in reverse order, hence the call to *rev*.

```
fun nextrun(run, [])     = (rev run, []: real list)
  | nextrun(run, x::xs) =
            if   x < hd run then (rev run, x::xs)
                            else nextrun(x::run, xs);
> val nextrun =
>   fn : real list * real list -> real list * real list
```

Runs are repeatedly taken and merged.

```
fun samsorting([],     ls, k) = hd(mergepairs(ls,0))
  | samsorting(x::xs, ls, k) =
        let val (run, tail) = nextrun([x], xs)
        in   samsorting(tail, mergepairs(run::ls,k+1), k+1)
        end;
> val samsorting =
>   fn : real list * real list list * int -> real list
```

The main sorting function is

```
fun samsort [] = []
  | samsort xs = samsorting(xs, [], 0);
> val samsort = fn : real list -> real list
```

The algorithm is both elegant and efficient. Even for our random data, with its short runs, the execution time is just 5 seconds.

Exercise 3.29 Express quick sort such that *quicker*(xs, *sorted*) accumulates the result in *sorted*, with no use of append.

Exercise 3.30 Write a function *find* such that *find*(xs, i) returns the ith smallest item in the list xs. This is called **selection**. Hoare's algorithm for selection is related to quick sort, and is much faster than sorting the list and returning the ith element.

Exercise 3.31 Generalize *find* above to *findrange*(xs, i, j), returning the list of the ith to jth smallest items in the list xs.

Exercise 3.32 Write a replacement for the function *nextrun*, finding both increasing and decreasing runs.

Summary of main points

Important functions from this chapter, most of them not predefined in Standard ML, are noted below.

Lists are constructed from the empty list (*nil* or []), using :: ('cons') to attach elements to the front.

The functions *null*, *hd* and *tl* analyse the structure of a list.

The function *length* counts the members of a list.

The functions *take* and *drop* detach an initial segment from a list.

The predefined infix operator @ concatenates (or appends) two lists.

The predefined function *rev* reverses a list.

The infix operator *mem* tests membership in a list.

The function *assoc* searches in a list of pairs (association list).

Equality polymorphism describes functions (like *mem* and *assoc*) that perform equality testing on their arguments.

A recursive function, using an argument to accumulate a result list, may avoid making inefficient calls to append.

4

Trees and Concrete Data

Concrete data consists of constructions that can be inspected, taken apart, or joined to form larger constructions. Lists are an example of concrete data. We can test whether or not a list is empty, and divide a non-empty list into its head and tail. New elements can be joined to a list. This chapter introduces several other forms of concrete data, including trees and logical propositions.

The ML **datatype** declaration defines a new type along with its **constructors**. In an expression, constructors create values of a datatype; in patterns, constructions describe how to take such values apart. A datatype can represent a class consisting of distinct subclasses — like Pascal's variant records, but without their complications and insecurities. A recursive datatype typically represents a tree. Functions on datatypes are defined by pattern-matching.

The special datatype *exn* is the type of **exceptions**, which stand for error conditions. Errors can be signalled and trapped. An exception handler tests for particular errors by pattern-matching.

Chapter outline

This chapter describes datatypes, pattern-matching, exception handling and trees. It contains the following sections:

The datatype declaration. Datatypes, constructors and pattern-matching are illustrated through examples. To represent the King and his subjects, a single type *person* comprises four classes of individual and associates appropriate information with each.

Exceptions. These represent a class of error values. Exceptions can be declared for each possible error. Raising an exception signals an error; handling the exception allows an alternative computation to be performed.

Trees. A tree is a branching structure. Binary trees are a generalization of lists having many applications, such as dictionaries.

Functional arrays and priority queues. A functional array is a mapping from integers to data; the update operation creates a new array. Binary trees can represent functional arrays as well as the data structure of heap sort, with reasonable efficiency.

A tautology checker. This is an example of elementary theorem proving. A datatype of propositions (boolean expressions) is declared. Functions convert propositions to Conjunctive Normal Form and test for tautologies.

The datatype declaration

A heterogeneous class consists of several distinct subclasses. A circle, a triangle and a square are all shapes, but of different kinds. A triangle might be represented by three points, a square by four points and a circle by its radius and centre.

For a harder problem, consider cataloguing all the inhabitants of the Kingdom by their class. These comprise the King, the Peers (or nobility), the Knights and the Peasants. For each we record appropriate information:

> The King is simply himself. There is nothing more to say.
> A Peer has a degree, territory and number in succession (as in 'the 7th Earl of Carlisle.')
> A Knight or Peasant has a name.

In weakly typed languages like Lisp and Prolog, these subclasses can be represented directly. We need only take care to distinguish Knights from Peasants; the others will differ naturally. In ML we could try

```
"King"
("Earl","Carlisle",7)      ("Duke","Norfolk",9)
("Knight","Gawain")        ("Knight","Galahad")
("Peasant","Jack Cade")    ("Peasant","Wat Tyler")
```

Unfortunately, these do not all have the same type! No ML function could handle both Kings and Peasants with this representation.

4.1   *The King and his subjects*

An ML type consisting of King, Peers, Knights and Peasants
is created by a **datatype** declaration:

```
datatype person = King
              | Peer of string*string*int
              | Knight of string
              | Peasant of string;
```

Five things are declared, namely the type *person* and its four **constructors**:

$$King : person$$

$$Peer : string \times string \times int \rightarrow person$$

$$Knight : string \rightarrow person$$

$$Peasant : string \rightarrow person$$

The type *person* consists precisely of the values built by its constructors. Note that *King* has type *person*, while the other constructors are functions that return something of that type. Thus
the following have type *person*:

```
King
Peer("Earl","Carlisle",7)      Peer("Duke","Norfolk",9)
Knight "Gawain"                Knight "Galahad"
Peasant "Jack Cade"            Peasant "Wat Tyler"
```

Furthermore, these values are distinct. No *person* can be both a
Knight and a *Peasant*; no *Peer* can have two different degrees.

Values of type *person*, like other ML values, may be arguments
and results of functions and may belong to data structures such as
lists:

```
val persons = [King, Peasant "Jack Cade", Knight "Gawain"];
> val persons = [King, Peasant "Jack Cade",
>                    Knight "Gawain"] : person list
```

Since each *person* is a unique construction, it can be taken apart.
A Standard ML function can be defined on a datatype through patterns involving the constructors. As with lists, there may be several
cases. A person's title depends upon his class and is constructed
using string concatenation (^):

```
fun title King               = "His Majesty the King"
  | title (Peer(deg,terr,_)) = "The " ^ deg ^ " of " ^ terr
  | title (Knight name)      = "Sir "^ name
  | title (Peasant name)     = name;
> val title = fn : person -> string
```

Each case is governed by a pattern with its own set of pattern variables. The *Knight* and *Peasant* cases each involve a variable called *name*, but these variables have separate scopes.

```
title(Peer("Earl", "Carlisle", 7));
> "The Earl of Carlisle" : string
title(Knight"Galahad");
> "Sir Galahad" : string
```

Patterns may be as complicated as necessary, combining tuples and the list constructors with datatype constructors. The function *sirs* returns the names of all the Knights in a list of persons:

```
fun sirs []                   = []
  | sirs ((Knight s) :: ps) = s :: (sirs ps)
  | sirs (p :: ps)          = sirs ps;
> val sirs = fn : person list -> string list
sirs persons;
> ["Gawain"] : string list
```

The cases of a function are considered in order. The third case (with pattern $p::ps$) is not considered if p is a *Knight*, and therefore must not be taken out of context. Some people prefer that the cases should be disjoint in order to assist mathematical reasoning. But replacing the case for $p::ps$ with separate cases for *King*, *Peer* and *Peasant* would make the function longer, slower and less readable. The third case of *sirs* makes perfect sense as a conditional equation:

$$sirs(p :: ps) = sirs(ps) \qquad \text{if } \forall s . p \neq Knight(s)$$

The ordering of cases is even more important when one *person* is compared with another. Rather than testing 16 cases, we test for each *true* case and take all the others for *false*, a total of 7 cases. Note the heavy use of wildcards in patterns.

```
fun superior (King,  Peer _)      = true
  | superior (King,  Knight _)    = true
  | superior (King,  Peasant _)   = true
  | superior (Peer _,  Knight _)  = true
  | superior (Peer _,  Peasant _) = true
  | superior (Knight _,  Peasant _) = true
  | superior _                    = false;
> val superior = fn : person * person -> bool
```

Exercise 4.1 Write an ML function to map persons to integers, mapping Kings to 4, Peers to 3, Knights to 2 and Peasants to 1. Write a function equivalent to *superior* that works by comparing the results of this mapping.

Exercise 4.2 Modify type *person* to add the constructor *Esquire*, whose arguments are a name and a village (both represented by strings). What is the type of this constructor? Modify function *title* to generate, for instance,

```
"John Smith, Esq., of Bottisham"
```

Modify *superior* to rank *Esquire* above *Peasant* and below *Knight*.

Exercise 4.3 Define a datatype of geometric figures such as triangles, rectangles, lines and circles. Define a function to compute the area of a figure.

4.2 Enumeration types

Letting strings denote degrees of nobility may be inadvisable. It does not prevent spurious degrees like `"butcher"` and `"madman"`. There are only five valid degrees; let them be the constructors of a new datatype:

```
datatype degree = Duke | Marquis | Earl | Viscount | Baron;
```

Now type *person* should be redefined, giving *Peer* the type *degree* × *string* × *int* → *person*.

Functions on type *degree* are defined by case analysis. What is the title of a lady of quality?

```
fun lady Duke     = "Duchess"
  | lady Marquis  = "Marchioness"
  | lady Earl     = "Countess"
  | lady Viscount = "Viscountess"
  | lady Baron    = "Baroness";
> val lady = fn : degree -> string
```

Accuracy being paramount in the Court and Social column, we cannot overestimate the importance of this example for electronic publishing.

A type like *degree*, consisting of a finite number of constants, is called an **enumeration type**. Another is the built-in type *bool*, which in effect is defined by

```
datatype bool = true | false;
```

The function *not* might be defined by cases:

```
fun not true = false
  | not false = true;
```

Datatypes are often represented compactly in storage. The internal values of an enumeration type are small integers.

! Beware of redefining a datatype. Each **datatype** declaration creates a
• new type distinct from all others. Suppose we have declared the type
degree and the function *lady*. Now, repeat the declaration of *degree*. This declares a new type with new constructors. Asking for the value of *lady(Duke)*
will elicit the type error 'expected type *degree*, found type *degree*.' Two different
types are now called *degree*. This exasperating situation can happen while a
program is being modified interactively. The surest remedy is to terminate the
ML session, start a new one, and load the program afresh.

Exercise 4.4   Define an enumeration type consisting of the names
of six different countries. Write a function to return the capital city
of each country as a string.

Exercise 4.5   Write functions of type *bool* × *bool* → *bool* for
boolean conjunction and disjunction. Use pattern-matching rather
than **andalso**, **orelse** or **if**. How many cases have to be tested
explicitly?

4.3   *Polymorphic datatypes*

Recall that *list* is a type operator taking one argument. Thus
list is not a type, while (*int*)*list* and ((*string* × *real*)*list*)*list* are. A
datatype declaration can introduce type operators. A fundamental
operator forms the disjoint sum of two types:

```
datatype ('a,'b) sum = In1 of 'a | In2 of 'b;
```

Three things are declared: the type operator *sum*, which takes two
arguments, and the constructors

$$In1 : \alpha \rightarrow (\alpha, \beta)sum$$
$$In2 : \beta \rightarrow (\alpha, \beta)sum$$

The type $(\alpha, \beta)sum$ is the disjoint sum of the types α and β. Its
values have the form $In1(x)$ for x of type α, or $In2(y)$ for y of
type β. It contains a copy of α and a copy of β. Observe that $In1$
and $In2$ can be viewed as labels that distinguish α from β.

The disjoint sum allows values of several types to be present where
normally only a single type is allowed. A list's elements must all
have the same type. If this type is (*string*, *person*)*sum* then an element could contain a string or a person, while type (*string*, *int*)*sum*
comprises strings and integers.

$$[In2\ King, In1\ \texttt{"Scotland"}] : ((string, person)sum)list$$
$$[In1\ \texttt{"tyrant"}, In2\ 1040] : ((string, int)sum)list$$

Pattern-matching for the disjoint sum tests whether $In1$ or $In2$ is present. The function $concat1$ concatenates all the strings included by $In1$ in a list:

```
fun concat1 []           = ""
  | concat1 ((In1 s)::l) = s ^ concat1 l
  | concat1 ((In2 _)::l) =      concat1 l;
> val concat1 = fn : (string, 'a) sum list -> string
concat1 [ In1 "0!", In2 (1040,1057), In1"Scotland" ];
> "0!Scotland" : string
```

Note that $In1$ "Scotland" has appeared with two different types, namely $(string, int \times int)sum$ and $(string, person)sum$. This is possible because its type is polymorphic:

```
In1 "Scotland";
> In1 "Scotland" : (string, 'a) sum
```

The disjoint sum can express all other non-recursive datatypes. The type *person* can be represented by

$$((unit, string \times string \times int)sum, (string, string)sum)sum$$

with constructors

$$King = In1(In1())$$
$$Peer(d, t, n) = In1(In2(d, t, n))$$
$$Knight(s) = In2(In1(s))$$
$$Peasant(s) = In2(In2(s))$$

These are valid as both expressions and patterns. Needless to say, type *person* is pleasanter. Observe how *unit*, the type whose sole element is (), represents the one King.

Exercise 4.6 What are the types of *King*, *Peer*, *Knight* and *Peasant* as defined above?

Exercise 4.7 Exhibit a correspondence between values of type $(\alpha, \beta)sum$ and certain values of type $(\alpha\ list) \times (\beta\ list)$ — those of the form $([x], [])$ or $([], [y])$.

4.4   *Pattern-matching with* **val**, **as**, **case**

A **pattern** is an expression consisting solely of variables, constructors and wildcards. The **constructors** comprise

> integer, real, boolean and string constants
> pairing, tupling and record formation
> list and datatype constructors

In a pattern, all names except constructors are variables. Any
meaning they may have outside the pattern is insignificant. The
variables in a pattern must be distinct. These conditions ensure
that values can be matched efficiently against the pattern and analysed uniquely to bind the variables.

Constructors absolutely must be distinguished from variables. In
this book, most constructors begin with a capital letter while most
variables are in lower case. However, the standard constructors *nil*,
true and *false* are also in lower case. A constructor name may be
symbolic or infix, such as : : for lists.

! *Mistakes in pattern-matching.* Typographical errors in patterns can be
hard to locate. The following version of the function *title* contains several
errors. Try to spot them before reading on:

```
fun title Kong              = "His Majesty the King"
  | title (Peer(deg,terr,_)) = "The " ^ deg ^ " of " ^ terr
  | title (Knightname)       = "Sir "^ name
  | title Peasant name       = name;
```

The first error is the misspelling of the constructor *King* as *Kong*. This is a
variable and matches all values, preventing further cases from being considered.
ML compilers warn if a function has a redundant case; this warning must be
heeded!

The second error is *Knightname*: the omission of a space again reduces a
pattern to a variable. Since the error leaves the variable *name* undefined, the
compiler should complain.

The third error is the omission of parentheses around *Peasant name*. The
resulting error messages could be incomprehensible.

Misspelled constructor functions are quickly detected, for

```
fun f (g x) = ...
```

is allowed only if *g* is a constructor. Other misspellings may not provoke any
warning. Omitted spaces before a wildcard, as in *Peer_*, are particularly obscure.

Exercise 4.8   Which simple mistake in *superior* would alter the
function's behaviour without making any case redundant?

Patterns in value declarations. The declaration

```
val P = E
```

defines the variables in the pattern P to have the corresponding
values of expression E. We have already used this to select com-

ponents from tuples (from Chapter 2):

```
val (xc,yc) = scalevec(4.0, a);
> val xc = 6.0 : real
> val yc = 27.2 : real
```

We may also write

```
val [x,y,z] = upto(1,3);
> val x = 1 : int
> val y = 2 : int
> val z = 3 : int
```

The declaration fails (raising an exception) if the value of the expression does not match the pattern. When the pattern is a tuple, type checking eliminates this danger.

The following declarations are valid because the values of the expressions match their patterns. They declare no variables.

```
val King = King;
val [1,2,3] = upto(1,3);
```

Constructor names cannot be declared for another purpose using **val**. In the scope of type *person*, the names *King*, *Peer*, *Knight* and *Peasant* are reserved as constructors. Declarations such as these, regarded as attempts at pattern-matching, will be rejected with a type error message:

```
val King = "Henry V";
val Peer = 925;
```

Layered patterns. A variable in a pattern may have the form

> *Id* **as** *P*

If the entire pattern (which includes the pattern P as a part) matches, then the value that matches P is also bound to the identifier *Id*. This value is viewed both through the pattern and as a whole. The function *nextrun* (from Chapter 3) can be coded

```
fun nextrun(run, [])          = ···
  | nextrun(run as r::_, x::xs) =
          if  x < r then (rev run, x::xs)
                    else nextrun(x::run, xs);
```

Here *run* and *r*::_ are the same list. We now may refer to its head as *r* instead of *hd run*. Whether it is more readable than the previous version is a matter for debate.

The case expression. This is another vehicle for pattern-matching
and has the form

$$\texttt{case } E \texttt{ of } P_1 \texttt{ => } E_1 \texttt{ | } \cdots \texttt{ | } P_n \texttt{ => } E_n$$

The value of E is matched successively against the patterns P_1,
..., P_n; if P_i is the first pattern to match then the result is the
value of E_i. Thus **case** is equivalent to an expression that defines
a function by cases and applies it to E. A typical **case** expression
tests for a few explicit values, concluding with a catch-all case:

```
case p-q of
    0 => "zero"
  | 1 => "one"
  | 2 => "two"
  | n => if n < 10 then "lots"  else  "lots and lots"
```

The function *merge* (from Chapter 3) can be recoded using **case**
to test the first argument before the second:

```
fun merge(xlist,ylist) : real list =
  case xlist of
      []     => ylist
    | x::xs => (case ylist of
                   [] => xlist
                 | y::ys => if x<=y  then x::merge(xs, ylist)
                                     else y::merge(xlist, ys));
```

In the recursive call, *xlist* and *x::xs* denote the same list — an
effect also obtainable through the pattern *xlist* **as** *x::xs*.

! *The scope of* **case**. No symbol terminates the **case** expression, so enclose
it in parentheses unless you are certain there is no ambiguity. Below,
the second line is part of the inner **case** expression, although the programmer
may have intended it to belong to the outer:

```
case x of 1 => case y of 0 => true | 1 => false
            | 2 => true;
```

The following declaration is not syntactically ambiguous, but many ML compilers
parse it incorrectly. The **case** expression should be enclosed in parentheses:

```
fun f [x] = case g x of 0 => true | 1 => false
  | f xs  = true;
```

Exercise 4.9 Express the function *title* using a **case** expression
to distinguish the four constructors of type *person*.

Exercise 4.10 Describe a simple method for removing all **case**
expressions from a program. Explain why your method does not
affect the meaning of the program.

Exceptions

A hard problem may be tackled by various methods, each of which succeeds in a fraction of the cases. There may be no better way of choosing a method than to try one and see if it succeeds. If the computation reaches a dead end, then the method fails — or perhaps determines that the problem is impossible. A proof method may make no progress or may reduce its goal to $0 = 1$. A numerical algorithm may suffer overflow or division by zero.

These outcomes can be represented by a datatype whose values are *Success(s)*, where *s* is a solution, *Failure* and *Impossible*. Dealing with multiple outcomes is complicated, as we saw with the topological sorting functions of Chapter 3. The function *cyclesort*, which returns information about success or failure, is more complex than *pathsort*, which expresses failure by calling *hd*[].

In ML, such 'illegal' values are called **exceptions**. An exception is **raised** (created) where the failure is discovered and **handled** (detected and analysed) elsewhere — possibly far away.

4.5   *Introduction to exceptions*

Exceptions are a datatype of error values that are treated specially in order to minimize explicit testing. When an exception is raised, it is transmitted by all ML functions until it is detected by an **exception handler**. Essentially a **case** expression, the exception handler specifies what to return for each kind of exception.

Suppose that functions *methodA* and *methodB* realize different methods for solving a problem, and that *show* displays a solution as a string. Using a datatype with constructors *Success*, *Failure* and *Impossible*, we can display the outcome of an attempted solution by nested case expressions. If *methodA* fails then *methodB* is tried, while if either reports that the problem is impossible then it is abandoned. In all cases, the result has the same type: *string*.

```
case methodA(problem) of
     Success s => show s
   | Failure    => (case methodB(problem) of
                          Success s => show s
                        | Failure    => "Both methods failed"
                        | Impossible => "No solution exists")
   | Impossible => "No solution exists"
```

Now try exception handling. Instead of a datatype of possible outcomes, declare exceptions *Failure* and *Impossible*:

```
exception Failure;
exception Impossible;
```

Functions *methodA* and *methodB* — and any functions they call within the scope of these exception declarations — can signal errors by code such as

```
if     ... then raise Impossible
else if ... then raise Failure
else (*compute successful result*)
```

The attempts to apply *methodA* and *methodB* involve two exception handlers:

```
show  (methodA(problem)
         handle Failure => methodB(problem))
      handle Failure    => "Both methods failed"
           | Impossible => "No solution exists"
```

The first handler traps *Failure* from *methodA*, and tries *methodB*. The second handler traps *Failure* from *methodB* and *Impossible* from either method. Function *show* is given the result of *methodA*, if successful, or else *methodB*.

Even in this simple example, exceptions give a shorter, clearer and faster program. Error propagation does not clutter our code.

4.6   *Declaring exceptions*

An exception name in Standard ML is a constructor of the built-in type *exn*. This is a datatype with a unique property: its set of constructors can be extended. The exception declaration

```
exception Failure;
```

makes *Failure* a new constructor of type *exn*.

While *Failure* and *Impossible* are constants, constructors can also be functions:

```
exception Failedbecause of string;
exception Badvalue of int;
```

Constructor *Failedbecause* has type *string* $\rightarrow$ *exn* while *Badvalue* has type *int* $\rightarrow$ *exn*. They create exceptions *Failedbecause*(*msg*), where *msg* is a message to be displayed, and *Badvalue*(*k*), where *k* may determine the method to be tried next.

Exceptions can be declared locally using **let**, even inside a recursive function. This can result in different exceptions having the same name and other complications. Whenever possible, declare exceptions at top level. The type of a top level exception must be monomorphic.

Values of type *exn* can be stored in lists, returned by functions, etc., like values of other types. In addition, they have a special role in the operations **raise** and **handle**.

4.7 *Raising exceptions*

Raising an exception creates an **exception packet** containing a value of type *exn*. If *Ex* is an expression of type *exn* and *Ex* evaluates to e, then

> **raise** *Ex*

evaluates to an exception packet containing e. Packets are not ML values; the only operations that recognize them are **raise** and **handle**. Type *exn* mediates between packets and ML values.

During evaluation, exception packets propagate under the call-by-value rule. If expression E returns an exception packet then that is the result of the application $f(E)$, for any function f. Thus $f(\textbf{raise } Ex)$ is equivalent to **raise** *Ex*. Incidentally, **raise** itself propagates exceptions, and so

> **raise** (*Badvalue* (**raise** *Failure*))

raises exception *Failure*.

Expressions in ML are evaluated from left to right. If E_1 returns a packet then that is the result of the pair (E_1, E_2); expression E_2 is not evaluated at all. If E_1 returns a normal value and E_2 returns a packet, then that packet is the result of the pair. The evaluation order matters when E_1 and E_2 raise different exceptions.

The evaluation order is also visible in conditional expressions:

> **if** E **then** E_1 **else** E_2

If E evaluates to *true* then only E_1 is evaluated. Its result, whether normal or not, becomes that of the conditional. Similarly, if E evaluates to *false* then only E_2 is evaluated. There is a third possibility. If the test E raises an exception then that is the result of the conditional.

Finally, consider the **let** expression

> **let val** P = E_1 **in** E_2 **end**

If E_1 evaluates to an exception packet then so does the entire **let** expression.

Exception packets are not propagated by testing. The ML system efficiently jumps to the correct exception handler if there is one, otherwise terminating execution.

Standard exceptions. ML has several built-in exceptions — mainly for errors from built-in functions — including the following:

> *Ln* is raised by *ln*(x) for $x \le 0$
> *Sqrt* is raised by *sqrt*(x) for $x < 0$
> *Ord* is raised by *ord*(s) where s is the empty string
> *Chr* is raised by *chr*(k) if $k < 0$ or $k > 255$
> *Interrupt* is raised if the program is interrupted externally
> *Io* signals errors during input and output operations

Failure of pattern-matching may raise the built-in exceptions *Match* or *Bind*. A function raises exception *Match* when applied to an argument matching none of its patterns. If a `case` expression has no pattern that matches, it also raises exception *Match*. The ML compiler warns in advance of this possibility when it encounters non-exhaustive patterns (not covering all values of the type).

Because many functions can raise *Match*, this exception conveys little information. To detect incorrect arguments to a function, declare a new exception and raise it in a final catch-all case.

The basic list functions *hd* and *tl* can be declared with exceptions *Hd* and *Tl* to indicate when they are wrongly applied.

```
exception Hd;
fun hd (x::_)   = x
  | hd []       = raise Hd;
> val hd = fn :  'a list -> 'a
exception Tl;
fun tl (_::xs)  = xs
  | tl []       = raise Tl;
> val tl = fn :  'a list -> 'a list
```

Less trivial is a function to return the nth element in a list, counting from 0:

```
exception Nth;
fun nth(x::_,   0) = x
  | nth(x::xs,  n) = if n>0  then   nth(xs,n-1)
                                    else   raise Nth
  | nth _           = raise Nth;
> val nth = fn :  'a list * int -> 'a
```

Evaluating $nth(l, n)$ raises exception *Nth* if $n < 0$ or if the list l has no nth element. In the latter case, the exception propagates up the recursive function calls.

```
nth(explode"At the pit of Acheron", 5);
> "e" : string
nth([1,2], 2);
> Exception Nth raised
```

The declaration **val** P = E raises exception *Bind* if the value of E does not match pattern P. This is usually poor style. If there is any possibility that the value will not match the pattern, the alternatives should be considered explicitly in a **case** expression:

$$\textbf{case } E \textbf{ of } P \texttt{ => } \cdots \texttt{ | } P_2 \texttt{ => } \cdots$$

4.8   *Handling exceptions*

An exception handler tests whether the result of an expression is an exception packet. If so, the packet's contents — a value of type *exn* — may be examined by cases. An expression that has an exception handler resembles the **case** construct:

$$E \textbf{ handle } P_1 \texttt{ => } E_1 \texttt{ | } \cdots \texttt{ | } P_n \texttt{ => } E_n$$

If E returns a normal value, then the handler simply passes this value on. On the other hand, if E returns a packet then its contents are matched against the patterns. If P_i is the first pattern to match then the result is the value of E_i, for $i = 1, \ldots, n$.

There is one major difference from **case**. If no pattern matches, then the handler propagates the exception packet rather than raising exception *Match*. A typical handler does not consider every possible exception.

Because exceptions are designed for complex and untidy tasks, elegant examples are scarce. Here is a contrived one. Suppose f is a function of type *int* → *int*. The following function computes the sum of a list's elements in positions i, $f(i)$, $f(f(i))$, $\ldots$. The sequence of integers terminates at the first value out of range, using exception *Nth*.

```
fun sumchain (l,n) = nth(l,n) + sumchain(l, f(n))
                  handle Nth=>0;
> val sumchain = fn : int list * int -> int
```

Better examples will occur later in the book as we tackle problems like parsing and unification.

!   *Pitfalls in exception handling.* An exception handler must be written with care, as with other forms of pattern matching. Never misspell an exception name; it will be taken as a variable and match all exceptions.

Be careful to give exception handlers the correct scope, since the ML compiler has no way of detecting whether they are in the intended location. In

   if E then E_1 else E_2 handle $\cdots$

the handler will only detect exceptions raised by E_2. Enclosing the conditional expression in parentheses brings it entirely within the scope of the handler. Similarly, in

   case E of P_1 => E_1 | $\cdots$ | P_n => E_n handle $\cdots$

the handler will only detect exceptions raised by E_n.

Exception handlers in case expressions can be syntactically ambiguous. Omitting the parentheses here would make the second line of the case expression become part of the handler:

   case f u of [x] => (g x handle _ => x)
                | xs => g u

4.9   *Objections to exceptions*

Exceptions can be a clumsy alternative to pattern-matching, as in this function for computing the length of a list:

```
fun len l =  1 + len(tl l) handle Tl => 0;
> val len = fn : 'a list -> int
```

Writing $\langle e \rangle$ for the packet containing exception value e, the evaluation of $len[1]$ goes like this:

$$len[1] \Rightarrow 1 + len(tl[1]) \text{ handle } Tl\text{=>}0$$
$$\Rightarrow 1 + len[] \text{ handle } Tl\text{=>}0$$
$$\Rightarrow 1 + (1 + len(tl[]) \text{ handle } Tl\text{=>}0) \text{ handle } Tl\text{=>}0$$
$$\Rightarrow 1 + (1 + len\langle Tl\rangle \text{ handle } Tl\text{=>}0) \text{ handle } Tl\text{=>}0$$
$$\Rightarrow 1 + (1 + \langle Tl\rangle \text{ handle } Tl\text{=>}0) \text{ handle } Tl\text{=>}0$$
$$\Rightarrow 1 + (\langle Tl\rangle \text{ handle } Tl\text{=>}0) \text{ handle } Tl\text{=>}0$$
$$\Rightarrow 1 + 0 \text{ handle } Tl\text{=>}0$$
$$\Rightarrow 1$$

This evaluation is more complicated than one for the obvious length function defined by pattern-matching. Test for different cases in advance, if possible, rather than trying them willy-nilly by exception handling.

Most proponents of lazy evaluation object to exception handling. Exceptions complicate the theory and can be abused, as we have just seen. The conflict is deeper. Exceptions are propagated under the call-by-value rule, while lazy evaluation follows call-by-need.

ML includes assignments and other commands, and exceptions can be hazardous in imperative programming. It is difficult to write correct programs when execution can be interrupted in arbitrary places.

Restricted to the functional parts of a program, exceptions can be understood as dividing the value space into ordinary values and exception packets. They are not strictly necessary in a programming language and could be abused, but they can also promote clarity and efficiency.

Exercise 4.11 Type *exn* does not admit the ML equality operator. Is this restriction justified?

Exercise 4.12 Describe a computational problem from your experience where exception handling would be appropriate. Write the skeleton of an ML program to solve this problem. Include the exception declarations and describe where exceptions would be raised and handled.

Trees

A **tree** is a branching structure consisting of **nodes** with **branches** leading to subtrees. Nodes may carry values, called **labels**. Despite the arboreal terminology, trees are usually drawn upside down:

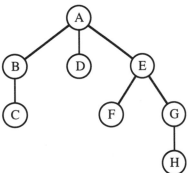

The node labelled A is the **root** of the tree, while codes C, D, F and H (which have no subtrees) are its **leaves**.

The type of a node determines the type of its label and how many subtrees it may have. A type of trees determines the types of its nodes. Two types of tree are especially important. The first has labelled nodes, each with one branch, terminated by an unlabelled leaf. Such trees are simply lists. The second type of tree differs from lists in that each labelled node has two branches instead of one. These are called **binary trees**.

When functional programmers work with lists, they can draw on a body of techniques and a library of functions. When they work with trees, they usually make all their own arrangements. This is a pity, for binary trees are ideal for many applications. The following sections apply them to efficient table lookup, arrays and priority queues. We develop a library of polymorphic functions for binary trees.

4.10   *A type for binary trees*

A binary tree has branch nodes with a label and two subtrees. Its leaves are unlabelled. To define binary trees in ML requires a recursive **datatype** declaration:

```
datatype 'a tree = Lf
                 | Br of 'a * 'a tree * 'a tree;
```

Recursive datatypes are understood exactly like non-recursive ones. Type α *tree* consists of all the values that can be made by *Lf* and *Br*. There is at least one α *tree*, namely *Lf*; and given two trees and a label of type α, we can make another tree. Thus *Lf* is the base case of the recursion.

Here is a tree labelled with strings:

```
val birnam =
  Br("The", Br("wood", Lf,
                       Br("of", Br("Birnam", Lf, Lf),
                              Lf)),
           Lf);
> val birnam = Br ("The", ..., Lf) : string tree
```

Here are some trees labelled with integers. Note how trees can be combined to form bigger ones.

```
val tree2 = Br(2, Br(1,Lf,Lf), Br(3,Lf,Lf));
> val tree2 = Br (2, Br (1,Lf,Lf), Br (3,Lf,Lf)) : int tree
val tree5 = Br(5, Br(6,Lf,Lf), Br(7,Lf,Lf));
> val tree5 = Br (5, Br (6,Lf,Lf), Br (7,Lf,Lf)) : int tree
val tree4 = Br(4, tree2, tree5);
> val tree4 =
> Br (4, Br (2, Br (1,Lf,Lf), Br (3,Lf,Lf)),
>        Br (5, Br (6,Lf,Lf), Br (7,Lf,Lf))) : int tree
```

Trees *birnam* and *tree*4 can be pictured as follows:

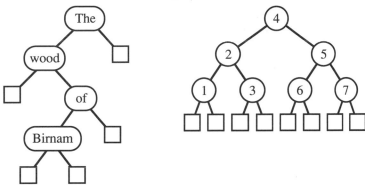

Leaves are shown as squares above, but will henceforth be omitted.

Tree operations are expressed by recursive functions with pattern-matching. The polymorphic function *count* returns the number of labels in a tree:

```
fun count Lf          = 0
  | count (Br(v,t1,t2)) = 1 + count t1 + count t2;
> val count = fn : 'a tree -> int
count birnam;
> 4 : int
count tree4;
> 7 : int
```

Another measure of the size of a tree is its *depth*: the length of the longest path from the root to a leaf.

```
fun depth Lf          = 0
  | depth (Br(v,t1,t2)) = 1 + maxl[depth t1, depth t2];
> val depth = fn : 'a tree -> int
depth birnam;
> 4 : int
depth tree4;
> 3 : int
```

Observe that *birnam* is rather deep for its count while *tree*4 is as shallow as possible. If t is a binary tree then

$$count(t) \leq 2^{depth(t)} - 1$$

If t satisfies $count(t) = 2^{depth(t)} - 1$ then it is a **full binary tree**. For instance, *tree*4 is a full binary tree of depth 3.

Informally speaking, a binary tree is **balanced** if at each node, both subtrees are of similar size. This concept can be made precise in various ways. The cost of reaching a node in a tree is proportional to its depth — for a balanced tree, to the logarithm of the number of elements. A full binary tree of depth 10 contains 1,023 branch nodes, all reachable in at most nine steps. A tree of depth 20 can contain over 10^6 elements. Balanced trees permit efficient access to large quantities of data.

Calling *fulltree*$(1, n)$ creates a full binary tree of depth n, labelling the nodes from 1 to 2^n:

```
fun fulltree (k,n) =
      if n=0 then Lf
            else Br(k, fulltree(2*k,   n-1),
                       fulltree(2*k+1, n-1));
> val fulltree = fn : int * int -> int tree
fulltree (1,3);
> Br (1, Br (2, Br (4,Lf,Lf), Br (5,Lf,Lf)),
>          Br (3, Br (6,Lf,Lf), Br (7,Lf,Lf))) : int tree
```

A function over trees, *reflect* forms the mirror image of a tree by exchanging left and right subtrees all the way down:

```
fun reflect Lf              = Lf
  | reflect (Br(v,t1,t2)) = Br(v, reflect t2, reflect t1);
> val reflect = fn : 'a tree -> 'a tree
reflect tree4;
> Br (4, Br (5, Br (7, Lf, Lf), Br (6, Lf, Lf)),
>          Br (2, Br (3, Lf, Lf), Br (1, Lf, Lf))) : int tree
```

Exercise 4.13   Write a function *fullsame*(x, n) to construct a full binary tree of depth n, labelling all nodes with x. How efficient is your function?

Exercise 4.14   A binary tree is **balanced** (by node count) if each node $Br(x, t_1, t_2)$ satisfies

$$\left| count(t_1) - count(t_2) \right| \leq 1.$$

The obvious recursive function to test whether a tree is balanced applies *count* at every subtree, performing much redundant computation. Write an efficient function to test whether a tree is balanced.

Exercise 4.15   Write a function that determines whether two arbitrary trees t and u satisfy

$$t = reflect(u).$$

The function should not build any new trees, so it should not call *reflect* or *Br*, although it may use *Br* in patterns.

Exercise 4.16 Lists need not have been built into ML. Give a `datatype` declaration of a type equivalent to α *list*.

Exercise 4.17 Define a datatype (α, β)*ltree* of labelled binary trees, where branch nodes carry a label of type α and leaves carry a label of type β.

Exercise 4.18 Define a datatype of trees where each branch node may have any finite number of branches. (Hint: use *list*.)

4.11 *Converting between lists and trees*

Consider the problem of making a list of a tree's labels. The labels must be arranged in some order. Three well-known orders, **preorder**, **inorder** and **postorder**, can be described by a recursive function over trees. Given a branch node, each puts the labels of the left subtree before those of the right; the orders differ only in the position of the label.

A preorder list places the label first:

```
fun preorder Lf            = []
  | preorder (Br(v,t1,t2)) = [v] @ preorder t1 @ preorder t2;
> val preorder = fn : 'a tree -> 'a list
preorder birnam;
> ["The", "wood", "of", "Birnam"] : string list
preorder tree4;
> [4, 2, 1, 3, 5, 6, 7] : int list
```

An inorder list places the label between the labels from the left and right subtrees, giving a strict left-to-right traversal:

```
fun inorder Lf            = []
  | inorder (Br(v,t1,t2)) = inorder t1 @ [v] @ inorder t2;
> val inorder = fn : 'a tree -> 'a list
inorder birnam;
> ["wood", "Birnam", "of", "The"] : string list
inorder tree4;
> [1, 2, 3, 4, 6, 5, 7] : int list
```

A postorder list places the label last:

```
fun postorder Lf            = []
  | postorder (Br(v,t1,t2)) = postorder t1 @ postorder t2 @ [v];
> val postorder = fn : 'a tree -> 'a list
postorder birnam;
> ["Birnam", "of", "wood", "The"] : string list
postorder tree4;
> [1, 3, 2, 6, 7, 5, 4] : int list
```

Although these functions are clear, they take quadratic time on badly unbalanced trees. The culprit is the appending (@) of long lists. It can be eliminated using an extra argument *vs* to accumulate the labels. The following versions perform exactly one cons (::) operation per branch node:

```
fun preord (Lf, vs)          = vs
  | preord (Br(v,t1,t2), vs) = v :: preord(t1, preord(t2,vs));

fun inord (Lf, vs)           = vs
  | inord (Br(v,t1,t2), vs)  = inord(t1, v::inord(t2,vs));

fun postord (Lf, vs)         = vs
  | postord (Br(v,t1,t2), vs)= postord(t1, postord(t2,v::vs));
```

These definitions are worth study; many functions are defined similarly. For instance, logical terms are essentially trees. The list of all the constants in a term can be built as above.

Now consider converting a list of labels to a tree. The concepts of preorder, inorder and postorder apply as well to this inverse operation. Even within a fixed order, one list can be converted to many different trees. The equation

$$preorder(t) = [1, 2, 3]$$

has five solutions in t:

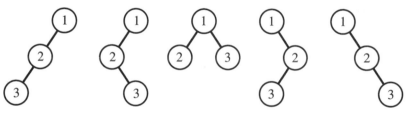

Only one of these trees is balanced. To construct balanced trees, divide the list of labels roughly in half. The subtrees may differ in size (number of nodes) by at most 1.

To make a balanced tree from a preorder list of labels, the first label is attached to the root of the tree:

```
fun balpreorder []      = Lf
  | balpreorder (x::xs) =
      let val k = length xs div 2
      in Br(x, balpreorder(take(k,xs)), balpreorder(drop(k,xs)))
      end;
> val balpreorder = fn : 'a list -> 'a tree
```

This function is an inverse of *preorder*.

```
balpreorder(explode"Macbeth");
> Br ("M", Br ("a", Br ("c", Lf, Lf), Br ("b", Lf, Lf)),
>        Br ("e", Br ("t", Lf, Lf), Br ("h", Lf, Lf)))
>    : string tree
implode(preorder it);
> "Macbeth" : string
```

To make a balanced tree from an inorder list, the label is taken from the middle. This resembles the top-down merge sort of Chapter 3:

```
fun balinorder [] = Lf
  | balinorder xs =
      let val k      = length xs div 2
          val y::ys = drop(k, xs)
      in  Br(y, balinorder (take(k,xs)), balinorder ys)
      end;
> val balinorder = fn : 'a list -> 'a tree
```

This function is an inverse of *inorder*.

```
balinorder(explode"Macbeth");
> Br ("b", Br ("a", Br ("M", Lf, Lf), Br ("c", Lf, Lf)),
>        Br ("t", Br ("e", Lf, Lf), Br ("h", Lf, Lf)))
>    : string tree
implode(inorder it);
> "Macbeth" : string
```

Exercise 4.19 Show the computation steps of *inorder*(*birnam*) and *inord*(*birnam*, []). For each, report how many cons operations are performed.

Exercise 4.20 Complete the following equations (in an interesting way) and explain why they are correct.

$$preorder(reflect(t)) = ?$$
$$inorder(reflect(t)) = ?$$
$$postorder(reflect(t)) = ?$$

Exercise 4.21 Write a function to convert a postorder list of labels to a balanced tree.

Exercise 4.22 The Function *balpreorder* constructs one tree from a preorder list of labels. Write a function that, given a list of labels, constructs the list of all trees that have those labels in preorder.

4.12   *Binary search trees*

A binary search tree implements a dictionary. Information can be associated with strings (or other search keys), and later retrieved. If it is reasonably balanced, a binary search tree is vastly more efficient than an association list of (*key, value*) pairs. The time required to search for a key among n items is order n for lists and order $\log n$ for binary search trees. The time required to update the tree is also of order $\log n$. An association list can be updated in constant time, but this does not compensate for the long search time.

In the worst case, binary search trees are actually slower than association lists. A series of updates can create a highly unbalanced tree. Search and update can take up to n steps for a tree of n items.

The keys in an association list may have any type with an equality test, but the keys in a binary search tree must come with a linear ordering. Strings, with alphabetic ordering, are the obvious choice. Each branch node of the tree carries a (*string, value*) pair; its left subtree holds only smaller strings; the right subtree holds only greater strings. The inorder list of labels puts the strings in alphabetic order.

Here is a binary search tree that is balanced and contains 5 items.

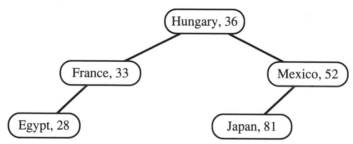

Three operations are defined on binary search trees:

> To **lookup** a string in the tree and return the value paired with it
>
> To **update** a tree with a new (*string, value*) pair, possibly altering an existing node
>
> To **insert** a new (*string, value*) pair into the tree, checking that the *string* is not already present

Unlike tree operations that might be coded in Pascal, the **update** and **insert** operations do not modify the current tree. Instead, they create a new tree. This is less wasteful than it sounds because the new tree shares most of its storage with the existing tree.

The **lookup** and **insert** operations may result in an error, so let us declare an exception:

```
exception Bsearch of string;
```

Lookup in a binary search tree is simple. At a branch node, look left if the item being sought is smaller than the current label, and right if it is greater. If the item is not found, the function raises exception *Bsearch*:

```
fun blookup (Br ((a,x),t1,t2), b: string) =
        if        b < a then blookup(t1, b)
        else if a < b then blookup(t2, b)
                    else x
  | blookup (Lf, b) = raise Bsearch("lookup: " ^ b);
> val blookup = fn : (string * 'a) tree * string -> 'a
```

Insertion of a (*string*, *value*) pair involves locating the correct position for the *string*, then inserting the *value*. As with *blookup*, comparing the string with the current label determines whether to look left or right. Here the result is a new branch node; one subtree is updated and the other borrowed from the original tree. If the string is found in the tree, an exception results.

```
fun binsert (Lf, b: string, y)          = Br((b,y), Lf, Lf)
  | binsert (Br((a,x),t1,t2), b, y)    =
        if b<a then    Br ((a,x), binsert(t1,b,y), t2)
        else
        if a<b then    Br ((a,x), t1, binsert(t2,b,y))
        else (*a=b*) raise Bsearch("insert: " ^ b);
> val binsert = fn : (string * 'a) tree * string * 'a
>                          -> (string * 'a) tree
```

In effect, *binsert* copies the path from the root of the tree to the new node. Function *bupdate* is identical apart from its result if the string is found in the tree.

The exception in *blookup* is easily eliminated because that function is iterative. Lookup could return the list $[x]$ if successful and $[]$ if not. The exception in *binsert* is another matter: since the recursive calls construct a new tree, returning a list of trees would be complicated. The insert operation could be implemented by lookup and update, doubling the number of comparisons.

Binary search trees are built from the empty tree (*Leaf*) by repeated updates or inserts. We construct a tree *ctree*1 containing

France and Egypt:

```
binsert(Lf, "France", 33);
> Br (("France",33), Lf, Lf) : (string*int) tree
val ctree1 = binsert(it, "Egypt", 20);
> val ctree1 = Br (("France",33), Br (("Egypt",20), Lf, Lf),
>                       Lf) : (string*int) tree
```

We insert Hungary and Mexico:

```
binsert(ctree1, "Hungary", 36);
> Br (("France",33), Br (("Egypt",20), Lf, Lf),
>     Br (("Hungary",36), Lf, Lf)) : (string*int) tree
binsert(it, "Mexico", 52);
> Br (("France",33), Br (("Egypt",20), Lf, Lf),
>     Br (("Hungary",36), Lf,
>         Br (("Mexico",52), Lf, Lf))) : (string*int) tree
```

By inserting Japan, we create the tree *ctree2* consisting of 5 items.

```
val ctree2 = bupdate(it, "Japan", 81);
> val ctree2 =
> Br (("France",33), Br (("Egypt",20), Lf, Lf),
>     Br (("Hungary",36), Lf,
>         Br (("Mexico",52), Br (("Japan",81), Lf, Lf),
>             Lf))) : (string*int) tree
```

Note that *ctree1* still exists, even though *ctree2* has been constructed from it.

```
blookup(ctree1, "France");
> 33 : int
blookup(ctree2, "Mexico");
> 52 : int
blookup(ctree1, "Mexico");
> Exception Bsearch "lookup: Mexico" raised
```

Inserting items at random can create unbalanced trees. There are functional algorithms for keeping trees balanced (Bird & Wadler, 1988), but simple methods are often faster in practice. If most of the insertions occur first, followed by many lookups, then it pays to balance the tree before the lookups. Since a binary search tree corresponds to a sorted inorder list, it can be balanced by converting it to inorder ...

```
inorder (ctree2);
> [("Egypt", 20), ("France", 33), ("Hungary", 36),
>  ("Japan", 81), ("Mexico", 52)] : (string * int) list
```

... then constructing a new tree:

```
val baltree = balinorder it;
> val baltree =
> Br(("Hungary", 36),
>    Br (("France", 33), Br (("Egypt", 20), Lf, Lf), Lf),
>    Br (("Mexico", 52), Br (("Japan", 81), Lf, Lf), Lf))
> : (string * int) tree
```

This is the tree illustrated at the beginning of the section.

Exercise 4.23   Draw the five trees that were created in the course of building *ctree2*.

Exercise 4.24   Write the function *bupdate* to update a binary search tree with a (*string, value*) pair.

Exercise 4.25   Give four examples of a binary search tree whose depth equals 5 and that contains only the 5 labels of *ctree2*. For each tree, show a sequence of insertions that creates it.

Functional arrays and priority queues

What is an array? To most programmers, an array is a block of storage cells, indexed by integers, that can be updated. Conventional programming skill mainly involves using arrays effectively. Since most arrays are scanned sequentially, the functional programmer can use lists instead. But many applications — hash tables and histograms are perhaps the simplest — require random access.

In essence, an array is a mapping defined on a finite range of the integers. The value associated with the integer k is written $A[k]$. Conventionally, an array is modified by the assignment command

$$A[k] := x,$$

changing the machine state such that $A[k] = x$. The previous value of $A[k]$ is lost. Updating in place is highly efficient, both in time and space, but it is hard to reconcile with functional programming.

A functional array provides a mapping from integers to values, with an update operation that creates a new array

$$B = update(A, k, x)$$

such that $B[k] = x$ and $B[i] = A[i]$ for all $i \neq k$. The array A continues to exist and additional arrays can be created from it.

Functional arrays can be implemented by binary trees. The position of subscript k in the tree is determined by starting at the root and repeatedly dividing k by 2 until it is reduced to 1. Each time the remainder equals 0, move to the left subtree; if the remainder equals 1, move to the right. For instance, subscript 12 is reached by left, left, right:

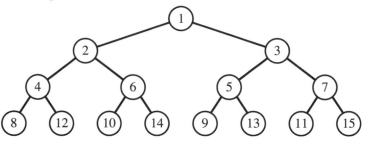

This representation allows the array to grow and shrink. It is possible to show that the binary tree is always balanced. Lookup and update to element k take order $\log k$ steps, which is the best possible time complexity for any data structure of unbounded size. Imperative arrays have a fast, constant access time regardless of their size. A binary tree of 1,000 elements may have acceptable access times, but one of 1,000,000 elements will be twice as slow.

Most Standard ML compilers provide imperative arrays, which will be used in a later chapter to implement functional arrays. That implementation gives fast, constant access time — if the array is used in an imperative style. Imperative arrays are so prevalent that functional applications require some imagination. If an editor represents text files by functional arrays, then it can easily provide an 'undo' command and maintain many different versions of a document. If a robot represents the state of its environment by a functional array, then while planning its next move it can consider many possible next states.

4.13   *Functional arrays*

Let us forbid arrays with gaps: element n may be defined only if elements 1 to $n-1$ are already defined. The upper bound of an array is the highest defined subscript position. An array may grow without limit, increasing the upper bound, or shrink, decreasing the upper bound. The lower bound is fixed at 1. The basic operations are lookup, update and hirem:

Lookup returns the value stored in the array at the subscript.

Update replaces the value stored in the array at the subscript, perhaps increasing the upper bound.

Hirem decreases the upper bound of the array, removing the highest subscript position.

This set of operations, loosely based on Dijkstra (1976), does not require the array to be initialized with arbitrary values or fix its size in advance. A program typically starts with an empty array and inserts elements as they are produced.

The ML functions resemble those for binary search trees. If the subscript is out of bounds they raise an exception.

```
exception Array;
```

The lookup function, *asub*, divides the subscript by 2 until 1 is reached. If the remainder is 0 then the function follows the left subtree, otherwise the right. It signals error if a leaf is reached.

```
fun asub (Lf, _)           = raise Array
  | asub (Br(v,t1,t2), k) =
        if k=1 then v
        else if k mod 2 = 0
                then asub (t1, k div 2)
                else asub (t2, k div 2);
> val asub = fn : 'a tree * int -> 'a
```

The update function, *aupdate*, also divides the subscript repeatedly by 2. When it reaches 1 it replaces the branch node by another branch with the new label. A leaf may be replaced by a branch, extending the array, provided no intervening nodes have to be generated. This is sufficient to represent arrays without gaps.

```
fun aupdate (Lf, k, w) =
        if k = 1 then Br (w, Lf, Lf)
        else   raise Array
  | aupdate (Br(v,t1,t2), k, w) =
        if k = 1 then Br (w, t1, t2)
        else if k mod 2 = 0
                then Br (v, aupdate(t1, k div 2, w),  t2)
                else Br (v,  t1,  aupdate(t2, k div 2, w));
> val aupdate = fn : 'a tree * int * 'a -> 'a tree
```

The result of *hirem*(*ta*, *n*) has a leaf in place of element *n*. An exception is raised if that element does not exist. Though valid only if *n* is the upper bound, *hirem* does not check this.

```
fun hirem (Lf, n)              = raise Array
  | hirem (Br(v,t1,t2), n) =
      if n = 1 then Lf
      else if n mod 2 = 0
              then Br (v,  hirem(t1, n div 2),  t2)
              else Br (v,  t1,  hirem(t2, n div 2));
> val hirem = fn : 'a tree * int -> 'a tree
```

The functions above perform only the tree manipulations.   For most applications, the array should be paired with its upper bound. Function *hiext* increases the upper bound by 1:

```
fun hiext((ta,n), v) = (aupdate(ta, n+1, v), n+1);
> val hiext = fn : ('a tree * int) * 'a -> 'a tree * int
```

By repeatedly applying *hiext* to a leaf, we build an array of the letters A to D.

```
hiext((Lf,0), "A");
> (Br ("A", Lf, Lf), 1) : string tree * int
hiext(it,"B");
> (Br ("A", Br ("B", Lf, Lf), Lf), 2) : string tree * int
hiext(it,"C");
> (Br ("A", Br ("B", Lf, Lf), Br ("C", Lf, Lf)), 3)
>   : string tree *int
val (tletters,n) = hiext(it,"D");
> val tletters = Br ("A", Br ("B", Br ("D", Lf, Lf), Lf),
>                        Br ("C", Lf, Lf)) : string tree
> val n = 4 : int
```

The tree *tletters* looks like this:

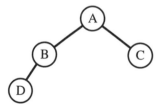

Updating element 4 of *tletters* does not affect that array, but creates a new array:

```
val tdag = aupdate(tletters, 4, "dagger");
> val tdag = Br ("A", Br ("B", Br ("dagger", Lf, Lf), Lf),
>                        Br ("C", Lf, Lf)) : string tree
asub(tletters,4);
> "D" : string
asub(tdag,4);
> "dagger" : string
```

Priority queues are a more substantial application. We shall shortly consider arrays of 10,000 elements.

Exercise 4.26   Write a function to create an array consisting of the value x in subscript positions 1 to n. Do not use *aupdate*: build the tree directly.

Exercise 4.27   Write a function to convert the array consisting of the values x_1, x_2, ..., x_n (in subscript positions 1 to n) to a list. Operate directly on the tree, without repeated subscripting.

Exercise 4.28   Implement sparse arrays, which may have arbitrary gaps between elements, by allowing empty labels in the tree.

Exercise 4.29   As mentioned above, a functional array really consists of a binary tree paired with its upper bound, an integer. Use the tree operations *asub*, *aupdate* and *hirem* to implement the corresponding operations on functional arrays. Subscript errors should be indicated by raising an exception containing the offending subscript and the upper bound.

4.14   *Priority queues*

A **priority queue** is an ordered collection of items. It supports the operations enqueue, largest and dequeue:

> **Enqueue** adds an item to the queue, returning a new queue.
> **Largest** returns the largest item in the queue.
> **Dequeue** returns a new queue, deleting the largest item.

In simulations, a priority queue selects the next event according to its stored time. In Artificial Intelligence, priority queues implement **best-first search**: attempted solutions to a problem are stored with priorities (assigned by a rating function) and the best attempt is chosen for further search.

If a priority queue is kept as a reverse sorted list, enqueue takes up to n steps for a queue of n items. This is far too slow. With a binary tree, enqueue and dequeue take order $\log n$ steps. Such a tree, called a **heap**, is the key to the well-known sorting algorithm **heap sort**. The labels are arranged such that no label is larger than a label above it in the tree. This **heap condition** puts the labels in no strict order, but does put the largest label at the root.

Conventionally, the tree is embedded in an array with the labels indexed as follows (Sedgewick, 1988):

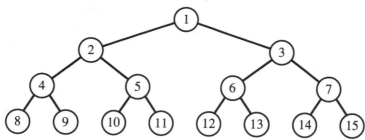

An *n*-item heap consists of nodes 1 to *n*. This indexing scheme always creates a tree of minimum depth. However, our indexing scheme for functional arrays also ensures minimum depth. Our functional priority queues are based on functional arrays. They call *asub* and *hirem* as well as manipulating trees directly. The resulting program is a hybrid of old and new ideas.

If the heap contains $n-1$ items, then an enqueue fills position *n*. (Remember, we are using the indexing scheme for functional arrays.) However, the new item may be too large to go into position *n* without violating the heap condition. It may end up higher in the tree, forcing smaller labels downwards. Function *upheap* resembles *aupdate*, but maintains the heap condition while filling position *n*.

```
fun upheap (Lf, n, w: real)      = Br (w, Lf, Lf)
  | upheap (Br(v,t1,t2), n, w) =   (* assume n>1 *)
      if v>w then
          if n mod 2 = 0
          then Br (v,  upheap(t1, n div 2, w),  t2)
          else Br (v,  t1,  upheap(t2, n div 2, w))
      else (* w>=v *)
          if n mod 2 = 0
          then Br (w, upheap(t1, n div 2, v), t2)
          else Br (w, t1, upheap(t2, n div 2, v));
> val upheap = fn : real tree * int * real -> real tree
```

The dequeue operation on an *n*-item heap must vacate position *n*, to keep the tree balanced, while removing the item at the root. Item *n* may be too small to go into the root without violating the heap condition. The item moves down the tree. At each branch node, it follows the larger of the labels on the subtrees. It stops when no subtree contains a greater label. A node may have no right subtree or no subtrees at all.

Function *downheap* performs this reshuffling while inserting an item w. Since the root label is replaced, the tree grows no larger. Observe the use of **case** to inspect the labels of $t1$ and $t2$.

```
fun downheap (Br(_,t1,t2), w: real) =
  case t1 of
      Lf              => Br(w,Lf,Lf)
    | Br(vl,_,_) =>
      (case t2 of
           Lf               => if w>vl then Br(w, t1, Lf)
                               else Br(vl, downheap(t1,w), Lf)
         | Br(vr,_,_)  =>
               if vl>=vr
               then if w>vl then Br(w, t1, t2)
                            else Br(vl, downheap(t1,w), t2)
               else if w>vr then Br(w, t1, t2)
                            else Br(vr, t1, downheap(t2,w)));
> val downheap = fn : real tree * real -> real tree
```

Exception *Heap* indicates an attempt to dequeue an element from the empty heap.

```
exception Heap;
```

Function *dequeue* calls *asub* to obtain item n, then *hirem* to dequeue that item, then *downheap* to put the item in the proper place. The case $n = 1$ is treated separately.

```
fun dequeue (hp,n) =
    if n>1 then (downheap(hirem(hp, n), asub(hp,n)), n-1)
    else if n=1 then (Lf,0)
                else raise Heap;
> val dequeue = fn : real tree * int -> real tree * int
```

Priority queues easily implement heap sort. Functions *upheaplist* and *heapoflist* convert a list into a heap.

```
fun upheaplist((hp,n), [])    = (hp,n)
  | upheaplist((hp,n), v::vs) =
        upheaplist((upheap(hp, n+1, v), n+1), vs);
> val upheaplist = fn : (real tree * int) * real list
>                               -> real tree * int
fun heapoflist vs = upheaplist((Lf,0), vs);
> val heapoflist = fn : real list -> real tree * int
```

Function *listofheap* repeatedly dequeues the next item to build a sorted list, while *heapsort* simply calls these functions.

```
fun listofheap ((hp as Br(v,_,_), n), vs) =
        listofheap(dequeue(hp,n), v::vs)
  | listofheap ((Lf,_), vs)                 = vs;
> val listofheap = fn : (real tree * int) * real list
>                         -> real list
fun heapsort vs = listofheap(heapoflist(vs), []);
> val heapsort = fn : real list -> real list
```

The time complexity of heap sort is optimal: it takes order $n \log n$ time to sort n items in the worst case. In practice, heap sort tends to be slower than other $n \log n$ algorithms. Recall our timing experiments of Chapter 3. Quick sort and merge sort can process 10,000 random numbers in 7 seconds or less, but *heapsort* takes 29 seconds. Although there are faster methods of sorting, heaps are ideal for representing priority queues.

To demonstrate how heaps work, build a small one and remove several items from it.

```
heapoflist [4.0, 2.0, 6.0, 1.0, 5.0, 8.0, 5.0];
> (Br (8.0, Br (6.0, Br (1.0, Lf, Lf), Br (2.0, Lf, Lf)),
>         Br (5.0, Br (4.0, Lf, Lf), Br (5.0, Lf, Lf))),
> 7) : real tree * int
dequeue it;
> (Br (6.0, Br (5.0, Br (1.0, Lf, Lf), Br (2.0, Lf, Lf)),
>         Br (5.0, Br (4.0, Lf, Lf), Lf)),
> 6) : real tree * int
```

ML's response has been indented to emphasize the structure of the binary trees. You might try drawing some of them. Let us apply *dequeue* twice more:

```
dequeue it;
> (Br (5.0, Br (2.0, Br (1.0, Lf, Lf), Lf),
>         Br (5.0, Br (4.0, Lf, Lf), Lf)),
> 5) : real tree * int
dequeue it;
> (Br (5.0, Br (2.0, Br (1.0, Lf, Lf), Lf),
>         Br (4.0, Lf, Lf)),
> 4) : real tree * int
```

Exercise 4.30   Draw diagrams of the heaps created by starting with the empty heap and inserting 4, 2, 6, 1, 5, 8 and 5 (as in the call to *heapoflist* above).

Exercise 4.31   Heap sort has been presented, but not a complete implementation of priority queues. Code the operations **enqueue** and **largest** in ML. What is the representation of a priority queue?

Exercise 4.32   Describe the functional array indexing scheme in terms of the binary notation for subscripts. Do the same for the conventional indexing scheme of heap sort.

Exercise 4.33   Write ML functions for lookup and update on functional arrays, represented by the conventional indexing scheme of heap sort. How do they compare with *asub* and *aupdate*?

A tautology checker

This section introduces elementary theorem proving. We define propositions and functions to convert them into various normal forms, obtaining a tautology checker for Propositional Logic. Rather than using binary trees, we define a datatype of propositions.

4.15   *Propositional Logic*

Propositional Logic deals with **propositions** constructed from atoms a, b, c, ..., by the connectives $\wedge$, $\vee$, $\neg$. A proposition may be

$\quad\quad \neg p$ a negation, 'not p'

$\quad\quad p \wedge q$ a conjunction, 'p and q'

$\quad\quad p \vee q$ a disjunction, 'p or q'

Propositions resemble boolean expressions and are represented by the datatype *prop*:

```
datatype prop = Atom of string
              | Neg  of prop
              | Conj of prop * prop
              | Disj of prop * prop;
```

The implication $p \rightarrow q$ is equivalent to $(\neg p) \vee q$. Here is a function to construct implications:

```
fun implies(p,q) = Disj(Neg p, q);
> val implies = fn : prop * prop -> prop
```

Our example is based on some important attributes — being rich, landed and saintly:

```
val rich   = Atom "rich"
and landed = Atom "landed"
and saintly = Atom "saintly";
```

Here are two assumptions about the rich, the landed and the saintly.

> Assumption 1 is *landed* → *rich*: the landed are rich.
> Assumption 2 is ¬(*saintly*∧*rich*): one cannot be both saintly and rich.*

A plausible conclusion is *landed* → ¬*saintly*: the landed are not saintly.

Let us give these assumptions and desired conclusion to ML:

```
val assumption1 = implies(landed, rich)
and assumption2 = Neg(Conj(saintly,rich));
> val assumption1 = Disj (Neg (Atom "landed"),
>                               Atom "rich")   : prop
> val assumption2 = Neg (Conj (Atom "saintly",
>                               Atom "rich"))   : prop
val concl = implies(landed, Neg saintly);
> val concl = Disj (Neg (Atom "landed"),
>                         Neg (Atom "saintly"))   : prop
```

If the conclusion follows from the assumptions, then the following proposition is a propositional theorem — a **tautology**. Let us declare it as a goal to be proved:

```
val goal = implies(Conj(assumption1,assumption2), concl);
> val goal =
> Disj (Neg(Conj (Disj (Neg(Atom "landed"),Atom "rich"),
>                       Neg(Conj (Atom "saintly",Atom "rich")))),
>        Disj (Neg(Atom "landed"),Neg(Atom "saintly")))
> : prop
```

In mathematical notation this is

$$((landed \to rich) \land \neg(saintly \land rich)) \to (landed \to \neg saintly)$$

For a more readable display, let us define a function for converting a proposition to a string.

```
fun show (Atom a)     = a
  | show (Neg p)      = "(~" ^ show p ^ ")"
  | show (Conj(p,q)) = "(" ^ show p ^ " & " ^ show q ^ ")"
  | show (Disj(p,q)) = "(" ^ show p ^ " | " ^ show q ^ ")";
> val show = fn : prop -> string
```

---

* This may be controversial, but the subject matter is in the finest tradition of mediæval logic.

Here is our goal:

```
show goal;
> "((~(((~landed) | rich) & (~(saintly & rich))))
>     | ((~landed) | (~saintly)))"   : string
```

Spaces and line breaks have been inserted in the above output to make it more legible, as elsewhere in this book.

Exercise 4.34 Write a version of *show* that suppresses needless parentheses. If ¬ has highest precedence and ∨ the lowest then all the parentheses in $((\neg a) \wedge b) \vee c$ are redundant. Since ∧ and ∨ are associative, suppress parentheses in $(a \wedge b) \wedge (c \wedge d)$.

Exercise 4.35 Write a function to evaluate a proposition using the standard truth tables. One argument should be a list of the true atoms, all others to be assumed false.

4.16 Negation Normal Form

Any proposition can be converted into **Negation Normal Form** (NNF), where ¬ is only applied to atoms, by pushing negations into conjunctions and disjunctions. Repeatedly replace

$$\neg\neg p \text{ by } p$$
$$\neg(p \wedge q) \text{ by } (\neg p) \vee (\neg q)$$
$$\neg(p \vee q) \text{ by } (\neg p) \wedge (\neg q)$$

Such replacements are sometimes called **rewrite rules**. First, consider whether they make sense. Are they unambiguous? Yes, because the left sides of the rules cover distinct cases. Will the replacements eventually stop? Yes, though the reasoning is subtle; while replacements can make the propositions grow, the negated parts shrink. How do we know when to stop? Here a single sweep through the proposition suffices.

Function *nnf* applies these rules literally. Where no rule applies, it simply makes recursive calls.

```
fun nnf (Atom a)          = Atom a
  | nnf (Neg (Atom a))    = Neg (Atom a)
  | nnf (Neg (Neg p))     = nnf p
  | nnf (Neg (Conj(p,q))) = nnf(Disj(Neg p, Neg q))
  | nnf (Neg (Disj(p,q))) = nnf(Conj(Neg p, Neg q))
  | nnf (Conj(p,q))       = Conj(nnf p, nnf q)
  | nnf (Disj(p,q))       = Disj(nnf p, nnf q);
> val nnf = fn : prop -> prop
```

Assumption 2, $\neg(\textit{saintly} \wedge \textit{rich})$, is converted to $\neg \textit{saintly} \vee \neg \textit{rich}$. Function *show* displays the result.

```
nnf assumption2;
> Disj (Neg (Atom "saintly"), Neg (Atom "rich")) : prop
show it;
> "((~saintly) | (~rich))" : string
```

The function *nnf* can be improved. Given $\neg(p \wedge q)$ it evaluates

$$nnf\,(Disj\,(Neg\,p, Neg\,q))$$

The recursive call then computes

$$Disj\,(nnf\,(Neg\,p), nnf\,(Neg\,q))$$

Making the function evaluate this expression directly saves a recursive call — similarly for $\neg(p \vee q)$.

We can make it still faster. A separate function to compute $nnf\,(Neg\,p)$ avoids the needless construction of negations. In mutual recursion, function *nnfpos p* computes the normal form of p while *nnfneg p* computes the normal form of $Neg\,p$.

```
fun nnfpos (Atom a)      = Atom a
  | nnfpos (Neg p)       = nnfneg p
  | nnfpos (Conj(p,q))   = Conj(nnfpos p, nnfpos q)
  | nnfpos (Disj(p,q))   = Disj(nnfpos p, nnfpos q)
and nnfneg (Atom a)      = Neg (Atom a)
  | nnfneg (Neg p)       = nnfpos p
  | nnfneg (Conj(p,q))   = Disj(nnfneg p, nnfneg q)
  | nnfneg (Disj(p,q))   = Conj(nnfneg p, nnfneg q);
```

4.17   Conjunctive Normal Form

The Conjunctive Normal Form of a proposition is the basis of our tautology checker and underlies the resolution method of theorem proving. Hardware designers know it as the maxterm representation of a Boolean expression.

A **literal** is an atom or its negation. A proposition is in **Conjunctive Normal Form** (CNF) if it has the form $p_1 \wedge \cdots \wedge p_m$, where each p_i is a disjunction of literals.

To check whether a proposition p is a tautology, reduce it to CNF, say $p_1 \wedge \cdots \wedge p_m$. If p is a tautology then so is p_i for $i = 1, \ldots, m$. Suppose p_i is $q_1 \vee \cdots \vee q_n$, where $q_1, \ldots, q_n$ are literals. If the literals include an atom and its negation then p_i is a tautology. Otherwise the atoms can be given truth values to falsify each literal in p_i, and therefore p is not a tautology.

To obtain CNF, start with a proposition in Negation Normal Form. Using the distributive law, push in disjunctions until they apply only to literals. Repeatedly replace

$p \vee (q \wedge r)$ by $(p \vee q) \wedge (p \vee r)$

$(q \wedge r) \vee p$ by $(q \vee p) \wedge (r \vee p)$

These replacements are less straightforward than those for Negation Normal Form. They are ambiguous — both of them apply to $(a \wedge b) \vee (c \wedge d)$ — but the resulting normal forms are logically equivalent. Termination is assured; although each replacement makes the proposition bigger, it replaces a disjunction by smaller disjunctions, and this cannot go on forever.

A disjunction may contain buried conjunctions; take for instance $a \vee (b \vee (c \wedge d))$. Our replacement strategy, given $p \vee q$, first puts p and q into CNF. This brings any conjunctions to the top. Then applying the replacements distributes the disjunctions into the conjunctions.

Calling $distrib(p, q)$ computes the disjunction $p \vee q$ in CNF, given p and q in CNF. If neither is a conjunction then the result is $p \vee q$, the only case where $distrib$ makes a disjunction. Otherwise it distributes into a conjunction.

```
fun distrib (p, Conj(q,r)) = Conj(distrib(p,q), distrib(p,r))
  | distrib (Conj(q,r), p) = Conj(distrib(q,p), distrib(r,p))
  | distrib (p, q)         = Disj(p,q)   (*no conjunctions*);
> val distrib = fn : prop * prop -> prop
```

The first two cases of $distrib$ overlap. If both p and q are conjunctions then $distrib(p, q)$ takes the first case, because ML matches patterns in order. This is a natural way to express the function.

As we can see, $distrib$ makes every possible disjunction from the parts available:

```
distrib (Conj(rich,saintly), Conj(landed, Neg rich));
> Conj (Conj (Disj (Atom "rich", Atom "landed"),
>             Disj (Atom "saintly", Atom "landed")),
>       Conj (Disj (Atom "rich", Neg (Atom "rich")),
>             Disj (Atom "saintly", Neg (Atom "rich"))))
> : prop
show it;
> "(((rich | landed) & (saintly | landed)) &
>   ((rich | (~rich)) & (saintly | (~rich))))" : string
```

The Conjunctive Normal Form of $p \wedge q$ is simply the conjunction of those of p and q. Function cnf is simple because $distrib$ does most of the work. The third case catches both *Atom* and *Neg*.

```
fun cnf (Conj(p,q)) = Conj (cnf p, cnf q)
  | cnf (Disj(p,q)) = distrib (cnf p, cnf q)
  | cnf p           = p     (*a literal*) ;
> val cnf = fn : prop -> prop
```

Finally, we convert the desired goal into CNF using *cnf* and *nnf*:

```
val cgoal = cnf (nnf goal);
> val cgoal = Conj (...,...) : prop
show cgoal;
> "((((landed | saintly) | ((~landed) | (~saintly))) &
>     (((~rich) | saintly) | ((~landed) | (~saintly)))) &
>    (((landed | rich) | ((~landed) | (~saintly))) &
>     (((~rich) | rich) | ((~landed) | (~saintly))))))"
>   : string
```

This is indeed a tautology. Each of the four disjunctions contains some *Atom* and its negation: *landed*, *saintly*, *landed* and *rich*, respectively. To detect this, function *positives* returns a list of the positive atoms in a disjunction, while *negatives* returns a list of the negative atoms. Unanticipated cases indicate that the proposition is not in CNF; an exception results.

```
exception NonCNF;
fun positives (Atom a)      = [a]
  | positives (Neg(Atom _)) = []
  | positives (Disj(p,q))   = positives p @ positives q
  | positives _             = raise NonCNF;
> val positives = fn : prop -> string list
fun negatives (Atom _)      = []
  | negatives (Neg(Atom a)) = [a]
  | negatives (Disj(p,q))   = negatives p @ negatives q
  | negatives _             = raise NonCNF;
> val negatives = fn : prop -> string list
```

Function *taut* performs the tautology check on any CNF proposition.* The final outcome is perhaps an anticlimax.

```
fun taut (Conj(p,q)) = taut p andalso taut q
  | taut p           = ([] <> inter(positives p, negatives p));
> val taut = fn : prop -> bool
taut cgoal;
> true : bool
```

* Recall that *inter* computes the intersection of two finite sets represented as lists (Chapter 3).

Exercise 4.36 A proposition in Conjunctive Normal Form can be represented as a list of lists of literals. The outer list is a conjunction; each inner list is a disjunction. Write functions to convert a proposition into CNF using this representation.

Exercise 4.37 Modify the definition of *distrib* so that no two cases overlap.

Exercise 4.38 A proposition is in **Disjunctive Normal Form** (DNF) if it has the form $p_1 \vee \cdots \vee p_m$, where each p_i is a conjunction of literals. A proposition is **inconsistent** if its negation is a tautology. Describe a method of testing whether a proposition is inconsistent that involves DNF. Code this method in ML.

Summary of main points

A **datatype** declaration creates a new type by combining several existing types.

A pattern consists of constructors and variables.

Exceptions are a general mechanism for responding to run-time errors.

Binary trees may represent many data structures, including dictionaries and functional arrays.

A recursive **datatype** declaration can define trees.

Pattern-matching can express transformations on logical formulae.

5

Functions and Infinite Data

The most powerful techniques of functional programming are those that treat functions as data. Most functional languages allow functions a full role in data structures, free of arbitrary restrictions. Like other values, functions may be arguments and results of other functions and may belong to pairs, lists and trees.

Procedural languages like Fortran and Pascal accept this idea as far as is convenient for the compiler writer. Functions may be arguments: say, the comparison to be used in sorting or a numerical function to be integrated. Even this restricted case is important.

A function is **higher-order** (or a **functional**) if it operates on other functions. For instance, the functional *map* applies a function to every element of a list, creating a new list. A sufficiently rich collection of functionals can express all functions without using variables. Functionals can be designed to construct parsers (see Chapter 9) and theorem proving strategies (see Chapter 10).

Lazy lists, whose elements are evaluated upon demand, can be implemented using functions as data. The tail of a lazy list is a function that, if called, produces another lazy list. A lazy list can be infinitely long and any finite number of its elements can be evaluated.

Chapter outline

The first half presents the essential programming techniques involving functions as data. The second half serves as an extended, practical example. Lazy lists can be represented in ML (despite its strict evaluation rule) by means of function values.

The chapter contains the following sections:

Functions as values. The **fn** notation can express a function without giving it a name. Any function of two arguments can be expressed as a 'curried' function of one argument, whose result is another function. Simple examples of higher-order functions include polymorphic sorting functions and numerical operators.

General-purpose functionals. Higher-order functional programming largely consists of using certain well-known functionals, which operate on lists or other recursive datatypes.

Sequences, or lazy lists. The basic mechanism for obtaining laziness in ML is demonstrated, using standard examples such as the Sieve of Eratosthenes. A harder problem is to combine a list of lists of integers into a single list of integers — if the input lists are infinite, they must be combined fairly such that no integers are lost.

Search strategies and lazy lists. The possibly infinite set of solutions to a search problem can be generated as a lazy list. The consumer of the solutions can be designed independently of the producer, which may employ any suitable search strategy.

Functions as values

Functions in ML are abstract values: they can be created; they can be applied to an argument; they can belong to other data structures. Nothing else is allowed. A function is given by patterns and expressions but taken as a 'black box' that transforms arguments to results.

5.1   *Anonymous functions with* **fn** *notation*

An ML function need not have a name. If x is a variable (of type α) and E is an expression (of type β) then the expression

    fn x => E

denotes a function of type $\alpha \to \beta$. Its argument is x and its body is E. This is like $\lambda x.E$ in the λ-calculus, which is described in

Chapter 9. Furthermore, the ML syntax allows pattern-matching: the expression

$$\textbf{fn } P_1 \texttt{ => } E_1 \text{ | } \cdots \text{ | } P_n \texttt{ => } E_n$$

denotes the function defined by the patterns $P_1, \ldots, P_n$. It has the same meaning as the **let** expression

$$\textbf{let fun } f(P_1) = E_1 \text{ | } \cdots \text{ | } f(P_n) = E_n \textbf{ in } f \textbf{ end}$$

provided f does not appear in the expressions $E_1, \ldots, E_n$. The **fn** syntax cannot express recursion.

For example, **fn** $n\texttt{=>}n\texttt{*2}$ is a function that doubles an integer. It can be applied to an argument; it can be given a name by a **val** declaration.

```
(fn n=>n*2)(9);
> 18 : int
val double = fn n=>n*2;
> val double = fn : int -> int
```

Many ML constructs are defined in terms of the **fn** notation. The conditional expression

$$\textbf{if } E \textbf{ then } E_1 \textbf{ else } E_2$$

abbreviates the function application

$$(\textbf{fn } true \texttt{ => } E_1 \text{ | } false \texttt{ => } E_2) \ (E)$$

The **case** expression is translated similarly.

Exercise 5.1 Express these functions using **fn** notation.

```
fun square(x) : real = x*x;
fun cons (x, y) = x::y;
fun null    []    = true
  | null (_::_) = false;
```

Exercise 5.2 Modify these function declarations to use **val** instead of **fun**:

```
fun area (r) = pi*r*r;
fun title(name) = "The Duke of " ^ name;
fun lengthvec (x,y) = sqrt(x*x + y*y);
```

5.2   *Curried functions*

A function can have only one argument. Hitherto, functions with multiple arguments have taken them as a tuple. Multiple arguments can also be realized by a function that returns another function as its result. This device is called **currying** after the logician H. B. Curry.* Consider the function

```
fun prefix pre =
    let fun cat post = pre^post
    in   cat   end;
> val prefix = fn : string -> (string -> string)
```

Using **fn** notation, *prefix* is the function

```
fn pre => (fn post => pre ^ post)
```

Given a string *pre*, the result of *prefix* is a function that concatenates *pre* to the front of its argument. For instance, *prefix*`"Sir "` is the function

```
fn post => "Sir " ^ post
```

It may be applied to a string:

```
prefix "Sir ";
> fn : string -> string
it "James Tyrrell";
> "Sir James Tyrrell" : string
```

Dispensing with *it*, both function applications may be done at once:

```
(prefix "Sir ")  "James Tyrrell";
> "Sir James Tyrrell" : string
```

This is a function call where the function is computed by an expression, namely *prefix*`"Sir "`.

Note that *prefix* behaves like a function of two arguments. It is a **curried function**. We now have two ways of representing a function with arguments of types α and β and result of type γ. A function over pairs has type $(\alpha \times \beta) \to \gamma$. A curried function has type $\alpha \to (\beta \to \gamma)$.

A curried function permits **partial application**. Applied to its first argument (of type α) its result is a function of type $\beta \to \gamma$.

---

* It has been credited to Schönfinkel, but **Schönfinkeling** has never caught on.

This function may have a general use: say, for addressing Knights.

```
val knightify = prefix "Sir ";
> val knightify = fn : string -> string
knightify "William Catesby";
> "Sir William Catesby" : string
knightify "Richard Ratcliff";
> "Sir Richard Ratcliff" : string
```

Other illustrious personages can be addressed similarly:

```
val dukify = prefix "The Duke of ";
> val dukify = fn : string -> string
dukify "Clarence";
> "The Duke of Clarence" : string
val lordify = prefix "Lord ";
> val lordify = fn : string -> string
lordify "Stanley";
> "Lord Stanley" : string
```

Syntax for curried functions. The above functions are declared by **val**, not **fun**. A **fun** declaration must have explicit arguments. There may be several arguments, separated by spaces, for a curried function. Here is an equivalent declaration of *prefix*:

```
fun prefix pre post = pre^post;
> val prefix = fn : string -> (string -> string)
```

A function call has the form $E\,E_1$, where E is an expression that denotes a function. Since

$$E\,E_1\,E_2\,\cdots\,E_n \text{ abbreviates } (\cdots((E\,E_1)\,E_2)\cdots)E_n$$

we may write   *prefix* `"Sir "` `"James Tyrrell"`   without parentheses. The expressions are evaluated from left to right.

The type of *prefix*, namely *string* $\rightarrow$ (*string* $\rightarrow$ *string*), may be written *string* $\rightarrow$ *string* $\rightarrow$ *string* because the function type symbol ($\rightarrow$) associates to the right.

An analogy with arrays. The choice between pairing and currying is analogous to the choice, in Pascal, between a 2-dimensional array and nested arrays.

```
A: array [1..20, 1..30] of integer
B: array [1..20] of array [1..30] of integer
```

The former array is subscripted $A[i,j]$, the latter as $B[i][j]$. Nested arrays permit partial subscripting: $B[i]$ is a 1-dimensional array.

Recursion. Curried functions may be recursive. Calling *replist n x* makes the list consisting of *n* copies of *x*:

```
fun replist n x = if n=0 then [] else x :: replist (n-1) x;
> val replist = fn : int -> 'a -> 'a list
replist 3 true;
> [true, true, true] : bool list
```

Recursion works by the usual evaluation rules, even with currying. The result of *replist* 3 is the function

$$\texttt{fn } x \Rightarrow \texttt{if } 3 = 0 \texttt{ then } [] \texttt{ else } x :: replist(3-1)x$$

Applying this to *true* produces the expression

$$true :: replist\ 2\ true$$

As evaluation continues, two further recursive calls yield

$$true :: true :: true :: replist\ 0\ true$$

The final call returns *nil* and the overall result is [*true, true, true*].

Now *replist n* is a function that makes *n*-element lists.

```
val list5 = replist 5;
> val list5 = fn : 'a -> 'a list
list5 "never";
> ["never","never","never","never","never"] : string list
```

Exercise 5.3   What functions result from partial application of the following curried functions?

```
fun plus i j : int = i+j;
fun cmin a b : real = if a<b then a else b;
fun pair x y = (x,y);
fun equals x y = (x = y);
```

Exercise 5.4   Is there any practical difference between the following two definitions of the function f? Assume that the function g and the curried function h are given.

```
fun f x y = h(g x) y;
fun f x = h(g x);
```

5.3   *Functions in data structures*

Functions and concrete datatypes play complementary roles in a data structure. Lists and trees provide the outer framework and organize the information, while functions hold potential computations. Although functions are represented by finite programs in the computer, we can often treat them as infinite objects.

Pairs and lists may contain functions as their components:*

```
(prefix, sin);
> (fn,fn) : (string -> string -> string) * (real -> real)
[op+, op-, op*, op div, op mod];
> [fn, fn, fn, fn, fn] : (int * int -> int) list
```

Functions stored in a data structure can be extracted and applied.

```
val titlefns = [dukify, lordify, knightify];
> val titlefns = [fn, fn, fn] : (string -> string) list
hd titlefns "Gloucester";
> "The Duke of Gloucester" : string
```

This looks like a curried function call: *hd titlefns* returns the function *dukify*. The polymorphic function *hd* has, in this example, the type

$$(string \rightarrow string)list \rightarrow (string \rightarrow string).$$

A binary search tree containing functions might be useful in a desk calculator program. Here the functions are addressed by name; a graphical calculator would store them in the data structure representing the buttons on the screen.

```
val funtree = binsert(binsert(binsert(Lf, "sin", sin),
                "cos", cos),    "arctan", arctan);
> val funtree =
> Br (("sin",fn),
>       Br (("cos",fn), Br(("arctan",fn),Lf,Lf), Lf),
>       Lf)    : (string * (real -> real)) tree
blookup(funtree,"cos") 0.0;
> 1.0 : real
```

The functions stored in the tree must have the same type, here *real* $\rightarrow$ *real*. Although different types can be combined into one datatype, this can be inconvenient. Typeless programming languages are more flexible than ML for storing functions as data.

Exercise 5.5 What type does the polymorphic function *blookup* have in the example above?

---

* Recall that the keyword **op** yields the value of an infix operator, as a function. Although some of these operators are overloaded, their types are constrained here by the integer operators *div* and *mod*.

5.4   *Functions as arguments and results*

The sorting functions of Chapter 3 are coded to sort real numbers. They can be generalized to an arbitrary ordered type by passing the ordering predicate ($\leq$) as an argument. Here is a polymorphic function for insertion sort:

```
fun insort lessequal =
    let fun ins (x, [])    = [x]
        |   ins (x, y::ys) =
                if lessequal(x,y) then x::y::ys
                                  else y :: ins (x,ys)
        fun sort []        = []
        |   sort (x::xs) = ins (x, sort xs)
    in   sort   end;
> val insort = fn : ('a * 'a -> bool) -> 'a list -> 'a list
```

Functions *ins* and *sort* are declared locally, referring to *lessequal*. Though it may not be obvious, *insort* is a curried function. Given an argument of type $\alpha \times \alpha \rightarrow bool$ it returns the function *sort*, which has type $\alpha\ list \rightarrow \alpha\ list$. The types of the ordering and the list elements must agree.

Integers can now be sorted. (Although the operator <= is overloaded, its type is constrained by the list of integers.)

```
insort (op<=) [5,3,7,5,9,8];
> [3,5,5,7,8,9] : int list
```

Passing the relation $\geq$ for *lessequal* gives a decreasing sort:

```
insort (op>=) [5,3,7,5,9,8];
> [9,8,7,5,5,3] : int list
```

Pairs of strings can be sorted using lexicographic ordering:

```
fun leq_stringpair ((a,b), (c,d): string*string) =
    a<c   orelse   (a=c andalso b<=d);
> val leq_stringpair =
>    fn : (string * string) * (string * string) -> bool
```

We sort a list of (family name, forename) pairs:

```
insort leq_stringpair
   [ ("Herbert","Walter"),        ("Plantagenet","Richard"),
     ("Plantagenet","Edward"),    ("Brandon","William"),
     ("Tyrrell","James"),         ("Herbert","John") ];
> [("Brandon", "William"), ("Herbert", "John"),
>  ("Herbert", "Walter"), ("Plantagenet", "Edward"),
>  ("Plantagenet", "Richard"), ("Tyrrell", "James")]
>  : (string * string) list
```

Functions are frequently passed as arguments in numerical computing. The following functional computes the summation $\sum_{i=0}^{m-1} f(i)$.
For efficiency, it uses an iterative function that refers to the arguments f and m:

```
fun summation f m =
    let fun sum (i,z) : real =
            if  i=m  then  z  else  sum (i+1, z + (f i))
    in  sum(0, 0.0)  end;
> val summation = fn : (int -> real) -> int -> real
```

The **fn** notation works well with functionals. Here it eliminates
the need to define a squaring function prior to computing the
sum $\sum_{k=0}^{9} k^2$:

```
summation (fn k => real(k*k)) 10;
> 285.0 : real
```

The double sum $\sum_{i=0}^{m-1} \sum_{j=0}^{n-1} g(i,j)$ is computed by

```
summation (fn i => summation (fn j => g(i,j)) n)
          m;
```

This looks like a translation of the $\sum$-notation into ML; the index variables i and j are bound by **fn**. The inner summation,
$\sum_{j=0}^{n-1} g(i,j)$, is a function of i. The function over j is the partial
application of g to i.

The partial application can be simplified by summing over a cur-
ried function h instead of g. The double sum $\sum_{i=0}^{m-1} \sum_{j=0}^{n-1} h\,i\,j$ is
computed by

```
summation (fn i => summation (h i) n)
          m;
```

Observe that *summation f* has the same type as f, namely *int* $\rightarrow$
real, and that $\sum_{i=0}^{m-1} \sum_{j=0}^{i-1} f(j)$ may be computed by

```
summation (summation f) m;
```

Exercise 5.6 Write a polymorphic function for top-down merge
sort, passing the ordering predicate ($\leq$) as an argument.

Exercise 5.7 Write a functional to compute the minimum value
$\min_{i=0}^{m-1} f(i)$ of a function f, where m is any given positive integer. Use the functional to express the two-dimensional minimum
$\min_{i=0}^{m-1} \min_{j=0}^{n-1} g(i,j)$, for positive integers m and n.

General-purpose functionals

Functional programmers often use higher-order functions to express programs clearly and concisely. Functionals to process lists have been popular since the early days of Lisp, appearing in infinite variety and under many names. They express operations that otherwise would require separate recursive function declarations. Similar recursive functionals can be defined for trees.

A comprehensive set of functionals provides an abstract language for expressing other functions. After reading this section, you may find it instructive to review previous chapters and simplify the function definitions using functionals.

5.5   *Sections*

Imagine applying an infix operator to only one operand, either left or right, leaving the other operand unspecified. This defines a function of one argument, called a **section**. Here are some examples in the notation of Bird & Wadler (1988):

("Sir "^) is the function *knightify*
(/2.0) is the function 'divide by 2'

Sections can be added to ML (rather crudely) by the functionals *secl* and *secr*:

```
fun secl x f y = f(x,y);
> val secl = fn : 'a -> ('a * 'b -> 'c) -> 'b -> 'c
fun secr f y x = f(x,y);
> val secr = fn : ('a * 'b -> 'c) -> 'b -> 'a -> 'c
```

These functionals are typically used with **op**, but may be applied to any function of suitable type. Here are some left sections:

```
val knightify = (secl "Sir " op^);
> val knightify = fn : string -> string
knightify"Geoffrey";
> "Sir Geoffrey" : string
val recip = (secl 1.0 op/);
> val recip = fn : real -> real
recip 5.0;
> 0.2 : real
```

Here is a right section for division by 2:

```
val halve = (secr op/ 2.0);
> val halve = fn : real -> real
halve 7.0;
> 3.5 : real
```

Exercise 5.8   Is there any similarity between sections and curried functions?

Exercise 5.9   What functions do the following sections yield? (Recall *take* and *inter* from Chapter 3; *take* removes elements from the head of a list while *inter* forms the intersection of two lists.)

```
secr op@ ["Richard"]
secr take ["heed", "of", "yonder", "dog!"]
secl 3 take
secl ["his", "venom", "tooth"] inter
```

5.6   *Combinators*

The theory of the λ-calculus is in part concerned with expressions known as **combinators**. Many combinators can be coded in ML as higher-order functions, and have practical applications.

Composition. The infix *o* (yes, the letter 'o') denotes function composition in Standard ML. It is defined as follows:

```
infix o;
fun (f o g) x = f (g x);
> val o = fn : ('b -> 'c) * ('a -> 'b) -> 'a -> 'c
```

Composition is familiar to mathematicians; $f \circ g$ is the function that applies g, then f, to its argument. Composition can express many functions, especially using sections. For instance, the functions

```
fn x => exp(~x)
fn a => "beginning" ^ a ^ "end"
fn x => 2.0 / (x-1.0)
```

can be expressed without mentioning their argument:

```
exp o ~
(secl"beginning" op^)  o  (secr op^ "end")
(secl 2.0 op/)  o  (secr op- 1.0)
```

To compute the sum $\sum_{k=0}^{9} \sqrt{k}$, the functions *sqrt* and *real* (which converts integers to reals) are composed. Composition is more readable than **fn** notation would be:

```
summation (sqrt o real) 10;
```

The combinators S, K and I. The identity combinator, I, simply returns its argument:

```
fun I x = x;
> val I = fn : 'a -> 'a
```

Composition of a function with *I* has no effect:

```
knightify o I o (prefix "William ") o I;
> fn : string -> string
it "Catesby";
> "Sir William Catesby" : string
```

The combinator *K* makes constant functions. Given *x* it makes the function that always returns *x*:

```
fun K x y = x;
> val K = fn : 'a -> 'b -> 'a
```

For a contrived demonstration of constant functions, let us compute the product $m \times z$ by the repeated addition $\sum_{i=0}^{m-1} z$:

```
summation (K 7.0) 5;
> 35.0 : real
```

The combinator *S* is a general form of composition:

```
fun S x y z = x z (y z);
> val S = fn : ('a -> 'b -> 'c) -> ('a -> 'b) -> 'a -> 'c
```

Every function in the λ-calculus can be expressed using just *S* and *K* — with no variables! David Turner (1979) has exploited this celebrated fact to obtain lazy evaluation: since no variables are involved, no mechanism is required for storing their values. Virtually all lazy functional compilers employ some refinement of this technique.

Here is a remarkable example of the expressiveness of *S* and *K*. The identity function *I* can be defined as *S K K*!

```
S K K 17;
> 17 : int
```

Exercise 5.10   Write the computation steps of *S K K* 17.

Exercise 5.11   Suppose we are given an expression *E* consisting of infix operators, constants and variables, with one occurrence of the variable *x*. Describe a method for expressing the function fn *x*=>*E* using *I*, sections and composition instead of fn.

5.7 *The list functionals* map *and* filter

The functional *map* applies a function to every element of a list, returning a list of the function's results:

$$map\, f\, [x_1, \ldots, x_n] = [f\, x_1, \ldots, f\, x_n]$$

One of ML's built-in functions, *map* can be defined as follows:

```
fun map f []      = []
  | map f (x::xs) = (f x) :: map f xs;
> val map = fn : ('a -> 'b) -> 'a list -> 'b list
map recip [0.1, 1.0, 5.0, 10.0];
> [10.0, 1.0, 0.2, 0.1] : real list
map size ["York","Clarence","Gloucester"];
> [4, 8, 10] : int list
```

The functional *filter* applies a predicate — a boolean-valued function — to a list. It returns a list of all elements satisfying the predicate, in their original order.

```
fun filter pred []      = []
  | filter pred (x::xs) =
        if pred(x) then x :: filter pred xs
                   else      filter pred xs;
> val filter = fn : ('a -> bool) -> 'a list -> 'a list
filter (fn a => size a = 4)
        ["Hie","thee","to","Hell","thou","cacodemon"];
> ["thee", "Hell", "thou"] : string list
```

Pattern-matching in curried functions works exactly as if the arguments were given as a tuple. Both functionals are curried: *map* takes a function of type $\alpha \to \beta$ to one of type $\alpha\, list \to \beta\, list$, while *filter* takes a function of type $\alpha \to bool$ to one of type $\alpha\, list \to \alpha\, list$.

Thanks to currying, these functionals work together for lists of lists. Observe that $map(map\, f)[l_1, l_2, \ldots, l_n]$ applies $map\, f$ to each list $l_1, l_2, \ldots$ It returns a list of lists of results.

```
map (map double) [[1], [2,3], [4,5,6]];
> [[2], [4, 6], [8, 10, 12]] : int list list
map (map (implode o rev o explode))
        [["When","he","shall","split"],
         ["thy","very","heart","with","sorrow"]];
> [["nehW", "eh", "llahs", "tilps"],
>  ["yht", "yrev", "traeh", "htiw", "worros"]]
> : string list list
```

Similarly, $map(filter\, pred)[l_1, l_2, \ldots, l_n]$ applies $filter\, pred$ to each of the lists $l_1, l_2, \ldots$ It returns a list of lists of elements satisfying the predicate *pred*.

```
map (filter (secr op< "m"))
    [["my","hair","doth","stand","on","end"],
     ["to","hear","her","curses"]];
> [["hair", "doth", "end"], ["hear", "her", "curses"]]
> : string list list
```

Many of the list functions of Chapter 3 can be coded trivially using *map* and *filter*. Our matrix transpose function becomes

```
fun transp ([]::_) = []
  | transp rows     = map hd rows :: transp (map tl rows);
> val transp = fn : 'a list list -> 'a list list
transp [["have","done","thy","charm"],
        ["thou","hateful","withered","hag!"]];
> [["have","thou"], ["done","hateful"],
>  ["thy","withered"], ["charm","hag!"]] : string list list
```

The intersection function becomes

```
fun inter(xs,ys) = filter (secr (op mem) ys) xs;
> val inter = fn : ''a list * ''a list -> ''a list
```

Exercise 5.12   Show how to replace an expression of the form

$$map\ f\ (map\ g\ xs),$$

where *f* and *g* are arbitrary functions, by an equivalent expression that calls *map* only once.

Exercise 5.13   Define the infix operator *andf* such that

$$filter\ (pred1\ andf\ pred2)\ xs$$

returns the same value as

$$filter\ pred1\ (filter\ pred2\ xs).$$

5.8   *The list functionals* takewhile *and* dropwhile
These functionals chop an initial segment from a list according to a predicate:

$$\underbrace{[x_0, \ldots, x_{i-1},}_{takewhile} \underbrace{x_i, \ldots, x_{n-1}]}_{dropwhile}$$

The initial segment, which consists of elements satisfying the predicate, is computed by *takewhile*:

```
fun takewhile pred []      = []
  | takewhile pred (x::xs) =
        if   pred x   then   x :: takewhile pred xs
                      else [];
> val takewhile = fn : ('a -> bool) -> 'a list -> 'a list
```

The remaining elements (if any) begin with the first one to falsify the predicate. This list is computed by *dropwhile*:

```
fun dropwhile pred []      = []
  | dropwhile pred (x::xs) =
        if   pred x   then   dropwhile pred xs
                      else   x::xs;
> val dropwhile = fn : ('a -> bool) -> 'a list -> 'a list
```

These two functionals can process text in the form of lists of characters. Here is a predicate to recognize lower case letters:

```
fun is_letter c = ("a" <= c) andalso (c <= "z");
> val is_letter = fn : string -> bool
```

Given this predicate, *takewhile* returns the first word from a sentence and *dropwhile* returns the remaining characters.

```
takewhile is_letter (explode"that deadly eye of thine");
> ["t", "h", "a", "t"] : string list
dropwhile is_letter (explode"that deadly eye of thine");
> [" ", "d", "e", "a", "d", "l", "y", ...] : string list
```

Since they are curried, *takewhile* and *dropwhile* combine with other functionals. For instance, *map*(*takewhile pred*) returns a list of initial segments.

5.9   *The list functionals* exists *and* forall

These functionals report whether some (or every) element of a list satisfies some predicate. They can be viewed as quantifiers over a list's elements:

```
fun exists pred []      = false
  | exists pred (x::xs) = (pred x)  orelse   exists pred xs;
> val exists = fn : ('a -> bool) -> 'a list -> bool
fun forall pred []      = true
  | forall pred (x::xs) = (pred x)  andalso  forall pred xs;
> val forall = fn : ('a -> bool) -> 'a list -> bool
```

By currying, these functionals convert a predicate over type α to a predicate over type α *list*. The membership test *x mem xs* can be expressed

```
fun x mem xs = exists (secl x op=) xs;
> val mem = fn : ''a * ''a list -> bool
```

The function *disjoint* tests whether two lists have no elements in common:

```
fun disjoint(xs,ys) =
        forall (fn x => forall (fn y => x<>y) ys) xs;
> val disjoint = fn : ''a list * ''a list -> bool
```

Because of their argument order, *exists* and *forall* are hard to read as quantifiers when nested; it is hard to see that *disjoint* tests 'for all x in xs and all y in ys, $x \neq y$'. However, *exists* and *forall* combine well with the other functionals. Useful combinations for lists of lists include

$$exists\,(exists\;pred)$$
$$filter\,(exists\;pred)$$
$$takewhile\,(forall\;pred)$$

5.10   *The list functionals* foldleft *and* foldright

These functionals apply a 2-argument function over the elements of a list. Their effect is best understood when the function is an infix operator:

$$foldleft\;\mathbf{op}\oplus (e, [x_1, x_2, \ldots, x_n]) = (\cdots((e \oplus x_1) \oplus x_2) \cdots \oplus x_n)$$

$$foldright\;\mathbf{op}\oplus ([x_1, x_2, \ldots, x_n], e) = (x_1 \oplus (x_2 \oplus \cdots (x_n \oplus e) \cdots))$$

These functionals are defined by

```
fun foldleft f (e, [])   = e
  | foldleft f (e, x::xs) = foldleft f (f(e,x), xs);
> val foldleft = fn : ('a * 'b -> 'a) -> 'a * 'b list -> 'a
fun foldright f ([],    e) = e
  | foldright f (x::xs, e) = f(x, foldright f (xs,e));
> val foldright = fn : ('a * 'b -> 'b) -> 'a list * 'b -> 'b
```

Numerous functions can be expressed using *foldleft* and *foldright*. The sum of a list of numbers is computed by repeated addition starting from 0:

```
fun sum xs = foldleft op+ (0,xs);
> val sum = fn : int list -> int
sum [1,2,3,4];
> 10 : int
```

The product is computed by repeated multiplication from 1:

```
foldleft op* (1, [1,2,3,4]);
> 24 : int
```

These definitions work because 0 and 1 are the **identity elements** of + and ×, respectively; in other words, $0 + k = k$ and $1 \times k = k$ for all k. Many applications of *foldleft* and *foldright* are of this sort.

A function of type $\alpha \times \beta \to \alpha$ associates to the left, and therefore suits *foldleft*. A function of type $\alpha \times \beta \to \beta$ associates to the right, and suits *foldright*. Since *foldleft* op+ has type $int \times int\ list \to int$, this function can be applied using *foldleft*. It adds a list of lists:

```
foldleft (foldleft op+) (0, [[1], [2,3], [4,5,6]]);
> 21 : int
```

This is more direct than $sum(map\ sum\ [[1], [2, 3], [4, 5, 6]])$, which forms the intermediate list of sums $[1, 5, 15]$.

List construction (the operator ::) nests to the right. Reversing its arguments makes it nest to the left. Through *foldleft*, it reverses lists efficiently:

```
fun revcons (l,x) = x::l;
> val revcons = fn : 'a list * 'a -> 'a list
foldleft revcons ([], explode"Richard");
> ["d", "r", "a", "h", "c", "i", "R"] : string list
```

An iterative length function is equally simple:

```
fun inc (n,x) = n+1;
> val inc = fn : int * 'a -> int
foldleft inc (0, explode"Margaret");
> 8 : int
```

The result of *foldright* op ⊕ (xs, e) can be visualized as replacing each :: by ⊕ and the final *nil* by e. To append the lists xs and ys, apply :: through *foldright* to each element of xs, starting with ys:

```
foldright op:: (["And","leave"],["out","thee?"]);
> ["And", "leave", "out", "thee?"] : string list
```

Applying append through *foldright* joins a list of lists, like the function *flat*; note that [] is the identity element of append:

```
foldright op@ ([[1], [2,3], [4,5,6]],    []);
> [1, 2, 3, 4, 5, 6] : int list
```

Applying the function *newmem* through *foldright* builds a 'set' of distinct elements:

```
foldright newmem (explode"Margaret",   []);
> ["M", "g", "a", "r", "e", "t"] : string list
```

To compute *map f xs*, apply a function based on :: and f:

```
fun map f xs = foldright (fn(x,l)=> f x::l) (xs,[]);
> val map = fn : ('a -> 'b) -> 'a list -> 'b list
```

Two calls to *foldright* compute the Cartesian product of two lists:

```
fun cartprod (xs, ys) =
        foldright (fn (x, pairs) =>
                foldright (fn (y,l) => (x,y)::l) (ys, pairs))
            (xs, []);
> val cartprod = fn : 'a list * 'b list -> ('a * 'b) list
```

Cartesian products can be computed more clearly by *map* and *flat*, at the expense of creating an intermediate list. First, declare a curried pairing function:

```
fun pair x y = (x,y);
> val pair = fn : 'a -> 'b -> 'a * 'b
```

A list of lists of pairs is created ...

```
map (fn a => map (pair a) ["Hastings","Stanley"])
    ["Lord","Lady"];
> [[("Lord", "Hastings"), ("Lord", "Stanley")],
>  [("Lady", "Hastings"), ("Lady", "Stanley")]]
> : (string * string) list list
```

... then flattened to form the Cartesian product:

```
flat it;
> [("Lord", "Hastings"), ("Lord", "Stanley"),
>  ("Lady", "Hastings"), ("Lady", "Stanley")]
> : (string * string) list
```

Both algorithms for Cartesian products can be generalized, replacing (x, y) by other functions of x and y, to express sets of the form

$$\{f(x, y) \mid x \in xs, \, y \in ys\}.$$

Exercise 5.14   Express the function *union* (Chapter 3) using functionals.

Exercise 5.15   Simplify the definition of matrix multiplication (Chapter 3) using functionals.

Exercise 5.16   Is *foldleft* op+ more efficient than *foldright* op+? What about *foldleft* op@ versus *foldright* op@? Discuss general approaches to such questions.

Exercise 5.17   Express *exists* using *foldleft* or *foldright*.

Exercise 5.18   Using functionals, express the conditional set expression

$$\{x - y \mid x \in xs, \, y \in ys, \, y < x\}$$

5.11 *More examples of recursive functionals*

Binary trees and other recursive types can be processed by recursive functionals. Even the natural numbers 0, 1, 2, ... can be viewed as a recursive type: their constructors are 0 and the successor function.

Powers of a function. If f is a function and $n \geq 0$ then f^n is the function such that

$$f^n(x) = \underbrace{f(\cdots f(f(x))\cdots)}_{n \text{ times}}$$

This is the function *repeat f n*:

```
fun repeat f  n  x =
    if n>0  then  repeat f (n−1) (f x)
               else  x;
> val repeat = fn : ('a -> 'a) -> int -> 'a -> 'a
```

Surprisingly many functions have this form. Repetition of the function *tl* is essentially *drop* (defined in Chapter 3):

```
repeat tl 5 (explode"I'll drown you in the malmsey-butt...");
> ["d", "r", "o", "w", "n", " ", "y", ...] : string list
```

The function *replist* (defined above in this chapter) is the repetition of a section:

```
repeat (secl"Ha!" op::) 5 [];
> ["Ha!", "Ha!", "Ha!", "Ha!", "Ha!"] : string list
```

Full binary trees with a constant label are created by

```
repeat (fn t=>Br("No",t,t)) 3 Lf;
> Br("No", Br("No", Br("No", Lf, Lf), Br("No", Lf, Lf)),
>          Br("No", Br("No", Lf, Lf), Br("No", Lf, Lf)))
> : string tree
```

A suitable function on pairs, when repeated, computes factorials:

```
fun factaux (k,p) = (k+1, k*p);
> val factaux = fn : int * int -> int * int
repeat factaux 5 (1,1);
> (6, 120) : int * int
```

Tree recursion. The functional *treerec*, for binary trees, is analogous to *foldright*. Recall that *foldright* op $\oplus$ (xs, e), figuratively speaking, replaces :: by $\oplus$ and *nil* by e in a list. Given a tree, *treerec* replaces each leaf by some value *leafval* and each branch by the application of a 3-argument function *branchfun*.

```
fun treerec (leafval, branchfun) =
    let fun h Lf               = leafval
        | h (Br(u,left,right)) = branchfun(u, h left, h right)
    in  h  end;
> val treerec =
>   fn : 'a * ('b * 'a * 'a -> 'a) -> 'b tree -> 'a
```

This functional can express many of the tree functions of the last chapter. The function *count* replaces each leaf by 0 and each branch by a function to add 1 to the counts of the subtrees:

```
val count = treerec(0, fn(_,c1,c2) => 1+c1+c2);
> val count = fn : 'a tree -> int
```

The function *depth* computes a maximum at each branch:

```
val depth = treerec(0, fn(_,d1,d2) => 1 + maxl[d1,d2]);
> val depth = fn : 'a tree -> int
```

Tree recursion over a reversed version of *Br* defines *reflect*:

```
fun revbranch (u,left,right) = Br(u,right,left);
> val revbranch = fn : 'a * 'a tree * 'a tree -> 'a tree
val reflect = treerec(Lf, revbranch);
> val reflect = fn : 'a tree -> 'a tree
```

To compute a preorder list, each branch joins its label to the lists for the subtrees:

```
fun joinpreorder (u,l1,l2) = [u] @ l1 @ l2;
> val joinpreorder = fn : 'a * 'a list * 'a list -> 'a list
val preorder = treerec([], joinpreorder);
> val preorder = fn : 'a tree -> 'a list
```

Operations on terms. The set of terms x, $f(x)$, $g(x,f(x))$, $\ldots$, which is generated by variables and function applications, corresponds to the ML datatype

```
datatype term = Var of string
            | Fun of string * term list;
```

The term $(x + u) - (y \times x)$ could be declared by

```
val tm = Fun("-", [Fun("+", [Var"x", Var"u"]),
                   Fun("*", [Var"y", Var"x"])]);
```

Though it is natural to represent a function's arguments as an ML list, the types *term* and *term list* must be regarded as mutually recursive. A typical function on terms will make use of a companion function on term lists. Fortunately, the companion function need not be declared separately; in most instances it can be expressed using list functionals.

If the ML function $f : string \rightarrow term$ defines a substitution from variables to terms, then *subst f* extends this over terms. Observe how *map f* applies the substitution to term lists.

```
fun subst f (Var a)        = f a
  | subst f (Fun(a,args))  = Fun(a, map (subst f) args);
> val subst = fn : (string -> term) -> term -> term
```

The list of variables in a term can be computed, again using *map*:

```
fun vars (Var a)        = [a]
  | vars (Fun(_,args))  = flat (map vars args);
> val vars = fn : term -> string list
vars tm;
> ["x", "u", "y", "x"] : string list
```

This is wasteful, however, as lists are repeatedly copied by *flat*. Instead, define a function *accumvars* with an argument to accumulate a list of variables. It can be extended to term lists using *foldright*:

```
fun accumvars(Var a, bs)        = a::bs
  | accumvars(Fun(_,args),bs) = foldright accumvars (args,bs);
> val accumvars = fn : term * string list -> string list
accumvars(tm,[]);
> ["x", "u", "y", "x"] : string list
```

Here is a demonstration. A trivial substitution, *replace t a* replaces the variable a by t while leaving other variables unchanged:

```
fun replace t a b = if a=b then t else Var b;
> val replace = fn : term -> string -> string -> term
```

Thus, *subst (replace t a) u* replaces a by t throughout the term u. Substituting $-z$ for x in *tm* yields the term $(-z + u) - (y \times -z)$:

```
subst(replace (Fun("-",[Var"z"])) "x") tm;
> Fun ("-",
>         [Fun ("+", [Fun ("-", [Var "z"]), Var "u"]),
>          Fun ("*", [Var "y", Fun ("-", [Var "z"])])]) : term
```

Now the list of variables contains z in place of x:

```
accumvars(it,[]);
> ["z", "u", "y", "z"] : string list
```

Exercise 5.19 Write a function *nf* such that *repeat nf* computes Fibonacci numbers.

Exercise 5.20   What is this function good for?

```
fun funny f 0 = I
  | funny f n = if n mod 2 = 0
                then funny (f o f) (n div 2)
                else funny (f o f) (n div 2) o f;
```

Exercise 5.21   What is the function *tf* good for?

```
fun F (v,f1,f2) vs = v :: f1 (f2 vs);
val tf = treerec(I, F);
```

Exercise 5.22   Consider counting the *Fun* nodes in a term. Express this as a function modelled on *vars*, then as a function modelled on *accumvars* and finally without using functionals.

Exercise 5.23   Note that the result of *vars tm* mentions x twice. Write a function to compute the list of variables in a term without repetitions. Can you find a simple solution using functionals?

Sequences, or lazy lists

Lazy lists are one of the most celebrated features of functional programming. The elements of a lazy list are not evaluated until their values are required by the rest of the program; thus a lazy list may be infinite. In lazy languages like Miranda, all data structures are lazy and infinite lists are commonplace in programs. In ML, which is not lazy, infinite lists are rare. This section describes how to express lazy lists in ML, representing the tail of a list by a function in order to delay its evaluation.

It is important to recognize the hazards of programming with lazy lists. Hitherto we have expected every function, from the greatest common divisor to priority queues, to deliver its result in finite time. Recursion was used to reduce a problem to simpler subproblems. Every recursive function included a base case where it would terminate.

Now we shall be dealing with potentially infinite results. We may view any finite part of an infinite list, but never the whole. We may add two infinite lists element by element to form a list of sums, but may not reverse an infinite list or find its smallest element. We shall define recursions that go on forever, with no base case. Instead of asking whether the program terminates, we can only ask whether the program generates each finite part of its result in finite time.

ML functions involving lazy lists are more complicated than their counterparts in a lazy language. By laying the mechanism bare, however, they may help us avoid some pitfalls. Mechanistic thinking should not be our only tool; computations over infinite values may exceed our powers of imagination. Domain theory (Paulson, 1987; Schmidt, 1986) gives a clearer picture of such computations.

5.12   *A type of sequences*

Lazy lists are traditionally called **streams**, but let us call them **sequences**.* Like a list, a sequence either is empty or contains a head and tail. The empty sequence is *Nil* and a non-empty sequence has the form $Cons(x, xf)$, where x is the head and xf is a function to compute the tail:

```
datatype 'a seq = Nil
                | Cons of 'a * (unit -> 'a seq);
```

Functions to return the head and tail of a sequence are easily defined. The tail function is applied to (), the sole value of type *unit*, to force evaluation of the tail; the argument conveys no information.

```
fun head(Cons(x,_)) = x;
> val head = fn : 'a seq -> 'a
fun tail(Cons(_,xf)) = xf();
> val tail = fn : 'a seq -> 'a seq
```

A head x and tail sequence xq are combined to form a longer sequence by $consq(x, xq)$:

```
fun consq(x,xq) = Cons(x, fn()=>xq);
> val consq = fn : 'a * 'a seq -> 'a seq
```

Note that $consq(x, E)$ is not evaluated lazily. ML evaluates the expression E, yielding say xq, and returns `Cons(x, fn()=>xq)`. So the **fn** inside *consq* does not delay the evaluation of the tail. To obtain lazy evaluation, we must write `Cons(x, fn()=>E)` instead of $consq(x, E)$. The explicit **fn** delays the evaluation of E, accomplishing a form of call-by-name.

For example, let us define the increasing sequence of integers

---

* A 'stream' in ML is an imperative input/output channel.

starting from k:

```
fun from k = Cons(k, fn()=> from(k+1));
> val from = fn : int -> int seq
from 1;
> Cons (1, fn) : int seq
```

The sequence starts with 1; here are some more elements:

```
tail it;
> Cons (2, fn) : int seq
tail it;
> Cons (3, fn) : int seq
```

Calling $takeq(n, xq)$ returns the first n elements of the sequence xq as a list:

```
fun takeq (0, xq)          = []
  | takeq (n, Nil)         = []
  | takeq (n, Cons(x,xf))  = x :: takeq (n-1, xf());
> val takeq = fn : int * 'a seq -> 'a list
takeq (7, from 30);
> [30, 31, 32, 33, 34, 35, 36] : int list
```

The computation of $takeq(2, from\ 30)$ proceeds as follows:

$$takeq(2, from\ 30)$$
$$\Rightarrow takeq(2, Cons(30, \mathtt{fn()=>}from(30 + 1)))$$
$$\Rightarrow 30 :: takeq(1, from(30 + 1))$$
$$\Rightarrow 30 :: takeq(1, Cons(31, \mathtt{fn()=>}from(31 + 1)))$$
$$\Rightarrow 30 :: 31 :: takeq(0, from(31 + 1))$$
$$\Rightarrow 30 :: 31 :: takeq(0, Cons(32, \mathtt{fn()=>}from(32 + 1)))$$
$$\Rightarrow 30 :: 31 :: []$$
$$\Rightarrow [30, 31]$$

Observe that the element 32 is computed but never used. Type $\alpha\ seq$ is not fully lazy; the head of a non-empty sequence is always computed. This defect can be cured at the cost of considerable extra complication.

Exercise 5.24   What is wrong with this version of *from*?

```
fun badfrom k = consq(k, badfrom(k+1));
```

Describe the computation steps of $takeq(2, badfrom\ 30)$.

Exercise 5.25   The type $\alpha\ lseq$, defined using mutual recursion, represents every sequence by a function and therefore prevents premature evaluation of the first element:

```
datatype 'a seqnode = Nil
              | Cons of 'a * 'a lseq
and      'a lseq     = Seq of unit -> 'a seqnode;
```

Code the functions *from* and *takeq* for this type of sequences.

5.13 *Elementary sequence processing*

For a function on sequences to be computable, each finite part of the output must depend on at most a finite part of the input. Evaluating elements of the output causes elements of the input to be evaluated.

Consider squaring a sequence of integers one by one. The tail of the output, when evaluated, applies *squares* to the tail of the input.

```
fun squares Nil : int seq = Nil
  | squares (Cons(x,xf)) = Cons(x*x, fn()=> squares (xf()));
> val squares = fn : int seq -> int seq
squares (from 1);
> Cons (1, fn) : int seq
takeq (10, it);
> [1, 4, 9, 16, 25, 36, 49, 64, 81, 100] : int list
```

Adding two sequences is similar. The tail of the output, when evaluated, adds the tails of the inputs. If either input sequence terminates, then so does the output.

```
fun addq (Cons(x,xf), Cons(y,yf)) =
              Cons(x+y, fn()=> addq(xf(), yf()))
  | addq _   : int seq              = Nil;
> val addq = fn : int seq * int seq -> int seq
addq (from 10000, squares (from 1));
> Cons (10001, fn) : int seq
takeq (5, it);
> [10001, 10005, 10011, 10019, 10029] : int list
```

The append function for sequences works like the one for lists. The elements of *appendq*(*xq, yq*) are first taken from *xq*; when *xq* becomes empty, elements are taken from *yq*.

```
fun appendq (Nil,    yq)    = yq
  | appendq (Cons(x,xf), yq) =
              Cons(x, fn()=> appendq(xf(), yq));
> val appendq = fn : 'a seq * 'a seq -> 'a seq
```

No elements of *yq* appear in the output unless *xq* is finite. A finite sequence can be built using *consq*.

```
val finiteq = consq(25, consq(10, Nil));
> Cons (25, fn) : int seq
appendq(finiteq, from 1415);
> Cons (25, fn) : int seq
takeq(3, it);
> [25, 10, 1415] : int list
```

Functionals for sequences. List functionals like *map* and *filter* can
be generalized to sequences. The function *squares* is an instance of
the functional *mapq*, which applies a function to every element of
a sequence:

```
fun mapq f Nil            = Nil
  | mapq f (Cons(x,xf)) = Cons(f x, fn()=> mapq f (xf()));
> val mapq = fn : ('a -> 'b) -> 'a seq -> 'b seq
```

To filter a sequence, successive tail functions are called until an
element is found to satisfy the given predicate. If no such element
exists, the computation will never terminate.

```
fun filterq pred Nil         = Nil
  | filterq pred (Cons(x,xf)) =
            if pred x then Cons(x, fn()=> filterq pred (xf()))
                      else filterq pred (xf());
> val filterq = fn : ('a -> bool) -> 'a seq -> 'a seq
filterq (fn n => n mod 10 = 7) (from 50);
> Cons (57, fn) : int seq
takeq(10,it);
> [57, 67, 77, 87, 97, 107, 117, 127, 137, 147] : int list
```

The function *from* is an instance of the functional *iterates*, which
generates sequences of the form $[x, f(x), f(f(x)), \ldots, f^k(x), \ldots]$:

```
fun iterates f x = Cons(x, fn()=> iterates f (f x));
> val iterates = fn : ('a -> 'a) -> 'a -> 'a seq
iterates(secr op/ 2.0) 1.0;
> Cons (1.0, fn) : real seq
takeq(5, it);
> [1.0, 0.5, 0.25, 0.125, 0.0625] : real list
```

To illustrate these functionals, let us turn to some elementary applications of sequences.

Random numbers. In Chapter 3 we generated a list of 10,000 random numbers for the sorting examples. However, seldom do we
know in advance how many random numbers are required. Conventionally, a random number generator is a procedure that stores

the 'seed' in a local variable. In a functional language, we can define
an infinite sequence of random numbers. This hides the implementation details and generates the numbers as they are required.

```
local val a = 16807.0  and   m = 2147483647.0
        fun nextrandom seed =
            let val t = a*seed
            in  t - m * real(floor(t/m))   end
    in
      fun randseq s = mapq (secr op/ m)
                              (iterates nextrandom (real s))
    end;
> val randseq = fn : int -> real seq
```

Observe how *iterates* generates a sequence of numbers, which *mapq*
divides by m. The random numbers are reals between 0 and 1,
exclusive. Using *mapq* we convert them to integers from 0 to 9:

```
mapq (floor o secl(10.0) op* ) (randseq 1);
> Cons (0, fn) : int seq
takeq (15, it);
> [0, 0, 1, 7, 4, 5, 2, 0, 6, 6, 9, 3, 5, 8, 0] : int list
```

Prime numbers. The sequence of prime numbers can be computed
by the Sieve of Eratosthenes.

Start with the sequence $[2, 3, 4, 5, 6, \ldots]$.

Take 2 as a prime. Delete all multiples of 2, since they cannot
be prime. This leaves the sequence $[3, 5, 7, 9, 11, \ldots]$.

Take 3 as a prime and delete its multiples. This leaves the
sequence $[5, 7, 11, 13, 17, \ldots]$.

Take 5 as a prime ....

At each stage, the sequence contains those numbers not divisible
by any of the primes generated so far. Therefore its head is prime,
and the process can continue indefinitely.

The function *sift* uses *filterq* to delete multiples from a sequence,
while *sieve* repeatedly sifts a sequence:

```
fun sift p = filterq (fn n => n mod p <> 0);
> val sift = fn : int -> int seq -> int seq
fun sieve (Cons(p,nf)) = Cons(p, fn()=>sieve(sift p (nf())));
> val sieve = fn : int seq -> int seq
```

The sequence *primes* results from *sieve* $[2, 3, 4, 5, \ldots]$. No primes beyond the first are generated until the sequence is inspected.

```
val primes = sieve (from 2);
> val primes = Cons (2, fn) : int seq
takeq(25,primes);
> [2, 3, 5, 7, 11, 13, 17, 19, 23, 29, 31, 37, 41, 43,
> 47, 53, 59, 61, 67, 71, 73, 79, 83, 89, 97] : int list
```

When we write programs such as these, ML types help to prevent confusion between sequences and tail functions. A sequence has type $\alpha\ seq$ while a tail function has type $unit \rightarrow \alpha\ seq$. We can insert a function call $\cdots$ () or a function abstraction `fn()=>`$\cdots$ in response to type error messages. Occasionally we must think harder than this to implement lazy evaluation correctly; we shall soon encounter a function definition that is type correct but does not delay evaluation, and therefore fails to terminate.

Exercise 5.26   Show the computation steps of

$$addq(from\ 5, squares(from\ 9)).$$

Exercise 5.27   Define a function that, given a positive integer k, transforms a sequence $[x_1, x_2, \ldots]$ into a new sequence by repeating each element k times:

$$[\underbrace{x_1, \ldots, x_1}_{k\ \text{times}}, \underbrace{x_2, \ldots, x_2}_{k\ \text{times}}, \ldots]$$

Exercise 5.28   Define a function to add adjacent elements of a sequence, transforming $[x_1, x_2, x_3, x_4, \ldots]$ to $[x_1 + x_2, x_3 + x_4, \ldots]$.

Exercise 5.29   Which of the list functionals *takewhile*, *dropwhile*, *exists* and *forall* can sensibly be generalized to infinite sequences? Code those that can be, and explain what goes wrong with the others.

5.14   *Numerical computing*

Sequences have applications in numerical analysis. This may seem surprising at first, but, after all, many numerical methods are based on infinite series. Why not express them literally?

Square roots are a simple example. Recall the Newton-Raphson method for computing the square root of some number a. Start with a positive approximation x_0. Compute further approximations by the rule

$$x_{k+1} = \left(\frac{a}{x_k} + x_k\right) / 2 \, ,$$

stopping when two successive approximations are sufficiently close. With sequences we can perform this computation directly.

The function *nextapprox* computes x_{k+1} from x_k. Repeated by the functional *iterates*, it computes the series of approximations.

```
fun nextapprox a x = (a/x + x) / 2.0;
> val nextapprox = fn : real -> real -> real
takeq(7, iterates (nextapprox 9.0) 1.0);
> [1.0, 5.0, 3.4, 3.023529412, 3.000091554, 3.000000001,
>  3.0] : real list
```

The simplest termination test is to stop when the absolute difference between two approximations is smaller than a given tolerance $\epsilon > 0$ (written *eps* below).*

```
fun within (eps:real) (Cons(x,xf)) =
      let val Cons(y,yf) = xf()
      in  if abs(x-y) <= eps then y
          else within eps (Cons(y,yf))
      end;
> val within = fn : real -> real seq -> real
```

Putting 10^{-6} for the tolerance and 1 for the initial approximation yields a square root function:

```
fun qroot a = within 1E~6 (iterates (nextapprox a) 1.0);
> val qroot = fn : real -> real
qroot 5.0;
> 2.236067977 : real
it*it;
> 5.0 : real
```

Would not a Fortran program be better? This example follows Hughes (1989) and Halfant & Sussman (1988), who show how 'interchangeable parts' involving sequences can be assembled into numerical algorithms. Each algorithm is tailor made to suit its application.

For instance, there are many termination tests to choose from. The absolute difference ($|x - y| < \epsilon$) tested by *within* is too strict

---

* The recursive call passes $Cons(y, yf)$ rather than $xf()$, which denotes the same sequence of values, to avoid calling $xf()$ twice. Our lists are not truly lazy, but employ a call-by-name rule.

for large numbers. We could test relative difference ($|x/y - 1| < \epsilon$)
or something fancier:

$$\frac{|x - y|}{(|x| + |y|)/2 + 1} < \epsilon$$

Sometimes it is prudent to test that three or more approximations
are sufficiently close.

Each termination test can be packaged as a function from sequences to reals. Techniques like Richardson extrapolation (for ac-
celerating the convergence of a series) can be packaged as functions
from sequences to sequences. These functions can be combined to
perform numerical differentiation, integration and so on.

Exercise 5.30   Compute the exponential function e^x by generating a sequence for the infinite sum

$$e^x = \frac{1}{0!} + \frac{x^1}{1!} + \frac{x^2}{2!} + \frac{x^3}{3!} + \cdots + \frac{x^k}{k!} + \cdots$$

Exercise 5.31   Write an ML function to take a value from a sequence using one of the other termination tests mentioned above.
Define a square root (or exponential) function using it.

5.15   *Interleaving and sequences of sequences*

If *xq* and *yq* are infinite sequences, consider forming the
infinite sequence of all pairs (x, y) with *x* from *xq* and *y* from *yq*.
This problem illustrates the subtleties of computing with infinities.

As remarked earlier in this chapter, a list of lists can be generated
using *map* with the curried pairing function *pair*. A sequence of
sequences can be generated similarly:

```
fun makeqq (xq,yq) = mapq (fn x=> mapq (pair x) yq) xq;
> val makeqq = fn : 'a seq * 'b seq -> ('a * 'b) seq seq
```

A sequence of sequences can be viewed using $takeqq((m, n), xqq)$.
This list of lists is the $m \times n$ upper left rectangle of *xqq*.

```
fun takeqq ((m,n), xqq) = map (secl n takeq) (takeq(m,xqq));
> val takeqq = fn : (int*int) * 'a seq seq -> 'a list list
makeqq (from 30, primes);
> Cons (Cons ((30, 2), fn), fn) : (int * int) seq seq
takeqq ((3,5), it);
> [[(30, 2), (30, 3), (30, 5), (30, 7), (30, 11)],
>  [(31, 2), (31, 3), (31, 5), (31, 7), (31, 11)],
>  [(32, 2), (32, 3), (32, 5), (32, 7), (32, 11)]]
> : (int * int) list list
```

The function *flat* appends the members of a list of lists, forming one list. What can be done with a sequence of infinite sequences? If *xq* is infinite then *appendq*(*xq*, *yq*) equals *xq*. To enumerate all the elements requires a function that combines infinite sequences fairly. The elements of two sequences can be **interleaved**:

```
fun interleave (Nil, yq)          = yq
  | interleave (Cons(x,xf), yq) =
        Cons(x, fn()=> interleave(yq, xf()));
> val interleave = fn : 'a seq * 'a seq -> 'a seq
takeq(10, interleave(from 0, from 50));
> [0, 50, 1, 51, 2, 52, 3, 53, 4, 54] : int list
```

In its recursive call, *interleave* exchanges the two sequences so that neither can exclude the other. Otherwise it resembles *appendq*.

Let us define a function *enumerate* to flatten a sequence of sequences of elements into a single sequence. Here is the idea. If the input sequence has head *xq* and tail *xqq*, recursively enumerate *xqq* and interleave the result with *xq*. If we take *flat* as a model we end up with the following definition, which is incorrect:

```
fun enumerate Nil            = Nil
  | enumerate (Cons(xq,xqf)) =
        interleave(xq, enumerate (xqf()));
> val enumerate = fn : 'a seq seq -> 'a seq
```

If the input to this function is infinite, ML will make an infinite series of recursive calls, generating no output. This definition would work in a lazy functional language, but with ML we must explicitly terminate the recursive calls as soon as some output can be produced. This requires a more complex case analysis. If the input sequence is non-empty, examine its head; if that is also non-empty then it contains an element for the output.

```
fun enumerate Nil                    = Nil
  | enumerate (Cons(Nil, xqf))       = enumerate (xqf())
  | enumerate (Cons(Cons(x,xf), xqf)) =
        Cons(x, fn()=> interleave(enumerate (xqf()), xf()));
> val enumerate = fn : 'a seq seq -> 'a seq
```

The second and third cases simulate the the incorrect definition's use of *interleave*, but the explicit fn()=>··· terminates the recursive calls.

Here is the sequence of all pairs of positive integers.

```
val pairqq = makeqq (from 1, from 1);
> val pairqq = Cons (Cons ((1, 1), fn), fn)
>    : (int * int) seq seq
takeq(15, enumerate pairqq);
> [(1, 1), (2, 1), (1, 2), (3, 1), (1, 3), (2, 2), (1, 4),
>   (4, 1), (1, 5), (2, 3), (1, 6), (3, 2), (1, 7), (2, 4),
>   (1, 8)]    : (int * int) list
```

We can be more precise about the order of enumeration. Consider the following definitions:

```
fun powof2 n = repeat double n 1;
> val powof2 = fn : int -> int
fun pack(i,j) = powof2(i-1) * (2*j - 1);
> val pack = fn : int * int -> int
```

This function, $pack(i, j) = 2^{i-1}(2j - 1)$, establishes a one-to-one correspondence between positive integers and pairs (i, j) of positive integers. Thus, the Cartesian product of two countable sets is a countable set. Here is a small table of this function:

```
val nqq = mapq (mapq pack) pairqq;
> val nqq = Cons (Cons (1, fn), fn) : int seq seq
takeqq ((4,6), nqq);
> [[1,   3,   5,   7,   9, 11],
>  [2,   6,  10,  14,  18, 22],
>  [4,  12,  20,  28,  36, 44],
>  [8,  24,  40,  56,  72, 88]] : int list list
```

Our enumeration decodes the packing function, returning the sequence of positive integers in their natural order:

```
takeq(12, enumerate nqq);
> [1, 2, 3, 4, 5, 6, 7, 8, 9, 10, 11, 12] : int list
```

It is not hard to see why this is so. Each interleaving takes half its elements from one sequence and half from another. Repeated interleaving distributes the places in the output sequence by powers of two, as in the packing function.

Exercise 5.32   Generate the sequence of all finite lists of positive integers. (Hint: first, define a function to generate the sequence of lists having a given length.)

Exercise 5.33   Show that for every positive integer k there are unique positive integers i and j such that $k = pack(i, j)$. What is $pack(i, j)$ in binary notation?

Exercise 5.34 Adapt the definition of type $\alpha\,seq$ to declare a type of infinite binary trees. Write a function *itr* that, applied to an integer n, constructs the tree whose root has the label n and the two subtrees $itr(2n)$ and $itr(2n+1)$.

Exercise 5.35 (Continuing the previous exercise.) Write a function to construct a sequence consisting of all the labels in a given infinite binary tree. In what order are the labels enumerated? Then write an inverse function that constructs an infinite binary tree whose labels are given by a sequence.

Search strategies and lazy lists

Theorem proving, planning and other Artificial Intelligence applications require search. There are many search strategies, each with its particular advantages.

Depth-first search is cheap, but it may follow a blind alley and run forever without finding any solutions.

Breadth-first search is **complete** — certain to find all the solutions — but it requires a huge amount of space.

Depth-first iterative deepening is complete and requires little space, but can be slow.

Best-first search must be guided by a function to estimate the distance from a solution.

By representing the set of solutions as a lazy list, the search strategy can be chosen independently from the process that consumes the solutions. The lazy list serves as a communication channel: the producer generates its elements and the consumer removes them. Because the list is lazy, its elements are not produced until the consumer requires them.

Figures 5.1 and 5.2 contrast the depth-first and breadth-first strategies, applying both to the same tree. The tree is portrayed at some point during the search, with subtrees not yet visited as triangles. Throughout this section, no tree node may have an infinite number of branches. Trees may have infinite depth.

In **depth-first search**, the subtrees below a node are visited from left to right. Each subtree is fully searched before its brother to the right is considered. The numbers in the figure show the order of the visits. Node 5 is reached because node 4 is a leaf, while four

Figure 5.1 *A depth-first search tree*

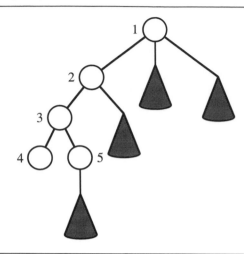

subtrees remain to be visited. If the subtree below node 5 is infinite, the other subtrees will never be reached: the strategy is incomplete. A famous application of depth-first search is Prolog's backtracking.

Breadth-first search visits all nodes at the current depth before moving on to the next depth. In Figure 5.2 it has explored the tree to three levels. Because of finite branching, all nodes will be reached: the strategy is complete. But an exponential number of nodes must typically be visited to reach a given depth. The list of subtrees to visit next may also grow exponentially. Breadth-first search is seldom practical.

5.16   *Search strategies in ML*

Infinite trees could be represented rather like infinite lists, namely as an ML datatype containing functions to delay evaluation. For the search trees of this section, however, a node's subtrees can be computed from its label. Trees over type α (with finite branching) are represented by a function *next* : $\alpha \to \alpha$ *list*, where *next x* is the list of the subtrees of *x*. Solutions are identified using a predicate over type α, a function *pred* : $\alpha \to$ *bool*.

Depth-first search can be implemented efficiently using a stack to hold the nodes to visit next. At each stage, the head *y* is removed from the stack and replaced by its subtrees, *next y*, which will be

Figure 5.2 *A breadth-first search tree*

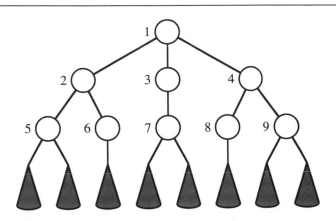

visited before other nodes in the stack. Node *y* is included in the output if it satisfies the predicate.

```
fun depthfirst (next,pred) x =
  let fun dfs []      = Nil
      | dfs(y::ys) =
            if pred y then Cons(y, fn()=> dfs(next y @ ys))
                      else dfs(next y @ ys)
  in  dfs [x]  end;
> val depthfirst =
>   fn : ('a -> 'a list) * ('a -> bool) -> 'a -> 'a seq
```

Breadth-first search stores the pending nodes on a queue, not on a stack. When *y* is visited, its successors in *next y* are put at the end of the queue.*

```
fun breadthfirst (next,pred) x =
  let fun bfs []      = Nil
      | bfs(y::ys) =
            if pred y then Cons(y, fn()=> bfs(ys @ next y))
                      else bfs(ys @ next y)
  in  bfs [x]  end;
> val breadthfirst =
>   fn : ('a -> 'a list) * ('a -> bool) -> 'a -> 'a seq
```

Other search strategies are obtained by modifying these functions.

---

* Stacks and queues are represented here by lists. Lists make efficient stacks, but using append as a queue operation is costly. Efficient queues are presented in Chapter 7.

For instance, **best-first search** employs a function for estimating the distance from any node to a solution node. The pending nodes are stored in a priority queue according to their estimated distance. The closest node is visited next. If the distance function is reasonably accurate, best-first search converges rapidly to a solution. See Rich (1983) for more information.

Exercise 5.36   Implement best-first search, as described above.

Exercise 5.37   Simplify *depthfirst* and *breadthfirst* by eliminating the argument *pred*, assuming that *pred x* is always *true*. What results when *filterq p* is applied to the outputs of these functions, where *p* is some other predicate?

5.17   *Generating palindromes*

Let us generate the sequence of palindromes over the alphabet $\{A, B, C\}$. Each node of the search tree will be a list l of these letters, with 3 branches to nodes `"A"::`l, `"B"::`l and `"C"::`l.

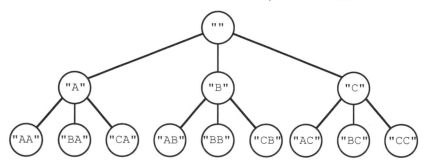

Function *nextlist* generates this tree.

```
fun nextlist l = ["A"::l, "B"::l, "C"::l];
> val nextlist = fn : string list -> string list list
```

A **palindrome** is a list that equals its own reverse. Let us define the corresponding predicate:

```
fun ispalindrome l = (l = rev l);
> val ispalindrome = fn : ''a list -> bool
```

Palindrome generation can, of course, be done by other means. As a search problem it has features in common with theorem proving. For instance, depth-first search clearly fails to find all solutions. In the following demonstration, *implode* joins the characters of each palindrome into a string:

```
depthfirst (nextlist,ispalindrome) [];
> Cons ([], fn) : string list seq
takeq(10, mapq implode it);
> ["", "A", "AA", "AAA", "AAAA", "AAAAA", "AAAAAA",
>  "AAAAAAA", "AAAAAAAA", "AAAAAAAAA"] : string list
```

Since the leftmost branch of the tree is infinite, depth-first search reaches nothing else. Breadth-first search is complete and generates all the palindromes:

```
breadthfirst (nextlist,ispalindrome) [];
> Cons ([], fn) : string list seq
takeq(15, mapq implode it);
> ["", "A", "B", "C", "AA", "BB", "CC", "AAA", "ABA",
>  "ACA", "BAB", "BBB", "BCB", "CAC", "CBC"] : string list
```

Depth-first search often fails for infinite search trees. If there is no solution on an infinite branch then it finds nothing at all. Let us start the search at the label B. There is only one palindrome of the form $AA\ldots AB$, and depth-first search considers no other strings:

```
depthfirst (nextlist,ispalindrome) ["B"];
> Cons (["B"], fn) : string list seq
```

The attempt to take more elements from this sequence ...

```
tail it;
```

... runs forever. Breadth-first search yields the sequence of palindromes ending in B:

```
breadthfirst (nextlist,ispalindrome) ["B"];
> Cons (["B"], fn) : string list seq
takeq(10, mapq implode it);
> ["B", "BB", "BAB", "BBB", "BCB", "BAAB", "BBBB", "BCCB",
>  "BAAAB", "BABAB"] : string list
```

Again, we see the importance of a complete search strategy.

5.18   *The 8 Queens Problem*

A classic problem is to place 8 Queens on a chess board so that no Queen may attack another. No two Queens may share a row, column or diagonal. Solutions may be found by examining all safe ways of placing new Queens on successive columns. The root of the search tree contains an empty board. There are 8 positions for a Queen in the first column, so there are 8 branches from the root to boards holding one Queen. Once a Queen has been placed in the first column, there are fewer than 8 safe positions for a Queen in the second column; branching decreases with depth in the tree. A board containing 8 Queens must be a leaf node.

Since the 8 Queens tree is finite, depth-first search finds all solutions. Most published solutions to the problem, whether imperative or functional, encode depth-first search directly. An imperative program, recording the occupation of rows and diagonals using boolean arrays, can find all solutions quickly. But let us view the 8 Queens problem more abstractly, as a means of demonstrating the different search strategies.

We can represent a board position by a list of row numbers. The list $[q_1, \ldots, q_k]$ stands for the board having Queens in row q_i of column i for $i = 1, \ldots, k$. Function *safequeen* tests whether a queen can safely be placed in row *newq* of the next column, forming the board $[newq, q_1, \ldots, q_k]$. (The other columns are essentially shifted to the left.) The new Queen must not be on the same row or diagonal as another Queen. Note that $|newq - q_i| = i$ exactly when *newq* and q_i share a diagonal.

```
fun safequeen oldqs newq =
    let fun nodiag (i, []) = true
      | nodiag (i, q::qs) =
            abs(newq-q)<>i andalso nodiag(i+1,qs)
    in  not (newq mem oldqs) andalso nodiag (1,oldqs)  end;
> val safequeen = fn : int list -> int -> bool
```

To generate the search tree, function *nextqueen* takes a board and returns the list of the safe board positions having a new Queen. Observe the use of *map* with a section and *filter* with a curried function. At this point, the 8 Queens problem is generalized to the n Queens problem, which is to place n Queens safely on an $n \times n$ board.

```
fun nextqueen n qs =
    map (secr op:: qs) (filter (safequeen qs) (upto(1,n)));
> val nextqueen = fn : int -> int list -> int list list
```

Let us define a predicate to recognize solutions. Since only safe board positions are considered, a solution is any board having n Queens.

```
fun isfull n qs = (length qs=n);
> val isfull = fn : int -> 'a list -> bool
```

Function *depthfirst* finds all 92 solutions for 8 Queens:

```
takeq(100, depthfirst (nextqueen 8, isfull 8) []);
> [[4, 2, 7, 3, 6, 8, 5, 1], [5, 2, 4, 7, 3, 8, 6, 1],
>   [3, 5, 2, 8, 6, 4, 7, 1], [3, 6, 4, 2, 8, 5, 7, 1],
>   [5, 7, 1, 3, 8, 6, 4, 2], [4, 6, 8, 3, 1, 7, 5, 2],
>   ...] : int list list
```

Since sequences are lazy, solutions can be demanded one by one. Depth-first search finds the first solution quickly. This is not so important for the 8 Queens problem, but the 15 Queens problem has over two million solutions. Here are some of them:

```
takeq(3, depthfirst (nextqueen 15, isfull 15) []);
> [[8, 11, 7, 15, 6, 9, 13, 4, 14, 12, 10, 2, 5, 3, 1],
>   [11, 13, 10, 4, 6, 8, 15, 2, 12, 14, 9, 7, 5, 3, 1],
>   [13, 11, 8, 6, 2, 9, 14, 4, 15, 10, 12, 7, 5, 3, 1]]
> : int list list
```

Imagine the design of an imperative program that could generate solutions upon demand. It would probably involve coroutines or communicating processes.

Function *breadthfirst* finds the solutions extremely slowly. Finding one solution takes nearly as long as finding all! The solutions reside at the same depth in the search tree; finding the first solution requires searching virtually the entire tree.

5.19 *Iterative deepening*

Depth-first iterative deepening combines some of the best properties of the other search procedures. Like depth-first search, it uses little space; like breadth-first search, it is complete. The strategy is to search the tree repeatedly, each time bounded by a finite depth. First it performs depth-first search down to some depth d, returning all solutions found. It then searches down to depth $2d$, returning all solutions found between depths d and $2d$. It then searches to depth $3d$, and so on. Since each search is finite, the strategy will eventually reach any depth.

The repeated searching is less wasteful than it may appear. Iterative deepening increases the time required to reach a given depth by no more than a constant factor, unless the tree branches very little. There are more nodes between depths kd and $(k+1)d$ than above kd (Korf, 1985). Recomputation eliminates the enormous queues that plague breadth-first search.

For simplicity, let us implement iterative deepening with $d = 1$. It yields the same result as breadth-first search, taking more time but using far less space.

Function *depthfirst* is not easily modified to perform iterative deepening because its stack contains nodes from various depths in the tree. The following search function has no stack; it visits each subtree in a separate recursive call. Argument *sf* of *dfs* accumulates the (possibly infinite!) sequence of solutions.

```
fun depthiter (next,pred) x =
  let fun dfs k (y, sf) =
          if k=0 then
                if  pred y  then  fn()=>Cons(y,sf)  else  sf
            else foldright (dfs (k-1)) (next y, sf)
      fun deepen k = dfs k (x, fn()=>deepen(k+1)) ()
  in  deepen 0  end;
> val depthiter =
>   fn : ('a -> 'a list) * ('a -> bool) -> 'a -> 'a seq
```

Let us examine this declaration in detail. Tail functions (of type $unit \rightarrow \alpha\ seq$) rather than sequences must be used in order to delay evaluation. Calling $dfs\ k\ (y, sf)\ ()$ constructs the sequence of all solutions found at depth k below node y, followed by the sequence $sf()$. There are two cases to consider.

If $k = 0$ then y is included in the output provided it satisfies the predicate.

If $k > 0$ then let $next\ y = [y_1, \ldots, y_n]$. These nodes, the subtrees of y, are supplied to *foldright*. The resulting sequence contains all solutions found at depth $k - 1$ below $y_1, \ldots, y_n$:

$$dfs(k - 1)(y_1, \ldots dfs(k - 1)(y_n, sf) \ldots)\,()$$

Calling *deepen k* creates a tail function to compute $deepen(k + 1)$ and passes it to *dfs*, which inserts the solutions found at depth k.

Let us try it on the previous examples. Iterative deepening generates the same sequence of palindromes as breadth-first search:

```
depthiter (nextlist, ispalindrome) [];
> Cons ([], fn) : string list seq
takeq(15, mapq implode it);
> ["", "A", "B", "C", "AA", "BB", "CC", "AAA", "ABA",
>  "ACA", "BAB", "BBB", "BCB", "CAC", "CBC"] : string list
```

It can also solve the 8 Queens problem, but slowly. With a larger depth interval d, iterative deepening recovers some of the efficiency of depth-first search, while remaining complete.

Exercise 5.38   Generalize the function *depthiter* to take the depth interval d as a parameter. Generate palindromes using $d = 5$. How does the result differ from those obtained by other strategies?

Exercise 5.39   Define a datatype of finite-branching search trees of possibly infinite depth, using a representation like that of sequences. Write a function to construct the tree generated by a parameter *next* : $\alpha \to \alpha$ *list*. Give an example of a tree that cannot be constructed in this way.

Summary of main points

An ML expression can evaluate to a function.

A curried function acts like a function of several arguments.

Higher-order functions reduce the need for separate function declarations.

A lazy list can contain an infinite number of elements, but only a finite number are ever evaluated.

Lazy lists, representing infinite series, are convenient for expressing numerical computations.

A lazy list connects a consumer to a producer, such that items are produced only when they have to be consumed.

6

Reasoning About Functional Programs

Most programmers know how hard it is to make a program work. In the 1970s, it became apparent that programmers could no longer cope with software projects that were growing ever more complex. Systems were delayed and cancelled; costs escalated. In response to this software crisis, several new methodologies have arisen — each an attempt to master the complexity of large systems.

Structured programming seeks to organize programs into simple parts with simple interfaces. An **abstract data type** lets the programmer view a data structure, with its operations, as a mathematical object. The next chapter, on modules, will say more about these topics.

Functional programming and **logic programming** aim to express computations directly in mathematics. The complicated machine state is made invisible; the programmer has to understand only one expression at a time.

Formal methods of program development are introduced in this chapter. Like the other responses to the software crisis, formal methods aim to increase our understanding. The first lesson is that a program only 'works' if it is **correct** with respect to its **specification**. Our minds cannot cope with the billions of steps in an execution. If the program is expressed in a mathematical form, however, then each stage of the computation can be described by a formula. Programs can be **verified** — proved correct — or **derived** from a specification. Most of the early work on program verification focused on Pascal and similar languages; functional programs are easier to reason about because they involve no machine state.

Chapter outline

The chapter presents proofs about functional programs, paying particular attention to induction. The proof methods are rigorous but informal. Their purpose is to increase our understanding of the programs.

The chapter contains the following sections:

Some principles of mathematical proof. A class of ML programs can be treated within elementary mathematics. Some integer functions are verified using mathematical induction.

Structural induction. This principle generalizes mathematical induction to lists and trees. Proofs about higher-order functions are presented.

A general induction principle. Several unusual inductive proofs are discussed. Well-founded induction provides a uniform framework for such proofs.

Specification and verification. The methods of the chapter are applied to an extended example: the verification of a merge sort function. Some limitations of verification are discussed.

Some principles of mathematical proof

The proofs in this chapter are conducted in a style typical of discrete mathematics. Most proofs are by induction. Much of the reasoning is equational, replacing equals by equals, although the logical connectives and quantifiers play a vital role.

6.1   *ML programs as mathematical objects*

Our proofs will treat Standard ML programs as mathematical entities subject to mathematical laws. A theory of the full language would be too complicated; let us restrict the form of programs. Only functional programs will be allowed; ML's imperative features will be forbidden.* Types will be interpreted as sets, which restricts the form of **datatype** declarations. Exceptions are forbidden, although it would not be hard to incorporate them into our framework. We shall allow only well-defined expressions. They must be legally typed, and must denote terminating computations.

---

* Chapter 8 discusses ML's references, assignments and input/output.

If all computations must terminate, recursive function definitions have to be restricted. Recall the function *facti*, declared as follows:

```
fun facti (n,p) =
      if n=0 then p  else  facti(n-1, n*p);
```

Recall from Chapter 2 that functional programs are computed by reduction:

$$facti(4,1) \Rightarrow facti(4-1, 4 \times 1) \Rightarrow facti(3,4) \Rightarrow \cdots \Rightarrow 24$$

Computing $facti(n,p)$ yields a unique result for all $n \geq 0$; thus $facti$ is a mathematical function satisfying these laws:

$$facti(0,p) = p$$
$$facti(n,p) = facti(n-1, n \times p) \qquad \text{for } n > 0$$

If $n < 0$ then $facti(n,p)$ produces a computation that runs forever; it is undefined, satisfying no laws at all. We may regard $facti(n,p)$ as meaningful only for $n \geq 0$, which is the function's **precondition**.

For another example, consider the following declaration:

```
fun undef(x) = undef(x)-1;
```

Since $undef(x)$ does not terminate for any x, we shall not regard it as meaningful. We may not adopt $undef(x) = undef(x) - 1$ as a law about numbers, for it is clearly false.

It is possible to introduce the value $\perp$ (called 'bottom') for the value of a nonterminating computation, and develop a **domain theory** for reasoning about arbitrary recursive function definitions (Schmidt, 1986). This theory interprets $undef$ as the function satisfying $undef(x) = \perp$ for all x. It turns out that $\perp - 1 = \perp$, so $undef(x) = undef(x) - 1$ means simply $\perp = \perp$, which is valid. But domain theory is complex and difficult. The value $\perp$ induces a partial ordering on all types. All functions in the theory must be monotonic and continuous over this partial ordering; recursive functions denote least fixed points. By insisting upon termination, we can work within elementary set theory.

Restricting ourselves to terminating computations entails some sacrifices. It is harder to reason about programs that do not aways terminate, such as interpreters. Nor can we reason about lazy evaluation — which is a pity, for using this sophisticated form of functional programming requires mathematical insights. Most functional programmers eventually learn some domain theory; there is no other way to understand what computation over an infinite list really means.

Logical notation. This chapter assumes you have some familiarity with the methods of mathematical proof. To fix the notation for logical formulae, here is a table of the connectives and quantifiers:

$$\neg\phi \qquad \text{not } \phi$$
$$\phi \wedge \psi \qquad \phi \text{ and } \psi$$
$$\phi \vee \psi \qquad \phi \text{ or } \psi$$
$$\phi \rightarrow \psi \qquad \phi \text{ implies } \psi$$
$$\phi \leftrightarrow \psi \qquad \phi \text{ if and only if } \psi$$
$$\forall x . \phi(x) \qquad \text{for all } x, \phi(x)$$
$$\exists x . \phi(x) \qquad \text{for some } x, \phi(x)$$

From highest to lowest precedence, the connectives are $\neg$, $\wedge$, $\vee$, $\rightarrow$, $\leftrightarrow$. An example of precedence in formulae:

$$P \wedge Q \rightarrow P \vee \neg R \text{ abbreviates } (P \wedge Q) \rightarrow (P \vee (\neg R))$$

Quantifiers have the widest possible scope to the right:

$$\forall x . P \wedge \exists y . Q \rightarrow R \text{ abbreviates } \forall x . (P \wedge (\exists y . (Q \rightarrow R)))$$

These symbols are used to construct formulae, not as a substitute for English. We may write 'for all x, the formula $\forall y . \phi(x, y)$ is true.'

6.2   *Mathematical induction and complete induction*

Let us begin with a review of mathematical induction. Suppose $\phi(n)$ is a property that we would like to prove for all natural numbers n (all non-negative integers). To prove it by induction, it suffices to prove two things: the **base case**, namely $\phi(0)$, and the **induction step**, namely that $\phi(k)$ implies $\phi(k+1)$ for all k.

The rule can be displayed as follows:

$$\frac{\phi(0) \qquad \phi(k+1)}{\phi(n)} \qquad \begin{array}{l} [\phi(k)] \\ \text{proviso: } k \text{ must not occur in} \\ \text{other assumptions of } \phi(k+1). \end{array}$$

In this notation, the **premises** appear above the line and the **conclusion** below. These premises are the base case and the induction step. The formula $\phi(k)$, which appears in brackets, is the **induction hypothesis**; it may be assumed while proving $\phi(k+1)$. The proviso means that k must be a new variable, not already present in other induction hypotheses (or other assumptions); thus k stands for an arbitrary value. This rule notation comes from **natural deduction**, a formal theory of proofs.

In the induction step, we prove $\phi(k + 1)$ under the assumption $\phi(k)$. We assume the very property we are trying to prove, but of k only. This may look like circular reasoning, especially since n and k are often the same variable (to avoid having to write the induction hypothesis explicitly). Why is induction sound? If the base case and induction step hold, then we have $\phi(0)$ by the base case and $\phi(1)$, $\phi(2)$, ..., by repeated use of the induction step. Therefore $\phi(n)$ holds for all n.

As a trivial example of induction, let us prove the following.

Theorem 1 *Every natural number is even or odd.*
Proof The inductive property is

$\qquad$ n is even or n is odd

which we prove by induction on n.

The base case, 0 is even or 0 is odd, is trivial: 0 is even.

In the induction step, we assume the induction hypothesis

$\qquad$ k is even or k is odd

and prove

$\qquad$ $k + 1$ is even or $k + 1$ is odd.

By the induction hypothesis, there are two cases: if k is even then $k+1$ is odd; if k is odd then $k+1$ is even. Since the conclusion holds in both cases, the proof is finished. $\qquad$ ∎

Notice that a black box marks the end of a proof.

This proof not only tells us that every natural number is even or odd, but contains a method for testing a given number. The test can be formalized in ML as a recursive function:

```
fun test 0  =  "even"
  | test n  =  if test(n-1) = "even" then "odd"
                                     else "even";
```

In some formal theories of constructive mathematics, a recursive function can be extracted automatically from every inductive proof (Constable et al., 1986). We shall not study such theories here, but shall try to learn as much as possible from our proofs. Mathematics would be barren indeed if each proof gave us nothing but a single formula. By sharpening the theorem, we can obtain more information from its proof.

Theorem 2 *Every natural number has the form $2m$ or $2m + 1$ for some natural number m.*

Proof   Since this property is fairly complicated, let us express it in logical notation:

$$\exists m \,.\, n = 2m \lor n = 2m + 1$$

The proof is by induction on n.

The base case is

$$\exists m \,.\, 0 = 2m \lor 0 = 2m + 1.$$

This holds with $m = 0$ since $0 = 2 \times 0$.

For the induction step, assume the induction hypothesis

$$\exists m \,.\, k = 2m \lor k = 2m + 1$$

and show (renaming m as m' to avoid confusion)

$$\exists m' \,.\, k + 1 = 2m' \lor k + 1 = 2m' + 1.$$

By the induction hypothesis, there exists some m such that either $k = 2m$ or $k = 2m + 1$. In either case we can exhibit some m' such that $k + 1 = 2m'$ or $k + 1 = 2m' + 1$.

If $k = 2m$ then $k + 1 = 2m + 1$, so $m' = m$.

If $k = 2m+1$ then $k+1 = 2m+2 = 2(m+1)$, so $m' = m+1$.

This concludes the proof.   ∎

Complete induction.   Mathematical induction reduces the problem $\phi(k)$ to the subproblem $\phi(k-1)$, if $k > 0$. Complete induction reduces $\phi(k)$ to the k subproblems $\phi(0)$, $\phi(1)$, ..., $\phi(k-1)$. It includes mathematical induction as a special case.

To prove $\phi(n)$ for all integer $n \geq 0$ by complete induction on n, it suffices to prove the following induction step:

$$\phi(k) \text{ assuming } \forall i < k \,.\, \phi(i)$$

The induction step comprises an infinite sequence of statements:

$\phi(0)$

$\phi(1)$ assuming $\phi(0)$

$\phi(2)$ assuming $\phi(0)$ and $\phi(1)$

$\phi(3)$ assuming $\phi(0), \phi(1)$ and $\phi(2)$

$\vdots$

Clearly it implies $\phi(n)$ for all n; complete induction is sound. The rule is portrayed as follows:

$$[\forall i < k . \phi(i)]$$
$$\frac{\phi(k)}{\phi(n)}$$

proviso: k must not occur in other assumptions of the premise.

We now consider a simple proof.

Theorem 3   *Every natural number $n \geq 2$ can be written as a product of prime numbers, $n = p_1 \cdots p_k$.*
Proof   By complete induction on n. There are two cases.

If n is prime then the result is trivial and $k = 1$.

If n is not prime then it is divisible by some natural number m such that $1 < m < n$. Since $m < n$ and $n/m < n$, we may appeal twice to the induction hypotheses of complete induction, writing these numbers as products of primes:

$$m = p_1 \cdots p_k \quad \text{and} \quad n/m = q_1 \cdots q_l$$

Now $n = m \times (n/m) = p_1 \cdots p_k q_1 \cdots q_l$.   ∎

This is the easy part of the Fundamental Theorem of Arithmetic. The hard part is to show that the factorization into primes is unique, regardless of the choice of m in the proof. As it stands, the proof provides a nondeterministic algorithm for factoring numbers into primes.

Exercise 6.1   The proof of Theorem 2 contains a method for dividing a number by 2. Formalize this method as an ML function.

Exercise 6.2   Prove, by induction, the basic theorem of integer division: if n and d are natural numbers with $d \neq 0$, then there exist natural numbers q and r such that $n = dq + r$ and $0 \leq r < d$. Express the corresponding division function in ML. How efficient is it?

Exercise 6.3   Show that if $\phi(n)$ can be proved by mathematical induction on n, then it can also be proved by complete induction.

Exercise 6.4   Show that if $\phi(n)$ can be proved by complete induction on n, then it can also be proved using mathematical induction. (Hint: use a different induction formula.)

6.3   *Simple examples of program verification*

A **specification** is a precise description of the properties required of a program execution. It specifies the result of the computation, not the method. The specification of sorting states that the output contains the same elements as the input, arranged in increasing order. Any sorting algorithm satisfies this specification. A specification (for the present purposes, at least) says nothing about performance.

Program verification means proving that a program satisfies its specification. The complexity of a realistic specification makes verification difficult. Each of the programs verified below has a trivial specification: the result is a simple function of the input. We shall verify ML functions to compute factorials, Fibonacci numbers and powers. These are all from Chapter 2.

The key step in these proofs is to formulate an induction suitable for the function. To be of any use, the induction hypothesis should be applicable to some recursive call of the function. The base case and induction step are simplified using function definitions, other mathematical laws and the induction hypothesis. If we are lucky, the simplified formula will be trivially true; if not, it may at least suggest a lemma to prove first.

Factorials. The iterative function *facti* was claimed in Chapter 2 to compute factorials. Let us prove that $facti(n, 1) = n!$ for all $n \geq 0$. Recall that $0! = 1$ and $n! = (n-1)! \times n$ for $n > 0$. The definition of *facti* was repeated in Section 6.1.

Induction on $facti(n, 1) = n!$ would lead nowhere because it says nothing about argument p of *facti*. The induction hypothesis would apply only for $p = 1$. We must discover a relationship involving $facti(n, p)$ and $n!$ that implies $facti(n, 1) = n!$ and that can be proved by induction. A good try is $facti(n, p) = n! \times p$, but this will not quite do. It refers to some particular n and p, but p varies in the recursive calls. The correct formulation has a universal quantifier:

$$\forall p \,.\, facti(n, p) = n! \times p$$

As an induction hypothesis about some fixed n, it asserts the equality for all p.

Theorem 4   *For every natural number n, $facti(n, 1) = n!$*

Proof This will follow by putting $p = 1$ in the following formula, which is proved by induction on n:

$$\forall p \,.\, facti(n, p) = n! \times p$$

By using n rather than k in the induction step, we can use this formula as the induction hypothesis.

For the base case we must show

$$\forall p \,.\, facti(0, p) = 0! \times p.$$

This holds because $facti(0, p) = p = 1 \times p = 0! \times p$.

For the induction step, the induction hypothesis is as stated above. We must show

$$\forall p \,.\, facti(n + 1, p) = (n + 1)! \times p.$$

Let us drop the universal quantifier and show the equality for arbitrary p. To simplify the equality, reduce the left side to the right side:

$$
\begin{aligned}
facti(n + 1, p) &= facti(n, (n + 1) \times p) &&[\textit{facti}] \\
&= n! \times ((n + 1) \times p) &&[\text{ind hyp}] \\
&= (n! \times (n + 1)) \times p &&[\text{associativity}] \\
&= (n + 1)! \times p &&[\text{factorial}]
\end{aligned}
$$

The comments in brackets are read as follows:

$$
\begin{aligned}
[\textit{facti}] \quad &\text{means 'by the definition of } \textit{facti'} \\
[\text{ind hyp}] \quad &\text{means 'by the induction hypothesis'} \\
[\text{associativity}] \quad &\text{means 'by the associative law for } \times \text{'} \\
[\text{factorial}] \quad &\text{means 'by the definition of factorials'}
\end{aligned}
$$

Other proofs adopt similar conventions.

Both sides are equal in the induction step. Observe that the quantified variable p of the induction hypothesis is replaced by $(n + 1) \times p$. ∎

Formal proofs should help us understand our programs. This proof explains the role of p in $facti(n, p)$. The induction formula is analogous to a **loop invariant** in imperative program verification. Since the proof depends on the associative law for $\times$, it suggests that $facti(n, 1)$ computes $n!$ by multiplying the same numbers in a different order. Later we shall generalize this to a theorem about transforming recursive functions into iterative functions.

Fibonacci numbers. Recall that the Fibonacci sequence is defined by $F_0 = 0$, $F_1 = 1$ and $F_n = F_{n-2} + F_{n-1}$ for $n \geq 2$. We shall prove that they can be computed by the function *itfib*:

```
fun itfib (n, prev, curr) : int =
    if n=1 then curr
    else itfib (n-1, curr, prev+curr);
```

Observing that $itfib(n, prev, curr)$ is defined for all $n \geq 1$, we set out to prove $itfib(n, 0, 1) = F_n$. As in the previous example, the induction formula must be generalized to say something about all the arguments of the function. There is no automatic procedure for doing this, but examining some computations of $itfib(n, 0, 1)$ reveals that *prev* and *curr* are always Fibonacci numbers. This suggests the relationship

$$itfib(n, F_k, F_{k+1}) = F_{k+n}.$$

Again, a universal quantifier must be inserted before induction.

Theorem 5   *For every integer $n \geq 1$, $itfib(n, 0, 1) = F_n$.*
Proof   This follows putting $k = 0$ in the following formula, which is proved by induction on n:

$$\forall k \,.\, itfib(n, F_k, F_{k+1}) = F_{k+n}$$

Since $n \geq 1$, the base case is to prove the above for $n = 1$:

$$\forall k \,.\, itfib(1, F_k, F_{k+1}) = F_{k+1}$$

This is immediate by the definition of *itfib*.

For the induction step, the induction hypothesis is given above; we must show

$$\forall k \,.\, itfib(n + 1, F_k, F_{k+1}) = F_{k+(n+1)}.$$

We prove this by simplifying the left side:

$$
\begin{aligned}
& itfib(n + 1, F_k, F_{k+1}) && \\
&= itfib(n, F_{k+1}, F_k + F_{k+1}) && [itfib] \\
&= itfib(n, F_{k+1}, F_{k+2}) && [\text{Fibonacci}] \\
&= F_{(k+1)+n} && [\text{ind hyp}] \\
&= F_{k+(n+1)} && [\text{arithmetic}]
\end{aligned}
$$

The induction hypothesis is applied with $k + 1$ in place of k, instantiating the quantifier.   ∎

This proof shows how pairs of Fibonacci numbers are generated successively. The induction formula is a key property of *itfib*, and is not at all obvious. It is good practice to state such a formula as a comment in each recursive function.

Powers. We now prove that $power(x, k) = x^k$ for every real number x and integer $k \geq 1$. Recall the definition of *power*:

```
fun power(x,k) : real =
    if k=1 then x
    else if k mod 2 = 0 then      power(x*x, k div 2)
                        else x * power(x*x, k div 2);
```

The proof will assume that ML's real arithmetic is exact, ignoring roundoff errors. It is typical of program verification to ignore the limitations of physical hardware. To demonstrate that *power* is suitable for actual computers would require an error analysis as well, which would involve much more work.

We must check that $power(x, k)$ is defined for $k \geq 1$. The case $k = 1$ is obvious. If $k \geq 2$ then we need to examine the recursive calls, which replace k by k *div* 2. These terminate because $1 \leq k$ *div* $2 < k$.

Since x varies during the computation of $power(x, k)$, the induction formula must have a quantifier:

$$\forall x . power(x, k) = x^k$$

However, ordinary mathematical induction is not appropriate. In $power(x, k)$ the recursive call replaces k by k *div* 2, not $k - 1$. We use complete induction in order to have an induction hypothesis for k *div* 2.

Theorem 6 *For every integer $k \geq 1$, $\forall x . power(x, k) = x^k$.*
Proof The formula is proved by complete induction on k.

Although complete induction has no separate base case, we may perform case analysis on k. Since $k \geq 1$, let us consider $k = 1$ and $k \geq 2$ separately.

Case $k = 1$. We must prove

$$\forall x . power(x, 1) = x^1.$$

This holds because $power(x, 1) = x = x^1$.

Case $k \geq 2$. We consider subcases. If k is even then $k = 2j$, and if k is odd then $k = 2j + 1$, for some integer j (namely k *div* 2). In both cases $1 \leq j < k$, so there is an induction hypothesis for j:

$$\forall x . power(x, j) = x^j$$

If $k = 2j$ then $k \bmod 2 = 0$ and

$$power(x, 2j) = power(x^2, j) \qquad\qquad [power]$$
$$= (x^2)^j \qquad\qquad [\text{ind hyp}]$$
$$= x^{2j}. \qquad\qquad [\text{arithmetic}]$$

If $k = 2j + 1$ then $k \bmod 2 = 1$ and

$$power(x, 2j + 1) = x \times power(x^2, j) \qquad\qquad [power]$$
$$= x \times (x^2)^j \qquad\qquad [\text{ind hyp}]$$
$$= x^{2j+1}. \qquad\qquad [\text{arithmetic}]$$

In both of these cases, the induction hypothesis is applied with x^2 in place of x.   ∎

Exercise 6.5   Verify that the function *introot* of Chapter 2 computes integer square roots.

Exercise 6.6   Recall *sqroot* of Chapter 2, which computes real square roots by the Newton-Raphson method. Discuss the problems involved in verifying this function.

Structural induction

Mathematical induction establishes $\phi(n)$ for all natural numbers n by considering how a natural number is constructed. Although there are infinitely many natural numbers, they are constructed in just two ways:

0 is a number.
If k is a number then so is $k + 1$.

Strictly speaking, we should introduce the successor function *suc* and reformulate the above:

If k is a number then so is $suc(k)$.

Addition and other arithmetic functions are then defined recursively in terms of 0 and *suc*, which are essentially the constructors of an ML datatype. **Structural induction** is a generalization of mathematical induction to datatypes such as lists and trees.

6.4   *Structural induction on lists*

Suppose $\phi(xs)$ is a property that we would like to prove for all lists xs. Let xs have type α *list* for some type α. To prove $\phi(xs)$ by structural induction, it suffices to prove two premises:

The base case is $\phi([\,])$.

The induction step is that $\phi(ys)$ implies $\phi(y :: ys)$ for all y of type α and ys of type α *list*. The induction hypothesis is $\phi(ys)$.

The rule can be displayed as follows:

$$\frac{\phi([\,]) \quad \overset{[\phi(ys)]}{\phi(y :: ys)}}{\phi(xs)} \qquad \text{proviso: } y \text{ and } ys \text{ must not occur in other assumptions of } \phi(y :: ys).$$

Why is structural induction sound? We have $\phi([\,])$ by the base case. Therefore, by the induction step, we have $\phi([y])$ for all y; the conclusion holds for all 1-element lists. Using the induction step again, the conclusion holds for all 2-element lists. Continuing this process, the conclusion $\phi(xs)$ holds for every n-element list xs; all lists are reached eventually. The rule can also be justified by mathematical induction on the length of the list.

To illustrate the rule, let us prove a fundamental property of lists.

Theorem 7 *No list equals its own tail.*

Proof The statement of the theorem can be formalized as follows:

$$\forall x \,.\, x :: xs \neq xs$$

This is proved by structural induction on the list xs.

The base case, $\forall x \,.\, [x] \neq [\,]$, is trivial by the definition of equality on lists. Two lists are equal if they have the same length and the corresponding elements are equal.

In the induction step, assume the induction hypothesis

$$\forall x \,.\, x :: ys \neq ys$$

and show (for arbitrary y and ys)

$$\forall x \,.\, x :: (y :: ys) \neq y :: ys.$$

By the definition of list equality, it is enough to show that the tails differ: to show $y :: ys \neq ys$. This follows by the induction hypothesis, putting y for the quantified variable x. Again, the quantifier in the induction formula is essential. ∎

This theorem does not apply to infinite lists, for $[1,1,1,\ldots]$ equals its own tail. The structural induction rules given here are sound for finite objects only. In domain theory, induction can be extended to infinite lists — but not for arbitrary formulae! The restrictions are complicated; roughly speaking, the conclusion holds for infinite lists only if the induction formula is a conjunction of equations. So $x :: xs \neq xs$ cannot be proved for infinite lists.

We shall prove some facts about the following list functions of Chapter 3. Each of these functions terminates for all arguments because each recursive call involves a shorter list.

The length of a list:

```
fun nlength []     = 0
  | nlength (x::xs) = 1 + nlength xs;
```

The infix operator @, which appends two lists:

```
fun []       @ ys = ys
  | (x::xs) @ ys = x :: (xs@ys);
```

The naïve reverse function:

```
fun nrev []     = []
  | nrev (x::xs) = (nrev xs) @ [x];
```

An efficient reverse function:

```
fun revto ([],   ys) = ys
  | revto (x::xs,ys) = revto (xs, x::ys);
```

Length and append. Here is an obvious property about the length of the concatenation of two lists.

Theorem 8 *For all lists xs and ys,*

$$nlength(xs \;@\; ys) = nlength\ xs + nlength\ ys$$

Proof By structural induction on xs. We avoid renaming this variable; thus, the above formula also serves as the induction hypothesis.

The base case is

$$nlength([] \;@\; ys) = nlength[] + nlength\ ys.$$

This holds because

$$
\begin{aligned}
nlength([] \;@\; ys) &= nlength\ ys & \text{[@]}\\
&= 0 + nlength\ ys & \text{[arithmetic]}\\
&= nlength[] + nlength\ ys. & \text{[nlength]}
\end{aligned}
$$

For the induction step, assume the induction hypothesis and show, for all x and xs, that

$$nlength((x :: xs) @ ys) = nlength(x :: xs) + nlength\ ys.$$

This holds because

$$
\begin{aligned}
&nlength((x :: xs) @ ys) \\
&= nlength(x :: (xs @ ys)) && [@] \\
&= 1 + nlength(xs @ ys) && [nlength] \\
&= 1 + (nlength\ xs + nlength\ ys) && [\text{ind hyp}] \\
&= (1 + nlength\ xs) + nlength\ ys && [\text{associativity}] \\
&= nlength(x :: xs) + nlength\ ys. && [nlength]
\end{aligned}
$$

We could have written $1 + nlength\ xs + nlength\ ys$, omitting parentheses, instead of applying the associative law explicitly. ∎

The proof brings out the correspondence between inserting the list elements and counting them. Induction on xs works because the base case and induction step can be simplified using function definitions. Induction on ys leads nowhere: try it.

Efficient list reversal. The function *nrev* is a mathematical definition of list reversal, while *revto* reverses lists efficiently. The proof that they are equivalent is similar to Theorem 4, the correctness of *facti*. In both proofs, the induction formula is universally quantified over an accumulating argument.

Theorem 9 *For every list xs, $\forall ys\,.\,revto(xs, ys) = nrev(xs) @ ys$.*
Proof By structural induction on xs, taking the above formula as the induction hypothesis. The base case is

$$\forall ys\,.\,revto([], ys) = nrev[]\,@\,ys.$$

It holds because

$$revto([], ys) = ys = []\,@\,ys = nrev[]\,@\,ys.$$

The induction step is to show, for arbitrary x and xs, the formula

$$\forall ys\,.\,revto(x :: xs, ys) = nrev(x :: xs)\,@\,ys.$$

Simplifying the right side of the equality yields

$$nrev(x :: xs)\,@\,ys = (nrev(xs)\,@\,[x])\,@\,ys. \qquad\qquad [nrev]$$

Simplifying the left side yields

$$revto(x :: xs, ys) = revto(xs, x :: ys) \qquad\qquad [revto]$$
$$= nrev(xs) \,@\, (x :: ys) \qquad\qquad [\text{ind hyp}]$$
$$= nrev(xs) \,@\, ([x] \,@\, ys). \qquad\qquad [@]$$

The induction hypothesis is applied with $x :: xs$ for the quantified variable ys.

Are we finished? Not quite: the parentheses do not agree. It remains to show

$$nrev(xs) \,@\, ([x] \,@\, ys) = (nrev(xs) \,@\, [x]) \,@\, ys.$$

This formula looks more complicated than the one we set out to prove. How shall we proceed? Observe that the formula is a special case of something simple and plausible: that @ is associative. We have only to prove

$$l_1 \,@\, (l_2 \,@\, l_3) = (l_1 \,@\, l_2) \,@\, l_3.$$

This routine induction is left as an exercise.   ∎

It would be tidier to prove each theorem in the correct order, making a flawless presentation. This example attempts to show how the need for a theorem is discovered. The hardest problem in a verification is recognizing what properties ought to be proved. The need here for the associative law may be obvious — but not if we are dazzled by the symbols, which happens all too easily.

Append and reverse. We now prove a relationship involving list concatenation and reversal.

Theorem 10   *For all lists xs and ys,*

$$nrev(xs \,@\, ys) = nrev\ ys \,@\, nrev\ xs.$$

Proof   By structural induction on xs. The base case is

$$nrev([] \,@\, ys) = nrev\ ys \,@\, nrev[].$$

This holds using the lemma $l \,@\, [] = l$, which is left as an exercise. The induction step is

$$nrev((x :: xs) \,@\, ys) = nrev\ ys \,@\, nrev(x :: xs).$$

This holds because
$$nrev((x :: xs) @ ys)$$
$$= nrev(x :: (xs @ ys)) \qquad [@]$$
$$= nrev(xs @ ys) @ [x] \qquad [nrev]$$
$$= nrev\ ys @ nrev\ xs @ [x] \qquad [\text{ind hyp}]$$
$$= nrev\ ys @ nrev(x :: xs). \qquad [nrev]$$
In $nrev\ ys @ nrev\ xs @ [x]$ we have implicitly applied the associativity of @ by omitting parentheses. ∎

These last two theorems show that *nrev*, though inefficient to compute, is a good specification of reversal. It permits simple proofs. A literal specification, like
$$reverse[x_1, x_2, \ldots, x_n] = [x_n, \ldots, x_2, x_1]\,,$$
would be most difficult to formalize. The function *revto* is not a good specification either; its performance is irrelevant and it is too complicated. Similarly, *nlength* is a good specification of the length of a list.

Exercise 6.7 Prove $xs @ [] = xs$ for every list xs, by structural induction.

Exercise 6.8 Prove $l_1 @ (l_2 @ l_3) = (l_1 @ l_2) @ l_3$ for all lists l_1, l_2 and l_3, by structural induction.

Exercise 6.9 Prove $nrev(nrev\ xs) = xs$ for every list xs.

Exercise 6.10 Show that $nlength\ xs = length\ xs$ for every list xs. (The function *length* was defined in Chapter 3.)

6.5   *Structural induction on trees*
In Chapter 4 we studied binary trees defined as follows:
```
datatype 'a tree = Lf
              | Br of 'a * 'a tree * 'a tree;
```
Binary trees admit a form of structural induction. In most respects, their treatment resembles that of lists. Suppose $\phi(t)$ is a property of trees, where t has type α *tree*. To prove $\phi(t)$ by structural induction, it suffices to prove two premises:

The base case is $\phi(Lf)$.
The induction step is to show that $\phi(t_1)$ and $\phi(t_2)$ imply $\phi(Br(x, t_1, t_2))$ for all x of type α and t_1, t_2 of type α *tree*. There are two induction hypotheses: $\phi(t_1)$ and $\phi(t_2)$.

The rule can be portrayed thus:

$$\frac{\phi(Lf) \qquad \phi(Br(x,t_1,t_2))}{\phi(t)} \quad \frac{[\phi(t_1),\ \phi(t_2)]}{}$$

proviso: x, t_1 and t_2 must not occur in other assumptions of $\phi(Br(x,t_1,t_2))$.

This structural induction rule is sound because it covers all the ways of building a tree. The base case establishes $\phi(Lf)$. Applying the induction step once establishes $\phi(Br(x,Lf,Lf))$ for all x, covering all trees containing one Br node. Applying the induction step twice establishes $\phi(t)$ where t is any tree containing two Br nodes. Further applications of the induction step cover larger trees.

We can also justify the rule by complete induction on the number of labels in the tree, because every tree is finite and its subtrees are smaller than itself. Structural induction is not sound in general for infinite trees.

We shall prove some facts about the following functions on binary trees, from Chapter 4.

The number of labels in a tree:
```
fun count Lf          = 0
  | count (Br(v,t1,t2)) = 1 + count t1 + count t2;
```

The depth of a tree:
```
fun depth Lf          = 0
  | depth (Br(v,t1,t2)) = 1 + maxl[depth t1, depth t2];
```

Reflection of a tree:
```
fun reflect Lf          = Lf
  | reflect (Br(v,t1,t2)) = Br(v, reflect t2, reflect t1);
```

The preorder listing of a tree's labels:
```
fun preorder Lf          = []
  | preorder (Br(v,t1,t2)) = [v] @ preorder t1 @ preorder t2;
```

The postorder listing of a tree's labels:
```
fun postorder Lf          = []
  | postorder (Br(v,t1,t2)) = postorder t1 @ postorder t2 @ [v];
```

Double reflection. We begin with an easy example: reflecting a tree twice yields the original tree.

Theorem 11 *For every binary tree t, reflect(reflect t) = t.*
Proof By structural induction on t. The base case is

$$reflect(reflect\ Lf) = Lf.$$

This holds by the definition of *reflect*:

$$reflect(reflect\ Lf) = reflect\ Lf = Lf$$

For the induction step we have the two induction hypotheses

$$reflect(reflect\ t_1) = t_1 \quad \text{and} \quad reflect(reflect\ t_2) = t_2$$

and must show

$$reflect(reflect(Br(x, t_1, t_2))) = Br(x, t_1, t_2).$$

Simplifying,

$$reflect(reflect(Br(x, t_1, t_2)))$$
$$= reflect(Br(x, reflect\ t_2, reflect\ t_1)) \qquad [reflect]$$
$$= Br(x, reflect(reflect\ t_1), reflect(reflect\ t_2)) \qquad [reflect]$$
$$= Br(x, t_1, reflect(reflect\ t_2)) \qquad [ind\ hyp]$$
$$= Br(x, t_1, t_2). \qquad [ind\ hyp]$$

Both induction hypotheses have been applied. We can observe the two calls of *reflect* cancelling each other. ∎

Preorder and postorder. If the concepts of preorder and postorder are obscure to you, then the following theorem may help. A key fact is Theorem 10, concerning *nrev* and @, which we have recently proved.

Theorem 12 *For every binary tree t,*

$$postorder(reflect\ t) = nrev(preorder\ t).$$

Proof By structural induction on t. The base case is

$$postorder(reflect\ Lf) = nrev(preorder\ Lf).$$

This is routine; both sides are equal to $[]$.

For the induction step we have the induction hypotheses

$$postorder(reflect\ t_1) = nrev(preorder\ t_1)$$
$$postorder(reflect\ t_2) = nrev(preorder\ t_2)$$

and must show

$$postorder(reflect(Br(x, t_1, t_2)))$$
$$= nrev(preorder(Br(x, t_1, t_2))).$$

First, we simplify the right hand side:

$$nrev(preorder(Br(x, t_1, t_2)))$$
$$= nrev([x] \mathbin{@} preorder\ t_1 \mathbin{@} preorder\ t_2) \qquad [preorder]$$
$$= nrev(preorder\ t_2) \mathbin{@}$$
$$\qquad nrev(preorder\ t_1) \mathbin{@} nrev[x] \qquad [\text{Theorem 10}]$$
$$= nrev(preorder\ t_2) \mathbin{@} nrev(preorder\ t_1) \mathbin{@} [x] \qquad [nrev]$$

Some steps have been skipped. Theorem 10 has been applied twice, to both occurrences of @, and $nrev[x]$ is simplified directly to $[x]$.

Now we simplify the left hand side:

$$postorder(reflect(Br(x, t_1, t_2)))$$
$$= postorder(Br(x, reflect\ t_2, reflect\ t_1)) \qquad [reflect]$$
$$= postorder(reflect\ t_2) \mathbin{@}$$
$$\qquad postorder(reflect\ t_1) \mathbin{@} [x] \qquad [postorder]$$
$$= nrev(preorder\ t_2) \mathbin{@} nrev(preorder\ t_1) \mathbin{@} [x] \qquad [\text{ind hyp}]$$

Thus, both sides are equal. ∎

Count and depth. We now prove a law relating the number of labels in a binary tree to its depth. The theorem is an inequality, reminding us that formal methods involve more than mere equations.

Theorem 13 *For every binary tree t, count $t \le 2^{depth\ t} - 1$.*
Proof By structural induction on t. The base case is

$$count\ Lf \le 2^{depth\ Lf} - 1.$$

It holds because

$$count\ Lf = 0 = 2^0 - 1 = 2^{depth\ Lf} - 1.$$

In the induction step the induction hypotheses are

$$count\ t_1 \le 2^{depth\ t_1} - 1 \quad \text{and} \quad count\ t_2 \le 2^{depth\ t_2} - 1$$

and we must demonstrate

$$count(Br(x, t_1, t_2)) \le 2^{depth(Br(x,t_1,t_2))} - 1.$$

First, simplify the right hand side:

$$2^{depth(Br(x,t_1,t_2))} - 1$$
$$= 2^{1+maxl[depth\ t_1, depth\ t_2]} - 1 \qquad [depth]$$
$$= 2 \times 2^{maxl[depth\ t_1, depth\ t_2]} - 1 \qquad [arithmetic]$$

Next, show that the left side is less than or equal to this:

$$count\,(Br(x, t_1, t_2))$$
$$= 1 + count\ t_1 + count\ t_2 \qquad\qquad [count]$$
$$\leq 1 + (2^{depth\ t_1} - 1) + (2^{depth\ t_2} - 1) \qquad\qquad [\text{ind hyp}]$$
$$= 2^{depth\ t_1} + 2^{depth\ t_2} - 1 \qquad\qquad [\text{arithmetic}]$$
$$\leq 2 \times 2^{\max\{depth\ t_1, depth\ t_2\}} - 1 \qquad\qquad [\text{arithmetic}]$$

We have a slight problem: max is the mathematical function for the maximum of a set, while *maxl* is an ML function on lists. The proof depends on their equivalence, or at least the special case $maxl[k_1, k_2] = \max\{k_1, k_2\}$, which is left as an exercise. ∎

It is usual to present this result as a mathematical property of trees, with *depth* and *count* as mathematical functions. The question of whether *maxl* really computes the maximum therefore does not arise. We should remember that ML is a programming language, not a notation for mathematics. Sets are not available in ML. The greatest element of a set is imperfectly expressed using lists. For instance, infinite sets are beyond reach — how could an ML function compute the maximum of an infinite list? Programming and pure mathematics are difficult to combine into one formal framework.

Problematical datatypes. Our simple methods do not admit all ML datatypes. Consider this declaration:

```
datatype lambda = F of lambda -> lambda;
```

The mathematics in this chapter is based on set theory. Since there is no set A that is isomorphic to the set of functions $A \to A$, we can make no sense of this declaration. In domain theory, this declaration can be interpreted because there is a domain D isomorphic to $D \to D$, which is the domain of **continuous** functions from D to D. Even in domain theory, no induction rule useful for reasoning about D is known. This is because the type definition involves recursion to the left of the function arrow ($\to$). We shall not consider datatypes involving functions.

The definition of type *term*, in Chapter 5, refers to lists:

```
datatype term = Var of string
              | Fun of string * term list;
```

Type *term* denotes a set of finite terms and satisfies a structural induction rule, but the rule is complicated by the involvement of lists in the type. Proofs are correspondingly messy.

Exercise 6.11   Formalize and prove: *No binary tree equals its own left subtree.*

Exercise 6.12   Prove *count*(*reflect t*) = *count t* for every binary tree *t*.

Exercise 6.13   Prove *nlength*(*preorder t*) = *count t* for every binary tree *t*.

Exercise 6.14   Prove *nrev*(*inorder*(*reflect t*)) = *inorder t* for every binary tree *t*.

Exercise 6.15   Define a function *leaves* to count the *Lf* nodes in a binary tree. Then prove *leaves t* = *count t* + 1 for all *t*.

Exercise 6.16   Verify the function *preord* of Chapter 4. In other words, prove *preord*(*t*, []) = *preorder t* for every binary tree *t*.

6.6   *Function values and functionals*

Our mathematical methods extend directly to proofs about higher-order functions (functionals). The notion of 'functions as values' is familiar to mathematicians. In set theory, for example, functions are sets and are treated no differently from other sets.

We can prove many facts about functionals without using any additional rules. The laws of the λ-calculus could be introduced for reasoning about ML's **fn** notation, although this will not be done here. Our methods, needless to say, apply only to pure functions — not to ML functions with side-effects.

Equality of functions. The **law of extensionality** can now be introduced. It states that functions f and g are equal if $f(x) = g(x)$ for all x (of suitable type). For instance, these three doubling functions are extensionally equal:

```
fun double1(n) = 2*n;
fun double2(n) = n*2;
fun double3(n) = (n-1)+(n+1);
```

The extensionality law is valid because the only operation that can be performed on an ML function is application to an argument.

Replacing f by g, if these functions are extensionally equal, does not affect the value of any application of f.*

A different concept of equality, called **intensional equality**, regards two functions as equal only if their definitions are identical. Our three doubling functions are all distinct under intensional equality. This concept resembles function equality in Lisp, where a function value is a piece of Lisp code that can be taken apart.

There is no general, computable method of testing whether two functions are extensionally equal. Therefore ML has no equality test for function values. Lisp tests equality of functions by comparing their internal representations.

We now prove a few statements about the following functions, which are reproduced from Chapter 5.

Function composition:

```
infix o;
fun (f o g) x = f (g x);
```

The functional *map*:

```
fun map f []        = []
  | map f (x::xs) = (f x) :: map f xs;
```

The associativity of composition. Our first theorem is trivial. It asserts that function composition is associative.

Theorem 14 *For all functions f, g and h (of appropriate type),*

$$(f \circ g) \circ h = f \circ (g \circ h).$$

Proof By the law of extensionality, it is enough to show

$$((f \circ g) \circ h)\, x = (f \circ (g \circ h))\, x$$

for all x. This holds because

$$
\begin{aligned}
((f \circ g) \circ h)\, x &= (f \circ g)(h\, x) \\
&= f(g(h\, x)) \\
&= f((g \circ h)\, x) \\
&= (f \circ (g \circ h))\, x.
\end{aligned}
$$

Each step holds by the definition of composition. ∎

---

* The extensionality law relies on our global assumption that functions terminate. ML distinguishes $\perp$ (the undefined function value) from $\lambda x.\perp$ (the function that never terminates when applied) although both functions yield $\perp$ when applied to any argument.

As stated, the theorem holds only for functions of appropriate type; the equation must be properly typed. Typing restrictions apply to all our theorems and will not be mentioned again.

The list functional map. Functionals enjoy many laws. Programs can be expressed using functionals for clarity, then transformed into more efficient programs. Here is a theorem about *map* and composition.

Theorem 15   *For all functions f and g,*

$$(map\ f) \circ (map\ g) = map\ (f \circ g).$$

Proof   By the extensionality law, this equality holds if

$$((map\ f) \circ (map\ g))\ xs = map\ (f \circ g)\ xs$$

for all xs. Using the definition of $\circ$, this can be simplified to

$$map\ f\ (map\ g\ xs) = map\ (f \circ g)\ xs$$

Since xs is a list, we may use structural induction. This formula will also be our induction hypothesis. The base case is

$$map\ f\ (map\ g\ []) = map\ (f \circ g)\ [].$$

It holds because both sides equal $[]$:

$$map\ f\ (map\ g\ []) = map\ f\ [] = [] = map\ (f \circ g)\ []$$

For the induction step, we assume the induction hypothesis and show (for arbitrary x and xs)

$$map\ f\ (map\ g\ (x :: xs)) = map\ (f \circ g)\ (x :: xs).$$

Straightforward reasoning yields

$$
\begin{aligned}
map\ f\ &(map\ g\ (x :: xs)) \\
&= map\ f\ ((g\ x) :: (map\ g\ xs)) && [map] \\
&= f(g\ x) :: (map\ f\ (map\ g\ xs)) && [map] \\
&= f(g\ x) :: (map\ (f \circ g)\ xs) && [\text{ind hyp}] \\
&= (f \circ g)(x) :: (map\ (f \circ g)\ xs) && [\circ] \\
&= map\ (f \circ g)\ (x :: xs). && [map]
\end{aligned}
$$

Despite the presence of function values, this proof is a routine structural induction. ∎

Exercise 6.17   Prove $map\ f\ (xs\ @\ ys) = (map\ f\ xs)\ @\ (map\ f\ ys)$.

Exercise 6.18   Prove $(map\ f) \circ nrev = nrev \circ (map\ f)$.

Exercise 6.19   Prove $foldright\ (\mathbf{op}\ ::)\ (xs, ys) = xs\ @\ ys$.

Exercise 6.20 Define a functional *maptree* on binary trees, satisfying the following equations (which you should prove):

$$(maptree\ f) \circ reflect = reflect \circ (maptree\ f)$$
$$(map\ f) \circ preorder = preorder \circ (maptree\ f)$$

A general induction principle

In a proof by structural induction on lists, we assume $\phi(xs)$ and show $\phi(x :: xs)$. Typically the induction formula involves a recursive list function such as *nrev*. The induction hypothesis, $\phi(xs)$, says something about $nrev(xs)$. Since $nrev(x :: xs)$ is defined in terms of $nrev(xs)$, we can deduce something about $nrev(x :: xs)$ to show $\phi(x :: xs)$.

Many list functions, like *nrev*, make their recursive calls on the tail of the list. This kind of recursion is called **structural recursion** by analogy with structural induction. However, other forms of recursion are also common. The function *maxl*, when applied to $m :: n :: ns$, calls itself on $m :: ns$ if $n < m$. Quick sort and merge sort divide a list into two smaller lists and sort these recursively. Matrix transpose and Gaussian elimination (as defined in Chapter 3 on lists of lists) make recursive calls on a submatrix with rows and columns deleted.

Most functions on trees are defined by structural recursion; their recursive calls involve a node's immediate subtrees. The function *nnf*, which converts a proposition into Negation Normal Form, is not structurally recursive. We shall prove theorems about *nnf* in this section.

Structural induction works best with functions that are structurally recursive. With other functions, **well-founded induction** is often superior. Well-founded induction is a powerful generalization of complete induction. Because the rule is abstract and seldom required in full generality, our proofs will be done by a special case: induction on size. For instance, the function *nlength* formalizes the size of a list. In the induction step we have to prove $\phi(xs)$ under the induction hypothesis

$$\forall ys\ .\ nlength\ ys < nlength\ xs \to \phi(ys).$$

Thus, we may assume $\phi(ys)$ provided ys is a shorter list than xs.

6.7   *Some proofs about foldleft*

The functional *foldleft* applies a 2-argument function over the elements of a list. Recall its definition from Chapter 5:

```
fun foldleft f (e, [])    = e
  | foldleft f (e, x::xs) = foldleft f (f(e,x), xs);
```

Although *foldleft* is defined by structural recursion — it is recursive in the tail of the list — structural induction seems inappropriate for proving the following theorem.

Theorem 16   *Suppose* $\oplus$ *is an infix operator that is associative and has right identity* e; *that is, for all* x, y *and* z,

$$x \oplus (y \oplus z) = (x \oplus y) \oplus z$$

$$x \oplus e = x.$$

Then for all y *and* xs,

$$y \oplus foldleft\ (\mathbf{op}\oplus)\ (e, xs) = foldleft\ (\mathbf{op}\oplus)\ (y, xs).$$

To see informally why this theorem holds, consider that if $xs = [x_1, x_2, \ldots, x_n]$ then it asserts

$$y \oplus (\cdots ((e \oplus x_1) \oplus x_2) \cdots \oplus x_n) = ((y \oplus x_1) \oplus x_2) \cdots \oplus x_n.$$

Since $\oplus$ is associative, we may erase the parentheses. Then, replacing $y \oplus e$ by y reduces both sides to $y \oplus x_1 \oplus x_2 \cdots \oplus x_n$.

We can see the notational advantage of working with an infix operator $\oplus$ instead of a function f. But the above 'proof' is rather sloppy. A proper proof must use induction.

Structural induction avails us little, however, since the induction step assumes

$$y \oplus foldleft\ (\mathbf{op}\oplus)\ (e, xs) = foldleft\ (\mathbf{op}\oplus)\ (y, xs)$$

and asks to show

$$y \oplus foldleft\ (\mathbf{op}\oplus)\ (e, x :: xs) = foldleft\ (\mathbf{op}\oplus)\ (y, x :: xs).$$

This simplifies to

$$y \oplus foldleft\ (\mathbf{op}\oplus)\ (e \oplus x, xs) = foldleft\ (\mathbf{op}\oplus)\ (y \oplus x, xs).$$

The induction hypothesis does not seem of any use, because e has changed to $e \oplus x$. Previously we solved such problems using a quantified induction formula. Quantification over e is impossible, however, because e is a constant: the identity element of $\oplus$.

At such an impasse, it is wise to study the informal proof. (Before you can prove something formally, you need to understand why it is true!) Imagine how the nested applications of $\oplus$ are regrouped, one by one. Regrouping can begin at the left or at the right; either way we obtain a valid proof.

Regrouping from the left replaces $(e \oplus x_1) \oplus x_2$ by $e \oplus (x_1 \oplus x_2)$ and $(y \oplus x_1) \oplus x_2$ by $y \oplus (x_1 \oplus x_2)$. Taking $x_1 \oplus x_2$ as a single element eliminates x_1 and x_2, reducing the number of elements by one. The step can be repeated. This argument corresponds to an induction on the length of the list. We now can prove Theorem 16.

Proof By induction on the length of the list xs in

$$y \oplus foldleft\,(\mathsf{op}\oplus)\,(e, xs) = foldleft\,(\mathsf{op}\oplus)\,(y, xs).$$

To obtain induction hypotheses, we may replace xs by any shorter list. Consider three cases:

If $xs = []$ then both sides of the equation equal y.

If $xs = [x]$ then both sides of the equation equal $y \oplus x$.

If $xs = x_1 :: x_2 :: ws$ then we must prove

$$y \oplus foldleft\,(\mathsf{op}\oplus)\,(e, x_1 :: x_2 :: ws)$$
$$= foldleft\,(\mathsf{op}\oplus)\,(y, x_1 :: x_2 :: ws).$$

First, use the definition of *foldleft* forwards and backwards:

$$
\begin{aligned}
&y \oplus foldleft\,(\mathsf{op}\oplus)\,(e, x_1 :: x_2 :: ws) \\
&= y \oplus foldleft\,(\mathsf{op}\oplus)\,(e \oplus x_1, x_2 :: ws) && [foldleft] \\
&= y \oplus foldleft\,(\mathsf{op}\oplus)\,((e \oplus x_1) \oplus x_2, ws) && [foldleft] \\
&= y \oplus foldleft\,(\mathsf{op}\oplus)\,(e \oplus (x_1 \oplus x_2), ws) && [\text{associativity}] \\
&= y \oplus foldleft\,(\mathsf{op}\oplus)\,(e, (x_1 \oplus x_2) :: ws) && [foldleft]
\end{aligned}
$$

Since $(x_1 \oplus x_2) :: ws$ is a shorter list than $x_1 :: x_2 :: ws$, it satisfies an induction hypothesis.

$$
\begin{aligned}
&= foldleft\,(\mathsf{op}\oplus)\,(y, (x_1 \oplus x_2) :: ws) && [\text{ind hyp}] \\
&= foldleft\,(\mathsf{op}\oplus)\,(y \oplus (x_1 \oplus x_2), ws) && [foldleft] \\
&= foldleft\,(\mathsf{op}\oplus)\,((y \oplus x_1) \oplus x_2, ws) && [\text{associativity}] \\
&= foldleft\,(\mathsf{op}\oplus)\,(y \oplus x_1, x_2 :: ws) && [foldleft] \\
&= foldleft\,(\mathsf{op}\oplus)\,(y, x_1 :: x_2 :: ws) && [foldleft]
\end{aligned}
$$

Using the associativity of $\oplus$ corresponds to an algorithm for regrouping the parentheses. ∎

The proof above performs regrouping from the left. To obtain an alternative proof, we regroup from the right, replacing

$$y \oplus ((\cdots (e \oplus x_1) \cdots) \oplus x_n) \quad \text{by} \quad (y \oplus (\cdots (e \oplus x_1) \cdots)) \oplus x_n.$$

Repeated replacements push the y inside until it collides with the e. Then $y \oplus e$ is replaced by y. To formalize the argument, we shall need the following facts about *foldleft*.

Theorem 17   *For every function f and all xs, ys and z,*

$$foldleft\ f\ (z, xs\ @\ ys) = foldleft\ f\ (foldleft\ f\ (z, xs), ys)$$

Proof   This is a routine induction, and is left as an exercise.   ∎

Theorem 18   *For every function f and all xs, x and z,*

$$foldleft\ f\ (z, xs\ @\ [x]) = f(foldleft\ f\ (z, xs), x)$$

Proof   By the previous theorem and the definition of *foldleft*.   ∎

Using this fact, which is reminiscent of the definition of *foldright*, we again prove Theorem 16.

Proof   We again employ induction on the length of xs in

$$y \oplus foldleft\ (\mathbf{op}\oplus)\ (e, xs) = foldleft\ (\mathbf{op}\oplus)\ (y, xs)$$

and assume induction hypotheses replacing xs by any shorter list. We now consider only two cases.

If $xs = []$ then both sides of the equation equal y.

If $xs = ws\ @\ [x]$ then we must prove

$$y \oplus foldleft\ (\mathbf{op}\oplus)\ (e, ws\ @\ [x]) = foldleft\ (\mathbf{op}\oplus)\ (y, ws\ @\ [x]).$$

This holds because

$$
\begin{aligned}
& y \oplus foldleft\ (\mathbf{op}\oplus)\ (e, ws\ @\ [x]) && \\
&= y \oplus (foldleft\ (\mathbf{op}\oplus)\ (e, ws) \oplus x) && \text{[Theorem 18]} \\
&= (y \oplus foldleft\ (\mathbf{op}\oplus)\ (e, ws)) \oplus x && \text{[associativity]} \\
&= foldleft\ (\mathbf{op}\oplus)\ (y, ws) \oplus x && \text{[ind hyp]} \\
&= foldleft\ (\mathbf{op}\oplus)\ (y, ws\ @\ [x]). && \text{[Theorem 18]}
\end{aligned}
$$

In the induction hypothesis, ws is shorter than $ws\ @\ [x]$.   ∎

As we can see from this example, structural induction may not be appropriate even for reasoning about a function that is structurally recursive. By studying informal proofs of the theorem, we have obtained two distinct formal proofs.

Exercise 6.21   (Guy Cousineau.) There is indeed a direct proof of Theorem 17 by structural induction if $\forall y$ is prefixed to the induction formula. Find this proof.

Exercise 6.22   Prove

$$foldright\ f\ (xs\ @\ ys, z) = foldright\ f\ (xs, foldright\ f\ (ys, z)).$$

Exercise 6.23 Suppose that $\odot$ satisfies, for all x, y and z,

$$x \odot (y \odot z) = (x \odot y) \odot z \quad \text{and} \quad e \odot x = x.$$

Prove that for all y and xs,

$$foldright\,(op\odot)\,(xs, e) \odot y = foldright\,(op\odot)\,(xs, y).$$

Exercise 6.24 Define the function h by

$$h(xs) = foldright\,f\,(xs, e)$$

and show

$$foldright\,(foldright\,f)\,(xss, e) = foldright\,f\,(map\,h\,xss, e).$$

Exercise 6.25 (Mike Fourman.) Suppose that $\oplus$ is associative, satisfying $x \oplus (y \oplus z) = (x \oplus y) \oplus z$ for all x, y and z. Prove that, for all y, z and xs,

$$y \oplus foldleft\,(op\oplus)\,(z, xs) = foldleft\,(op\oplus)\,(y \oplus z, xs).$$

Use this result to prove Theorem 16.

6.8 *Computing normal forms*

The tautology checker of Chapter 4 contains functions to compute certain normal forms of propositions. Because these functions involve unusual recursions, structural induction seems inappropriate. First, let us recall some definitions.

The definition of *prop*, the datatype of propositions, is

```
datatype prop = Atom of string
        | Neg   of prop
        | Conj of prop * prop
        | Disj of prop * prop;
```

Function *nnf* computes the Negation Normal Form of a proposition. It is practically a literal rendering of the rewrite rules for this normal form, and has complex patterns.

```
fun nnf (Atom a)          = Atom a
  | nnf (Neg (Atom a))    = Neg (Atom a)
  | nnf (Neg (Neg p))     = nnf p
  | nnf (Neg (Conj(p,q))) = nnf(Disj(Neg p, Neg q))
  | nnf (Neg (Disj(p,q))) = nnf(Conj(Neg p, Neg q))
  | nnf (Conj(p,q))       = Conj(nnf p, nnf q)
  | nnf (Disj(p,q))       = Disj(nnf p, nnf q);
```

The mutually recursive functions *nnfpos* and *nnfneg* compute the same normal form, but more efficiently:

```
fun nnfpos (Atom a)      = Atom a
  | nnfpos (Neg p)       = nnfneg p
  | nnfpos (Conj(p,q))   = Conj(nnfpos p, nnfpos q)
  | nnfpos (Disj(p,q))   = Disj(nnfpos p, nnfpos q)
and nnfneg (Atom a)      = Neg (Atom a)
  | nnfneg (Neg p)       = nnfpos p
  | nnfneg (Conj(p,q))   = Disj(nnfneg p, nnfneg q)
  | nnfneg (Disj(p,q))   = Conj(nnfneg p, nnfneg q);
```

We must verify that these functions terminate. The functions *nnfpos* and *nnfneg* are structurally recursive — recursion is always applied to an immediate constituent of the argument — and therefore terminate. For *nnf*, termination is not so obvious. Consider $nnf(Neg(Conj(p,q)))$, which makes a recursive call on a large expression. But this reduces in a few steps to

$$Disj(nnf(Neg\ p), nnf(Neg\ q)).$$

So the recursive calls after $Neg(Conj(p,q))$ involve the smaller propositions $Neg\ p$ and $Neg\ q$. The other complicated pattern, $Neg(Disj(p,q))$, behaves similarly. In every case, recursive computations in *nnf* involve smaller and smaller propositions, and therefore terminate.

Let us prove that *nnfpos* and *nnf* are equal. The termination argument suggests that theorems involving *nnf p* should be proved by induction on the size of p. Let us write $nodes(p)$ for the number of *Neg*, *Conj* and *Disj* nodes in p. This function can easily be coded in ML.

Theorem 19   *For all propositions p, nnf p = nnfpos p.*
Proof   By mathematical induction on $nodes(p)$, taking as induction hypotheses $nnf\ q = nnfpos\ q$ for all q such that $nodes(q) < nodes(p)$. We consider seven cases, corresponding to the definition of *nnf*.

If $p = Atom\ a$ then

$$nnf(Atom\ a) = Atom\ a = nnfpos(Atom\ a).$$

If $p = Neg(Atom\ a)$ then $nnf(Neg(Atom\ a))$

$$= Neg(Atom\ a) = nnfpos(Neg(Atom\ a)).$$

If $p = Conj(r, q)$ then

$\quad nnf(Conj(r, q))$

$\quad\quad = Conj(nnf\ r, nnf\ q)$ \hfill [*nnf*]

$\quad\quad = Conj(nnfpos\ r, nnfpos\ q)$ \hfill [ind hyp]

$\quad\quad = nnfpos(Conj(r, q)).$ \hfill [*nnfpos*]

The case $p = Disj(r, q)$ is similar.

$\quad$If $p = Neg(Conj(r, q))$ then

$\quad nnf(Neg(Conj(r, q)))$

$\quad\quad = nnf(Disj(Neg\ r, Neg\ q))$ \hfill [*nnf*]

$\quad\quad = Disj(nnf(Neg\ r), nnf(Neg\ q))$ \hfill [*nnf*]

$\quad\quad = Disj(nnfpos(Neg\ r), nnfpos(Neg\ q))$ \hfill [ind hyp]

$\quad\quad = nnfneg(Conj(r, q))$ \hfill [*nnfneg*]

$\quad\quad = nnfpos(Neg(Conj(r, q))).$ \hfill [*nnfpos*]

We have induction hypotheses for $Neg\ r$ and $Neg\ q$ because they are smaller, as measured by *nodes*, than $Neg(Conj(r, q))$.

$\quad$The case $p = Neg(Disj(r, q))$ is similar.

$\quad$If $p = Neg(Neg\ r)$ then

$\quad nnf(Neg(Neg\ r))$

$\quad\quad = nnf\ r$ \hfill [*nnf*]

$\quad\quad = nnfpos\ r$ \hfill [ind hyp]

$\quad\quad = nnfneg(Neg\ r)$ \hfill [*nnfneg*]

$\quad\quad = nnfpos(Neg(Neg\ r)).$ \hfill [*nnfpos*]

An induction hypothesis applies since r contains fewer nodes than $Neg(Neg\ r)$. ∎

The Conjunctive Normal Form. We now consider a different question: whether computing the Conjunctive Normal Form preserves the meaning of a proposition. A **truth valuation** for propositions is a predicate that respects the connectives:

$$Tr(Neg\ p) \leftrightarrow \neg Tr(p)$$
$$Tr(Conj(p, q)) \leftrightarrow Tr(p) \wedge Tr(q)$$
$$Tr(Disj(p, q)) \leftrightarrow Tr(p) \vee Tr(q)$$

The predicate is completely determined by its valuation of atoms, $Tr(Atom\ a)$. To show that the normal forms preserve truth for all valuations, we make no assumptions about which atoms are true.

Most of the work of computing Conjunctive Normal Forms is performed by *distrib*:

```
fun distrib (p, Conj(q,r)) = Conj(distrib(p,q), distrib(p,r))
  | distrib (Conj(q,r), p) = Conj(distrib(q,p), distrib(r,p))
  | distrib (p, q)         = Disj(p,q)  (*no conjunctions*);
```

This function is awkward in its case analysis and its recursive calls.

The first two cases overlap if both arguments in $distrib(p, q)$ are conjunctions. Because ML tries the first case before the second, the second case cannot simply be taken as an equation. There seems to be no way of making the cases separate except to write nearly every combination of one *Atom*, *Neg*, *Disj* or *Conj* with another: at least 13 cases seem necessary. To avoid this, take the second case of *distrib* as a conditional equation; if p does not have the form $Conj(p_1, p_2)$ then

$$distrib(Conj(q, r), p) = Conj(distrib(q, p), distrib(r, p)).$$

The computation of $distrib(p, q)$ may make recursive calls affecting either p or q. It terminates because every call reduces the value of $nodes(p) + nodes(q)$. We shall use this measure for induction.

The purpose of $distrib(p, q)$ is to compute a proposition equivalent to $Disj(p, q)$, but in Conjunctive Normal Form. Its correctness can be stated as follows.

Theorem 20   *For all propositions p, q and truth valuations Tr,*
$$Tr(distrib(p, q)) \leftrightarrow Tr(p) \vee Tr(q).$$

Proof   We prove this by induction on $nodes(p) + nodes(q)$. The induction hypothesis is
$$Tr(distrib(p', q')) \leftrightarrow Tr(p') \vee Tr(q')$$
for all p' and q' such that
$$nodes(p') + nodes(q') < nodes(p) + nodes(q).$$
The proof considers the same cases as in the definition of *distrib*.

If $q = Conj(q', r)$ then
$$Tr(distrib(p, Conj(q', r)))$$

$\leftrightarrow Tr(Conj(distrib(p, q'), distrib(p, r)))$ [*distrib*]

$\leftrightarrow Tr(distrib(p, q')) \wedge Tr(distrib(p, r))$ [*Tr*]

$\leftrightarrow (Tr(p) \vee Tr(q')) \wedge (Tr(p) \vee Tr(r))$ [ind hyp]

$\leftrightarrow Tr(p) \vee (Tr(q') \wedge Tr(r))$ [distributive law]

$\leftrightarrow Tr(p) \vee Tr(Conj(q', r)).$ [*Tr*]

The induction hypothesis has been applied twice using these facts:

$$nodes(p) + nodes(q') < nodes(p) + nodes(Conj(q', r))$$
$$nodes(p) + nodes(r) < nodes(p) + nodes(Conj(q', r))$$

We may now assume that q is not a *Conj*. If $p = Conj(p', r)$ then the conclusion follows as in the previous case. If neither p nor q is a *Conj* then

$$Tr(distrib(p, q)) \leftrightarrow Tr(Disj(p, q)) \qquad [distrib]$$
$$\leftrightarrow Tr(p) \lor Tr(q). \qquad [Tr]$$

The conclusion holds in every case. ∎

The proof exploits the distributive law of $\lor$ over $\land$, as might be expected. The overlapping cases in *distrib* do not complicate the proof at all. On the contrary, they permit a concise definition of this function and a simple case analysis.

Exercise 6.26 State and justify a rule for structural induction on values of type *prop*. To demonstrate it, prove the following formula by structural induction on p:

$$nnf\ p = nnfpos\ p \land nnf(Neg\ p) = nnfneg\ p$$

Exercise 6.27 Define a predicate *Isnnf* on propositions such that $Isnnf(p)$ holds exactly when p is in Negation Normal Form. Prove $Isnnf(nnf\ p)$ for every proposition p.

Exercise 6.28 Let Tr be an arbitrary truth valuation for propositions. Prove $Tr(nnf\ p) \leftrightarrow Tr(p)$ for every proposition p.

6.9 *Well-founded induction and recursion*

Our treatment of induction is rigorous enough for the informal proofs we have been performing, but is not formal enough to be automated. Many induction rules can be formally derived from mathematical induction alone. A more uniform approach is to adopt the rule of **well-founded induction**, which includes most other induction rules as instances.

Well-founded relations. The relation $\prec$ is **well-founded** if there exist no infinite decreasing chains

$$\cdots \prec x_n \prec \cdots \prec x_2 \prec x_1.$$

For instance, 'less than' ($<$) on the natural numbers is well-founded. 'Less than' on the integers is not well-founded: there exists the decreasing chain

$$\cdots < -n < \cdots < -2 < -1.$$

'Less than' on the rational numbers is not well-founded either; consider

$$\cdots < \frac{1}{n} < \cdots < \frac{1}{2} < \frac{1}{1}.$$

Observe that we have to state the domain of the relation — the set of values it is defined over — and not simply say that $<$ is well-founded.

Another well-founded relation is the **lexicographic ordering** of pairs of natural numbers, defined by

$$(i',j') \prec_{\text{lex}} (i,j) \quad \text{if and only if} \quad i' < i \lor (i' = i \land j' < j).$$

To see that $\prec_{\text{lex}}$ is well-founded, suppose there is an infinite decreasing chain

$$\cdots \prec_{\text{lex}} (i_n, j_n) \prec_{\text{lex}} \cdots \prec_{\text{lex}} (i_2, j_2) \prec_{\text{lex}} (i_1, j_1).$$

If $(i',j') \prec_{\text{lex}} (i,j)$ then $i' \leq i$. Since $<$ is well-founded on the natural numbers, the decreasing chain

$$\cdots \leq i_n \leq \cdots \leq i_2 \leq i_1$$

reaches some constant value i after say M steps: thus $i_n = i$ for all $n \geq M$. Now consider the strictly decreasing chain

$$\cdots < j_{M+n} < \cdots < j_{M+1} < j_M.$$

This must eventually terminate at some constant value j after say N steps: thus $(i_n, j_n) = (i, j)$ for all $n \geq M + N$. At this point the chain of pairs becomes constant, contradicting our assumption that it was decreasing under $\prec_{\text{lex}}$.

Similar reasoning shows that lexicographic orderings for triples, quadruples and so forth, are well-founded. The lexicographic ordering is not well-founded for lists of natural numbers; it admits an infinite decreasing chain:

$$\cdots \prec [\underbrace{1, 1, \ldots, 1, 2}_{length=n}] \prec \cdots \prec [1, 2] \prec [2]$$

Another sort of well-founded relation is given by a **measure function**. If f is a function into the natural numbers, then there is a well-founded relation $\prec_f$ defined by

$$x \prec_f y \quad \text{if and only if} \quad f(x) < f(y).$$

Clearly, if there were an infinite decreasing chain

$$\cdots \prec_f x_n \prec_f \cdots \prec_f x_2 \prec_f x_1$$

then there would be an infinite decreasing chain

$$\cdots < f(x_n) < \cdots < f(x_2) < f(x_1)$$

in the natural numbers, which is impossible. Here f typically 'measures' the size of something. The well-founded relations $\prec_{nlength}$ and $\prec_{count}$ compare lists and trees by size. Our proof about *distrib* used the measure $nodes(p) + nodes(q)$ on pairs (p, q) of propositions.

The demonstration that $\prec_f$ is well-founded applies just as well if $<$ is replaced by any other well-founded relation. For instance, f could return pairs of natural numbers to be compared by $\prec_{\text{lex}}$. Similarly, the construction of $\prec_{\text{lex}}$ may be applied to any existing well-founded relations. There are several ways of constructing well-founded relations from others. Frequently we can show that a relation is well-founded by construction, without having to argue about decreasing chains.

Well-founded induction. Let $\prec$ be a well-founded relation over some type α, and $\phi(x)$ a property to be proved for all x of type α. To prove it by well-founded induction, it suffices to prove, for all y, the following induction step:

$$\text{if } \phi(y') \text{ for all } y' \prec y \text{ then } \phi(y)$$

The rule may be portrayed as follows:

$$\frac{[\forall y' \prec y \,.\, \phi(y')]}{\phi(y)} \qquad \text{proviso: } y \text{ must not occur in other}$$
$$\overline{\phi(x)} \qquad\qquad \text{assumptions of the premise.}$$

The rule is sound by contradiction: if $\phi(x)$ is false for any x then we obtain an infinite decreasing chain in $\prec$. By the induction step we know that $\forall y' \prec x \,.\, \phi(y')$ implies $\phi(x)$. If $\neg\phi(x)$ then $\neg\phi(y_1)$ for some $y_1 \prec x$. Repeating this argument for y_1, we get $\neg\phi(y_2)$

for some $y_2 \prec y_1$. We then get $y_3 \prec y_2$, and so forth.*

Complete induction is an instance of this rule, where $\prec$ is the well-founded relation $<$ (on the natural numbers). Our other induction rules are instances of well-founded induction for suitable choices of $\prec$.

The predecessor relation on the natural numbers, where $m \prec_N n$ just if $m + 1 = n$, is obviously well-founded. Now consider proving $\phi(y)$ under the induction hypothesis $\forall y' \prec_N y . \phi(y')$. There are two cases:

If $y = 0$ then, since $y' \prec_N 0$ never holds, we must prove $\phi(0)$ outright.

If $y = k + 1$ then $y' \prec_N k + 1$ holds just if $y' = k$, so we may assume $\phi(k)$ when proving $\phi(k + 1)$.

Therefore, well-founded induction over $\prec_N$ is precisely mathematical induction.

Structural induction is obtained similarly. Let $\prec_L$ be the relation on lists such that $xs \prec_L ys$ just if $x :: xs = ys$ for some x. Informally, $xs \prec_L ys$ means that xs is the tail of ys. Induction on $\prec_L$, which is clearly well-founded, yields structural induction on lists. Let $\prec_T$ be the relation on trees such that $t' \prec_T t$ just if $Br(x, t', t'') = t$ or $Br(x, t'', t') = t$ for some x and t''. Well-founded induction on this 'subtree of' relation yields structural induction on trees.

A well-founded relation given by a measure function yields induction on the size of an object. In reasoning about *distrib*, induction on the size of the pair (p, q) saves us from performing nested structural inductions on q and then p.

Well-founded induction can also simulate induction on a quantified formula, as when we proved

$$\forall p . facti(n, p) = n! \times p$$

by mathematical induction. It suffices to prove $facti(n, p) = n! \times p$ by well-founded induction on the pair (n, p) under the relation $\prec_{fst}$,

---

* Infinite decreasing chains are intuitively appealing, but other definitions of well-foundedness permit simpler proofs. For instance, $\prec$ is well-founded just if every non-empty set contains a $\prec$-minimal element. There also exist definitions suited for constructive logic.

where

$$(n', p') \prec_{fst} (n, p) \quad \text{if and only if} \quad n' + 1 = n.$$

Although many induction principles can be derived from mathematical induction alone, the derivations typically involve quantifiers. Well-founded induction makes significant proofs possible within quantifier-free logic.

Well-founded recursion. Let $\prec$ be a well-founded relation over some type α. If f is a function with formal parameter x that makes recursive calls $f(y)$ only if $y \prec x$, then $f(x)$ terminates for all x. In this case, f is defined by **well-founded recursion** on $\prec$.

Informally, $f(x)$ terminates because, since there are no infinite decreasing chains in $\prec$, there can be no infinite recursion. A completely formal justification of well-founded recursion is extremely complex; besides termination, it must show that $f(x)$ is uniquely defined. Suppes (1972, page 197) treats the simpler case of transfinite recursion.

For most of our recursive functions, the well-founded relation is obvious. If $n > 0$ then $fact(n)$ recursively calls $fact(n-1)$, so $fact$ is defined by well-founded recursion on the predecessor relation, $\prec_N$. When $facti(n, p)$ recursively calls $facti(n-1, n \times p)$ it changes the second argument; its well-founded relation is $\prec_{fst}$. The list functions *nlength*, @ and *nrev* are recursive over the 'tail of' relation, $\prec_L$.

Proving that a function terminates suggests a useful form of induction for it — recall our proofs involving *nnf* and *distrib*. If a function is defined by well-founded recursion on $\prec$, then its properties can often be proved by well-founded induction on $\prec$.

Well-founded relations are central to the Boyer & Moore (1979) Theorem Prover. It accepts functions defined by well-founded recursion and employs elaborate heuristics to choose the right relation for well-founded induction. Its logic is quantifier-free, but as we have seen, this is not a fatal restriction. Several major proofs have been performed in this system.

Recursive program schemes. Well-founded relations permit reasoning about program schemes. Suppose that p and g are functions and that $\oplus$ is an infix operator, and consider the ML declarations

```
fun f1(x)   =  if p(x)  then  e  else  f1(g x) ⊕ x;
fun f2(x,y) =  if p(x)  then  y  else  f2(g x, x ⊕ y);
```

Suppose that we are also given a well-founded relation $\prec$ such that $g(x) \prec x$ for all x such that $p(x) = false$. We then know that $f1$ and $f2$ terminate, and can prove theorems about them.

Theorem 21 *Suppose $\oplus$ is an infix operator that is associative and has identity e; that is, for all x, y and z,*

$$x \oplus (y \oplus z) = (x \oplus y) \oplus z$$

$$e \oplus x = x = x \oplus e.$$

Then for all x and a we have $f2(x, e) = f1(x)$.

Proof It suffices to prove the following formula, then put $y = e$:

$$\forall y \,.\, f2(x, y) = f1(x) \oplus y.$$

This holds by well-founded induction over $\prec$. There are two cases.
  If $p(x) = true$ then

$$\begin{aligned} f2(x, y) &= y & [f2] \\ &= e \oplus y & [\text{identity}] \\ &= f1(x) \oplus y. & [f1] \end{aligned}$$

  If $p(x) = false$ then

$$\begin{aligned} f2(x, y) &= f2(g\,x, x \oplus y) & [f2] \\ &= f1(g\,x) \oplus x \oplus y & [\text{ind hyp}] \\ &= f1(x) \oplus y. & [f1] \end{aligned}$$

The induction hypothesis applies because $g(x) \prec x$. We have implicitly used the associativity of $\oplus$.   ∎

  Thus we can transform a recursive function ($f1$) into an iterative function with an accumulator ($f2$). The theorem can be applied to the computation of factorials. Put

$$\begin{aligned} e &= 1 \\ \oplus &= \times \\ g(x) &= x - 1 \\ p(x) &= (x = 0) \\ \prec &= \prec_N \end{aligned}$$

Then $f1$ is the factorial function while $f2$ is the function *facti*. The theorem is a generalization of Theorem 4.

Our approach to program schemes is simpler than resorting to domain theory, but is less general. In domain theory it is simple to prove that any ML function of the form

```
fun h x = if p x then x else h(h(g x));
```

satisfies $h(h\,x) = h\,x$ for all x — regardless of whether the function terminates. Our approach cannot easily handle this. What well-founded relation should we use to demonstrate the termination of the nested recursive call in h?

Exercise 6.29 Recall the function *fst*, such that $fst(x,y) = x$ for all x and y. Give an example of a well-founded relation that uses *fst* as a measure function.

Exercise 6.30 Consider the function *ack*:

```
fun ack(0,n)   = n+1
  | ack(m,0)   = ack(m-1, 1)
  | ack(m,n)   = ack(m-1, ack(m,n-1));
```

Use a well-founded relation to show that $ack(m,n)$ is defined for all natural numbers m and n. Prove $ack(m,n) > m + n$ by well-founded induction.

Exercise 6.31 Give an example of a well-founded relation that is not transitive. Show that if $\prec$ is well-founded then so is $\prec^+$, its transitive closure.

Exercise 6.32 Consider the function *half*:

```
fun half 0 = 0
  | half n = half(n-2);
```

Show that this function is defined by well-founded recursion. Be sure to specify the domain of the well-founded relation.

Exercise 6.33 Show that well-founded induction on the 'tail of' relation $\prec_L$ is equivalent to structural induction for lists.

Specification and verification

Sorting is a good example for program verification: it is simple but not trivial. Considerable effort is required just to specify what sorting is. Most of our previous correctness proofs concerned the equivalence of two functions, and took little more than a page. Proving the correctness of the function *tmergesort* takes most of this section, even though many details are omitted.

First, consider a simpler specification task: the Greatest Common Divisor. If m and n are natural numbers then k is their GCD just if k divides both m and n exactly, and is the greatest number to do so. Given this specification, it is not hard to verify an ML function that computes the GCD by Euclid's Algorithm:

```
fun gcd(m,n) =
      if m=0 then   n   else gcd(n mod m, m);
```

The simplest approach is to observe that the specification defines a mathematical function:

$$GCD(m, n) = \max\{k \mid k \text{ divides both } m \text{ and } n\}$$

The value of $GCD(m, n)$ is uniquely defined unless $m = n = 0$, when the maximum does not exist; we need **not** know whether $GCD(m, n)$ is computable. Using simple number theory it is possible to prove these facts:

$$GCD(0, n) = n \qquad\qquad \text{for } n > 0$$
$$GCD(m, n) = GCD(n \bmod m, m) \qquad\qquad \text{for } m > 0$$

A trivial induction proves that $gcd(m, n) = GCD(m, n)$ for all natural numbers m and n not both zero. We thereby learn that $GCD(m, n)$ is computable.

A sorting function is not verified like this. It is not practical to define a mathematical function *sorting* and to prove *tmergesort*$(xs) = $ *sorting*(xs). Sorting involves two different correctness properties, which can be considered separately:

    1 The output must be an ordered list.
    2 The output list must be some rearrangement of the elements of the input list.

All too often in program verification, some of the correctness properties are ignored. This is dangerous. A function can satisfy property 1 by returning the empty list, or property 2 by returning its input unchanged. Either property alone is useless.

The specification does not have to specify the output uniquely. We might specify that a compiler generates correct code, but should not specify the precise code to generate in each case. This would be too complicated and would forbid code optimizations. We might specify that a database system answers queries correctly, but should not specify the precise storage layout.

The next sections will prove that *tmergesort* is correct, in the sense that it returns an ordered rearrangement of its input. Let us recall some functions from Chapter 3. Proving that they terminate is left as an exercise.

The list utilities *take* and *drop*:

```
fun take (i, [])    = []
  | take (i, x::xs) = if i>0 then x::take(i-1,xs)
                             else [];
fun drop (_, [])    = []
  | drop (i, x::xs) = if i>0 then drop (i-1, xs)
                             else x::xs;
```

The merging function:

```
fun merge([],ys)         = ys : real list
  | merge(xs,[])         = xs
  | merge(x::xs, y::ys) =
        if x<=y then x::merge(xs,   y::ys)
                else y::merge(x::xs,   ys);
```

The top-down merge sort:

```
fun tmergesort []  = []
  | tmergesort [x] = [x]
  | tmergesort xs  =
        let val k = length xs div 2
        in   merge(tmergesort (take(k,xs)),
                   tmergesort (drop(k,xs)))
        end;
```

6.10 *An ordering predicate*

The predicate *ordered* expresses that the elements of a list are in increasing order under $\leq$:

$ordered([])$

$ordered([x])$

$ordered(x :: y :: ys) \leftrightarrow x \leq y \wedge ordered(y :: ys).$

Note that $ordered(x :: xs)$ implies $ordered(xs)$. We now prove that merging two ordered lists yields another ordered list.

Theorem 22   *For all lists xs and ys,*

$$ordered(xs) \wedge ordered(ys) \rightarrow ordered(merge(xs, ys)).$$

Proof   By induction on the value of *nlength xs* + *nlength ys*.

If $xs = []$ or $ys = []$ then the conclusion follows by the definition of *merge*. So assume $xs = x :: xs'$ and $ys = y :: ys'$ for some xs' and ys'. We may assume

$$ordered(x :: xs') \quad \text{and} \quad ordered(y :: ys')$$

and must show

$$ordered(merge(x :: xs', y :: ys')).$$

Consider the case where $x \leq y$. (The case where $x > y$ is similar and is left as an exercise.) By the definition of *merge*, it remains to show

$$ordered(x :: merge(xs', y :: ys')).$$

Because we know $ordered(xs')$, we may apply the induction hypothesis, obtaining

$$ordered(merge(xs', y :: ys')).$$

We are nearly there, having only to show $x \leq u$, where u is the head of $merge(xs', y :: ys')$. Determining the head requires further case analysis.

If $xs' = []$ then $merge(xs', y :: ys') = y :: ys'$. Its head is y and we have already assumed $x \leq y$.

If $xs' = v :: vs$ then there are two subcases:

> If $v \leq y$ then $merge(xs', y :: ys') = v :: merge(vs, y :: ys')$. The head is v and $x \leq v$ follows from $ordered(xs)$ since $xs = x :: v :: vs$.
>
> If $v > y$ then $merge(xs', y :: ys') = y :: merge(xs', ys')$. The head is y and we have assumed $x \leq y$.   ∎

The proof is surprisingly tedious. Perhaps *merge* is less straightforward than it looks. Anyway, we are now ready to show that *tmergesort* returns an ordered list.

Theorem 23   *For every list xs, ordered(tmergesort xs).*
Proof   By induction on the length of *xs*. If $xs = []$ or $xs = [x]$ then the conclusion is obvious, so assume *nlength xs* ≥ 2.

Let $k = (nlength\ xs)\ div\ 2$. Then $1 \leq k < nlength\ xs$. It is easy to show these inequalities:

$$nlength(take(k, xs)) = k < nlength\ xs$$
$$nlength(drop(k, xs)) = nlength\ xs - k < nlength\ xs$$

By the induction hypotheses, we obtain corresponding facts:

$$ordered(tmergesort(take(k, xs)))$$
$$ordered(tmergesort(drop(k, xs)))$$

Since both arguments of *merge* are ordered, the conclusion follows by the previous theorem. ∎

Exercise 6.34   Fill in the details of the proofs in this section.

Exercise 6.35   Write another predicate to define the notion of ordered list, and prove that it is equivalent to *ordered*.

6.11   *Expressing rearrangement through multisets*

If the output of the sort is a rearrangement of the input, then there is a function, called a **permutation**, that maps element positions in the input to the corresponding positions in the output. To show the correctness of sorting, we could provide a method of exhibiting the permutation. However, we do not need so much information; it would complicate the proof. This specification is too concrete.

We could show that the input and output of the sort contained the same set of elements, not considering where each element was moved. Unfortunately, this approach accepts [1,1,1,1,2] as a valid sorting of [2,1,2]. Sets do not take account of repeated elements. This specification is too abstract.

Multisets are a good way to specify sorting. A multiset is a collection of elements that takes account of their number but not of their order. The multisets $\{1, 1, 2\}_{\mathcal{M}}$ and $\{1, 2, 1\}_{\mathcal{M}}$ are equal; they differ from $\{1, 2\}_{\mathcal{M}}$. Multisets are often called **bags**, for reasons that should be obvious. Here are some ways of forming multisets:

∅, the empty bag, contains no elements.
$\{u\}_{\mathcal{M}}$, the singleton bag, contains one occurrence of u.
$b_1 \uplus b_2$, the bag union of b_1 and b_2, contains all elements in the bags b_1 and b_2 (accumulating repetitions of elements).

Rather than assume bags as primitive, let us represent them as functions into the natural numbers. If b is a bag then $b(x)$ is the number of occurrences of x in b. Thus, for all x,

$$\emptyset(x) = 0$$

$$\{u\}_{\mathcal{M}}(x) = \begin{cases} 0 & \text{if } u \neq x \\ 1 & \text{if } u = x \end{cases}$$

$$(b_1 \uplus b_2)(x) = b_1(x) + b_2(x).$$

These laws are easily checked:

$$b_1 \uplus b_2 = b_2 \uplus b_1$$

$$(b_1 \uplus b_2) \uplus b_3 = b_1 \uplus (b_2 \uplus b_3)$$

$$\emptyset \uplus b = b.$$

Let us define a function to convert lists into bags:

$$bag[] = \emptyset$$

$$bag(x :: xs) = \{x\}_{\mathcal{M}} \uplus bag\ xs.$$

The 'rearrangement' correctness property can finally be specified:

$$bag(tmergesort\ xs) = bag\ xs$$

A preliminary proof. To illustrate reasoning about multisets, we shall work through a proof. It is a routine induction.

Theorem 24   *For every list xs and integer k,*

$$bag(take(k, xs)) \uplus bag(drop(k, xs)) = bag\ xs.$$

Proof   By structural induction on the list xs. In the base case,

$$
\begin{aligned}
& bag(take(k, [])) \uplus bag(drop(k, [])) \\
&= bag[] \uplus bag[] && [take, drop] \\
&= \emptyset \uplus \emptyset && [bag] \\
&= \emptyset && [\uplus] \\
&= bag[]. && [bag]
\end{aligned}
$$

For the induction step, we must prove

$$bag(take(k, x :: xs)) \uplus bag(drop(k, x :: xs)) = bag(x :: xs).$$

If $k > 0$ then

$$
\begin{aligned}
& bag(take(k, x :: xs)) \uplus bag(drop(k, x :: xs)) \\
&= bag(x :: take(k-1, xs)) \uplus \\
& \quad bag(drop(k-1, xs)) && [take, drop] \\
&= \{x\}_{\mathcal{M}} \uplus bag(take(k-1, xs)) \uplus \\
& \quad bag(drop(k-1, xs)) && [bag] \\
&= \{x\}_{\mathcal{M}} \uplus bag\ xs && [\text{ind hyp}] \\
&= bag(x :: xs). && [bag]
\end{aligned}
$$

If $k \leq 0$ then

$$bag(take(k, x :: xs)) \uplus bag(drop(k, x :: xs))$$
$$= bag[] \uplus bag(x :: xs) \qquad\qquad\qquad [take, drop]$$
$$= \emptyset \uplus bag(x :: xs) \qquad\qquad\qquad\qquad\quad [bag]$$
$$= bag(x :: xs). \qquad\qquad\qquad\qquad\qquad\quad [\uplus]$$

Therefore, the conclusion holds for every integer k.   ∎

The next step is to show that *merge* combines the elements of its arguments when forming its result.

Theorem 25   *For all lists xs and ys,*

$$bag(merge(xs, ys)) = bag\ xs \uplus bag\ ys.$$

Proof   By induction on the value of *nlength xs* + *nlength ys*.

If $xs = []$ or $ys = []$ then the conclusion is immediate, so assume $xs = x :: xs'$ and $ys = y :: ys'$ for some xs' and ys'. We must prove

$$bag(merge(x :: xs', y :: ys')) = bag(x :: xs') \uplus bag(y :: ys').$$

If $x \leq y$ then

$$bag(merge(x :: xs', y :: ys'))$$
$$= bag(x :: merge(xs', y :: ys')) \qquad\qquad\qquad [merge]$$
$$= \{x\}_{\mathcal{M}} \uplus bag(merge(xs', y :: ys')) \qquad\qquad\quad [bag]$$
$$= \{x\}_{\mathcal{M}} \uplus bag\ xs' \uplus bag(y :: ys') \qquad\qquad [\text{ind hyp}]$$
$$= bag(x :: xs') \uplus bag(y :: ys'). \qquad\qquad\qquad\quad [bag]$$

The case $x > y$ is similar.   ∎

Finally, we prove that merge sort preserves the bag of elements given to it.

Theorem 26   *For every list xs, bag(tmergesort xs) = bag xs.*
Proof   By induction on the length of xs. The only difficult case is where $nlength\ xs \geq 2$. As in Theorem 23, the induction hypotheses apply to $take(k, xs)$ and $drop(k, xs)$:

$$bag(tmergesort(take(k, xs))) = bag(take(k, xs))$$
$$bag(tmergesort(drop(k, xs))) = bag(drop(k, xs))$$

Therefore
$$bag(tmergesort\ xs)$$
$$= bag(merge(tmergesort(take(k, xs)),$$
$$\qquad tmergesort(drop(k, xs)))) \qquad\qquad [tmergesort]$$
$$= bag(tmergesort(take(k, xs)))\ \uplus$$
$$\qquad bag(tmergesort(drop(k, xs))) \qquad\qquad [\text{Theorem 25}]$$
$$= bag(take(k, xs))\ \uplus\ bag(drop(k, xs)) \qquad\qquad [\text{ind hyp}]$$
$$= bag\ xs. \qquad\qquad [\text{Theorem 24}]$$

This concludes the verification of *tmergesort*.   ∎

Exercise 6.36   Verify that $\uplus$ is commutative and associative. (Hint: recall the extensional equality of functions.)

Exercise 6.37   Prove that insertion sort preserves the bag of elements it is given. In particular, prove these facts:
$$bag(ins(x, xs)) = \{x\}_{\mathcal{M}}\ \uplus\ bag\ xs$$
$$bag(insort\ xs) = bag\ xs$$

Exercise 6.38   Modify merge sort to suppress repetitions: each input element should appear exactly once in the output. Formalize this property and state the theorems required to verify it.

6.12   *The significance of verification*

We could now announce that *tmergesort* has been verified — but would this mean anything? What, exactly, have we established about *tmergesort*? Formal verification has three fundamental limitations:

1 The model of computation may be inaccurate. Typically the hardware is assumed to be infallible. A model can be designed to cope with specific errors, like arithmetic overflow, rounding errors, or running out of store. However, a computer can fail in unanticipated ways. What if somebody takes an axe to it?

2 The specification of the program may be incomplete or incorrect. Design requirements are difficult to formalize, especially if they pertain to the real world. Safety-critical systems — in aircraft, nuclear reactors and railways — have to deal with complex physical events.

3 Our proofs may contain errors. Automated theorem proving can reduce but not eliminate the likelihood of error. All human efforts may have flaws, even our principles of mathematics. This is not merely a philosophical problem. Many errors have been discovered in theorem provers, in proof rules and in published proofs.

Apart from these fundamental limitations, there is a practical one: formal proof is tedious. Look back over the proofs in this chapter; usually they take great pains to prove something elementary. Now consider verifying a compiler. The specification will be gigantic, comprising the syntax and semantics of a programming language along with the complete instruction set of the target machine. The compiler will be a large program. The proof should be divided into parts, separately verifying the parser, the type checker, the intermediate code generator and so forth. There may only be time to verify the most interesting part of the program: say, the code generator. So the 'verified' compiler could fail due to faulty parsing. Cohn (1989b) discusses these problems in the context of hardware verification, taking as an example her proofs about the Viper microprocessor.

Let us not be too negative. The painstaking work of verification does yield rewards. Cohn (1989a) proves a great deal, although not everything, about the Viper chip. Bevier et al. (1989) have verified a complete, although tiny, computer system. Lakatos (1976) argues that we can learn from partial, even faulty, proofs.

The act of writing a formal specification often reveals ambiguities and inconsistencies in the design requirements. Since design errors are far more serious than coding errors, writing a specification is valuable even if the code will not be verified. Many companies go to great expense to produce specifications that are rigorous, if not strictly formal.

Most programs are incorrect, and an attempted proof often pinpoints the error. To see this, insert an error into any program verified in this chapter, and work through the proof again. The proof should fail, and the location of this failure should indicate the precise conditions under which the modified program fails.

A correctness proof is a detailed explanation of a program's workings. If the proof is simple, we can go through it line by line, reading it as a series of snapshots of the execution. The inductive step traces what happens at a recursive function call. A large proof may consist of many theorems, explaining the program's anatomy. For instance, *merge* combines the elements of two ordered lists, building another ordered list.

Specification and verification yield a fuller knowledge of the program and its task. This leads to increased confidence in the system. Formal proof does not eliminate the need for systematic testing, especially for a safety-critical system. Testing is the only way to investigate whether the computational model and the formal specification accurately reflect the real world. However, while testing can detect errors, it cannot guarantee success; nor does it provide insights into how a program works.

Summary of main points

Many functional programs can be given a meaning within elementary mathematics. Higher-order functions can be handled, but not lazy evaluation or infinite data structures.

The proof that a function terminates has the same general form as most other proofs about the function.

Mathematical induction applies to recursive functions over the natural numbers.

Structural induction applies to recursive functions over lists and trees.

Well-founded induction and recursion handle a wide class of terminating computations.

The specification is the most important part of a program correctness proof.

Although proofs can be fallible, they usually convey valuable information.

7

Modules

Structured programming is an approach to the design of complex software. It seeks to structure a large program as a system of simple parts, connected by simple interfaces. It is not, as commonly supposed, merely a campaign to abolish the go to command. Functional programs have no go to's, but they still deserve to be well organized.

Standard ML programs can be organized into **modules**. A module is either a **structure** or a **functor**.

A **structure** is a collection of declarations, typically of items that serve a common purpose. These may include types, values and other structures. Since structures may be grouped into larger structures, a software system can be designed as a hierarchy. A structure can be treated as a unit, no matter how complex it is internally.

A **signature** consists of type checking information about each item declared in a structure. It lists the types; it lists the values, with their types; it lists the substructures, with their signatures. Just as different values can have the same type, different structures can have the same signature.

A **functor** is a mapping from structures to structures. The body of the functor defines a structure in terms of a formal parameter, which is specified by a signature. Applying the functor substitutes an actual structure into the body. Functors allow separate compilation and can express generic definitions.

Chapter outline

This chapter presents the main features of modules and shows how they can be used in practice. It does not cover every detail, however. The chapter contains the following sections:

Queues, an abstract type. The concept of abstract type is introduced. For example, queues can be represented in several ways; a program that uses an abstract type of queues is independent of their representation.

Structures. The three different queue representations are expressed as structures. This packages each representation into a separate environment, with uniform naming conventions for the components of each structure.

Signatures of structures. Signatures are presented for the three queue representations. Another signature defines queues as an abstract type. More complicated examples are then considered: binary trees, tables, arrays and priority queues.

Functors over structures. Tables and priority queues are implemented for an arbitrary ordered type; a functor takes the type and its ordering, and returns a suitable structure. Using functors, program units can be coded independently.

A review of the modules system. The syntax of modules is presented systematically. Structures, signatures and functors are discussed as aspects of a single design.

Queues, an abstract type

A **queue** is a sequence whose elements may be inserted only at the end and removed only from the front. Queues enforce a first-in-first-out (FIFO) discipline. They provide the following operations:

$empty$ — the empty queue

$enqueue(q, x)$ — the queue obtained by inserting x on the end of q

$qnull(q)$ — the boolean test of whether q is empty

$qhd(q)$ — the front element of q

$dequeue(q)$ — the queue obtained by removing the front element of q

$Qerror$ — the exception raised by qhd and $dequeue$ if the queue is empty

These queue operations are functional; *enqueue* and *dequeue* create new queues rather than modifying existing queues. The names have been chosen to avoid clashes with the list functions *null* and *hd* (of Chapter 3); structures allow greater freedom to choose names. We shall discuss several ways of representing queues and defining their operations in ML, eventually finding an efficient representation.

If several programmers work on a large program, they could inadvertently implement queues several times. Even if the programmers discover their duplication of effort, eliminating it may prove impractical. It is unlikely that everyone will have discovered the most efficient representation.

Queues should be defined as an **abstract type**, hiding its internal representation. An abstract type allows no operations other than the ones named in its definition. Its representation can be changed — perhaps to a more efficient one — without affecting the rest of the program. Abstract types make programs easier to understand and modify.

7.1   *Representing queues as lists*

Representation 1, perhaps the most obvious, stores a queue as the list of its elements. We can declare a type abbreviation:

```
type 'a queue = 'a list;
```

This makes α *queue* a synonym for α *list*. (Recall how in Chapter 2 we made *vec* a synonym for *real* $\times$ *real*.) Since a value of type α *queue* can be used with any list operations, the type name is little more than a comment.

Function *enqueue* uses append; *dequeue* uses pattern-matching:

```
exception Qerror;

fun enqueue(q,x) = q @ [x];

fun dequeue(x::q) = q
  | dequeue []     = raise Qerror;
```

The other queue operations are implemented easily and efficiently. Unfortunately, *enqueue*(q, x) takes time proportional to the length of q. For many applications, this is too slow.

7.2   *Representing queues as a new datatype*

Representation 2 defines α *queue* as a datatype with constructors *empty* and *enqueue*:

```
datatype 'a queue = empty
                  | enqueue of 'a queue * 'a;
```

The operation *enqueue*(q, x) now takes constant time, independent of the length of q, but *qhd*(q) and *dequeue*(q) are slow. Recursive functions must be defined to reach or remove the first element of a queue. The operation *dequeue*(q) copies the remaining elements of q.

```
fun qhd (enqueue(empty,x)) = x
  | qhd (enqueue(q,x))     = qhd q
  | qhd empty              = raise Qerror;

fun dequeue (enqueue(empty,x)) = empty
  | dequeue (enqueue(q,x))     = enqueue(dequeue q, x)
  | dequeue empty              = raise Qerror;
```

Pattern-matching on *enqueue*(q, x) permits the removal of the last element of the queue, which violates its FIFO discipline. Thus, although α *queue* is a new type, it is not an abstract type.

Representation 2 gains little by defining a new datatype. It is essentially no different from representing a queue by a reversed list. Then

$$enqueue(q, x) = x :: q,$$

while *dequeue* is a recursive function to remove the last element from a list. We could call this Representation 2a.

7.3   *Representing queues as pairs of lists*

Representation 3 (Burton, 1982) stores a queue as pair of lists. The pair

$$([x_1, x_2, \ldots, x_m], [y_1, y_2, \ldots, y_n])$$

denotes the queue

$$x_1 x_2 \cdots x_m y_n \cdots y_2 y_1.$$

The queue has a front part and a rear part. The elements of the rear part are stored in reverse order so that new ones can quickly be added to the end of the queue; *enqueue*(q, y) modifies the queue thus:

$$(xs, [y_1, \ldots, y_n]) \mapsto (xs, [y, y_1, \ldots, y_n])$$

The elements of the front part are stored in correct order so that they can quickly be removed from the queue; *dequeue(q)* modifies the queue thus:

$$([x_1, x_2, \ldots, x_m], ys) \mapsto ([x_2, \ldots, x_m], ys)$$

When the front part becomes empty, the rear part is reversed and moved to the front:

$$([], [y_1, y_2, \ldots, y_n]) \mapsto ([y_n, \ldots, y_2, y_1], [])$$

The rear part then accumulates further elements until the front part is again emptied. A queue is in **normal form** provided it does not have the form

$$([], [y_1, y_2, \ldots, y_n])$$

for $n \geq 1$. The queue operations ensure that their result is in normal form. Therefore, inspecting the first element of a queue does not perform a reversal. A normal queue is empty if its front part is empty.

To implement this method, let us declare α *queue* as a datatype:

```
datatype 'a queue = Queue of ('a list * 'a list);
```

A type abbreviation could have been used. The **datatype** declaration yields a new type with the constructor *Queue*; this helps to emphasize occurrences of queues.* Later we shall turn α *queue* into an abstract type by hiding the constructor, breaking the connection between queues and pairs of lists.

A queue is normalized (put into normal form) using *norm*:

```
fun norm (Queue([],tails)) = Queue(rev tails, [])
  | norm q                 = q;
```

A queue must be normalized every time an element is added or removed.

```
fun enqueue(Queue(heads,tails), x) =
        norm(Queue(heads, x::tails));
fun dequeue(Queue(x::heads,tails)) = norm(Queue(heads,tails))
  | dequeue(Queue([],_))           = raise Qerror;
```

Although the use of reverse may seem expensive, the cost of an *enqueue* or *dequeue* operation is constant when averaged over the lifetime of the queue. At most two cons (::) operations are performed per queue element, one when it is put on the rear part and

---

* A single constructor costs nothing at run-time on most ML systems.

one when it is moved to the front part. The main drawback of
this representation is that the conses are not evenly distributed.
When normalization takes place, the reverse operation could cause
an unexpected delay.

Balanced trees can represent queues without such delays, but
they are complicated and slower on average. Representation 3 is
simple and efficient, and can be recommended for most situations
requiring functional queues.

Exercise 7.1   Under Representation 1, how much time does it
take to build an *n*-element queue by applying *enqueue* operations
to the empty queue?

Exercise 7.2   Discuss the relative merits of the three representations of functional queues. For example, are there any circum-
stances under which Representation 1 might be more efficient than
Representation 3?

Exercise 7.3   Code Representation 2a in ML.

Exercise 7.4   A queue is conventionally represented using an array, with indexes to its first and last elements. Are the functional
arrays of Chapter 4 suitable for this purpose? How would it compare with the other representations of functional queues?

Structures

A collection of related declarations can be packaged as a
structure. The items in a structure observe a uniform naming
convention. Suppose that list utilities are grouped in the structure *List*. Items known inside the structure as *null*, *hd* and *tl*
are known outside by the compound names *List.null*, *List.hd* and
List.tl. We no longer have to give the queue operations distinctive
names, as we did in the previous section. If structure *Queue* contains items called *null*, *hd* and *deq*, then these are known outside as
Queue.null, *Queue.hd* and *Queue.deq*, with no name clash between
List.hd and *Queue.hd*.

In this section, queues are defined using structures, but not as
abstract data types. Structures are only a means of grouping declarations. Signatures and functors permit the hiding of information,
which is necessary for data abstraction.

7.4   *A structure for queues as lists*

The declarations in a structure are enclosed within **struct** and **end**. The structure *Queue*1, for Representation 1 of queues, is declared as follows:

```
structure  Queue1 =
  struct
  type 'a  T = 'a  list;
  exception  E;

  val  empty = [];

  fun  enq(q,x) = q @ [x];

  fun  null(x::q) = false
    |  null _      = true;

  fun  hd(x::q) = x
    |  hd []      = raise E;

  fun  deq(x::q) = q
    |  deq []      = raise E;
  end;
```

Shorter names have been chosen than in the previous section, taking advantage of the compound names of items in the structure. The type of queues is simply $\alpha\ T$; outside the structure it is $\alpha\ Queue1.T$, a reasonable name for a type of queues. (When the purpose of a structure is to define a type, that type is commonly called T.) Its exception is called *Queue*1.*E*, the enqueue operation is called *Queue*1.*enq*, and so forth.

Declaring this structure hardly differs from declaring its items separately, except that a structure declaration is taken as a unit and introduces compound names. Each item behaves as if it were declared separately; there is no distinction between queues and lists.

```
Queue1.deq ["We","happy","few"];
> ["happy", "few"] : string list
```

7.5   *A structure for queues as a new datatype*

Now let us declare *Queue2*, a structure for Representation 2
of queues:

```
structure Queue2 =
  struct
  datatype 'a  T  = empty
                  | enq of 'a  T * 'a;
  exception E;

  fun null (enq _) = false
    | null empty   = true;

  fun hd (enq(empty,x)) = x
    | hd (enq(q,x))       = hd q
    | hd empty            = raise E;

  fun deq (enq(empty,x)) = empty
    | deq (enq(q,x))       = enq(deq q, x)
    | deq empty            = raise E;
  end;
```

Its type of queues, α *Queue2.T*, is a datatype with constructors
Queue2.empty and *Queue2.enq*. These compound names are valid
only after the declaration, when the name *Queue2* begins its scope;
inside the structure declaration, *Queue2* does not denote anything.
Of course, a structure may use compound names to refer to components of another structure.

Although structures *Queue1* and *Queue2* declare the same names,
their differences are visible outside. The function *Queue1.null* may
be applied to any list, while *Queue2.null* may only be applied to
values of type α *Queue2.T*. Both *Queue1.enq* and *Queue2.enq* are
functions, but *Queue2.enq* is a constructor and may appear in patterns.

```
fun last(Queue2.enq(q,x)) = x;
> val last = fn : 'a Queue2.T -> 'a
```

The function *last* returns the last element of a queue. Its definition
depends upon Representation 2. Declarations like these, scattered
throughout a program, could make it virtually impossible to change
the representation of queues.

7.6 *A structure for queues as pairs of lists*

Finally, let us implement Representation 3 through a structure declaration:

```
structure Queue3 =
  struct
  datatype 'a T =  Queue of ('a list * 'a list);
  exception E;

  val empty = Queue([],[]);

  fun norm (Queue([],tails))  = Queue(rev tails,  [])
    | norm q                  = q;

  fun enq(Queue(heads,tails),  x)
        = norm(Queue(heads,  x::tails));

  fun null(Queue([],[])) = true
    | null _             = false;

  fun hd(Queue(x::_,_)) = x
    | hd(Queue([],_))   = raise E;

  fun deq(Queue(x::heads,tails))  = norm(Queue(heads,tails))
    | deq(Queue([],_))            = raise E;
  end;
```

This contains items not present in the other structures: the constructor *Queue3.Queue* and the function *Queue3.norm*. Pattern-matching with the constructor *Queue* gives access to the representation of a queue as a front part and a rear part. Inside the structure, such access is essential for defining the queue operations. Outside the structure, tampering with this information could violate the FIFO discipline of the queue. Calling *Queue3.norm* outside the structure can serve no purpose.

! *Constructors cannot be redeclared.* We cannot call the empty queue *nil* under Representation 3. Because *nil* is a constructor (for the datatype of lists), the value declaration

```
val nil = ...
```

is viewed as an attempt at pattern-matching — not as a redeclaration of *nil*. The scope of a constructor can be restricted by enclosing its **datatype** declaration within a structure; the constructor *Queue2.enq* does not prevent our declaring *enq* as a value outside that structure.

Exercise 7.5 Can the empty queue be called *nil* under Representation 1? What about Representation 2?

7.7   *The* **open** *declaration*

Compound names like *Queue2.hd* can grow excessively long when structures are nested. Suppose that the structure declarations given above are actually part of a larger structure declaration:

```
structure AllQueues =
  struct
  structure Queue1 = struct ... end;
  structure Queue2 = struct ... end;
  structure Queue3 = struct ... end;
  end;
```

The structures *Queue1*, *Queue2* and *Queue3* are then components of *AllQueues*. The compound name *Allqueues.Queue2* refers to *Queue2*, while *Allqueues.Queue2.hd* refers to a function in *Queue2*. **Opening** a structure declares its items so that they are known by their simple names.

The syntax of an **open** declaration is

> **open** *Id*

where *Id* is the (possibly compound) name of a structure. Only one level of a structure is opened at a time. After declaring

> **open** *Allqueues*;

we may write *Queue2* and *Queue2.hd* instead of *Allqueues.Queue2* and *Allqueues.Queue2.hd*. If we go on to declare

> **open** *Queue2*;

we may write *T* and *null* instead of *Queue2.T* and *Queue2.null*. In the scope of this **open** declaration, *enq* denotes a constructor and may not be redeclared as a value.

Since **open** is a declaration, its scope may be limited using **let** or **local**. Below, *Queue3* is opened to define the function *qtake*, which mentions *null*, *hd* and *deq* without the prefix *Queue3*:

```
local open Queue3
in
  fun qtake(i,q) =
      if null q orelse i<=0 then []
      else (hd q) :: qtake(i-1, deq q)
end;
> val qtake = fn : int * 'a Queue3.T -> 'a list
```

A structure dependent on *Queue3* could have an **open** declaration:

```
struct
open  Queue3;
...  empty  ...  enq  ...  null  ...  hd
end
```

As these examples show, **open** can cause obscurity. Our queue structures have been designed to exploit compound names; the simple names of the items are too short. Opening several structures can declare hundreds of names at a stroke. Unless these names are descriptive, we may not be able to remember which structure they belong to — especially if some structures have names in common.

However, **open** is indispensable in large programs. Most structures are not elegant pearls, but chunks of a program. No matter how carefully we divide a program into structures, they will often be arbitrary. Compound names are then obstructive rather than informative, and **open** conveniently does away with them.

Infix operators in structures. Infix directives issued inside a structure have no effect outside. When a structure is opened, its names are made visible as ordinary identifiers, not as infix operators. To make them into infix operators again, new infix directives are required. If the infix directives are issued before the structure declaration, then they will have global effect, visible both inside the structure and afterwards. Some compilers extend Standard ML by causing **open** to restore the infix status of identifiers.

A compound name can never become an infix operator. Only simple names are permitted in an infix directive.

Exercise 7.6 Declare a structure *List* consisting of list utilities like *length* and *rev* (see Chapter 3).

Exercise 7.7 What is the effect of the following declaration?

```
open  Queue3;   open  Queue2;
```

Signatures of structures

Although the structures *Queue*1, *Queue*2 and *Queue*3 differ, they are equivalent in certain respects. They all implement queues, which could be proved using a mathematical specification of queues. Let us consider a weaker sense in which the structures are equivalent. Each is an instance of the following **signature**:

```
signature QUEUE =
  sig
  type 'a  T                         (*type of queues*)
  exception E                        (*for errors in hd, deq*)
  val empty : 'a  T                  (*the empty queue*)
  val enq   : 'a  T * 'a -> 'a  T    (*add to end*)
  val null  : 'a  T -> bool          (*test for empty queue*)
  val hd    : 'a  T -> 'a            (*return front element*)
  val deq   : 'a  T -> 'a  T         (*remove from front*)
  end;
```

This declaration gives the name $QUEUE$ to the signature enclosed within the brackets **sig** and **end**. The comments after each item are not required, but make the signature more informative to readers. A structure is an **instance** of this signature provided it declares (in any order):

a polymorphic type $\alpha\ T$
an exception E
a value *empty* of type $\alpha\ T$
a value *enq* of type $\alpha\ T \times \alpha \to \alpha\ T$
a value *null* of type $\alpha\ T \to bool$
a value *hd* of type $\alpha\ T \to \alpha$
a value *deq* of type $\alpha\ T \to \alpha\ T$

Consider each structure in turn. In *Queue*1, type $\alpha\ T$ abbreviates $\alpha\ list$, and the values have the correct types under this abbreviation. In *Queue*2, type $\alpha\ T$ is a datatype and *empty* and *enq* are constructors. In *Queue*3, type $\alpha\ T$ is again a datatype; the structure declares everything required by signature $QUEUE$, and the additional items *Queue* and *norm*. An instance of a signature may contain items not specified in the signature.

Names free in a signature. Each entry in a signature is called a **specification**. Names introduced by a specification become visible in the rest of the signature; the type T is specified and later employed to specify the type of *empty*. Predefined names are also visible in a signature; *bool* is used in the type of *null*. Predefined names are said to be **pervasive**: they are visible everywhere.

A name that occurs in a signature and that has not been specified there is said to be **free** in that signature. The only name occurring free in *QUEUE* is *bool*.

David MacQueen wrote the original proposal for Standard ML modules (Harper et al., 1986). He proposed that signatures could not refer to names declared elsewhere in a program, except names of other signatures. A signature could refer to structures specified within the same signature, but not to free-standing structures. Thus, every signature was completely self-contained, and every structure carried with it the structures and types it depended upon. This restriction, the **signature closure rule**, was eventually relaxed to give programmers greater freedom.

Since signature closure is an aid to modularity, we shall adhere to it in this book. Some compilers enforce the rule for separately compiled modules.

7.8   *The inferred signature of a structure*

A structure declaration does not have to mention a signature explicitly, as in the declarations of *Queue1*, *Queue2* and *Queue3*. ML then infers a signature containing maximal information about the structure.

Signature *QUEUE1* is equivalent to the signature inferred for structure *Queue1*. Observe that the types of values involve type α *list* instead of α *T*, as in signature *QUEUE*.

```
signature QUEUE1 =
  sig
  type 'a T
  exception E
  val empty : 'a list
  val enq   : 'a list * 'a -> 'a list
  val null  : 'a list -> bool
  val hd    : 'a list -> 'a
  val deq   : 'a list -> 'a list
  end;
```

The signature inferred for *Queue2* specifies α *T* as a datatype with constructors *empty* and *enq*; constructors are not specified again as values. The signature could be declared as follows:

```
signature QUEUE2 =
  sig
  datatype 'a T = empty | enq of 'a T * 'a
  exception E
  val null : 'a T -> bool
  val hd   : 'a T -> 'a
  val deq  : 'a T -> 'a T
  end;
```

The signature inferred for structure *Queue3* again specifies $\alpha\ T$ as a datatype — not merely a type, as in signature *QUEUE*. All items in the structure are specified, including *Queue* and *norm*.

```
signature QUEUE3 =
  sig
  datatype 'a T = Queue of 'a list * 'a list
  exception E
  val empty : 'a T
  val enq   : 'a T * 'a -> 'a T
  val null  : 'a T -> bool
  val hd    : 'a T -> 'a
  val deq   : 'a T -> 'a T
  val norm  : 'a T -> 'a T
  end;
```

These signatures are far more concrete and specific than *QUEUE*. No structure can be an instance of more than one of them. Consider *QUEUE*1 and *QUEUE*3. Function *hd* must have type $\alpha\ list \to \alpha$ to satisfy *QUEUE*1; it must have type $\alpha\ T \to \alpha$ to satisfy *QUEUE*3, which also specifies that $\alpha\ T$ is a datatype clearly different from $\alpha\ list$.

On the other hand, each signature has many different instances. A structure can satisfy the specification **val** $x:T$ by declaring x to be any value of type T. It can satisfy the specification **type** T by declaring T to be any type. (However, it can satisfy a **datatype** specification only by an identical **datatype** declaration.) A structure may include items not specified in the signature. Thus, a signature defines a class of structures.

Interesting relationships hold among these classes. We have already seen that *QUEUE*1, *QUEUE*2 and *QUEUE*3 are disjoint. The latter two are contained in *QUEUE*; an instance of *QUEUE*2 or *QUEUE*3 is an instance of *QUEUE*. An instance of *QUEUE*1 is an instance of *QUEUE* only if it makes type $\alpha\ T$ equivalent to

α *list.* These containments can be shown in a Venn diagram:

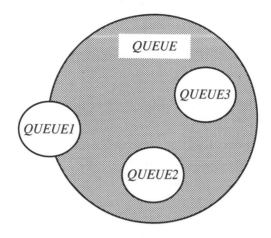

The empty structure. The structure

```
struct end
```

consists of no items and is called the **empty structure**. Its signature is the empty signature:

```
sig end
```

The empty structure is mainly used as the argument of a functor. In that role it is analogous to the empty tuple (), which is mainly used when a function does not depend on the value of its argument.*

Exercise 7.8 Declare a structure that has signature *QUEUE*1 and that implements queues by a different representation from that of *Queue*1.

Exercise 7.9 Declare a structure that has signature *QUEUE* but does not implement queues. After all, the signature specifies only the types of the queue operations, not their other properties.

Exercise 7.10 Which structures are instances of the empty signature?

---

* An example is the function representing the tail of a sequence; see Chapter 5.

7.9   *Signature constraints on a structure*

Different views of a structure, with varying degrees of abstraction, can be obtained using different signatures. A structure can be given an explicit signature when it is first defined, or a signature constraint can be imposed later. Let us constrain our existing queue structures:

```
structure S1:  QUEUE = Queue1
and        S2:  QUEUE = Queue2
and        S3:  QUEUE = Queue3;
```

This simultaneous declaration — which could easily have been written as three separate declarations — makes $S1$, $S2$ and $S3$ denote the same structures as $Queue1$, $Queue2$ and $Queue3$, respectively. However, the new structures are constrained to have the signature $QUEUE$. The types $\alpha\, Queue2.T$ and $\alpha\, S2.T$ are identical, yet $Queue2.empty$ is a constructor while $S2.empty$ may only be used as a value. The structures $Queue3$ and $S3$ are identical, yet $Queue3.norm$ is a function while $S3.norm$ means nothing.

A signature constraint may hide components, but they are still present. This can hardly be called abstraction. Structure $S1$ does not hide its representation at all; type $\alpha\, S1.T$ is identical to α *list*.

```
S1.deq ["We","band","of","brothers"];
> ["band", "of", "brothers"] : string S1.T
```

Structures $S2$ and $S3$ may seem more abstract, because they declare the type $\alpha\, T$ and hide its constructors. Without the constructors, pattern-matching is not available to take apart values of the type and disclose the representation. However, the constructor $Queue3.Queue$ may be used in a pattern to take apart a value of type $\alpha\, S3.T$:

```
val Queue3.Queue(heads,tails) =
      S3.enq(S3.enq(S3.empty,"Saint"), "Crispin");
> val heads = ["Saint"] : string list
> val tails = ["Crispin"] : string list
```

The concrete structure, $Queue3$, provides a loophole into its abstract view, $S3$. To hide the constructors completely, there must be no concrete view in existence. This can be ensured by including the signature constraint in the original structure declaration:

```
structure S:QUEUE = struct ... end
```

The structure enclosed by **struct** and **end** cannot be viewed directly — only via structure S, which has signature $QUEUE$. This signature constraint cannot be circumvented.

Data abstraction is compromised in another way. In ML, abstract types do not admit equality testing; for each of our queue structures, type $\alpha\ T$ admits equality. Equality of abstract values may not coincide with equality of their representations. Under Representation 3, the values $([1, 2], [])$ and $([1], [2])$ denote the same queue, but the equality test says they are different.

Exercise 7.11 Assuming Representation 3, show how two different representations of the same queue value could be created using only the abstract queue operations.

7.10 *Specifying trees and their applications*

Binary trees were exploited (in Chapter 4) to define lookup tables, functional arrays and priority queues. These present a complex problem of organization:

Binary trees should be packaged with their basic utilities.

Tables and functional arrays should be defined as abstract types represented by binary trees.

Priority queues should be defined as an abstract type represented by functional arrays, but their definition relies on the tree representation of arrays.

A structure will be defined simply to package the array operations, as an intermediate stage in defining the abstract types for functional arrays and priority queues. In the section on functors, tables and priority queues will be defined as generic data structures.

A structure for trees. We begin by defining a structure *Tree*, containing the **datatype** declaration and a few functions. Everything in the structure is made visible outside. First, we define a signature — not to hide anything, but to document the contents of the structure.

```
signature TREE =
  sig
  datatype 'a T = Lf  |  Br of 'a * 'a T * 'a T
  val count : 'a T -> int
  val depth : 'a T -> int
  val reflect : 'a T -> 'a T
  end;
```

Since the structure is declared with signature constraint *TREE*,
the ML compiler checks that the structure matches this signature.

```
structure Tree : TREE =
  struct
  datatype 'a T = Lf
                | Br of 'a * 'a T * 'a T;

  fun count Lf            = 0
    | count (Br(v,t1,t2)) = 1 + count t1 + count t2;

  fun depth Lf            = 0
    | depth (Br(v,t1,t2)) = 1 + maxl[depth t1, depth t2];

  fun reflect Lf            = Lf
    | reflect (Br(v,t1,t2)) = Br(v, reflect t2, reflect t1);
  end;
```

Substructures. Arrays can be represented by trees, exploiting the
binary expansion of the subscripts. Chapter 4 presents the functions *asub*, which looks up an array element, *aupdate*, which updates an element, and *hirem*, which removes an element.

Including these functions in structure *Tree* would be simpler than
the approach taken here. Simpler still, in the short term, would
be to dispense with modules altogether. Let us make the effort
to organize our code, not make a giant structure containing every
imaginable tree operation. Consider the following signature of array
operations:

```
signature ARRAYOPS =
  sig
  structure Tree: TREE
  exception E
  val sub    : 'a Tree.T * int -> 'a
  val update : 'a Tree.T * int * 'a -> 'a Tree.T
  val hirem  : 'a Tree.T * int -> 'a Tree.T
  end;
```

A structure having this signature must declare an exception *E* and
functions *sub*, *update* and *hirem*. It does not declare an abstract
type; the functions are viewed as operations on trees. The structure
must declare a substructure *Tree*. If the line

```
structure Tree: TREE
```

were removed from *ARRAYOPS*, the signature would still be valid.
However, it would depend on the structure *Tree* already declared,

since it mentions α *Tree.T* in the types of the functions.

The only names free in *ARRAYOPS* refer to the pervasive type *int* and the signature *TREE*. The structure name *Tree* is not free in *ARRAYOPS* since it is specified there, while *Tree.T* is just a component of *Tree*. In short, *ARRAYOPS* follows the signature closure rule. When this rule is followed, an entire system can be specified using signatures. The executable code can be written later.

A concrete structure for arrays. In the structure for the array operations, some of the code has been omitted since it is identical to that in Chapter 4:

```
structure ArrayOps : ARRAYOPS =
  struct
  structure Tree = Tree;
  exception E;
  local open Tree
    in
    fun sub (Lf, _) = raise E
      | sub (Br(v,t1,t2), k) =
            if k=1 then v
            else if k mod 2 = 0
                  then sub (t1, k div 2)
                  else sub (t2, k div 2);
    fun update ... ;
    fun hirem ... ;
    end
  end;
```

Let us examine this carefully. The line

```
structure Tree = Tree;
```

may seem to do nothing, but actually it redeclares *Tree* as an item of structure *ArrayOps*. Without this line, *ArrayOps* would not match the signature *ARRAYOPS*.

The declaration

```
open Tree
```

allows the constructors to be written as *Lf* and *Br*, without compound names. It is enclosed within **local** so that *Lf*, *Br* and the other items in *Tree* will not be included in the structure *ArrayOps*. The signature constraint would hide these items anyway; using **local** is an aid to clarity.

Arrays as an abstract type. The structure *Array* (Figure 7.1) neatly packages the array operations just defined. An array of n elements consists of a tree paired with the number n, and admits subscripts from 1 to n. The functions *sub*, *update* and *hirem* call their namesakes in *ArrayOps*. An additional function, *hiext*, adds an element to an array and increases its upper bound. The empty array is called *empty*. Exceptions *Sub*, *Update* and *Hirem* signal errors in the corresponding functions.

Signature *ARRAY* specifies the array type $\alpha\ T$, the array operations and the exceptions. The simultaneous exception specification could have been written as three separate specifications.

```
signature ARRAY =
  sig
  type 'a  T
  exception Sub and  Update and  Hirem
  val empty : 'a  T
  val sub    : 'a  T * int -> 'a
  val update : 'a  T * int * 'a -> 'a  T
  val hiext  : 'a  T * 'a -> 'a  T
  val hirem  : 'a  T -> 'a  T
  end;
```

Structure *Array* depends only on *ArrayOps*, through which it refers to *Tree*. Such dependencies between structures will stand out more clearly when we use functors. Note the long compound names, like *ArrayOps.Tree.Lf*.

Observe that $\alpha\ T$ is a datatype with one constructor — which is hidden — rather like the type for representing queues as pairs of lists. Hiding the constructors of a datatype is a common trick for defining abstract types in ML, but it is not really satisfactory. It only works because datatypes are treated differently from other types. Each **datatype** declaration creates a fresh type distinct from all others. Outside the structure, no declaration can create a type identical to $\alpha\ T$, which is therefore protected from pattern matching. To that extent, the representation is hidden.

Type $\alpha\ T$ admits equality, so it is not abstract. Luckily, in this case, equality of representations coincides with equality of the abstract values.

Exercise 7.12 State which names appear free in each of these signatures: *QUEUE*1, *QUEUE*2, *QUEUE*3, *TREE* and *ARRAY*.

Figure 7.1 *Arrays as an abstract type*

```
structure Array : ARRAY =
  struct
  datatype 'a T = Array of 'a ArrayOps.Tree.T * int;
  exception Sub and Update and Hirem;

  val empty = Array(ArrayOps.Tree.Lf, 0);

  fun sub (Array(t,n), k) =
      if 1<=k andalso k<=n then ArrayOps.sub(t,k)
      else raise Sub;

  fun update (Array(t,n), k, w) =
      if 1<=k andalso k<=n then Array(ArrayOps.update(t,k,w), n)
      else raise Update;

  fun hiext (Array(t,n), w) = Array(ArrayOps.update(t,n+1,w), n+1);

  fun hirem(Array(t,n)) =
      if n>0 then Array(ArrayOps.hirem(t,n) , n-1)
      else raise Hirem;
  end;
```

Exercise 7.13 Extend signature $QUEUE$ to specify the functions *length*, for returning the number of elements in a queue, and *equal*, for testing whether two queues consist of the same sequence of elements. Extend the structures $Queue1$, $Queue2$ and $Queue3$ with declarations of these functions.

Exercise 7.14 Explain how an **open** declaration could be inserted in *Array* to shorten the compound names in that structure. Discuss the pros and cons of this idea.

Exercise 7.15 Declare an instance of the following signature:

```
sig
structure Oak: TREE
exception E
val sub    : 'a Oak.T * int -> 'a
val update : 'a Oak.T * int * 'a -> 'a Oak.T
val hirem  : 'a Oak.T * int -> 'a Oak.T
end;
```

Functors over structures

Sorting is possible for any type whose elements have a linear ordering,* but the sorting functions of Chapter 3 accept only real numbers. The priority queue functions of Chapter 4 are also restricted to real numbers. Binary search trees are polymorphic in the type of elements that may be stored, but the search keys must be strings. In each of these cases, the type restriction is due to the use of a particular < relation.

Declarations that presume the existence of certain operations (like <) can be written using a functor. The body of a functor can refer to an arbitrary type with its ordering, packaged as a structure. We can make actual types and orderings into structures and supply them to the functor. Applying the functor creates a structure for a specific case of the generic algorithm.

Functors make structures from other structures. Besides expressing generic algorithms, they permit a modular style of programming. Units of a program can be coded separately as functors; applying the functors links the units together.

Higher-order functions can replace functors in simple situations. A polymorphic sorting function could well take the < relation as an argument. However, making the priority queue operations take < as an argument seems clumsy.

7.11   *Ordered types as structures*

A mathematician defines an ordered set as a pair $(A, <)$, where A is a set and < is a relation on A that is transitive and so forth. In Standard ML the idea is similar, although the notation is slightly more cumbersome. The signature *ORDER* specifies a type T and a function *less* of type $T \times T \to bool$:

```
signature ORDER =
  sig
  type T
  val less: T*T -> bool
  end;
```

The specification 'type T' is essential. If it were omitted, as in the signature

```
sig  val less: T*T -> bool  end
```

---

* An ordering < is **linear** if for all x and y either $x < y$, $x = y$, or $x > y$.

then the type of *less* would refer to some type T already present in the program. As it stands, signature *ORDER* allows any type to be packaged with a relation; its only free name is *bool*.

The following three structures are instances of *ORDER*, where T is *string*, *int* and *real*, respectively. In each, *less* is the ML infix operator $<$ with its type constrained to resolve overloading.*

```
structure StringOrder: ORDER =
  struct
  type T = string;
  val less: string*string -> bool = op <
  end
and       IntOrder: ORDER =
  struct
  type T = int;
  val less: int*int -> bool = op <
  end
and       RealOrder: ORDER =
  struct
  type T = real;
  val less: real*real -> bool = op <
  end;
```

We are not restricted to the predefined meanings of the operator $<$. 'Less than' can be defined for other types, such as pairs of integers under lexicographic ordering.

```
structure IntPairOrder: ORDER =
  struct
  type T = int*int;
  fun less((x1,y1): T, (x2,y2): T) =
        x1<x2 orelse (x1=x2 andalso y1<y2)
  end;
```

7.12   *A functor for tables*

Given some ordered type and a definition of binary trees, we shall define binary search trees over that ordering. More formally, suppose that *Order* is a structure of signature *ORDER* and that *Tree* is a structure of signature *TREE*. Our functor will define a structure for tables in terms of *Order* and *Tree*. Applying the

---

* Many Standard ML compilers extend the language definition by letting $<$ compare strings, using lexicographic ordering.

functor to actual structures will create another structure containing the table operations, implemented by binary search trees.

Making structure *Tree* an argument of the functor is not strictly necessary — there will probably be only one such structure in the program — but allows the functor to be independent of any existing structure. Making structure *Order* an argument is essential, of course, if we are to define tables for various orderings.

The result signature. When designing a functor, the signature of its resulting structure should be carefully considered. The following signature is suitable for an abstract type of lookup tables:

```
signature TABLE =
  sig
  type key                             (*type of keys*)
  type 'a T                            (*type of tables*)
  exception Lookup                     (*errors in lookup*)
  val empty : 'a T                     (*the empty table*)
  val lookup : 'a T * key -> 'a        (*look in table*)
  val update : 'a T * key * 'a -> 'a T (*modify table*)
  end;
```

An instance of *TABLE* is a structure declaring two types:

key, the type of search keys

$\alpha\ T$, the type of tables whose elements have type α

The structure will also declare the table operations with appropriate types, such as

$lookup : \alpha\ T \times key \rightarrow \alpha.$

The function *lookup* takes a table and a key, and returns an element of the table. The signature specifies the type *key* so that it can specify the types of the table operations.

Nothing in signature *TABLE* betrays that binary trees or ordered types might be involved. We may adopt any representation.

The functor declaration. Figure 7.2 presents a functor *TableFUN*, which generates instances of signature *TABLE*. The formal parameters are the structures *Order* and *Tree*. The formal parameter list is, in fact, a signature specification; the functor may be applied to any structure containing *Order* and *Tree* as substructures.

The body of the functor declares functions on binary trees that are almost identical to those in Chapter 4. However, it never refers

Figure 7.2 *A functor for tables as binary search trees*

```
functor TableFUN (structure Order: ORDER and Tree: TREE)
        : TABLE =
  struct
  type key = Order.T;
  type 'a T = (key * 'a) Tree.T;
  exception Lookup;

  local open Tree
    in
    val empty = Lf;

    fun lookup (Br ((a,x),t1,t2), b) =
          if       Order.less(b,a) then   lookup(t1, b)
          else if Order.less(a,b) then   lookup(t2, b)
          else x
      | lookup (Lf, b) = raise Lookup;

    fun update (Lf, b, y) = Br((b,y), Lf, Lf)
      | update (Br((a,x),t1,t2), b, y) =
          if Order.less(b,a)
          then Br ((a,x),   update(t1,b,y),   t2)
          else if Order.less(a,b)
          then Br ((a,x),   t1,   update(t2,b,y))
          else (*a=b*) Br ((a,y),t1,t2);
    end
  end;
```

---

to the built-in operator $<$; instead of $b < a$ it has $Order.less(b, a)$. The 'less than' test is taken from *Order*, and has to be. Because type *Order.T* is a component of a formal parameter, the only operations involving this type are those given in signature *ORDER*. The operator $<$ is undefined for type *Order.T*. Equality testing on *Order.T* is also forbidden. In short, *Order.T* behaves like an abstract type within the functor body.

The body declares the types *key* and α *T*, as it must do to satisfy the signature. They are only type abbreviations.

A functor application. Applying the functor *TableFUN* to the structures *StringOrder* and *Tree* creates a structure of tables with strings for keys. The actual parameter list is, in fact, the body of a structure; the brackets **struct** and **end** are omitted.

```
structure StringTab =
    TableFUN(structure  Order=StringOrder and  Tree=Tree);
```

Using compound names or an **open** declaration, tables can be created and searched:

```
local open StringTab in
val tab = update(update(update(update(update(empty,
                "Crecy",1346),
            "Poitiers",1356),
          "Agincourt",1415),
        "Trafalgar",1805),
      "Waterloo",1815)
end;
> val tab = Br (("Crecy", 1346),
>               Br (("Agincourt", 1415), Lf, Lf),
>               Br (("Poitiers", 1356), Lf,  Br ...))
>    : int StringTab.T
StringTab.lookup(tab,"Poitiers");
> 1356 : int
```

Sadly, *TableFUN* does not define an abstract type. Signature *TABLE* specifies no details about the representation of type $\alpha\,T$, but ML regards $\alpha\,StringTab.T$ as the type $(string \times \alpha)\,Tree.T$. Patterns involving the tree constructors *Lf* and *Br* can take apart a table:

```
val Tree.Br(a,t1,t2) = tab;
> val a = ("Crecy", 1346) : string * int
> val t1 = Br (("Agincourt", 1415), Lf, Lf)
>             : (string * int) StringTab.T
> val t2 = Br (("Poitiers", 1356), Lf,  Br ...)
>             : (string * int) StringTab.T
```

The ML equality test may be applied to type $\alpha\,T$ if α is an equality type. This violates data abstraction; one table can be represented by many different trees. If *TableFUN* declared $\alpha\,T$ as a datatype, the type would be protected outside the structure from pattern-matching — but not from equality testing. A datatype is fine for structure *Array*, but would somewhat complicate *TableFUN*.

Exercise 7.16   Which names are free in signature *TABLE*?

Exercise 7.17   Write a new version of *TableFUN* where a table is represented by a list of (*key*, *element*) pairs ordered by the keys.

Exercise 7.18   Extend *TABLE* and *TableFUN* to include a function *insert*, which behaves like *update* save that it raises exception *Insert* if the given key is already in the table.

7.13   *A functor for priority queues*

There are many similarities between the definitions of tables and priority queues. Again, we are given two structures, *Order* of signature *ORDER* and *ArrayOps* of signature *ARRAYOPS*. Again, one of the structures (*ArrayOps*) is a formal parameter of the functor only for the sake of modularity, while *Order* is expected to stand for various ordered types.

One difference between tables and priority queues is the role of the ordering. For tables, the ordering is involved only in our implementation. For priority queues, the ordering is part of the very concept. A priority queue, remember, accumulates elements as they are given and returns them largest element first.

The result signature. Because the ordering is part of the concept of priority queue, the signature makes it explicit:

```
signature PQUEUE =
  sig
  structure Order: ORDER      (*ordering for elements*)
  type T                      (*type of priority queues*)
  exception E                 (*for errors in hd, deq*)
  val empty: T                (*the empty queue*)
  val enq  : T * Order.T -> T (*insert into queue*)
  val null : T -> bool        (*test for empty*)
  val hd   : T -> Order.T     (*return front element*)
  val deq  : T -> T           (*remove from front*)
  end;
```

An instance of *PQUEUE* is a structure containing a substructure *Order* of signature *ORDER*. The instance also contains a type *T*, which is the type of priority queues; elements stored in a queue have type *Order.T*. The insertion operation

$$enq : T \times Order.T \rightarrow T$$

takes a priority queue and a new element, returning another priority queue. The priority queue operations are named like the analogous queue operations, where the elements are imagined to be in decreasing order. Thus *hd* returns the largest element of a priority queue while *deq* removes that element.

Signature *PQUEUE* could have specified a type *elem* rather than
the structure *Order*, and specified *enq* to have the type $T \times elem \rightarrow$
T. That approach was suitable for signature *TABLE*, where the
ordering had to be hidden. Because *PQUEUE* specifies *Order*, each
priority queue structure *PQueue* carries its ordering with it. We
may write

$$PQueue.Order.less(x, y)$$

to test whether x is less than y under the given ordering.

The functor declaration. Figure 7.3 presents the functor to create
priority queues. The definition of *upheap* is omitted in order to
save space.

Structure *Order* is declared in the body by the line

        structure *Order* = *Order*;

This declaration is required because the result signature specifies
a substructure *Order*. (Compare with the declaration of *Tree* in
ArrayOps.)

The functor contains the declaration

        open *ArrayOps.Tree*

to allow direct reference to the constructors *Lf* and *Br* of *Tree.T*,
which is specified as a datatype. The heap functions *upheap* and
downheap use *Order.less* as the ordering on type *Order.T*. To
improve readability, the infix operator << is declared and made
equivalent to *Order.less*. The priority queue functions *enq* and *deq*
use the heap and array functions.

A priority queue is represented much like an abstract array as
declared in structure *Array*. It consists of a tree paired with the
number of elements currently stored. The type of priority queues
is a datatype with one constructor, *PQueue*. Observe how *PQueue*
makes occurrences of priority queues stand out in the functor body.
This use of a datatype promotes clarity.

Exercise 7.19   Which names appear free in signature *PQUEUE*?

Exercise 7.20   Write a new version of *PQueueFUN* where a priority queue is represented by a decreasing list.

Exercise 7.21   Write a functor *SortingFUN* whose argument is
an instance of signature *ORDER* and whose result implements both

Figure 7.3 *The priority queue functor*

```
functor PQueueFUN (structure Order: ORDER
                   and        ArrayOps: ARRAYOPS) : PQUEUE =
  struct
  structure Order = Order;
  datatype T = PQueue of Order.T ArrayOps.Tree.T * int;
  exception E;

  local open ArrayOps.Tree
        infix <<
        fun v<<w = Order.less(v,w)
  in
  fun upheap ...

  fun downheap (Br(_,t1,t2), w) =
    case t1 of  Lf => Br(w,Lf,Lf)
      | Br(v1,_,_) =>
          (case t2 of
              Lf => if v1<<w then Br(w, t1, Lf)
                    else Br(v1, downheap(t1,w), Lf)
            | Br(v2,_,_) =>
                if v1<<v2
                then if v2<<w then Br(w, t1, t2)
                             else Br(v2, t1, downheap(t2,w))
                else if v1<<w then Br(w, t1, t2)
                             else Br(v1, downheap(t1,w), t2) );

  val empty = PQueue(Lf,0);

  fun enq(PQueue(t,n), w) = PQueue(upheap(t,n+1,w), n+1);

  fun null (PQueue(Br _, _)) = false
    | null (PQueue(Lf,    _)) = true;

  fun hd (PQueue(Br(w,_,_), n)) = w
    | hd (PQueue(Lf,          _)) = raise E;

  fun deq (PQueue(t,n)) =
        if n>1 then PQueue(downheap(ArrayOps.hirem(t,n),
                                    ArrayOps.sub(t,n)),
                          n-1)
        else if n=1 then empty
        else raise E;
  end
  end;
```

---

quick sort and merge sort. What is the point of providing more than one sorting algorithm?

Exercise 7.22   If $<_\alpha$ is an ordering on type α and $<_\beta$ is an ordering on type β then the lexicographic ordering $<_{\alpha \times \beta}$ on type $\alpha \times \beta$ is defined by $(a', b') <_{\alpha \times \beta} (a, b)$ if and only if

$$a' <_\alpha a \vee (a' = a \wedge b' <_\beta b).$$

Write a functor *LexOrderFUN*, with formal parameters *OrderA* and *OrderB* of signature *ORDER*, and with result signature *ORDER*, to yield the lexicographic ordering based on *OrderA* and *OrderB*.

7.14   *Sharing constraints*

Applying *PQueueFUN* to the structures *StringOrder* and *ArrayOps* creates a structure for priority queues of strings.

```
structure StringPQ =
    PQueueFUN (structure Order    = StringOrder
            and          ArrayOps = ArrayOps);
```

Elements can be inserted into a queue and removed from it.*

```
StringPQ.enq(StringPQ.empty, "Agincourt");
> ? : StringPQ.T
StringPQ.enq(it, "Crecy");
val pq = StringPQ.enq(it, "Poitiers");
> val pq = ? : StringPQ.T
```

Since the elements of the priority queue *pq* are strings, an element may be supplied as a search key in *StringTab.lookup*.

```
StringTab.lookup(tab, StringPQ.hd pq);
> 1356 : int
```

A generic algorithm might employ a priority queue whose elements are keys into a table, where the keys may have any ordered type. The corresponding functor (call it *SharFUN*) would take the structures as formal parameters:

$$PQueue : PQUEUE$$
$$Table : TABLE$$

The functor might make declarations like

```
fun lookhead(tab, pq) = Table.lookup(tab, PQueue.hd pq);
```

---

* The ML compiler used here prints ? for the value of priority queues, since *StringPQ.T* is a datatype whose constructor is hidden.

But is this valid? Consider the types of the functions involved:

$$PQueue.hd : PQueue.T \rightarrow PQueue.Order.T$$

$$Table.lookup : \alpha\ Table.T \times Table.key \rightarrow \alpha$$

The call of *Table.lookup* is permissible only if *PQueue.Order.T* is the same type as *Table.key*. These types might coincide when functor *SharFUN* is applied to actual structures; for *StringPQ* and *StringTab*, the common type is *string*. In other cases, the types might not coincide. Let *IntPQ* be a structure for priority queues of integers:

```
structure IntPQ =
    PQueueFUN(structure Order    = IntOrder
              and        ArrayOps = ArrayOps);
```

Functor *SharFUN* must not be applied to *IntPQ* and *StringTab* and cause the integer returned by *IntPQ.hd* to be treated like a string by *StringTab.lookup*.

The requirement that the two types coincide can be enforced using a **sharing constraint** in the functor declaration:

```
functor SharFUN(structure PQueue : PQUEUE
                and        Table  : TABLE
                sharing type PQueue.Order.T  = Table.key) =
    struct
    fun lookhead(tab, pq)  = Table.lookup(tab, PQueue.hd pq);
    end;
```

In the body of the functor, the constraint guarantees that the two types are identical. The type checker, using this information, accepts the declaration of *lookhead*. When the functor is applied to actual structures, the ML compiler will insist that the sharing constraint is satisfied — that the two types really are the same.

Sharing constraints for structures. When functors are used to combine the components of a system, sharing constraints may be required on common substructures. Here is a sketch of a typical situation. Problems are the input of structure *In*, while solutions are the output of structure *Out*. The two components communicate via a priority queue of goals, in structure *PQueue*. Structure *Main* coordinates the program via *In* and *Out*. These four structures are related as shown:

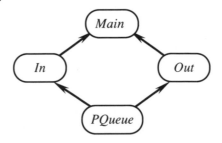

Suppose that *In* and *Out* have the following signatures:

```
signature IN =
  sig
  structure PQueue: PQUEUE
  type problem
  val goals: problem -> PQueue.T
  end
and        OUT =
  sig
  structure PQueue: PQUEUE
  type solution
  val solve: PQueue.T -> solution
  end;
```

A functor to combine *In* and *Out* might look like this:

```
functor MainFUN (structure In: IN and Out: OUT
                 sharing In.PQueue = Out.PQueue) =
  struct
  fun tackle(p) = Out.solve(In.goals p)
  end;
```

Because the structures *In.PQueue* and *Out.PQueue* are declared as sharing, the types *In.PQueue.T* and *Out.PQueue.T* are identical in the functor body.

When building the system, the same structure *PQueue* must be incorporated into *In* and *Out*. The functor *MainFUN* will then accept *In* and *Out* as arguments, since they will satisfy the sharing constraint.

Understanding sharing constraints. Sharing is one of the most difficult aspects of Standard ML modules. A type error is the usual warning that a sharing constraint might be necessary. In our previous example, omitting the constraint might cause the error 'type conflict between *In.PQueue.T* and *Out.PQueue.T*'. Unfortunately, some compilers produce cryptic error messages.

The type error could be eliminated by imposing a sharing constraint on those types:

> sharing type *In.PQueue.T* = *Out.PQueue.T*

The structure sharing constraint actually used in *MainFUN* is preferable; it conveys more information than a type sharing constraint. It implies that the substructures *In.PQueue.Order* and *Out.PQueue.Order* are also shared.

Every structure generated through struct...end is assigned a unique internal name. A structure retains its internal name as it is passed to functors and taken as a substructure of other structures. ML enforces sharing constraints on structures by checking that they have the same internal name. If the struct...end is the body of a functor, it generates a fresh structure (with a distinct internal name) every time the functor is applied.

Types are treated like structures in sharing constraints. Each datatype declaration generates a fresh type with a unique internal name. Type checking and sharing constraints compare these internal names.

Exercise 7.23 Declare an instance of *TABLE* that may be passed with *IntPQ* to *SharFUN*, satisfying the sharing constraint.

Exercise 7.24 Suppose that the functors *InFUN* and *OutFUN* are declared as follows:

```
functor InFUN (structure PQueue: PQUEUE): IN =
   struct
   structure PQueue = PQueue;
   fun goals ... ;
   end
and OutFUN (structure PQueue: PQUEUE): OUT =
   struct
   structure PQueue = PQueue;
   fun solve ... ;
   end;
```

By applying these functors, declare structures that may be given to *MainFUN*. Then declare structures that have the required signatures but violate the functor's sharing constraint.

Exercise 7.25 The functors *InFUN* and *OutFUN* declared above incorporate the formal parameter *PQueue* into the result structure.

Modify these functors to generate a fresh instance of *PQUEUE* instead. How will this affect *MainFUN*?

7.15   *Functors and modular design*

In the functors *TableFUN* and *PQueueFUN*, one of the formal parameters is the structure *Order*. The possibility of supplying different structures for *Order* is the main reason for expressing tables and priority queues as functors. Each of the functors has another formal parameter (*Tree* and *ArrayOps*, respectively) to ensure that no actual structures are mentioned in the functor bodies. A functor may refer to existing structures and functors — just as a function may refer to global variables — but many ML programmers avoid this.

If all program units are coded as functors then they can be written and compiled separately. First, the signatures are declared. Program units are then coded from the top down, or from the bottom up, or (if there are several programmers) at the same time. Each functor refers to signatures, but not to structures or other functors. When a functor is compiled, error messages may reveal mistakes and omissions in the signatures. Revised signatures can be checked by recompiling the functors.

Once all the functors have been written and compiled, applying them generates a structure for each program unit. The final structure contains the executable program. A functor can be modified, recompiled and a new system built, without recompiling the other functors, provided no signatures have changed. Applying the functors amounts to linking the program units. Different configurations of a system can be built.

Functors for binary trees. Suppose we have entered a fresh ML session. To express the binary tree examples in the all-functors style, begin by declaring the signatures:

```
signature TABLE    = ...;
signature TREE     = ...;
signature ARRAYOPS = ...;
signature ARRAY    = ...;
signature ORDER    = ...;
signature PQUEUE   = ...;
```

Since a signature may refer to others, the declarations must be made in a correct order. Signature *TREE* must be declared before *ARRAYOPS*. Since our functors do not refer to each other, they can be declared in any order. The functors *PQueueFUN* and *TableFUN* can be declared now:

```
functor PQueueFUN ...;
functor TableFUN ...;
```

The previous declaration of the structure *Array* can be modified into a functor declaration with *ArrayOps* as its formal parameter. The body of the functor, enclosed within **struct**...**end**, is exactly as it was in the structure declaration.

```
functor ArrayFUN (structure ArrayOps: ARRAYOPS)
        : ARRAY = struct ... end;
```

Similarly, the declaration of structure *ArrayOps* can be made into a functor declaration with *Tree* as its formal parameter. Again, the contents of the structure becomes the body of the functor.

```
functor ArrayOpsFUN (structure Tree: TREE)
        : ARRAYOPS = struct ... end;
```

Even structure *Tree* can be made into a functor, although it requires no formal parameters. Since a functor's parameter list is the specification of a signature, functor *TreeFUN* specifies the empty signature.

```
functor TreeFUN () : TREE = struct ... end;
```

Now that all the functors have been declared, let us build the structures. Functor *TreeFUN* can be given an empty argument list, generating the structure *Tree*. Strictly speaking, the functor is applied to the empty structure.

```
structure Tree = TreeFUN();
```

Next, structures *ArrayOps* and *Array* are generated by functor applications:

```
structure ArrayOps = ArrayOpsFUN (structure Tree=Tree);
structure Array = ArrayFUN (structure ArrayOps=ArrayOps);
```

The structure *StringOrder* can be declared like before:

```
structure StringOrder = ...;
```

Now structures *StringTab* and *StringPQ* can be declared, as they were before, by functor applications:

```
structure StringTab = TableFUN (structure ...);
structure StringPQ = PQueueFUN (structure ...);
```

Figure 7.4 *Structures and functors involving trees*

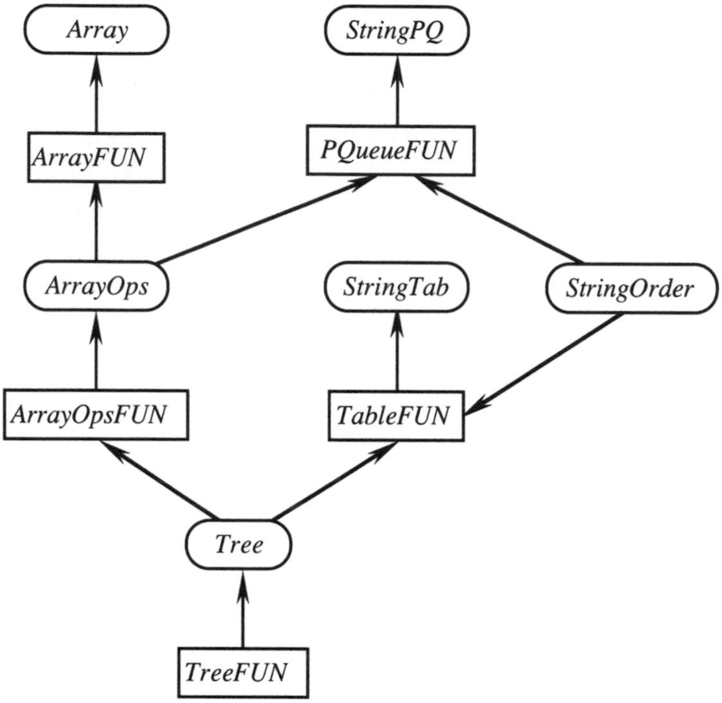

Figure 7.4 shows the complete system, with structures as rounded boxes and functors as square boxes. Most of the structures were created by functors, but *StringOrder* was written directly.

Programming with functors unfortunately requires many sharing constraints. Functor application may be inefficient on some ML systems; you may end up with two copies of the program in the machine, once as functors and once as structures.

Functors and abstract types. In the all-functors style of programming, each functor refers to structures only as formal parameters. Suppose that *FUN* is a functor whose formal parameters include a structure *Table* of signature *TABLE*. Since *Table* is a formal parameter rather than a real structure, nothing is known about it apart from its signature. In the body of *FUN*, type α *Table.T* behaves like an abstract type — it has no constructors that could allow pattern-matching, and equality testing is forbidden.

But even the all-functors style does not completely hide the representation of an abstract type. Structures are created when the functors are finally applied. There is no way of executing the program without creating structures, and structures are not abstract, as we have seen previously for *String Tab*.

Standard ML completely hides the internal representation of its built-in types; a program cannot view a real number as a bit pattern. Abstract types defined by the programmer deserve to be equally secure. The **abstype** declaration achieves secure data abstraction, but that 15-year-old construct ought to be superseded by modules and does not feature in this book. New 'abstraction' declarations are being considered as an extension to the modules system, and are implemented in some compilers.

Exercise 7.26 Write a functor with no formal parameters and result signature *QUEUE*, implementing Representation 3 of queues.

Exercise 7.27 Specify a signature *SEQUENCE* for an abstract type of lazy lists, and implement the type by writing a functor with result signature *SEQUENCE*. Write a functor that takes instances of *QUEUE* and *SEQUENCE*, and defines searching functions like *depthfirst* and *breadthfirst* (Chapter 5).

A review of the modules system

This section brings together the concepts of structures, signatures and functors, presenting a view of the modules system as a whole. It begins with a description of the syntax, gives another example of a functor and concludes with the mathematical origins of the concepts.

7.16 *The syntax of signatures and structures*

This book aims to teach programming techniques, not to describe Standard ML in full. Modules involve a great deal of syntax, however; here is a systematic description of their main features.

In the syntax definitions, an optional phrase is enclosed in square brackets. A repeatable phrase (occurring at least once) is indicated informally using three dots (...). For example, in

$$\textbf{structure } Id_1\big[:Sig_1\big]{=}Str_1 \textbf{ and } \ldots \textbf{ and } Id_n\big[:Sig_n\big]{=}Str_n$$

the signature constraint ':*Sig*' is optional. Simultaneous declarations are separated by the keyword **and**.

Syntax of signatures. A signature has the form

> **sig** *Spec* **end**

where a *Spec* is a specification of types, values, exceptions, structures and sharing constraints.

A value specification of the form

> **val** $Id_1 : T_1$ **and** ... **and** $Id_n : T_n$

specifies values named $Id_1, \ldots, Id_n$ with types $T_1, \ldots, T_n$, respectively. Several values and their types can be specified simultaneously.

Types may be specified (simultaneously) by

> **type** $\left[\mathit{TypeVars}_1\right] Id_1$ **and** ... **and** $\left[\mathit{TypeVars}_n\right] Id_n$

or by

> **eqtype** $\left[\mathit{TypeVars}_1\right] Id_1$ **and** ... **and** $\left[\mathit{TypeVars}_n\right] Id_n$

An **eqtype** specification introduces equality types. In a functor body, a type specified by **eqtype** admits equality testing. Every instance of the signature must declare this identifier to be an actual type that admits equality. An example of **eqtype** appears at the end of this section.

In both **type** and **eqtype** specifications, a type is given by optional type variables (*TypeVars*) followed by an identifier, exactly as may appear on the left side of a type declaration. A **datatype** specification has the same syntax as a **datatype** declaration.

Exceptions, with optional types, can be specified by

> **exception** $Id_1 \left[\textbf{of } T_1\right]$ **and** ... **and** $Id_n \left[\textbf{of } T_n\right]$

Structures, with their signatures, are specified by

> **structure** $Id_1 : Sig_1$ **and** ... **and** $Id_n : Sig_n$

Sharing constraints have the form

> **sharing** $\left[\textbf{type}\right] Id_1 = Id_2 = \cdots = Id_n$

The identifiers $Id_1, \ldots, Id_n$ are specified to share. If the keyword **type** is present then they must be type identifiers; otherwise they must be structure identifiers. Sharing constraints typically appear in a functor's formal parameter list, which is given as a signature specification.

Syntax of structures. A structure can be created by a declaration (which may declare substructures) enclosed by the brackets **struct** and **end**:

> **struct** *D* **end**

A structure can also be given by a functor application:

> *FunctorId* (*Str*)

The functor named *FunctorId* is applied to the structure *Str*. This is the primitive syntax for functor application, but it is not used in our examples, since it allows only one argument. We have used a derived form of functor application instead, where the argument is a declaration:

> *FunctorId* (*D*)

This abbreviates the functor application

> *FunctorId* (**struct** *D* **end**)

and is analogous to writing a tuple as the argument of a function for the effect of multiple arguments.

7.17   *The syntax of module declarations*

Signature, structure and functor declarations are not allowed within expressions. Structures may be declared inside other structures, but functor declarations must not be nested.

A signature declaration makes the identifiers $Id_1, \ldots, Id_n$ denote the signatures $Sig_1, \ldots, Sig_n$, respectively:

> **signature** $Id_1 = Sig_1$ **and** $\ldots$ **and** $Id_n = Sig_n$

A structure declaration makes the identifier Id_i denote the structure Str_i (optionally specifying the signature Sig_i), for $1 \leq i \leq n$:

> **structure** $Id_1 \left[: Sig_1 \right] = Str_1$ **and** $\ldots$ **and** $Id_n \left[: Sig_n \right] = Str_n$

The primitive syntax for a functor declaration is

> **functor** *Id* (*Id'* : *Sig'*) $\left[: Sig \right]$ = *Str*

where *Id* is the name of the functor, *Id'* and *Sig'* are the name and signature of the formal parameter, structure *Str* is the body and *Sig* is an optional signature constraint.

The derived syntax for a functor declaration, which gives the effect of multiple arguments, has the form

> **functor** *Id* (*Spec*) $\left[:Sig\right]$ = *Str*

The formal parameter list is given by the specification *Spec*. The functor still takes one argument, a structure whose signature is determined by *Spec*. The formal parameter is implicitly opened in the body of the functor, making its components visible. These complicated arrangements permit a functor to take any number of arguments, which need not be structures.

! *Functor declarations.* The primitive syntax is more concise when there is one argument, since it avoids creating another structure. On the other hand, using both syntaxes in a program may lead to confusion. The declaration

> **functor** *ArrayFUN* (**structure** *ArrayOps*: *ARRAYOPS*) ...

is an example of the derived syntax. Since the functor takes only one argument, a structure, it can be declared using the primitive syntax:

> **functor** *ArrayFUN2* (*ArrayOps*: *ARRAYOPS*) ...

These declarations differ only by the keyword **structure** in the formal parameter list, which could be omitted by accident. The functors must be called differently:

> *ArrayFUN* (**structure** *ArrayOps* = *ArrayOps*)
> *ArrayFUN2* (*ArrayOps*)

7.18   *An alternative functor for tables*

The following example illustrates two aspects of the modules syntax. It uses an **eqtype** specification, and declares a functor using the derived syntax. Lookup tables were previously implemented by binary search trees. Association lists are a simpler but slower representation:

```
functor AlistFUN (eqtype key) : TABLE =
  struct
  type key   = key;
  type 'a T = (key * 'a) list;
  exception Lookup;

  val empty = [];

  fun lookup ([], a)            = raise Lookup
    | lookup ((x,y)::pairs, a) =
        if a=x then  y  else  lookup(pairs, a);

  fun update (pairs, b, y) = (b,y)::pairs;
  end;
```

The derived functor syntax lets us view *AlistFUN* as a functor whose formal parameter is a type, not a structure. Type *key* is specified as an **eqtype**. Within the body of *AlistFUN*, equality testing is permitted on type *key*. Here is an application:

```
structure StringIntAlist = AlistFUN(type key=string*int);
```

We may apply the functor to *string* × *int* because this type admits equality. The type *int* → *int*, for example, would be rejected.

Exercise 7.28 Assuming the declarations of *TreeFUN* and *Array* given in this chapter, discuss whether *TreeFUN(Array)* is a valid functor application or not.

Exercise 7.29 Write a version of *AlistFUN* that does not involve **eqtype**. Instead, it should employ a signature similar to *ORDER*.

7.19   *The use of structures, signatures and functors*
      The following analogy between Standard ML's modules language and core language is often remarked:

structure ∼ value

signature ∼ type

functor ∼ function

A better analogy for modules involves abstract algebra, which inspired the terminology of structures, signatures and functors.

Mathematicians frequently package a set with its operations to form a single object. We have already seen ordered sets packaged as $(A, <)$. Abstract algebra defines the notion of a group $(G, 0, +, -)$, a ring $(R, 0, +, -, \times)$, a field and so forth. These are known as **algebraic structures**.

A group consists of a set G with an element 0 and binary operations + and −, satisfying certain laws like $0 + x = x$. A ring is a group that includes a binary operation × and satisfies additional laws. A field is a ring that includes a binary operation / and satisfies yet more laws. An **algebraic signature** specifies the names of the operations and the laws that they must satisfy.

The rational numbers, the real numbers and the complex numbers are examples of fields. The integers are an example of rings. The rotations of an object can be viewed as a group. Every field can be viewed as a ring by forgetting about its / operation. The rational, real and complex numbers were known before the notion of field was invented. Groups, rings and fields classify mathematical structures so that general definitions can be made.

For example, two square matrices of the same size can be added and multiplied; for all $n > 0$, the set of $n \times n$ matrices forms a ring. The components of a matrix are usually real numbers, but matrix addition and multiplication require only addition and multiplication of the components. Matrices can thus be generalized from the real numbers to an arbitrary ring. Since matrices form a ring, the construction 'take R to the set of $n \times n$ matrices over R' is a **functor** from rings to rings.

Polynomials over a single variable x form another ring:

$$a_n x^n + \cdots + a_1 x + a_0$$

The coefficients a_0, a_1, ..., a_n are typically real numbers. Addition and multiplication of polynomials requires only addition and multiplication of the coefficients; they could belong to any ring. The construction 'take R to the set of polynomials in x over R' is another functor from rings to rings. These (algebraic) functors can be combined; given a ring R, we can form the ring of matrices of polynomials over R.

The discussion above is mathematical, but similar ideas are established in computer science. Consider device-independent input/output: programmers assume a uniform set of input/output operations, which must be implemented by each device. Expressing numerical algorithms independently of particular kinds of numbers (like rational, real and complex) is a practical problem in programming. The ML concept of functor, though weaker than its algebraic counterpart, suffices for these programming tasks.

Exercise 7.30   Write Standard ML signatures for the notions of group, ring and field.

Exercise 7.31   Define a structure implementing the rational numbers as an abstract data type, represented perhaps by pairs of integers with no common factor. (Remember the function *gcd*.)

Exercise 7.32   Write an ML functor that, given an integer $n > 0$ and a ring, creates a ring of $n \times n$ matrices. It should implement matrix addition and multiplication in terms of the ring operations.

Exercise 7.33   Write an ML functor that, given a string x (to serve as the name of the variable) and a ring, creates a ring of polynomials. It should implement polynomial addition and multiplication in terms of the ring operations.

Summary of main points

A structure is a collection of declarations, typically a program unit.

A signature specifies type-checking information, defining a class of structures.

A functor is a mapping from structures to structures.

Functors can express generic algorithms and permit program units to be written and compiled separately.

Sharing constraints may be necessary to ensure that certain subcomponents of a system are identical.

An abstract data type consists of a type together with an explicit set of operations, which are the only means by which to compute with values of that type.

8

Imperative Programming in ML

Standard ML is not a purely functional language. Its imperative features include references, arrays and commands for input and output. These features are not inherently incompatible with functional programming. If they are used in a disciplined manner, large parts of the program will be purely functional.

References and arrays can be used to implement functions and data structures that exhibit purely functional behaviour. We shall code sequences (lazy lists) using references to store each element — thereby avoiding wasteful recomputation, which is a defect of the sequences of Chapter 5. We shall code functional arrays (where updating creates a new array) with the help of imperative arrays. This representation of functional arrays can be far more efficient than the binary trees of Chapter 4.

Chapter outline

This chapter describes reference types and imperative arrays, with examples of their use in data structures. ML's input and output facilities are presented.

The chapter contains the following sections:

Reference types. References stand for storage locations and can be created, updated and inspected. Reference types complicate the notion of polymorphism.

References in data structures. Three large examples are presented. We modify our type of sequences to store computed elements internally. Ring buffers illustrate how references can represent linked data structures. *V*-arrays exploit imperative programming techniques in a functional data structure.

Input and output. Channels, carrying streams of characters, connect an ML program to input and output devices. The primitive operations easily suffice for simple text processing. A more interesting example is a program for pretty printing.

Reference types

References in ML are essentially store addresses. They correspond to the variables of Pascal and similar languages, and serve as pointers in linked data structures. For control structures, ML provides **while-do** loop commands; the **if-then-else** and **case** expressions also work for imperative programming. The section concludes by explaining the interaction between reference types and polymorphism.

8.1   *References and their operations*

All values computed during the execution of an ML program reside for some time in the machine store. To functional programmers, the store is nothing but a device inside the computer; they never have to think about the store until they run out of it. With imperative programming the store is visible. An ML reference denotes the address of a location in the store. Each location contains a value, which can be replaced by another value by an assignment. A reference is itself a value.

The constructor *ref* creates references. When applied to a value *v*, it allocates a new address with *v* for its initial contents, and returns a reference to this address. Although *ref* is an ML function, it is not a function in the mathematical sense because it returns a new address every time it is called.

The function !, when applied to a reference, returns its contents. This operation is called **dereferencing**. Clearly ! is not a mathematical function; its result depends upon the state.

The assignment $E_1 := E_2$ evaluates E_1, which must return a reference, and E_2. It updates the address denoted by E_1 with the value denoted by E_2. Syntactically, := is a function and $E_1 := E_2$ is an expression, although it updates the state. Its value is always (), which has type *unit*.

Here is a simple example of these primitives:

```
val p = ref 5
and q = ref 2;
> val p = ref 5 : int ref
> val q = ref 2 : int ref
```

The references *p* and *q* are declared with initial contents 5 and 2.

```
(!p,!q);
> (5, 2) : int * int
p := !p + !q;
> () : unit
(!p,!q);
> (7, 2) : int * int
```

The assignment changes the contents of *p* to 7. Note the word 'contents'! The assignment does not change the value of *p*, which is a fixed address in the store; it changes the contents of that address. We may use *p* and *q* like integer variables in Pascal, except that dereferencing is explicit. We must write !*p* to get the contents of *p*, since *p* by itself denotes an address.

!   *Keep symbolic names separate.* The operators ! and :=, like +, −, * and so on, are symbolic names and must not be run together. It is a common error to write expressions like these:

       p:=!p+1   2*!q

ML will complain that the symbolic names :=! and *! have not been declared. The solution is to insert spaces:

       p := !p+1   2 * !q

References in data structures. Because references are ML values, they may belong to tuples, lists, etc.

```
val refs = [p,q,p];
> val refs = [ref 7, ref 2, ref 7] : int ref list
q := 1346;
> () : unit
refs;
> [ref 7, ref 1346, ref 7] : int ref list
```

The first and third elements of *refs* denote the same address as *p*, while the second element is the same as *q*. ML compilers print the value of a reference as *ref c*, where *c* is its contents, rather than printing the address as a number. So assigning to *q* affects how *refs* is printed. Let us assign to the head of the list:

```
hd refs := 1415;
> () : unit
refs;
> [ref 1415, ref 1346, ref 1415] : int ref list
(!p,!q);
> (1415, 1346) : int * int
```

Because the head of *refs* is *p*, assigning to *hd refs* is the same as assigning to *p*.

References to references are also allowed:

```
val refp = ref p
and refq = ref q;
> val refp = ref (ref 1415) : int ref ref
> val refq = ref (ref 1346) : int ref ref
```

The following assignment updates the contents (*q*) of *refq* with the contents (1415) of the contents (*p*) of *refp*. Here *refp* and *refq* behave like Pascal pointer variables.

```
!refq := !(!refp);
> () : unit
(!p,!q);
> (1415, 1415) : int * int
```

Equality of references. The ML equality test is valid for all references, regardless of the type of their contents. Two references are equal precisely if they denote the same address. The following tests verify that *p* and *q* are distinct references, and that the head of *refs* equals *p*, not *q*:

```
p=q;
> false : bool
hd refs = p;
> true : bool
hd refs = q;
> false : bool
```

In Pascal, two pointer variables are equal if they happen to contain the same address; an assignment makes two pointers equal. The ML notion of reference equality may seem peculiar, for if *p* and *q* are distinct references then nothing can make them equal (short of redeclaring them). In imperative languages, where all variables can be updated, a pointer variable really involves two levels of reference. The usual notion of pointer equality is like comparing the contents of *refp* and *refq*, which are references to references:

```
!refp = !refq;
> false : bool
refq := p;
> () : unit
!refp = !refq;
> true : bool
```

At first, *refp* and *refq* contain different values, *p* and *q*. Assigning the value *p* to *refq* makes *refp* and *refq* have the same contents; both 'pointer variables' refer to *p*.

When two references are equal, like *p* and *hd refs*, assigning to one affects the contents of the other. This situation, called **aliasing**, can cause great confusion. Aliasing can occur in procedural languages; in a procedure call, a global variable and a formal parameter may denote the same address.

Cyclic data structures. Circular chains of references arise in many situations. Suppose that we declare *cp* to refer to the successor function on the integers, and dereference it in the function *cfact*.

```
val cp = ref (fn k => k+1);
> val cp = ref fn : (int -> int) ref
fun cfact n = if n=0 then 1 else n * !cp(n-1);
> val cfact = fn : int -> int
```

Each time *cfact* is called, it takes the current contents of *cp*. Initially this is the successor function, and $cfact(8) = 8 \times 8 = 64$:

```
cfact 8;
> 64 : int
```

Let us update *cp* to contain *cfact*. Now *cfact* refers to itself via *cp*. It becomes a recursive function and computes factorials:

```
cp := cfact;
> () : unit
cfact 8;
> 40320 : int
```

Updating a reference to create a cycle is sometimes called 'tying the knot'. Many functional language interpreters implement recursive functions exactly as shown above, creating a cycle in the execution environment.

Exercise 8.1 True or false: if $E_1 = E_2$ then *ref* E_1 = *ref* E_2.

Exercise 8.2 Define the function +:= such that +:= *Id E* has the same effect as *Id* := !*Id* + *E*, for integer *E*.

8.2   *Control structures*

ML does not distinguish commands from expressions. A command is an expression that updates the state when evaluated. Most commands have type *unit* and return (). Viewed as an imperative language, ML provides only basic control structures.

The expression

$$\texttt{if } E \texttt{ then } E_1 \texttt{ else } E_2$$

can be viewed as a conditional command. It executes E_1 if E has the value *true*, and E_2 if E has the value *false*. Note that E may also update the state. Similarly, the `case` expression serves as a conditional control structure.

In the function call $E_1\,E_2$ and the n-tuple $(E_1, E_2, \ldots, E_n)$, the expressions are evaluated from left to right. If E_1 changes the state, it could affect the outcome of E_2.

A series of commands can also be executed by the expression

$$(E_1; E_2; \ldots; E_n)$$

When this expression is evaluated, the expressions E_1, E_2, ..., E_n are evaluated from left to right. The result is the value of E_n; the values of the other expressions are discarded. Because of the other uses of the semicolon in ML, this construct must always be enclosed in parentheses unless it forms the body of a `let` expression:

$$\texttt{let } D \texttt{ in } E_1; E_2; \ldots; E_n \texttt{ end}$$

For iteration, the expression

$$\texttt{while } E_1 \texttt{ do } E_2$$

resembles Pascal's `while` command. If E_1 evaluates to *false* then the command terminates; if E_1 evaluates to *true* then E_2 is evaluated and the command is executed again. The `while` command has type *unit*, so E_2 is evaluated purely for its effect on the state.

Exceptions and commands. When an exception is raised, the normal flow of execution is interrupted. An exception handler is chosen, as described in Chapter 4, and control resumes there. This could be dangerous; an exception could occur at any time, leaving the state in an abnormal condition. The following exception handler traps any exception, tidies up the state, and re-raises the exception. The variable e is a trivial pattern (of type *exn*) to match all exceptions:

```
handle e => (... (*tidy up actions*)...; raise e)
```

Simple examples. ML can imitate procedural programming languages. The following procedures, apart from the explicit dereferencing (the ! operation), could have been written in Pascal or C. The function *ifact* computes factorials using local references *resultp* and *ip*, returning the final contents of *resultp*.

```
fun ifact n =
  let val resultp = ref 1
      and ip      = ref 0
  in  while !ip < n do (ip      := !ip + 1;
                        resultp := !resultp * !ip);
      !resultp
  end;
> val ifact = fn : int -> int
```

Although calling *ifact* allocates new references, this state change is invisible outside. The value of *ifact*(*E*) is a mathematical function of the value of *E*.

```
ifact 6;
> 720 : int
```

In procedural languages, a procedure may have reference parameters in order to modify variables in the calling program. In Standard ML, a reference parameter is literally a formal parameter of reference type. We can transform *ifact* into a procedure *pfact* that takes *resultp* as a reference parameter.

```
fun pfact (n, resultp) =
  let val ip = ref 0
  in  resultp := 1;
      while !ip < n do (ip      := !ip + 1;
                        resultp := !resultp * !ip)
  end;
> val pfact = fn : int * int ref -> unit
```

Calling *pfact*(*n*, *resultp*) assigns the factorial of *n* to *resultp*:

```
pfact (5,p);
> () : unit
p;
> ref 120 : int ref
```

These two functions demonstrate the imperative style, but a pure recursive function is the clearest and probably the fastest way to compute factorials. More realistic imperative programs appear later in this chapter.

Most commands return the value () of type *unit*. From now on, the boring response

```
> () : unit
```

will no longer be shown.

Exercise 8.3   Expressions $(E_1; E_2; \ldots; E_n)$ and **while** E_1 **do** E_2 are derived forms in ML, which means they are defined by translation to other expressions. Describe suitable translations.

Exercise 8.4   Write an imperative version of the function *sqroot* of Chapter 2, which computes real square roots by the Newton-Raphson method.

Exercise 8.5   Write an imperative version of the function *fib* of Chapter 2, which computes Fibonacci numbers efficiently.

8.3   *Polymorphic references*

References have been a notorious source of insecurity ever since they were introduced to programming languages. Often, no type information was kept about the contents of a reference; a character code could be interpreted as a real number. Pascal prevents such errors, ensuring that each reference contains values of one fixed type, by having a distinct type 'pointer to τ' for each type τ. In ML, the problem is harder: what does the type τ *ref* mean if τ is polymorphic? Unless we are careful, the contents of this reference could change over time.

An imaginary session. The following session, which is illegal in Standard ML, demonstrates what could go wrong if references were naïvely added to the type system. We begin by declaring the identity function:

```
fun I x = x;
> val I = fn : 'a -> 'a
```

Since I is polymorphic, it may be applied to arguments of any types. Now let us create a reference to I:

```
val fp = ref I;
> val fp = ref fn : ('a -> 'a) ref
```

With its polymorphic type $(\alpha \to \alpha)ref$, we should be able to apply the contents of *fp* to arguments of any types:

```
(!fp true, !fp 5);
> (true, 5) : bool * int
```

Equally, its polymorphic type permits assigning a function of type $bool \to bool$ to *fp*:

```
fp := not;
!fp 5;
> ERROR! ERROR! THAT DOES NOT COMPUTE!!
```

Applying *not* to the integer 5 is a run-time type error, but ML is supposed to detect all type errors at compile-time. Obviously something has gone wrong in this session, but where? The type checking of polymorphic references has been studied by many people, including Luis Damas and Robin Milner (1982). Mads Tofte (1990) has recently published a lucid analysis. Tofte blames the creation of polymorphic references, rather than assignments, for the difficulties. His approach has been adopted in Standard ML, and therefore the declaration of *fp* above is illegal.

Weak type variables. The problem with *fp* is that the type of its contents varies over time. To ensure that this type remains fixed, a reference may be polymorphic only in a weak sense. Let us introduce a new set of type variables $\underline{\alpha}$, $\underline{\beta}$, $\underline{\gamma}$, ... These are called **weak** or **imperative** type variables; in contrast, ordinary type variables are called **strong** or **applicative**. The operations on references have the following types:

$$ref : \underline{\alpha} \to \underline{\alpha}ref$$
$$! : \alpha ref \to \alpha$$
$$(\mathbf{op} :=) : \alpha ref \times \alpha \to unit.$$

Observe that the type of *ref* involves a weak type variable, while the other operations have strong type variables. Only the creation of references is restricted. A polymorphic function can inspect and update existing references.

Weak type variables range over the weakly polymorphic types, which are any types containing no strong type variables. In particular, every monotype is weakly polymorphic. The function *ref* has types such as the following:

$$int \rightarrow int\ ref$$
$$(bool \rightarrow bool) \rightarrow (bool \rightarrow bool)ref$$
$$(\underline{\beta} \times real) \rightarrow (\underline{\beta} \times real)ref$$

Note that $\underline{\beta}$ is a weak type variable. The declaration of *fp* is illegal because *ref* does not have this type, with its strong type variable:

$$(\alpha \rightarrow \alpha) \rightarrow (\alpha \rightarrow \alpha)ref$$

Weak type variables keep track of all calls to *ref* that could occur in the evaluation of an expression. In this they resemble equality type variables, which keep track of equality tests. If an expression involves both *ref* and equality testing, its type could involve weak equality type variables. Fortunately, the 'weak' and 'equality' attributes can be understood separately.

Polymorphic declarations. Consider the value declaration

```
val Id = E
```

where the type of E contains weak type variables. When this declaration is evaluated, it could create new *ref* cells. These must not be treated as polymorphic. Since it is impossible to predict at compile-time whether E will allocate references, ML adopts a simple and safe rule:

1 If E is an identifier or is a function in **fn** notation, then it certainly does not allocate references. (The body of a function is not executed until an argument is supplied.)

2 If E is a function application or anything else, then it may allocate references.

If case 2 holds of a top level declaration, it is illegal:

```
val fp = ref I;
> Error: imperative type variables in declaration
```

Any monomorphic type constraint makes it legal:

```
val fp = ref (I: bool -> bool);
> val fp = ref fn : (bool -> bool) ref
```

If case 2 holds for a declaration inside a **let** expression, then each weak type variable in the type of E is effectively frozen; it can be replaced by only one type in the body of the **let**. For instance,

```
let val fp = ref I
in   fp := not; !fp 5  end;
```

is illegal because *ref I* involves the weak type variable α, which cannot stand for *bool* and *int* at the same time. The expression

```
let val fp = ref I
in  (!fp true, !fp 5)  end;
```

is illegal for the same reason. Observe that if we could evaluate this expression anyway, the result would be $(true, 5)$ with no run-time error. Finally

```
let val fp = ref I
in  fp := not; !fp true  end;
> false : bool
```

is legal because α stands for the type *bool*. Strictly speaking, *fp* has the monomorphic type $(bool \rightarrow bool)ref$.

Imperative list reversal. We now consider an example with real polymorphism. The function *irev* reverses a list imperatively. It uses one reference to scan down the list and another to accumulate the elements in reverse.

```
fun irev l =
   let val resultp = ref []
       and lp      = ref l
   in  while not (null (!lp)) do
            (resultp := hd(!lp) :: !resultp;
             lp      := tl(!lp));
         !resultp
   end;
> val irev = fn : '_a list -> '_a list
```

Weak type variables in Standard ML begin with the characters '_ (or ''_ for a weak equality type variable), and *irev* has the type $\alpha\ list \rightarrow \alpha\ list$. The variables *lp* and *resultp* have type $(\alpha\ list)ref$; the weak type variable α is fixed in the body of the **let**. ML accepts *irev* as a polymorphic function because it is declared using **fun**. A **fun** declaration is shorthand for a **val** declaration involving **fn** notation, and therefore comes under case 1.

As we can verify, *irev* is indeed polymorphic:

```
irev [25,10,1415];
> [1415, 10, 25] : int list
irev (explode("Montjoy"));
> ["y", "o", "j", "t", "n", "o", "M"] : string list
```

However, the following expressions are rejected:

```
irev [];
irev [I];
```

What is wrong here? An expression E at top level is equivalent to the declaration val $it=E$, and can be rejected by case 2. These expressions are rejected because their types, α *list* and $(\alpha \rightarrow \alpha)$ *list*, contain weak type variables. Actually these expressions are safe, and a more complicated type system might accept them.

If type checking is performed at compile-time, then it must make conservative assumptions about what could happen at run-time. Type checking rejects many programs that could be executed safely. The expression $hd[5, true] + 3$ evaluates safely to 8 despite being ill-typed. Many modern languages employ compile-time type checking; programmers accept these restrictions in order to be free from type errors at run-time.

Polymorphic references involve complex rules and their restrictions can seem arbitrary. Early ML compilers forbade polymorphic references altogether, allowing the function *ref* to have only monomorphic types. Some compilers provide various degrees of weak type variables. The type system of Standard ML seems adequate for defining polymorphic functions. The inability to define polymorphic objects like *irev*[I] matters little in practice.

The type checking of polymorphic references in Standard ML is probably secure. Tofte (1990) proved its correctness for a subset of ML and there is no reason to doubt that it is correct for the full language. Standard ML has been defined with great care to avoid insecurities and other semantic defects; in this regard, the language is practically in a class by itself.

Other uses of weak type variables. Weak type variables are involved in the type checking of imperative arrays, which are essentially collections of references. They are also involved with polymorphic exceptions, although exceptions do not involve the store. Consider the following nonsense:

```
exception Poly of 'a;          (* illegal!! *)
(raise Poly true) handle Poly x => x+1;
```

If this expression could be evaluated, it would attempt to evaluate $true + 1$, a run-time error. When a polymorphic exception is declared, ML must ensure that it is used with only one type. It suffices to treat each new exception like a reference involving the given type. Therefore, the type of a top level exception must be monomorphic and the type of a locally declared exception must not involve strong type variables.

Exercise 8.6   Is this expression legal? What does *WI* do?

```
let fun WI x = !(ref x)
in  (WI false, WI "Clarence")  end
```

Exercise 8.7   Which of these declarations are legal? Which could, if evaluated, lead to a run-time type error?

```
val funs = [ref];

val lp  =  let fun nilp x = ref []  in  nilp()  end;
```

Exercise 8.8   The simultaneous assignment

$$V_1, V_2, \ldots, V_n := E_1, E_2, \ldots, E_n$$

first evaluates the expressions, then assigns their values to the corresponding references. For instance $x, y := {!y}, {!x}$ exchanges the contents of x and y. Write an ML function to perform simultaneous assignments. It should have the (strongly) polymorphic type

$$(\alpha\,ref)\,list \times \alpha\,list \to unit.$$

References in data structures

Standard ML includes imperatives for practical reasons. Imperative programming is the most natural way to perform input and output. Some programs are specifically concerned with managing a state; a chess program must keep track of where the pieces are! Some efficient data structures, such as hash tables, work by updating arrays and pointers. Imperative methods make programs hard to understand and should only be employed when there is no functional alternative.

Linked data structures are a typical application of references. This section presents two such examples: doubly-linked circular lists and a highly efficient form of functional array. We begin with something simpler: sequences that store elements after they are computed.

8.4   *Sequences, or lazy lists*

Under the representation given in Chapter 5, the tail of a sequence is a function to compute another sequence. Each time the tail is inspected, a possibly expensive function call is repeated. This inefficiency can be eliminated. Represent the tail of a sequence by a reference, which initially contains a function and is later updated with the function's result. Sequences so implemented exploit imperative operations, but when viewed from outside are purely functional.

An abstract type of sequences. Lazy lists are implemented by the functor of Figure 8.1. Type $\alpha\,T$ has three constructors: *Nil* for the empty sequence, *Cons* for non-empty sequences, and *Delay* to permit delayed evaluation of the tail. A sequence of the form

$$Cons(x, ref(Delay\ xf)),$$

where *xf* has type *unit* $\to$ $\alpha\,T$, begins with *x* and has the sequence *xf*() for its remaining elements. Note that *Delay xf* is contained in a reference; applying *force* to this reference updates it to contain the value of *xf*(), removing the *Delay*.

The function *null* tests whether a sequence is empty, while *hd* and *tl* return the head and tail of a sequence. Because *tl* calls *force*, a sequence's outer constructor cannot be *Delay*. Inside functor *ImpSeqFUN*, functions on sequences may exploit pattern-matching; outside, they must use *null*, *hd* and *tl* because the constructors are hidden. The structure hides the implementation details, providing an abstract type with the following signature:

```
signature SEQUENCE =
  sig
  type 'a T
  exception E
  val empty   :   'a T
  val cons    :   '_a * (unit -> '_a T) -> '_a T
  val null    :   'a T -> bool
  val hd      :   'a T -> 'a
  val tl      :   'a T -> 'a T
  val take    :   int * 'a T -> 'a list
  val append  :   '_a T * '_a T -> '_a T
  val map     :   ('a -> '_b) -> 'a T -> '_b T
  val cycle   :   ((unit -> '_a T) -> '_a T) -> '_a T
  end;
```

Figure 8.1 *Lazy lists using references*

```
functor ImpSeqFUN () : SEQUENCE =
  struct
  datatype 'a T  = Nil
                 | Cons of 'a * ('a T) ref
                 | Delay of unit -> 'a T;

  exception E;

  val empty = Nil;
  fun cons(x,xf) = Cons(x, ref(Delay xf));

  fun force xp =
        case !xp of
            Delay xf => (xp := xf(); !xp)
          | xq => xq;

  fun null Nil = true
    | null (Cons _) = false;

  fun hd Nil = raise E
    | hd (Cons(x,_)) = x;

  fun tl Nil = raise E
    | tl (Cons(_,xp)) = force xp;

  fun take (0, xq) = []
    | take (n, Nil) = []
    | take (n, Cons(x,xp)) = x :: take (n-1, force xp);

  fun append (Nil,    yq) = yq
    | append (Cons(x,xp), yq) =
          cons(x, fn()=> append(force xp, yq));

  fun map f Nil  = Nil
    | map f (Cons(x,xp)) =
          cons(f x, fn()=> map f (force xp));

  fun cycle seqfn =
      let val knot = ref Nil
      in  knot := seqfn (fn()=> !knot); !knot  end;

  end;
```

Some of the functions are weakly polymorphic. The type of *cons* has weak type variables because it calls *ref*. The functions that call *cons*, like *append*, also have weak type variables. The function *cycle* also calls *ref*; it is explained below.

First, apply the functor to create a structure for sequences:

```
structure Seq = ImpSeqFUN();
```

Cyclic sequences. The function *cycle* creates cyclic sequences by tying the knot. Here is a sequence whose tail is itself:

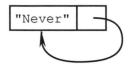

This behaves like the infinite sequence **"Never"**, **"Never"**, ..., but occupies a tiny amount of space in the computer. It is created by

```
Seq.cycle(fn xf => Seq.cons("Never", xf));
> Cons ("Never", ref (Delay fn)) : string T
Seq.take(5, it);
> ["Never","Never","Never","Never","Never"] : string list
```

When *cycle* is applied to some function *seqfn*, it creates the reference *knot* and supplies it to *seqfn* (packaged as a function). The result of *seqfn* is a sequence that, as its elements are computed, eventually refers to the contents of *knot*. Updating *knot* to contain this very sequence creates a cycle.

Cyclic sequences can compute Fibonacci numbers in an amusing fashion. Let *add* be a function that adds two sequences of integers, returning a sequence of sums. To illustrate reference polymorphism, *add* is coded in terms of a function to join two sequences into a sequence of pairs:

```
fun pairs (xq,yq) =
        Seq.cons((Seq.hd xq, Seq.hd yq),
                  fn()=>pairs(Seq.tl xq, Seq.tl yq));
> val pairs = fn : '_a T * '_b T -> ('_a * '_b) T
fun add (xq,yq): int Seq.T = Seq.map op+ (pairs(xq,yq));
> val add = fn : int T * int T -> int Seq.T
```

Observe that *pairs* is weakly polymorphic. The type constraint in *add* is necessary because + is overloaded.

The sequence of Fibonacci numbers can be defined using *cycle*:

```
val fib = Seq.cycle(fn fibf =>
    Seq.cons(1, fn()=>
        Seq.cons(1, fn()=>
            add(fibf(), Seq.tl(fibf())))));
> val fib = Cons (1, ref (Delay fn)) : int T
```

This definition is cyclic. The sequence begins 1, 1, and the remaining elements are obtained by adding the sequence to its tail:

$$add(fib, Seq.tl\,fib)$$

Initially, *fib* can be portrayed as follows:

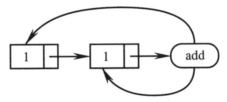

When the third element of *fib* is inspected by *tl* (*tl fib*), *add* computes a 2 and *force* updates the sequence as follows:

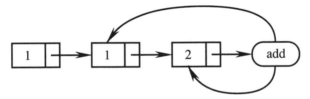

When the next element is inspected, *fib* becomes

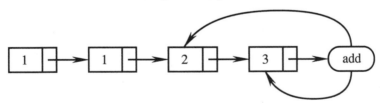

Because the sequence is cyclic and retains computed elements, each Fibonacci number is computed only once. This is reasonably fast. If Fibonacci numbers were defined recursively using the sequences of Chapter 5, the cost of computing the nth element would be exponential in n.

Exercise 8.9   The Hamming problem is to enumerate all integers of the form $2^i 3^j 5^k$ in increasing order. Define a cyclic sequence consisting of these numbers. Hint: define a function to merge increasing sequences, and consider the following diagram:

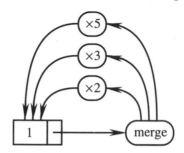

Exercise 8.10   The function *iterates* generates sequences of the form $[x, f(x), f(f(x)), \ldots, f^k(x), \ldots]$. Implement this function such that it creates a cyclic sequence.

Exercise 8.11   Discuss the difficulty showing whether a cyclic sequence is correct — that it generates a sequence of values satisfying a given specification. Comment on the following sequence:

```
val fib2 = Seq.cycle(fn fibf =>
            Seq.cons(1, fn()=> add(fibf(), Seq.tl(fibf()))));
```

Exercise 8.12   Why does the type of *map* involve both weak and strong type variables?

8.5   *Ring Buffers*

A doubly-linked list can be read forwards or backwards, and allow elements to be inserted or deleted at any point. It is circular if it closes back on itself:

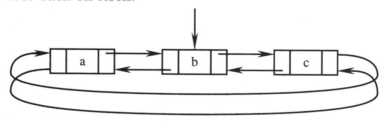

This imperative data structure, sometimes called a **ring buffer**, should be familiar to most programmers. We implement it here to make a comparison between references in Standard ML and pointer variables in procedural languages. Let us define an abstract type with the following signature:

```
signature RINGBUF =
  sig
  type 'a T
  exception E
  val empty     :  unit -> '_a T
  val null      :  'a T -> bool
  val label     :  'a T -> 'a
  val moveleft  :  'a T -> unit
  val moveright :  'a T -> unit
  val insert    :  '_a T * '_a -> unit
  val delete    :  'a T -> 'a
  end;
```

A ring buffer has type $\alpha\, T$ and is a reference into a doubly-linked list; the operations that create ring buffers are weakly polymorphic. Empty ring buffers are created by calling the function *empty*. Compare with the empty sequence *Seq.empty*, which contains no references and is polymorphic.

The function *null* tests whether a ring buffer is empty, *label* returns the label of the current node, and *moveleft*/*moveright* move the pointer to the left/right of the current node. As shown below, *insert*(*buf*, *e*) inserts a node labelled *e* to the left of the current node. Two links are redirected to the new node; their initial orientations are shown by crossed arrows and their final orientations by dashed arrows:

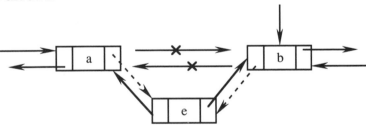

The function *delete* removes the current node and moves the pointer to the right. Its value is the label of the deleted node.

The code, which appears in Figure 8.2, is much as it might be written in Pascal. Each node of the doubly-linked list has type $\alpha\, buf$, which contains a label and references to the nodes on its left and right. Given a node, the functions *left* and *right* return these references.

The constructor *Empty* represents an empty list and serves as

Figure 8.2 *Ring buffers as doubly-linked lists*

```
structure Ringbuf : RINGBUF =
  struct
  datatype 'a buf = Empty | Node of 'a buf ref * 'a * 'a buf ref;
  datatype 'a T = Ptr of 'a buf ref;
  exception E;

  fun left (Node(lp,_,_)) = lp
    | left Empty = raise E;

  fun right (Node(_,_,rp)) = rp
    | right Empty = raise E;

  fun empty () = Ptr(ref Empty);

  fun null (Ptr p) = case !p of
          Empty => true
        | Node(_,x,_) => false;

  fun label (Ptr p) = case !p of
          Empty => raise E
        | Node(_,x,_) => x;

  fun moveleft (Ptr p) = (p := !(left(!p)));

  fun moveright (Ptr p) = (p := !(right(!p)));

  fun insert (Ptr p, x) =
      case !p of
          Empty =>
              let val lp = ref Empty
                  and rp = ref Empty
                  val new = Node(lp,x,rp)
              in  lp := new;  rp := new;  p := new  end
        | Node(lp,_,_) =>
              let val new = Node(ref(!lp), x, ref(!p))
              in  right(!lp) := new;  lp := new  end;

  fun delete (Ptr p) =
      case !p of
          Empty => raise E
        | Node(lp,x,rp) =>
              (if left(!lp) = lp then p := Empty
               else (right(!lp) := !rp;  left (!rp) := !lp;
                     p := !rp);
               x)
  end;
```

---

a placeholder, like Pascal's **nil** pointer. If *Node* were the only constructor of type α *buf*, no value of that type could be created. Consider the code for *insert*. When the first node is created, its left and right pointers initially contain *Empty*. They are then updated to contain the node itself.

Bear in mind that reference equality in ML differs from the usual notion of pointer equality. The function *delete* must check whether the only node of a buffer is about to be deleted. It cannot determine whether *Node*(lp, x, rp) is the only node by testing whether $lp = rp$, as a Pascal programmer might expect. That equality will always be false in a properly constructed buffer; each link field must be a distinct reference so that it can be updated independently. The test *left*$(!lp) = lp$ is correct. If the node on the left (namely $!lp$) and the current node have the same left link, then they are the same node and that is the only node in the buffer.

Here is a small demonstration of ring buffers. First, let us create an empty buffer. Because the function *empty* is weakly polymorphic, we must constrain its result to some monotype, here *string*.

```
val buf: string Ringbuf.T = Ringbuf.empty();
> val buf = Ptr (ref Empty) : string Ringbuf.T
Ringbuf.insert(buf, "They");
```

If only *insert* and *delete* are performed, then a ring buffer behaves like an imperative queue; elements can be inserted and later retrieved in the same order.

```
Ringbuf.insert(buf, "shall");
Ringbuf.delete buf;
> "They" : string
Ringbuf.insert(buf, "be");
Ringbuf.insert(buf, "famed");
Ringbuf.delete buf;
> "shall" : string
Ringbuf.delete buf;
> "be" : string
Ringbuf.delete buf;
> "famed" : string
```

Exercise 8.13 Modify *delete* to return a boolean value instead of a label: *true* if the modified buffer is empty and otherwise *false*.

Exercise 8.14 Which of the following equalities are suitable for testing whether *Node*(lp, x, rp) is the only node in a ring buffer?

$$!lp =\, !rp \qquad right(!lp) = lp \qquad right(!lp) = rp$$

Exercise 8.15   Compare the following insertion function with *insert*; does it have any advantages or disadvantages?

```
fun insert2 (Ptr p, x) =
    case !p of
        Empty          => p := Node(p,x,p)
      | Node(lp,_,_) =>
            let val new = Node(lp,x,p)
            in  right(!lp) := new;   lp := new end;
```

Exercise 8.16   Code a version of *insert* that inserts the new node to the right of the current point, rather than to the left.

Exercise 8.17   Show that if a value of type α *Ringbuf.T* (with a strong type variable) could be declared, a run-time type error could ensue.

8.6   *Imperative arrays and functional arrays*

Arrays are not specified in *The Definition of Standard ML*, but implementors have agreed to provide a structure *Array* with the following signature:

```
signature ARRAY =
  sig
  eqtype 'a array
  exception Subscript and Size
  val array     :   int * '_a -> '_a array
  val arrayoflist :  '_a list -> '_a array
  val tabulate   :   int * (int -> '_a) -> '_a array
  val sub        :   'a array * int -> 'a
  val update     :   'a array * int * 'a -> unit
  val length     :   'a array -> int
  end;
```

These are the operations for imperative arrays:

array(n, x) creates an n-element array with x stored in each cell. An n-element array admits subscripts from 0 to $n-1$. Each array has a fixed size.

arrayoflist$[x_0, x_1, \ldots, x_{n-1}]$ creates an n-element array with x_k stored in cell k, for $k = 0, \ldots, n - 1$.

tabulate(n, f) creates an n-element array with $f(k)$ stored in cell k, for $k = 0, \ldots, n - 1$.

sub(A, k) returns the contents of cell k of array A.

update(A, k, x) updates cell k of array A to contain x.

length(A) returns the number of elements in array A.

Exception *Subscript* is raised if a subscript is out of range, while *Size* is raised upon any attempt to create an array of negative size.

The functions *array* and *arrayoflist* are weakly polymorphic because they create cells that can be updated. These arrays suffice for all the usual applications. Arrays of arrays may be created, like in Pascal, to serve as multi-dimensional arrays.

Representing functional arrays. Holmström and Hughes have developed a hybrid representation of functional arrays, exploiting imperative arrays and association lists. An association list consisting of (*index, contents*) pairs has a functional update operation: simply add a new pair to the front of the list. Update is fast, but lookup requires an expensive search. Introducing an imperative array, called the **vector**, makes lookups faster (Aasa et al., 1988).

Initially, a functional array is represented by a vector. Update operations build an association list in front of the vector, indicating differences between the current contents of the vector and the values of various arrays. Consider two cells i and j of a functional array A, with $i \neq j$, and suppose $A[i] = u$ and $A[j] = v$. Now perform some functional updates. Obtain B from A by storing x in position i; obtain C from B by storing y in position j:

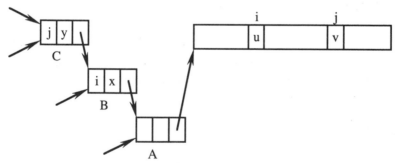

Other links into A, B and C are shown; these come from arrays created by further updating. The arrays form a tree, called a **version tree** since its nodes are 'versions' of the vector. Unlike ordinary trees, its links point towards the root rather than away from it. The root of the tree is A, which is a dummy node linked to the vector. The dummy node contains the only direct link into the vector, in order to simplify the re-rooting operation.

Re-rooting the version tree. Although C has the correct value, with $C[i] = x$, $C[j] = y$ and the other elements like in A, lookups to C are slower than they could be. If C is the most heavily used version of the vector, then the root of the version tree ought to be moved to C. The links from C to the vector are reversed; the updates indicated by those nodes are executed in the vector; the previous contents of those vector cells are recorded in the nodes.

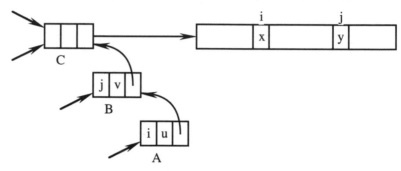

This operation does not affect the values of the functional arrays, but lookups to A become slower while lookups to C become faster. The dummy node is now C. Nodes of the version tree that refer to A, B, or C likewise undergo a change in lookup time, but not in value. Re-rooting does not require locating those other nodes. If there are no other references to A or B then the ML storage allocator will reclaim them.

An implementation. Figure 8.3 shows an ML structure declaration for version tree arrays, called *v*-arrays for short. It is based on Aasa et al. (1988) and has the following signature:

```
signature VARRAY =
  sig
  type 'a T
  exception E
  val array       :  int * '_a -> '_a T
  val reroot      :  'a T -> 'a T
  val sub         :  'a T * int -> 'a
  val just_update :  '_a T * int * '_a -> '_a T
  val update      :  '_a T * int * '_a -> '_a T
  end;
```

The type of *v*-arrays is $\alpha\ T$, which is a datatype with constructors *Modif* and *Vector*. A *Modif*, for modification node, is a record

Figure 8.3 *Functional arrays as version trees*

```
structure Varray : VARRAY =
  struct
  datatype 'a T = Modif of {limit: int,
                            index: int ref,
                            elem: 'a ref,
                            next: 'a T ref}
              | Vector of 'a Array.array;
  exception E;

  fun array (n,x) =
      if n <= 0  then  raise E
      else  Modif{limit=n, index=ref 0, elem=ref x,
                  next=ref(Vector(Array.array(n,x)))};

  fun reroot (va as Modif{index, elem, next,...}) =
      case !next of
        Vector _ => va   (*have reached root*)
      | Modif _ =>
          let val Modif{index=bindex, elem=belem, next=bnext,...} =
                    reroot (!next)
              val Vector vec = !bnext
          in  bindex := !index;
              belem := Array.sub(vec, !index);
              Array.update(vec, !index, !elem);
              next := !bnext;
              bnext := va;
              va
          end;

  fun sub (Modif{index,elem,next,...}, i) =
      case !next of
        Vector vec => Array.sub(vec,i)
      | Modif _ =>    if !index=i  then  !elem
                                   else  sub(!next,i);

  fun just_update(va as Modif{limit,...}, i, x) =
      if 0<=i andalso i<limit
      then Modif{limit=limit, index= ref i,
                 elem=ref x, next=ref va}
      else raise E;

  fun update(va,i,x) = reroot(just_update(va,i,x));
  end;
```

with four fields. The upper limit of the v-array is stored for sub-script checking. The other fields are references to an index, an element and the next v-array; these are updated during re-rooting. A *Vector* contains the imperative array. The constructors are hidden to protect the representation of type $\alpha\ T$.

Calling $array(n, x)$ constructs a v-array consisting of a vector and a dummy node. The recursive function *reroot* performs re-rooting. The subscript operation $sub(va, i)$ searches in the nodes for i and if necessary looks up that subscript in the vector. The function *just_update* simply creates a new node, while *update* follows this operation by re-rooting at the new array.

Programs frequently use functional arrays in an imperative style, discarding the previous value of the array after each update. In this case, we should re-root after each update. If many versions of a functional array are active then version trees could be inefficient; only one version can be represented by the vector. In this case, we should represent functional arrays by binary trees, like in Chapter 4. Binary trees would also allow an array to grow and shrink.

Aasa et al. (1988) describe v-arrays, with experimental results. For several essentially imperative algorithms, v-arrays prove to be more efficient than other representations of functional arrays. At their best, v-arrays can perform lookups and updates in constant time, although more slowly than imperative arrays. Quick sort on v-arrays turns out to be no faster than quick sort on lists, suggesting that arrays should be reserved for tasks requiring random access. Lists are efficient for processing elements sequentially.

Exercise 8.18   Add a function *arrayoflist* to structure *Varray*, to create a v-array from a list.

Exercise 8.19   Add a function *copy* to structure *Varray*, such that $copy(va)$ creates a new v-array having the same value as va.

Exercise 8.20   Define a structure *Array2* for imperative arrays of 2 dimensions, with components analogous to those of *Array*.

Exercise 8.21   Define a structure *Varray2* for v-arrays of 2 dimensions, with components analogous to those of *Varray*.

Exercise 8.22   What are the contents of the dummy node? Could an alternative representation of v-arrays eliminate this node?

Input and output in Standard ML

Functional programming and input/output are fundamentally incompatible. Displays, printers and discs have a state; their operations are imperative. Although many people are investigating methods for communication between the outside world and purely functional programs, no simple solution appears to be forthcoming.

8.7 *The input/output primitives*

Standard ML's input and output primitives are imperative. A **stream** connects an external device to the program for transmitting characters. There are two kinds of streams. An **input** stream is connected to a producer of data, such as the keyboard; characters may be read from it until the producer terminates the stream. An **output** stream is connected to a consumer of data, such as a printer; characters may be sent to it.

These facilities are rudimentary. The *Definition* does not even provide an operation for converting a string like "3.14159" to a real number. Some compilers provide the conversion from real numbers to strings — as well as advanced facilities like parser generators and window management. The input and output primitives are shown in the following signature:

```
signature IO =
  sig
  type instream and outstream
  exception Io of string
  val std_in       :  instream
  val open_in      :  string -> instream
  val close_in     :  instream -> unit
  val input        :  instream * int -> string
  val lookahead    :  instream -> string
  val end_of_stream :  instream -> bool
  val std_out      :  outstream
  val open_out     :  string -> outstream
  val close_out    :  outstream -> unit
  val output       :  outstream * string -> unit
  end;
```

Here is a brief description of these items:

Input streams have type *instream* while output streams have type *outstream*. These types do not admit equality.

open_in(*s*) and *open_out*(*s*) create a stream connected to the file or device named *s*.

close_in(*is*) and *close_out*(*os*) terminate a stream, disconnecting it from its device. The stream may no longer transmit characters. An input stream may be closed by its device, for example upon end of file.

input(*is*, *n*) removes up to *n* characters from stream *is* and returns them as a string. If the stream has closed with fewer than *n* characters, then only these characters are returned. The input operation waits until *n* characters are available or the stream closes.

lookahead(*is*) returns the same value as *input*(*is*, 1) but does not remove any characters from the stream. It waits until a character is available or the stream is closed.

end_of_stream(*is*) is *true* if the stream *is* is empty and has been closed; it is exactly equivalent to *lookahead*(*is*) = "".

output(*os*, *s*) writes the characters of string *s* to the stream *os*, provided it has not been closed.

std_in and *std_out*, the standard input and output streams, are connected to the terminal in an interactive session.

Exception *Io* is raised in the event of errors, with a message like 'No such file.'

Two other functions, *print* and *makestring*, are no longer part of Standard ML but are provided by many compilers. Calling *print*(*x*) prints the value of *x* on the terminal, while *makestring*(*x*) converts *x* to a string. These functions are overloaded; typically *x* may have the type *real*, *int* or *bool*.

```
makestring 4;
> "4" : string
makestring (sqrt 2.0);
> "1.414213562" : string
print (sqrt 2.0);
> 1.4142135621.414213562 : real
```

Exercise 8.23 Explain the response to the call to *print* above. (Hint: the value of *print*(*x*) is *x*.)

Exercise 8.24 Compare Standard ML's input and output facilities with those of Pascal, C, or a similar language. How far could ML's facilities be extended without compromising security?

8.8   *Example: simple text processing*

To demonstrate ML's input/output primitives, here is a program to read a series of lines and print the first word of each line.

The function *input_line* reads the next line from a stream and returns it, including the final newline character, as a string. It works by reading single characters until it reads a newline or finds that the input has closed (as indicated by the empty string). Remember that calling *input*(*is*, 1) has the side effect of removing a character from *is*:

```
fun input_line is =
  let fun getstring s =
        case input(is,1) of
            ""   => s               (*input has closed*)
          | "\n" => s^"\n"          (*end of line*)
          | c    => getstring(s^c)
  in   getstring "" end;
> val input_line = fn : instream -> string
```

The function *is_letter* recognizes letters, both upper and lower case:

```
fun is_letter c =
  "A" <= c  andalso  c <= "Z"  orelse
  "a" <= c  andalso  c <= "z";
> val is_letter = fn : string -> bool
```

The function *getword* returns the first 'word' — series of letters — in a string. The string is converted to a list by *explode* and each letter is concatenated to the current word.

```
local fun get ([], word) = word
        | get (c::cs, word)=
              if is_letter c then get(cs, word^c) else word
  in
  fun getword s = get(explode s, "")
  end;
> val getword = fn : string -> string
```

The function *firstwords*, given an input stream and an output stream, repeatedly reads a line from the input and writes the first word to the output:

```
fun firstwords (is, os) =
  while not (end_of_stream is) do
    output(os, getword(input_line is) ^ "\n");
> val firstwords = fn : instream * outstream -> unit
```

Suppose the file **Harry** holds some lines by Henry V, from his message to the French shortly before the battle of Agincourt:

```
My people are with sickness much enfeebled,
my numbers lessened, and those few I have
almost no better than so many French...
But, God before, we say we will come on!
```

Let *infile* be an input stream to **Harry**, and apply *firstwords* to it:

```
val infile = open_in("Harry");
> val infile = ? : instream
firstwords(infile,std_out);
> My
> my
> almost
> But
```

The output appears at the terminal because *std_out* has been given as the output stream. We can make *firstwords* read from and write to the terminal:

```
firstwords(std_in,std_out);
If we may pass, we will.
> If
If we be hindered...
> If
```

Purely functional languages perform input and output via lazy lists of characters. Our example must be coded carefully under that approach. Otherwise the output may appear too soon — as soon as we have typed the first word. Interactive input/output is easy in Standard ML.

Exercise 8.25   Modify *firstwords* to prompt for each input line from the terminal. Ensure that it prints the prompt before demanding input.

Exercise 8.26   Write an ML program to count how many characters, words and lines are contained in a file.

8.9   *A pretty printer*

Programs and mathematical formulae are easier to read if they are laid out with line breaks and indentation to emphasize their structure. The tautology checker of Chapter 4 includes the function *show*, which converts a proposition to a string. If the string is too long to fit on one line, we usually see something like

Figure 8.4 *Output of the pretty printer*

```
((~((((~landed) | rich) &
      (~(saintly & rich)))) |
 ((~landed) | (~saintly)))

((((landed | saintly) |
   ((~landed) | (~saintly))) &
  (((~rich) | saintly) |
   ((~landed) |
    (~saintly)))) &
 (((landed | rich) |
   ((~landed) | (~saintly))) &
  (((~rich) | rich) |
   ((~landed) | (~saintly)))))


((~((((~landed) | rich) & (~(saintly & rich)))) |
 ((~landed) | (~saintly)))

((((landed | saintly) | ((~landed) | (~saintly))) &
  (((~rich) | saintly) | ((~landed) | (~saintly)))) &
 (((landed | rich) | ((~landed) | (~saintly))) &
  (((~rich) | rich) | ((~landed) | (~saintly)))))
```

---

this (for a margin of 30):

```
((((landed | saintly) | ((~lan
ded) | (~saintly))) & (((~rich
) | saintly) | ((~landed) | (~
saintly)))) & (((landed | rich
) | ((~landed) | (~saintly)))
& (((~rich) | rich) | ((~lande
d) | (~saintly)))))
```

Figure 8.4 shows the rather better display produced by a pretty printer. Two propositions (including the one above) are formatted to margins of 30 and 60. Finding the ideal presentation of a formula may require judgement and taste, but a simple scheme for pretty printing gives surprisingly good results.

The pretty printer accepts a piece of text decorated with information about nesting and allowed break points. Let us indicate nesting by angle brackets (⟨⟩) and possible line breaks by a vertical bar (|). An expression of the form $\langle e_1 \ldots e_n \rangle$ is called a **block**. For instance, the block

$$\langle\!\langle \; \texttt{a} \; * \; | \; \texttt{b} \; \rangle \; - \; | \langle \; (\; \langle \; \texttt{c} \; + \; | \; \texttt{d} \; \rangle \;) \; \rangle\!\rangle$$

represents the string `a*b-(c+d)`. It allows line breaks after the characters `*`, `-` and `+`.

When parentheses are suppressed according to operator precedences, correct pretty printing is essential. The nesting structure of the block corresponds to the formula

$$(a \times b) - (c + d) \quad \text{rather than} \quad a \times (b - (c + d)).$$

If `a*b-(c+d)` does not fit on one line, then it should be broken after the `-` character; outer blocks are broken before inner blocks.

The pretty printing algorithm keeps track of how much space remains on the current line. When it encounters a break, it determines how many characters there are until the next break in the same block or in an enclosing block. (Thus it ignores breaks in inner blocks.) If that many characters will not fit on the current line, then the algorithm prints a new line, indented to match the beginning of the current block.

The algorithm does not insist that a break should immediately follow every block. In the previous example, the block

$$\langle \; \texttt{c} \; + \; | \; \texttt{d} \; \rangle$$

is followed by a `)` character; the string `d)` cannot be broken. Determining the distance until the next break is therefore somewhat involved.

The pretty printer has the signature

```
signature PRETTY =
  sig
  type T
  val blo : int * T list -> T
  val str : string -> T
  val brk : int -> T
  val pr  : outstream * T * int -> unit
  end;
```

and provides slightly fancier primitives than those just described:

T is the type of symbolic expressions, namely blocks, strings and breaks.

$blo(i, [e_1, \ldots, e_n])$ creates a block containing the given expressions, and specifies that the current indentation be increased by i. This indentation will be used if the block is broken.

$str(s)$ creates an expression containing the string s.

$brk(l)$ creates a break of length l; if no line break is required then l spaces will be printed instead.

$pr(os, e, m)$ prints expression e on stream os with a right margin of m.

Figure 8.5 presents the pretty printer as a functor. Observe that *Block* stores the total size of a block, as computed by *blo*. Also, *after* holds the distance from the end of the current block to the next break.

The pretty printer is inspired by Oppen (1980). Oppen's algorithm is complicated but requires little storage; it can process an enormous file, storing only a few linefuls. Our pretty printer is adequate for displaying theorems and other computed results that easily fit in store.

The output shown in Figure 8.4 was produced by extending the tautology checker (Chapter 4) as follows:

```
structure Pretty = PrettyFUN();
open Pretty;

fun prettyshow (Atom a)    = str a
  | prettyshow (Neg p)     =
        blo(1, [str"(~", prettyshow p, str")"])
  | prettyshow (Conj(p,q)) =
        blo(1, [str"(", prettyshow p, str" &",
                brk 1, prettyshow q, str")"])
  | prettyshow (Disj(p,q)) =
        blo(1, [str"(", prettyshow p, str" |",
                brk 1, prettyshow q, str")"]);
> val prettyshow = fn : prop -> T
```

Calling *pr* with the result of *prettyshow* does the pretty printing.

Exercise 8.27 Give an example of how a block of the form

$$\langle\langle E_1 \; * \; | \; E_2 \rangle \; - \; | \langle \; (\; \langle E_3 \; + \; | \; E_4 \rangle \;) \; \rangle \rangle$$

could be pretty printed with a line break after the * character and none after the − character. How serious is this problem? Suggest a modification to the algorithm to correct it.

Figure 8.5 *The pretty printer*

```
functor PrettyFUN () : PRETTY =
  struct
  datatype T = Block of T list * int * int
             | String of string
             | Break of int;

    fun breakdist(Block(_,_,len)::es, after) = len + breakdist(es,after)
      | breakdist(String s :: es, after) = size s + breakdist(es,after)
      | breakdist(Break _ :: es, after) = 0
      | breakdist([], after) = after;

    fun pr (os, e, margin) =
     let val space = ref margin
         fun blanks 0 = ()
           | blanks n = (output(os," ");   space := !space - 1;
                         blanks(n-1))
         fun newline () = (output(os,"\n");   space := margin)

         fun printing ([], _, _) = ()
           | printing (e::es, blockspace, after) =
             (case e of
                  Block(bes,indent,len) =>
                      printing(bes, !space-indent, breakdist(es,after))
                | String s => (output(os,s);   space := !space - size s)
                | Break len =>
                    if len + breakdist(es,after) <= !space
                    then blanks len
                    else (newline();   blanks(margin-blockspace));
              printing (es, blockspace, after))
     in  printing([e], margin, 0);   newline()  end;

    fun length (Block(_,_,len)) = len
      | length (String s) = size s
      | length (Break len) = len;

    val str = String and   brk = Break;

    fun blo (indent,es) =
      let fun sum([], k) = k
            | sum(e::es, k) = sum(es, length e + k)
      in  Block(es,indent, sum(es,0))   end;
  end;
```

Exercise 8.28 Implement a new kind of block, with 'consistent breaks': unless the entire block fits on the current line, all of its breaks are forced. For instance, consistent breaking of

$$\langle \texttt{ if } E \mid \texttt{ then } E_1 \mid \texttt{ else } E_2 \rangle$$

would produce
```
if E
then E₁
else E₂
```
and never
```
if E then E₁
else E₂
```

Exercise 8.29 Write a purely functional version of the pretty printer. Instead of writing to a stream, it should return a list of strings. Does the functional version have any practical advantages?

Exercise 8.30 The Fortran statement

```
FORMAT (' Input =', I6, ' Output =', F8.2)
```

describes a line of text beginning with the string ' Input =', followed by an integer taking up 6 characters, followed by the string ' Output =', followed by a floating point (real) number taking up 8 characters, with 2 digits to the right of the decimal point. A file written under a Fortran format can be read under the same format. Discuss how this kind of formatted input/output could be implemented in ML. How would formats and data be represented?

Summary of main points

References denote modifiable cells in the store, like the variables and pointers of procedural languages.

In ML, variables cannot be updated; only references and arrays can be updated.

The function *ref*, which creates a reference cell, is weakly polymorphic; the type of a cell cannot change at run-time.

Cyclic data structures, like ring buffers, can be constructed using references.

A function can exploit imperative features while exhibiting purely functional behaviour.

Input and output commands transmit characters between the ML program and external devices.

9

Writing Interpreters for the λ-Calculus

This chapter brings together all the concepts we have learned so far. For an extended example, it presents a collection of ML modules to implement the λ-calculus as a primitive functional programming language. Terms of the λ-calculus can be parsed, evaluated and the result displayed. It is hardly a practical language; computing the factorial of four takes minutes! However, its implementation involves many fundamental techniques: parsing, representing bound variables and reducing expressions to normal form. These techniques can be applied to theorem proving and computer algebra.

Chapter outline

We consider parsing and two interpreters for λ-terms, with an overview of the λ-calculus. The chapter contains the following sections:

A functional parser. An ML functor implements top-down recursive descent parsing. Parsers can be combined using infix operators that resemble the symbols for combining grammatical phrases.

The λ-calculus. This is a formal model of computation. Terms of the λ-calculus can be evaluated using either the call-by-value or the call-by-name rule for function application. Substitution must be performed carefully, avoiding variable name clashes.

Representing λ-terms in ML. Substitution, parsing and pretty printing are implemented using ML functors.

The λ-calculus as a programming language. Typical data structures of functional languages, including infinite lists, are encoded in the λ-calculus. The evaluation of recursive functions is demonstrated.

A functional parser

Before discussing the λ-calculus, let us consider how to write scanners and parsers in a functional style. The parser described below complements the pretty printer of the previous chapter. Using these tools, ML programs can read and write λ-terms, ML types and logical formulae.

9.1   *A library module*

This chapter and the next demonstrate the use of Standard ML modules, presenting programs that consist entirely of signatures and functors. Previous chapters have assumed declarations of utility functions like *take* and *drop*. Henceforth a functor will refer only to ML's pervasive identifiers, like *rev* and *map*, and to the functor's formal parameters. All the library functions required below are packaged into a structure having signature *BASIC*:

```
infix mem;

signature BASIC =
  sig
  exception Lookup
  exception Nth
  val minl     : int list -> int
  val maxl     : int list -> int
  val take     : int * 'a list -> 'a list
  val drop     : int * 'a list -> 'a list
  val nth      : 'a list * int -> 'a
  val mem      : ''a * ''a list -> bool
  val newmem   : ''a * ''a list -> ''a list
  val lookup   : (''a * 'b) list * ''a -> 'b
  val filter   : ('a -> bool) -> 'a list -> 'a list
  val exists   : ('a -> bool) -> 'a list -> bool
  val forall   : ('a -> bool) -> 'a list -> bool
  val foldleft : ('a * 'b -> 'a) -> 'a * 'b list -> 'a
  val foldright: ('a * 'b -> 'b) -> 'a list * 'b -> 'b
  end;
```

Here is a brief description of the functions, most of which have appeared earlier in the book:

minl(*ns*) returns the minimum of the integers in *ns*.

Figure 9.1 *The basic library functor*

```
functor BasicFUN () : BASIC =
  struct
  fun minl [m]  : int = m
    | minl(m::n::ns) = if m<n then minl(m::ns) else minl(n::ns);

  fun maxl [m]  : int = m
    | maxl(m::n::ns) = if m>n then maxl(m::ns) else maxl(n::ns);

  fun take (n, []) = []
    | take (n, x::xs) =  if n>0 then x::take(n-1,xs) else [];
  fun drop (_, [])    = []
    | drop (n, x::xs) = if n>0 then drop (n-1, xs) else x::xs;

  exception Nth;
  fun nth (l,n) =      (*numbers the list elements [x0,x1,x2,...] *)
        case drop(n,l) of [] => raise Nth
                      | x::_ => x;

  fun x mem []   =  false
    | x mem (y::l)  =  (x=y) orelse (x mem l);
  fun newmem(x,xs) = if x mem xs then  xs    else  x::xs;

  exception Lookup;
  fun lookup ([], a) = raise Lookup
    | lookup ((x,y)::pairs, a) = if a=x then y else lookup(pairs, a);

  fun filter pred [] = []
    | filter pred (x::xs) =
        if pred(x) then x :: filter pred xs else  filter pred xs;

  fun exists pred []      = false
    | exists pred (x::xs) = (pred x)  orelse  exists pred xs;

  fun forall pred []      = true
    | forall pred (x::xs) = (pred x)  andalso  forall pred xs;

  fun foldleft f (e, [])    = e
    | foldleft f (e, x::xs) = foldleft f (f(e,x), xs);

  fun foldright f ([],    e) = e
    | foldright f (x::xs, e) = f(x, foldright f (xs,e));
  end;
```

maxl(*ns*) returns the maximum of the integers in *ns*.

take(*i*, *xs*) returns the first *i* elements of *xs* ($i \geq 0$).

drop(*i*, *xs*) returns all but the first *i* elements of *xs* ($i \geq 0$).

nth([$x_0, \ldots, x_{n-1}$], *i*) returns element x_i if $0 \leq i < n$ and raises exception *Nth* otherwise.

x mem *xs* returns *true* if *x* is an element of *xs*. The directive **infix** *mem* is pervasive since it is made at top level.

newmem(*x*, *xs*) returns the 'set' $\{x\} \cup xs$, inserting *x* only if it is not already a member of *xs*.

lookup([$(x_1, y_1), \ldots, (x_n, y_n)$], *x*) returns y_k if $x = x_k$ (for the least *k*), and raises exception *Lookup* if there is no such *k*, namely if *x* is not found in the list.

filter pred xs returns the list of all *x* in *xs* with *pred x* = *true*.

exists pred xs = *true* if *pred x* = *true* for some *x* in *xs*.

forall pred xs = *true* if *pred x* = *true* for every *x* in *xs*.

foldleft f (e, [$x_1, \ldots, x_n$]) = $f(\ldots f(e, x_1) \ldots, x_n)$.

foldright f ([$x_1, \ldots, x_n$], e) = $f(x_1, \ldots f(x_n, e) \ldots)$.

The functor *BasicFUN* (Figure 9.1) can create an instance *Basic* of this signature. By taking *Basic* as a parameter, any functor can have access to the library, and most functors will do so.

Perhaps it would be simpler to add these functions to the ML environment, making them pervasive; some ML compilers allow this. However, if a project accumulates a vast library of definitions, they should be structured into modules. It would be unwise to introduce hundreds of pervasive names.

Exercise 9.1   Sketch the design of a library consisting of separate modules for integer arithmetic, real arithmetic, strings, lists and trees. Give a fragment of each signature and the corresponding fragment of each functor. Give examples of 'generic' operations that ought to be implemented for all the types in the library.

9.2   *Scanning, or lexical analysis*

A parser seldom operates directly on a string of characters. The characters are first **scanned**: processed into **tokens** such as keywords, identifiers, special symbols and numbers. The parser is supplied a list of tokens.

This two-level approach simplifies the grammar used for parsing. The scanner removes spaces, line breaks and comments in some uniform fashion, leaving the parser to deal with more complex matters of syntax. Scanning can be performed by a finite-state machine. Such a machine, controlled by character-indexed arrays, can run extremely fast. If we expect to scan only small inputs then we can make do with naïve list processing.

A lexical analyser is a structure with the following signature:

```
signature LEXICAL =
  sig
  datatype token = Id of string | Key of string
  val scan : string -> token list
  end;
```

A *token* is either an identifier or a keyword; this simple scanner does not recognize numbers. Calling *scan* performs lexical analysis on a string and returns the resulting list of tokens.

To classify tokens as identifiers or keywords, the scanner must be supplied with an instance of the signature *KEYWORD*:

```
signature KEYWORD =
  sig
  val alphas  : string list
  and symbols : string list
  end;
```

The list *alphas* must contain all the alphanumeric keywords (like `"if"` and `"let"`) of the language to be parsed, while *symbols* must contain the symbolic keywords (like `"("` and `")"`). The two kinds of keywords are treated differently.

A string of alphanumeric characters is scanned as far as possible — until it is not followed by another letter or digit. It is classified as a keyword if it belongs to *alphas*, and as an identifier otherwise.

A string of symbolic characters is scanned until it matches some element of *symbols*, or until it is not followed by another symbolic character. It is always classified as a keyword. For instance, if `"("` belongs to *symbols* then the string `"(("` is scanned as two `"("` tokens, and as one `"(("` token otherwise.

Functor *LexicalFUN* implements the scanner (Figure 9.2). Its main concession to efficiency is that *scanning* is an iterative function, accumulating tokens while it processes the list of characters. The remainder of the functor consists of routine list processing. Its formal parameters are *Basic* and *Keyword*; observe that the library module is **open** in the functor body.

Figure 9.2 *The lexical analysis functor*

```
functor LexicalFUN (structure Basic: BASIC
                    and       Keyword: KEYWORD) : LEXICAL =
  struct
  local open Basic in
  datatype token = Key of string  |  Id of string;

  fun is_letter_or_digit c =
      "A"<=c andalso c<="Z" orelse
      "a"<=c andalso c<="z" orelse
      "0"<=c andalso c<="9";
  val specials = explode"!@#$%^&*()+-=[]:\"|;'\,./?`_~<>";
  fun alphanum (id, c::cs) =
        if is_letter_or_digit c
        then  alphanum (id^c, cs)
        else  (id, c::cs)
    | alphanum (id, []) = (id, []);

  fun tokenof a = if a mem Keyword.alphas then Key(a) else Id(a);

  fun symbolic (sy, c::cs) =
        if sy mem Keyword.symbols orelse not (c mem specials)
        then  (sy, c::cs)
        else  symbolic (sy^c, cs)
    | symbolic (sy, []) = (sy, []);

  fun scanning (toks, []) = rev toks     (*end of chars*)
    | scanning (toks, c::cs) =
        if is_letter_or_digit c
        then (*identifier or keyword*)
            let val (id, cs2) = alphanum(c, cs)
            in  scanning (tokenof id :: toks, cs2)   end
        else if c mem specials
        then (*symbolic keyword*)
            let val (sy, cs2) = symbolic(c, cs)
            in  scanning (Key sy :: toks, cs2)   end
        else (*skip spaces, line breaks, strange characters*)
            scanning (toks, cs);

  fun scan a = scanning([], explode a);
  end
end;
```

Exercise 9.2 Modify the scanner to recognize decimal numerals in the input. Let a new constructor *Num* : *integer* → *token* return the value of a string of digits.

Exercise 9.3 Modify the scanner to ignore comments. The comment brackets, such as "(*" and "*)", should be supplied as additional components of the structure *Keyword*.

9.3   *A toolkit for top-down parsing*

Many programmers know that a top-down recursive descent parser closely resembles the grammar that it parses. There are procedures for all the syntactic phrases, and their mutually recursive calls precisely mirror the grammar rules.

The resemblance is closer in functional programming. Higher-order functions can express syntactic operations such as concatenation of phrases, alternative phrases and repetition of a phrase. With an appropriate choice of infix operators, a functional parser can be coded to look almost exactly like a set of grammar rules. Do not be fooled; the program has all the limitations of top-down parsing. In particular, a **left-recursive** grammar rule such as

$$exp = exp \ "*"$$

makes the parser run forever! Compiler books such as Aho, Sethi & Ullman (1986) advise on coping with these limitations. Some ML systems provide access to sophisticated parser generators, but top-down parsing suffices for our purposes.

This approach to functional parsing has been understood for a long time. Burge (1975) contains one of the earliest published descriptions. Reade (1989) gives a more modern account. Frost & Launchbury (1989) use the method to parse a subset of English for a question-answering system.

Outline of the approach. Suppose that the grammar includes a certain class of phrases whose meanings can be represented by values of type α. A **parser** for such phrases must be a function of type

$$token \ list \ \rightarrow \ \alpha \times token \ list,$$

henceforth abbreviated as type $\alpha \ phrase$. When the parser is given a list of tokens that begins with a valid phrase, it removes those tokens and computes their meaning as a value of type α. The parser returns the pair of this meaning and the remaining tokens. If the token list does not begin with a valid phrase, then the parser rejects it by raising exception *SynError*.

Not all functions of type α *phrase* are parsers. A parser must only remove tokens from the front of the token list; it must not insert tokens, or modify the token list in any other way.

To implement complex parsers, we define some primitive parsers and some operations for combining parsers.

Parsing primitive phrases. The trivial parsers recognize an identifier, a specific keyword, or the empty phrase. They remove no more than one token from their input:

> The parser *id*, of type *string phrase*, removes an *Id* token from its input and returns this identifier as a string (paired with the tail of the token list).
>
> The parser \$*a* has type *string phrase* if *a* is a string. It removes the keyword token *Key a* from its input and returns *a* paired with the tail of the token list.
>
> The parser *empty* has the polymorphic type (α *list*) *phrase*. It returns [] paired with the original token list.

The first two of these reject their input unless it begins with the required token, while *empty* always succeeds.

Alternative phrases. The parser *ph*1||*ph*2 accepts all the phrases that are accepted by either of the parsers *ph*1 or *ph*2. This parser, when supplied with a list of tokens, passes them to *ph*1 and returns the result if successful. If *ph*1 rejects the tokens then *ph*2 is attempted.

If *ph*1 and *ph*2 have type α *phrase* then so does *ph*1||*ph*2.

Consecutive phrases. The parser *ph*1−−*ph*2 accepts a *ph*1 phrase followed by a *ph*2 phrase. This parser, when supplied with a list of tokens, passes them to *ph*1. If *ph*1 parses a phrase and returns $(x, toks2)$ then the remaining tokens ($toks2$) are passed to *ph*2. If *ph*2 parses a phrase and returns $(y, toks3)$ then *ph*1−−*ph*2 returns $((x, y), toks3)$. Note that $toks3$ consists of the tokens remaining after both parses. If either parser rejects its input then so does *ph*1−−*ph*2.

Thus, the meaning of *ph*1−−*ph*2 is the pair of the meanings of *ph*1 and *ph*2, applied to consecutive segments of the input. If *ph*1 has type α *phrase* and *ph*2 has type β *phrase* then *ph*1−−*ph*2 has type $(\alpha \times \beta)$ *phrase*.

Modifying the meaning. The parser *ph*>>*f* accepts the same inputs as *ph*, but returns $(f(x), toks)$ when *ph* returns $(x, toks)$. Thus, it assigns the meaning $f(x)$ when *ph* assigns the meaning x. If *ph* has type α *phrase* and f has type $\alpha \to \beta$ then *ph*>>*f* has type β *phrase*.

Repetition. To illustrate these operators, let us code a parsing functional. If *ph* is any parser then *repeat ph* will parse zero or more repetitions of *ph*:

```
fun repeat ph toks = (    ph -- repeat ph >> (op::)
                     || empty     ) toks;
```

The precedences of the infix operators are −−, >>, || from highest to lowest. The body of *repeat* consists of two parsers joined by ||, resembling the obvious grammatical definition: a repetition of *ph* is either a *ph* followed by a repetition of *ph*, or is empty.

The parser *ph* −− *repeat ph* returns $((x, xs), toks)$, where *xs* is a list. The operator >> applies a list 'cons' (the operator ::), converting the pair (x, xs) to $x :: xs$. In the second line, *empty* yields [] as the meaning of the empty phrase. In short, *repeat ph* constructs the list of the meanings of the repeated phrases. If *ph* has type α *phrase* then *repeat ph* has type $(\alpha \ list)$ *phrase*.

! *Beware of infinite recursion.* Can the declaration of *repeat* be simplified by omitting *toks* from both sides? No — calling *repeat ph* would immediately produce a recursive call to *repeat ph*, resulting in disaster:

```
fun repeat ph = ph -- repeat ph >> (op::) || empty;
```

Mentioning the formal parameter *toks* is a device to delay evaluation of the body of *repeat* until it is given a token list; the inner *repeat ph* is normally given a shorter token list and therefore terminates. Lazy evaluation would eliminate the need for this device.

9.4   *The ML code of the parser*

Infix directives for the operators −−, >> and || assign appropriate precedences to them (the exact numbers are arbitrary):

```
infix 5 --;
infix 3 >>;
infix 0 ||;
```

Figure 9.3 *The parsing functor*

```
functor ParseFUN (Lex: LEXICAL) : PARSE =
  struct
  type token = Lex.token;
  exception SynError of string;

  (*Phrase consisting of the keyword 'a' *)
  fun $a (Lex.Key b :: toks) =
        if a=b then (a,toks) else raise SynError a
    | $a _ = raise SynError "Symbol expected";

  fun id (Lex.Id a :: toks) = (a,toks)
    | id toks = raise SynError "Identifier expected";

  fun (ph>>f) toks =
      let val (x,toks2) = ph toks
      in  (f x, toks2)  end;

  fun (ph1 || ph2) toks = ph1 toks  handle SynError _ => ph2 toks;

  fun (ph1 -- ph2) toks =
      let val (x,toks2) = ph1 toks
          val (y,toks3) = ph2 toks2
      in  ((x,y), toks3)  end;

  fun empty toks = ([],toks);

  fun repeat ph toks = (   ph -- repeat ph >> (op::)
                        || empty      ) toks;

  fun infixes (ph,prec_of,apply) =
    let fun over k toks = next k (ph toks)
        and next k (x, Lex.Key a :: toks) =
              if prec_of a < k then (x, Lex.Key a :: toks)
              else next k ((over (prec_of a) >> apply a x) toks)
          | next k (x, toks) = (x, toks)
    in  over 0  end;

  (*Scan and parse, checking that no tokens remain*)
  fun reader ph a =
    (case ph (Lex.scan a) of
         (x, []) => x
       | (_,_::_) => raise SynError "Extra characters in phrase");
  end;
```

Functor *ParseFUN* (Figure 9.3) implements the parser. The functor declaration has the primitive form that takes exactly one argument structure, in this case *Lex*. Its result signature is *PARSE*:

```
signature PARSE =
  sig
  exception SynError of string
  type token
  val reader : (token list -> 'a * 'b list) -> string -> 'a
  val --    : ('a -> 'b * 'c) * ('c -> 'd * 'e) ->
                'a -> ('b * 'd) * 'e
  val >>    : ('a -> 'b * 'c) * ('b -> 'd) -> 'a -> 'd * 'c
  val ||    : ('a -> 'b) * ('a -> 'b) -> 'a -> 'b
  val $     : string -> token list -> string * token list
  val empty : 'a -> 'b list * 'a
  val id    : token list -> string * token list
  val infixes :
     (token list -> 'a * token list) * (string -> int) *
     (string -> 'a -> 'a -> 'a) -> token list -> 'a * token list
  val repeat : ('a -> 'b * 'a) -> 'a -> 'b list * 'a
  end;
```

You may notice that many of the types in this signature differ from those given in the previous section. The abbreviation

$$\alpha\ phrase\ =\ token\ list \rightarrow \alpha \times token\ list$$

is not used,* and more importantly, some of the types in the signature are more general than is necessary for parsing. They are not restricted to token lists.

ML often assigns a function a type that is more polymorphic than we expect. If we specify the signature prior to coding the functor — which is a disciplined style of software development — then any additional polymorphism is lost. I prefer to code the body of the functor first, then construct the signature from the types that ML assigns. The resulting signature is more general and concise than it would be otherwise, although with the disadvantage of depending upon a particular implementation.

Signature *PARSE* specifies the type *token* in order to specify the types of *id* and other items. Accordingly, *ParseFUN* declares the type *token* to be equivalent to *Lex.token*.

The function *reader* packages a parser for outside use. Calling

---

* A signature cannot make type abbreviations.

reader ph a scans the string *a* into tokens and supplies them to the parsing function *ph*. If there are no tokens left then *reader* returns the meaning of the phrase; otherwise it signals a syntax error.

Parsing infix operators. The function *infixes* constructs a parser for infix operators, when supplied with the following arguments:

> *ph* recognizes the atomic phrases that are to be combined by the operators.
>
> *prec_of* gives the precedences of the operators, returning −1 for all keywords that are not infix operators.
>
> *apply* combines the meanings of phrases; *apply a x y* applies the operator *a* to operands *x* and *y*.

The resulting parser recognizes an input like

$$ph \oplus ph \otimes ph \ominus ph \oslash ph$$

and groups the atomic phrases according to the precedences of the operators. It employs the mutually recursive functions *over* and *next*.

Calling *over k* parses a series of phrases, separated by operators of precedence *k* or above. In *next k* (*x, toks*) the argument *x* is the meaning of the preceding phrase and *k* is the governing precedence. The call does nothing unless the next token is an operator *a* of precedence *k* or above; in this case, tokens are recursively parsed by *over*(*prec_of a*) and their result combined with *x*. The result and the remaining tokens are then parsed under the original precedence *k*.

The algorithm does not handle parentheses; this should be done by *ph*. Chapter 10 demonstrates the use of *infixes*.

Writing a backtracking parser. A grammar is **ambiguous** if some token list admits more than one parse. Burge (1975) describes a parsing method similar to ours except that a parsing function returns a sequence (lazy list) of successful outcomes. Inspecting elements of this sequence causes backtracking over all parses of the input.

The parser *ph1*−−*ph2* returns the sequence of all possible ways of parsing a *ph1* followed by a *ph2*. It applies *ph1* to the input, which yields a sequence of (*x, toks2*) pairs. For each element of this sequence it applies *ph2* to *toks2*, obtaining a sequence of

(y, *toks*3) pairs. Finally it returns the sequence of all successful outcomes ((x, y), *toks*3). For each outcome, the meaning (x, y) consists of a pair of meanings returned by *ph*1 and *ph*2.

A parser rejects its input by returning the empty sequence rather than by raising an exception. Note that if *ph*1 rejects its input or if *ph*2 rejects each of the outcomes of *ph*1 then *ph*1−−*ph*2 yields the empty sequence, rejecting its input.

This is an enjoyable exercise in sequence processing, but it suffers from the drawbacks of backtracking parsers: it is slow and handles errors poorly. It can take exponential time to parse the input; bottom-up parsing would be much faster. If the input contains a syntax error, a backtracking parser returns no information other than an empty sequence. Our parser can easily be made to report the exact location of a syntax error.

Backtracking is valuable in theorem proving. A 'tactic' for finding proofs can be expressed as a function that takes a goal and returns a sequence of solutions. Tactics can be combined to form effective search procedures. The next chapter presents this technique, which is related to our treatment of parsing functions.

Exercise 9.4   Give an example of a parser *ph* such that, for all inputs, *ph* terminates successfully but *repeat ph* runs forever.

Exercise 9.5   A **parse tree** is a tree representing the structure of a parsed token list. Each node stands for a phrase, with branches to its constituent symbols and subphrases. Modify our parsing method so that it constructs parse trees. Declare a suitable type *partree* of parse trees such that each parsing function can have type

$$token\ list \rightarrow partree \times token\ list.$$

Code the operators ||, −−, *id*, $, *empty* and *repeat*; note that >> no longer serves any purpose.

Exercise 9.6   Modify the parsing method to generate a sequence of successful results, as described above.

Exercise 9.7   Code the parsing method in a procedural style, where each parsing 'function' has type *unit* → α and updates a reference to a token list by removing tokens from it. Does the procedural approach have any drawbacks, or is it superior to the functional approach?

Exercise 9.8 Modify signature *PARSE* to specify a substructure *Lex* of signature *LEXICAL* rather than a type *token*, so that other signature items can refer to the type *Lex.token*. Modify the functor declaration accordingly.

Exercise 9.9 When an expression contains several infix operators of the same precedence, does *infixes* associate them to the left or to the right? Modify this function to give the opposite association. Describe an algorithm to handle a mixture of left and right-associating operators.

9.5   *Example: parsing and displaying types*

The parser and pretty printer will now be demonstrated using a grammar for ML types. For purposes of the example, ML's type system can be simplified by dropping record and product types. There are two forms of type to consider:

Types such as *int*, *bool list* and $(\alpha \, list) \rightarrow (\beta \, list)$ consist of a **type constructor** applied to zero or more **type arguments**. Above, the type constructor *int* is applied to zero arguments; *list* is applied to the type *bool*; and $\rightarrow$ is applied to the types $\alpha \, list$ and $\beta \, list$. ML adopts a postfix syntax for most type constructors, but $\rightarrow$ has an infix syntax. Internally, such types can be represented by a string paired with a list of types.

A type can consist merely of a type variable. This can be represented by a string.

A basic structure for types has the following signature:

```
signature TYPE =
  sig
  datatype typ = Con of string * typ list | Var of string
  val pr   : typ -> unit
  val read : string -> typ
  end;
```

It contains three components:

The datatype *typ* comprises the two forms of type, with *Con* for type constructors and *Var* for type variables.

Calling *pr T* prints the type *T* at the terminal.

The function *read* converts a string to a type.

Functor *TypeFUN* (Figure 9.4) creates an instance of this signature given structures *Parse* and *Pretty*. For simplicity, it only treats $\rightarrow$;

Figure 9.4 *Parsing and displaying* ML *types*

```
functor TypeFUN (structure Parse: PARSE
                 and        Pretty: PRETTY) : TYPE =
  struct
  datatype typ = Con of string * typ list
               | Var of string;

  local (** Parsing **)
    fun makefun ((S,_),T) = Con("->",[S,T]);
    open Parse
    fun typ toks =
      (    atom -- $"->" -- typ                    >> makefun
      || atom
      ) toks
    and atom toks =
      (    $"'" -- id                              >> (Var o op^)
      || $"(" -- typ -- $")"                       >> (#2 o #1)
      ) toks;
  in
    val read = reader typ
  end;
  local (** Display **)
    open Pretty
    fun typ (Var a) = str a
      | typ (Con("->",[S,T])) =
              blo(0, [atom S, str " ->", brk 1, typ T])
    and atom (Var a) = str a
      | atom T = blo(1, [str"(", typ T, str")"]);
  in
    fun pr T = Pretty.pr (std_out, typ T, 50)
  end
end;
```

---

the treatment of other constructors is left as an exercise. The grammar distinguishes atomic types from other types:

$$Type = Atom\ \text{->}\ Type$$
$$|\ Atom$$

$$Atom = \text{'}\ Id$$
$$|\ (\ Type\ )$$

This treats $\rightarrow$ as an infix operator that associates to the right. It

interprets 'a->'b->'c as 'a->('b->'c) rather than ('a->'b)->'c
because 'a -> 'b is not an *Atom*.

The functor body consists of two **local** declarations, one for parsing and one for printing. Each declares mutually recursive functions *typ* and *atom* corresponding to the grammar.

Parsing of types. Using the top-down parsing operators, the function definitions in the parser are practically identical to the grammar rules. The operator >>, which applies a function to a parser's result, appears three times. Function *typ* uses >> to apply *makefun* to the result of the first grammar rule. This combines the three constituents of the phrase — a type, an arrow and another type — into a function type.

Both cases of *atom* involve >>, with two mysterious functions. During parsing of the type variable 'a, in the first case, >> applies *Var o op^* to the pair ("'", "a"). This function consists of *Var* composed with string concatenation; it concatenates the strings to "'a" and returns the type *Var* "'a".

In the second case of *atom*, parsing the phrase (*Type*) calls the function (#2 *o* #1). Recall (from Chapter 2) that an ML expression of the form #k, where k is a positive integer constant, denotes a function to select the kth component of any n-tuple such that $k \leq n$. The function (#2 *o* #1) selects the second component of the first component of its argument, mapping $((x, y), z)$ to y. When parsing types, it is applied to $(("(", T), ")")$ and yields T.

The parsing functions mention the argument *toks* to avoid looping (like *repeat* above) and because a **fun** declaration must mention an argument.

Pretty printing of types. The same mutual recursion works for displaying as for parsing. Functions *typ* and *atom* both convert a type into a symbolic expression for the pretty printer, but *atom* encloses its result in parentheses unless it is just an identifier. Parentheses appear only when necessary; too many parentheses are confusing.

The pretty printing operations *blo*, *str* and *brk* are used in typical fashion to describe blocks, strings and breaks. Function *atom* calls *blo* with an indentation of one to align subsequent breaks past the left parenthesis. Function *typ* calls *blo* with an indentation of zero, since it includes no parentheses; after the string " ->", it calls *brk* 1 to make a space or a line break.

The function *pr* writes to the terminal (channel *std_out*), giving a right margin of fifty.

Trying some examples. Let us create structures for the library, the lexical analyser, the parser, the pretty printer and types. These structures will also be used for the λ-calculus examples. Structure *LamKey* defines the keywords for lexical analysis.

```
structure Basic   = BasicFUN();
structure LamKey =
    struct val alphas  = []
           and symbols = ["(", ")", "'", "->"]
    end;
structure Lex = LexicalFUN (structure Basic    = Basic
                            and          Keyword = LamKey);
```

Below, *ParseFUN* is given its one argument using the primitive syntax for functor application. The other functors use the derived syntax, where the argument is the body of a structure.

```
structure Parse   = ParseFUN(Lex);
structure Pretty  = PrettyFUN();
structure Type    = TypeFUN (structure Parse = Parse
                             and          Pretty = Pretty);
```

We can enter types, note their internal representations (as values of *typ*) after parsing, and check that they are displayed correctly:

```
Type.read"'a->'b->'c";
> Con ("->", [Var "'a", Con ("->", [Var "'b", Var "'c"])])
>  : Type.typ
Type.pr it;
> 'a -> 'b -> 'c
Type.read"('a->'b)->'c";
> Con ("->", [Con ("->", [Var "'a", Var "'b"]), Var "'c"])
>  : Type.typ
Type.pr it;
> ('a -> 'b) -> 'c
```

Exercise 9.10 Implement parsing and pretty printing of arbitrary type constructors. First, define a grammar for ML's postfix syntax, as in the examples

```
'c list list            (string,int) sum
('a -> 'b) list         'a list -> 'b list
```

Parentheses are optional when a type constructor is applied to one argument not involving the arrow; thus `'a -> 'b list` stands for `'a -> (('b) list)` rather than `('a -> 'b) list`.

Exercise 9.11   Use the parsing primitives to implement a parser for propositions — type *prop* of Chapter 4.

The λ-calculus

Turing machines, recursive functions and register machines are formal models of computation (Boolos & Jeffrey, 1980). The λ-calculus, developed by Alonzo Church, is one of the earliest models and perhaps the most realistic. It can express computations over pairs, lists and trees (even infinite ones) and higher-order functions. Most functional languages are nothing more than elaborated forms of the λ-calculus, and their implementations are founded in λ-calculus theory.

Church's thesis asserts that the effectively computable functions are precisely those functions that can be computed in the λ-calculus. Because 'effective' is a vague notion, Church's thesis cannot be proved, but the λ-calculus is known to have the same power as the other models of computation. Functions coded in these models can be computed effectively, given sufficient time and space, and nobody has exhibited a computable function that cannot be coded in these models.

This section gives a brief introduction to the λ-calculus. Gordon (1988b) describes it for computer scientists; Barendregt (1984) is the comprehensive reference.

9.6   *λ-terms and λ-reductions*

The λ-calculus is a simple formal theory of functions. Its terms, called λ-terms, are constructed recursively from variables x, y, z, ... and other λ-terms. Let t, u, ... stand for arbitrary λ-terms. They may take one of the following forms:

$$x \quad \text{a variable}$$
$$(\lambda x.t) \quad \text{functional } \textbf{abstraction}$$
$$(t\ u) \quad \text{function } \textbf{application}$$

A term t_1 is a **subterm** of t_2 if t_1 is contained in t_2 or is identical to it. For instance, y is a subterm of $(\lambda z.(z\ y))$.

In the abstraction $(\lambda x.t)$, we call x the **bound variable** and t the **body**. Every occurrence of x in t is **bound** by the abstraction. Conversely, an occurrence of a variable y is **free** if it is not bound — if it is not contained within the body of some abstraction $(\lambda y.u)$. For example, x occurs bound and y occurs free in $(\lambda z.(\lambda x.(y\,x)))$. From now on, let a, b, c, ... denote free variables.

The names of bound variables have little significance; if they are renamed consistently in an abstraction, the new abstraction will be equivalent to the old. Free variables are significant, however; thus a is distinct from b while $(\lambda x.x)$ is equivalent to $(\lambda y.y)$. These principles are known throughout mathematics. In the integral $\int_a^b f(x)\,dx$, the variables a and b are free while x is bound. In the product $\Pi_{k=0}^n p(k)$, the variable n is free while k is bound.

The abstraction $(\lambda x.t)$ represents the function f with $f(x) = t$ for all x. Applying $(\lambda x.t)$ to an argument u yields the term that results when u is substituted for all free occurrences of x in t. Write the result of this substitution as $t[u/x]$. Substitution involves some delicate points, but let us leave them for later.

λ-conversions. These are rules for transforming a λ-term while preserving its intuitive meaning. Conversions should not be confused with equations such as $x + y = y + x$, which are statements about known arithmetic operations. The λ-calculus is not concerned with previously existing mathematical objects. The λ-terms themselves are the objects, and the λ-conversions are symbolic transformations upon them.

Most important is *β*-**conversion**, which transforms a function application by substituting the argument into the body:

$$((\lambda x.t)u) \Rightarrow_\beta t[u/x]$$

In this example, the argument is $(g\,a)$:

$$((\lambda x.((f\,x)x))(g\,a)) \Rightarrow_\beta ((f(g\,a))(g\,a))$$

Here is an example of two successive β-conversions:

$$((\lambda z.(z\,a))(\lambda x.x)) \Rightarrow_\beta ((\lambda x.x)a) \Rightarrow_\beta a$$

An α-**conversion** renames the bound variable in an abstraction:

$$(\lambda x.t) \Rightarrow_\alpha (\lambda y.t[y/x])$$

The abstraction over x is transformed into an abstraction over y,

and x is replaced by y. Examples:
$$(\lambda x.a\, x) \Rightarrow_\alpha (\lambda y.a\, y)$$
$$(\lambda x.(x(\lambda y.(y\, x)))) \Rightarrow_\alpha (\lambda z.(z(\lambda y.(y\, z))))$$

Two λ-terms are **equivalent** if they can be transformed into identical terms using α-conversions (possibly applied to subterms). Intuitively, we may assume that bound variables are renamed whenever this becomes necessary.

Notation. Nested abstractions and applications can be abbreviated:
$$(\lambda x_1.(\lambda x_2.\ldots(\lambda x_n.t)\ldots))\quad \text{as}\quad (\lambda x_1 x_2\ldots x_n.t)$$
$$(\ldots(t_1 t_2)\ldots t_n)\quad \text{as}\quad (t_1 t_2 \ldots t_n)$$

The outer parentheses are dropped when the term is not enclosed in another term or is the body of an abstraction. For example,

$$(\lambda x.(x(\lambda y.(y\, x)))) \text{ can be written as } \lambda x.x(\lambda y.y\, x).$$

Reduction to normal form. A **reduction step** $t \Rightarrow u$ transforms t to u by applying a β-conversion to any subterm of t. If a term admits no reductions then it is in **normal form**. To **normalize** a term means to apply reductions until a normal form is reached.

The **Church-Rosser Theorem** states that no two sequences of reductions, starting from one λ-term, can reach distinct (non-equivalent) normal forms. This theorem tells us that the normal form of a term can usefully be regarded as its value, since it is independent of the order in which reductions are performed.

For instance, $(\lambda x.a\, x)((\lambda y.b\, y)c)$ has two different reduction sequences, both leading to the same normal form. The affected subterm is underlined at each step:
$$\underline{(\lambda x.a\, x)((\lambda y.b\, y)c)} \Rightarrow a(\underline{(\lambda y.b\, y)c}) \Rightarrow a(b\, c)$$
$$(\lambda x.a\, x)(\underline{(\lambda y.b\, y)c}) \Rightarrow \underline{(\lambda x.a\, x)(b\, c)} \Rightarrow a(b\, c)$$

Many λ-terms have no normal form. For instance, $(\lambda x.x\, x)(\lambda x.x\, x)$ reduces to itself by β-conversion. Any attempt to normalize this term must fail to terminate:
$$\underline{(\lambda x.x\, x)(\lambda x.x\, x)} \Rightarrow \underline{(\lambda x.x\, x)(\lambda x.x\, x)} \Rightarrow \cdots$$

A term t can have a normal form even though certain reduction sequences never terminate. Typically, t contains a subterm u that has no normal form, but u can be erased by a reduction step. For example, the reduction sequence

$$(\lambda y.a)((\lambda x.x\,x)(\lambda x.x\,x)) \Rightarrow a$$

reaches normal form instantly, erasing the term $(\lambda x.x\,x)(\lambda x.x\,x)$. This corresponds to a **call-by-name** treatment of functions: the argument is not evaluated but simply substituted into the body of the function. Attempting to normalize the argument generates a nonterminating reduction sequence:

$$(\lambda y.a)((\lambda x.x\,x)(\lambda x.x\,x)) \Rightarrow (\lambda y.a)((\lambda x.x\,x)(\lambda x.x\,x)) \Rightarrow \cdots$$

Evaluating the argument prior to substitution into the function body corresponds to a **call-by-value** treatment of function application. In this example, the call-by-value strategy never reaches the normal form. The reduction strategy corresponding to call-by-name evaluation always reaches a normal form if one exists.

You may well ask, in what sense is $\lambda x.x\,x$ a function? It can be applied to any object and applies that object to itself! In classical mathematics, a function can only be defined over some previously existing set of values. The λ-calculus does not deal with functions as they are classically understood. Dana Scott has constructed models in which every abstraction, including $\lambda x.x\,x$, denotes a function (Barendregt, 1984). However, this chapter regards the λ-calculus from a purely symbolic point of view.

9.7 *Preventing variable capture in substitution*

Substitution must be defined carefully, for otherwise the conversions could go wrong. For instance, the term $\lambda x\,y.y\,x$ ought to behave like a curried function that, when applied to arguments t and u, returns $u\,t$ as its result. For all λ-terms t and u, we should expect to have the reductions

$$(\lambda x\,y.y\,x)t\,u \Rightarrow (\lambda y.y\,t)u \Rightarrow u\,t.$$

The following reduction sequence is certainly wrong:

$$(\lambda x\,y.y\,x)y\,b \Rightarrow (\lambda y.y\,y)b \Rightarrow b\,b \ ???$$

The β-conversion of $(\lambda x\,y.y\,x)y$ to $\lambda y.y\,y$ is incorrect because the free variable y has become bound. The substitution has **captured** this free variable. By first renaming the bound variable y to z, the reduction can be performed safely:

$$(\lambda x\,z.z\,x)y\,b \Rightarrow (\lambda z.z\,y)b \Rightarrow b\,y$$

In general, the substitution $t[u/x]$ will not capture any variables provided no free variable of u is bound in t.

If bound variables are represented literally, then the substitution algorithm must sometimes rename bound variables of t to avoid capturing free variables. Renaming is complicated and can be inefficient. It is essential that the new names do not appear elsewhere in the term. Preferably they should be similar to the names that they replace; nobody wants to see a variable called G6620094.

De Bruijn's name-free representation. Changing the representation of λ-terms can simplify the substitution algorithm. The name x of a bound variable serves only to match each occurrence of x with its binding λx so that reductions can be performed correctly. If these matches can be made by other means, then the names can be abolished. N. G. de Bruijn (1972) achieves this using the nesting depth of abstractions. Each occurrence of a bound variable is represented by an index, giving the number of abstractions lying between it and its binding abstraction. Two λ-terms are equivalent — differing only by α-conversions — if and only if their name-free representations are identical.

In the name-free notation, no variable name appears after the λ symbol and bound variable indices appear as numbers. The first occurrence of x in the body of $\lambda x.(\lambda y.x)x$ is represented by 1 because it is enclosed in an abstraction over y. The second occurrence of x is not enclosed in any other abstraction and is represented by 0. Therefore the name-free representation of $\lambda x.(\lambda y.x)x$ is $\lambda.(\lambda.1)0$.

Here is a term where the bound variables occur at several nesting depths:

$$\lambda x.x(\lambda y.x\, y(\lambda z.x\, y\, z))$$

Viewing the term as a tree emphasizes its nesting structure:

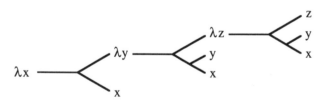

In the name-free notation, the three occurrences of x are represented by 0, 1 and 2:

$$\lambda.0(\lambda.1\,0(\lambda.2\,1\,0))$$

De Bruijn developed the name-free notation for his AUTOMATH system; it is also used in Isabelle (Paulson, 1990). It is a good data structure for variable binding, but is unreadable as a notation. The user-supplied variable names should be retained for later display, so that the user sees the traditional notation.

Operations such as abstraction and substitution are easily performed in the name-free representation.

Abstraction. Suppose that t is a λ-term that we would like to abstract over all free occurrences of the variable x, constructing the abstraction $\lambda x.t$. Take, for instance, $x(\lambda y.a\,x\,y)$, which in the name-free notation is

$$x(\lambda.a\,x\,0).$$

To bind all occurrences of x, we must replace them by the correct indices, here 0 and 1, and insert a λ symbol:

$$\lambda.0(\lambda.a\,1\,0)$$

This can be performed by a recursive function on terms that keeps count of the nesting depth of abstractions. Each occurrence of x is replaced by an index equal to its depth.

Substitution. To perform the β-conversion

$$(\lambda x.t)u \Rightarrow_\beta t[u/x],$$

the term t must be recursively transformed, replacing all the occurrences of x by u. In the name-free notation, x could be represented by several different indices. The index is initially 0 and increases with the depth of abstractions in t. For instance, the conversion

$$(\lambda x.x(\lambda y.a\,x\,y))b \Rightarrow_\beta b(\lambda y.a\,b\,y)$$

becomes

$$(\lambda.0(\lambda.a\,1\,0))b \Rightarrow_\beta b(\lambda.a\,b\,0)$$

in the name-free notation. Observe that x has index 0 in the outer abstraction and index 1 in the inner one.

Performing β-conversion on a subterm $(\lambda x.t)u$ is more complex. The argument u may contain variables bound outside, namely indices with no matching abstraction in u. These indices must be increased by the current nesting depth before substitution into t; this ensures that they refer to the same abstractions afterwards.

For instance, in

$$\lambda z.(\lambda x.x(\lambda y.x))(a\ z) \Rightarrow_\beta \lambda z.a\ z(\lambda y.a\ z),$$

the argument $a\ z$ is substituted in two places, one of which lies in the scope of λy. In the name-free approach, $a\ z$ receives two different representations:

$$\lambda.(\lambda.0(\lambda.1))(a\ 0) \Rightarrow_\beta \lambda.a\ 0(\lambda.a\ 1)$$

Exercise 9.12   Show all the reduction sequences for normalizing the term $(\lambda f.f(f\ a))((\lambda x.x\ x)((\lambda y.y)(\lambda y.y)))$.

Exercise 9.13   For each term, show its normal form or demonstrate that it has none:

$$(\lambda f\ x\ y.f\ x\ y)(\lambda u\ v.u)$$
$$(\lambda x.f(x\ x))(\lambda x.f(x\ x))$$
$$(\lambda x\ y.y\ x)(\lambda x.f(f\ x))(\lambda x.f(f(f(f\ x))))$$
$$(\lambda x.x\ x)(\lambda x.x)$$

Exercise 9.14   Give the name-free representation of each of the following terms:

$$\lambda x\ y\ z.x\ z(y\ z)$$
$$\lambda x\ y.(\lambda z.x\ y\ z)y\ x$$
$$\lambda f.(\lambda x.f(\lambda y.x\ x\ y))(\lambda x.f(\lambda y.x\ x\ y))$$
$$(\lambda p\ x\ y.p\ x\ y)(\lambda x\ y.y)\ a\ b$$

Exercise 9.15   Consider a representation of λ-terms that designates bound variables internally by unique integers. Give algorithms for constructing λ-terms and for performing substitution.

Representing λ-terms in ML

Implementing the λ-calculus in ML is straightforward under the name-free representation. The following sections present ML programs for abstraction and substitution, and for parsing and pretty printing λ-terms.

9.8   *The fundamental operations*

The name-free representation, with its operations, is implemented by functor *LambdaFUN* (Figure 9.5). The functor has the following result signature:

```
signature LAMBDA_NAMELESS =
  sig
  datatype term = Free    of string
                | Bound of int
                | Abs     of string*term
                | Apply of term*term;
  val abstract : int -> string -> term -> term
  val subst    : int -> term -> term -> term
  val inst     : (string * term) list -> term -> term
  end;
```

Datatype *term* comprises free variables (as strings), bound variables (as indices), abstractions and applications. Each *Abs* node stores the bound variable name for use in printing.

Calling *abstract i b t* converts each occurrence of the free variable *b* in *t* to the index *i* (or a greater index within nested abstractions). Usually $i = 0$ and the result is immediately enclosed in an abstraction to match this index. Recursive calls over abstractions in *t* have $i > 0$.

Calling *subst i u t* substitutes *u* for the bound variable index *i* in *t*. Usually $i = 0$ and *t* is the body of an abstraction in the β-conversion $(\lambda x.t)u$. The case $i > 0$ occurs during recursive calls over abstractions in *t*. All indices exceeding *i* are decreased by one in order to compensate for the removal of that index.

Calling *inst* $[(b_1, t_1), \ldots, (b_n, t_n)]$ *t* repeatedly replaces each free variable b_i in *t* by the corresponding term t_i until the result no longer contains occurrences of $b_1, \ldots, b_n$. The list of (*string*, *term*) pairs forms an **environment** of definitions; *inst* expands all the definitions in a term. This is called **instantiation**.

Signature *LAMBDA_NAMELESS* is concrete, revealing all the internal details. Many values of type *term* are **improper**: they do not correspond to real λ-terms because they contain unmatched bound variable indices. In particular, *Bound i* for any *i* does not correspond to a λ-term. Moreover, *abstract* returns improper terms and *subst* expects them. An abstract signature for the λ-calculus would provide operations upon λ-terms themselves, hiding their representation.

Figure 9.5 *The name-free representation of λ-terms*

```
functor LambdaFUN (Basic: BASIC) : LAMBDA_NAMELESS =
  struct
  local open Basic in
  datatype term = Free  of string
                | Bound of int
                | Abs   of string*term
                | Apply of term*term;

  fun abstract i b (Free a) = if a=b then  Bound i  else  Free a
    | abstract i b (Bound j) = Bound j
    | abstract i b (Abs(a,t)) = Abs(a, abstract (i+1) b t)
    | abstract i b (Apply(t,u)) = Apply(abstract i b t, abstract i b u);

  fun shift 0 d u = u
    | shift i d (Free a) = Free a
    | shift i d (Bound j) = if j>=d then Bound(j+i) else Bound j
    | shift i d (Abs(a,t)) = Abs(a, shift i (d+1) t)
    | shift i d (Apply(t,u)) = Apply(shift i d t, shift i d u);

  fun subst i u (Free a)  = Free a
    | subst i u (Bound j) =
          if j<i then      Bound j          (*locally bound*)
          else if j=i then shift i 0 u
          else (*j>i*)     Bound(j-1)        (*non-local to t*)
    | subst i u (Abs(a,t)) = Abs(a, subst (i+1) u t)
    | subst i u (Apply(t1,t2)) = Apply(subst i u t1, subst i u t2);

  fun inst env (Free a) = (inst env (lookup(env,a))
                              handle Lookup => Free a)
    | inst env (Bound i) = Bound i
    | inst env (Abs(a,t)) = Abs(a, inst env t)
    | inst env (Apply(t1,t2)) = Apply(inst env t1, inst env t2);
  end
end;
```

Function *shift* is local to the functor because it is called only by *subst*. Calling *shift i d u* adds i to all the unmatched indices j in u such that $j \geq d$. Initially $d = 0$ and d is increased in recursive calls over abstractions in u. Before substituting some term u into another term, any unmatched indices in u must be shifted.

Function *inst* substitutes for free variables, not bound variables. It expects to be given proper λ-terms having no unmatched indices. It therefore does not keep track of the nesting depth or call *shift*.

Exercise 9.16 Define a signature for the λ-calculus that hides its internal representation. It should specify predicates to test whether a λ-term is a variable, an abstraction or an application, and specify functions for abstraction and substitution. Sketch the design of two structures, employing two different representations of λ-terms, that would have this signature.

9.9   *Parsing λ-terms*

In order to apply the parser and pretty printer, we require a grammar for λ-terms, including the abbreviations for nested abstractions and applications. The following grammar distinguishes between ordinary terms and atomic terms. A per cent sign (%) serves as the λ symbol:

$$Term \; = \; \% \; Id \; Id^* \; Term$$
$$| \; Atom \; Atom^*$$

$$Atom \; = \; Id$$
$$| \; (\; Term \;)$$

Note that *phrase** stands for zero or more repetitions of *phrase*. A term consisting of several Atoms, such as *a b c d*, abbreviates the nested application $(((a\,b)c)d)$. A more natural grammar would define the phrase class *Applic*:

$$Applic \quad = \; Atom$$
$$| \; Applic \; Atom$$

Then we could replace the *Atom Atom** in *Term* by *Applic*. Unfortunately, the second grammar rule for *Applic* is left-recursive and would cause our parser to loop. Eliminating this left recursion in the standard way yields our original grammar.

Functor *ParseLamFUN* (Figure 9.6) takes structures *Parse* and *Lambda*, containing the parser and the datatype *term*. It returns a structure having signature *PARSELAM*:

```
signature PARSELAM =
  sig
  type term
  val abslist   : string list * term -> term
  val applylist : term * term list -> term
  val read      : string -> term
  end;
```

Figure 9.6 *The λ-calculus parser*

```
functor ParseLamFUN (structure Parse: PARSE
                and Lambda: LAMBDA_NAMELESS) : PARSELAM =
  struct
  local open Parse  open Lambda  in
  type term = term;

  fun abslist([],    t) = t
    | abslist(b::bs, t) = Abs(b, abstract 0 b (abslist(bs, t)));

  fun applylist(t, []) = t
    | applylist(t, u::us) = applylist(Apply(t,u), us);

  fun makelambda ((((_,b),bs),_),t) = abslist(b::bs,t)

  fun term toks =
    (    $"%" -- id -- repeat id -- $"." -- term   >> makelambda
     || atom -- repeat atom                        >> applylist
    ) toks
  and atom toks =
    (    id                                        >> Free
     || $"(" -- term -- $")"                       >> (#2 o #1)
    ) toks;

  val read = reader term;
  end
  end;
```

Although the functor's only purpose is to parse λ-terms, the signature contains several components:

> Type *term* is specified for use elsewhere in the signature.
> *abslist*($[x_1, \ldots, x_n], t$) creates the abstraction $\lambda x_1 \ldots x_n.t$.
> *applylist*($t, [u_1, \ldots, u_n]$) creates the application $t\, u_1 \ldots u_n$.
> The function *read* converts a string to a λ-term.

The body of the functor is straightforward. The functor employs *abslist* and *applylist* for parsing and returns them because they could have other uses.

Exercise 9.17 In function *makelambda*, why does the pattern contain so many parentheses? What values are supplied to its wildcard (_) variables?

Exercise 9.18 What is the result of parsing "%x x.x(%x x.x)"?

9.10   *Displaying* λ-*terms*
Functor *DispLamFUN* (Figure 9.7) implements pretty printing for λ-terms. It takes structures *Basic*, *Pretty* and *Lambda* —
containing the library, the pretty printer and the datatype *term* —
and yields a result with signature *DISPLAM*:

```
signature DISPLAM =
  sig
  type term
  val rename  : string list * string -> string
  val stripabs : term -> string list * term
  val pr       : term -> unit
  end;
```

The signature specifies several components:

As in *PARSELAM*, type *term* must be included.
rename([$a_1, \ldots, a_n$], *a*) suffixes prime (') characters to *a* so
    that it differs from each of $a_1, \ldots, a_n$.
stripabs analyses an abstraction into its bound variables and
    body, as described below.
Calling *pr t* prints the term *t* at the terminal.

Even with the name-free representation, bound variables may have
to be renamed when a term is displayed. The normal form of
(λ*xy.x*)*y* is shown as %y' . y, not as %y. y. Function *stripabs* and
its auxiliary function *strip* handle abstractions. Given λ$x_1 \ldots x_m.t$,
the bound variables are renamed to differ from all free variables
in *t*. The new names are substituted into *t* as free variables. Thus,
all indices are eliminated from a term as it is displayed.

The mutually recursive functions *term*, *applic* and *atom* prepare
terms for pretty printing. A *Free* variable is displayed literally. A
Bound variable index should never be encountered unless it has no
matching *Abs* node (indicating that the term is improper). For
an *Abs* node, the bound variables are renamed; then *foldleft* joins
them into a string, separated by spaces. An *Apply* node is displayed
using *applic*, which corresponds to the grammatical phrase *Applic*
mentioned in the previous section. Finally, *atom* encloses a term
in parentheses unless it is simply an identifier.

Exercise 9.19   How will the normal form of (λ*x y.x*)(λ*y.y*) be
displayed? Modify *DispLamFUN* to ensure that, when a term is
displayed, no variable name is bound twice in overlapping scopes.

Figure 9.7 *The λ-calculus pretty printer*

```
functor DisplLamFUN (structure Basic: BASIC and Pretty: PRETTY
                and Lambda: LAMBDA_NAMELESS) : DISPLAM =
  struct
  local open Basic  open Pretty  open Lambda  in
  type term = Lambda.term;

  fun vars (Free a) = [a]
    | vars (Bound i) = []
    | vars (Abs(a,t)) = vars t
    | vars (Apply(t1,t2)) = vars t1 @ vars t2;

  fun rename (bs,a) =
        if  a mem bs  then  rename (bs, a ^ "'")  else  a;

  fun strip (bs, Abs(a,t)) =
          let val b = rename (vars t, a)
          in  strip (b::bs, subst 0 (Free b) t)  end
    | strip (bs, u) = (rev bs, u);

  fun stripabs t = strip ([],t);

  fun spacejoin (a,b) = a ^ " " ^ b;

  fun term (Free a) = str a
    | term (Bound i) = str "??UNMATCHED INDEX??"
    | term (t as Abs _) =
          let val (b::bs,u) = stripabs t
              val binder = foldleft spacejoin ("%" ^ b, bs) ^ ". "
          in  blo(0, [str binder, term u])  end
    | term t = blo(0, applic t)
  and applic (Apply(t,u)) = applic t @ [brk 1, atom u]
    | applic t        = [ atom t ]
  and atom (Free a) = str a
    | atom t = blo(1, [str"(", term t, str")"]);

  fun pr t = Pretty.pr (std_out, term t, 50);
  end
end;
```

Exercise 9.20   Terms can be displayed without substituting free variables for bound variables. Instead, maintain a list of the bound variables of the abstractions enclosing the current subterm. To display the term *Bound i*, locate the *i*th name in the list. Modify *DisplLamFUN* accordingly.

The λ-calculus as a programming language

Despite its simplicity, the λ-calculus is rich enough to model the full range of functional programming. Data structures such as pairs and lists can be processed under either call-by-value or call-by-name evaluation strategies. After a brief discussion of these topics we shall demonstrate them using ML. See Gordon (1988b) for a more detailed discussion.

First, we must make some definitions.

Write $t \Rightarrow^* u$ whenever t can be transformed into u by zero or more reduction steps. If u is in normal form then $t \Rightarrow^* u$ can be viewed as evaluating t to obtain the result u. Of course, not every evaluation strategy may succeed in finding this normal form.

Write $t_1 = t_2$ whenever there is some term u (not necessarily in normal form!) such that $t_1 \Rightarrow^* u$ and $t_2 \Rightarrow^* u$. If $t_1 = t_2$ then both terms have the same normal form, if any. Viewing normal forms as values, $t_1 = t_2$ means that t_1 and t_2 have the same value.

Write $t_1 \equiv t_2$ whenever t_1 and t_2 are equivalent — identical apart from renaming of bound variables. If a is a free variable then the definition 'a abbreviates t' is also written $a \equiv t$.

9.11 *Data structures in the λ-calculus*

We now consider how to encode boolean values, ordered pairs, natural numbers and lists. The codings given below are arbitrary; all that matters is that the data structures and their operations satisfy certain standard properties. An encoding of the booleans must define the truth values *true* and *false* and the conditional operator *if* as λ-terms, satisfying (for all t and u)

> *if true t u* $= t$
>
> *if false t u* $= u$

Once we have two distinct truth values and the conditional operator, we can define negation, conjunction and disjunction. Analogously, the ML compiler may represent *true* and *false* by any bit patterns provided the operations behave properly.

The booleans. The booleans can be coded by defining

> $true \equiv \lambda x\ y.x$
>
> $false \equiv \lambda x\ y.y$
>
> $if \equiv \lambda p\ x\ y.p\ x\ y$

The necessary properties are easily verified. For instance:
$$if\ true\ t\ u \equiv (\lambda p\ x\ y.p\ x\ y)true\ t\ u$$
$$\Rightarrow (\lambda x\ y.true\ x\ y)t\ u$$
$$\Rightarrow (\lambda y.true\ t\ y)u$$
$$\Rightarrow true\ t\ u$$
$$\Rightarrow (\lambda y.t)u$$
$$\Rightarrow t$$

This establishes $if\ true\ t\ u \Rightarrow^* t$ and therefore $if\ true\ t\ u = t$.

Ordered pairs. An encoding must specify a function *pair* (to construct pairs) and projection functions *fst* and *snd* (to select the components of a pair). The usual encoding is
$$pair \equiv \lambda x\ y\ f.f\ x\ y$$
$$fst \equiv \lambda p.p\ true$$
$$snd \equiv \lambda p.p\ false$$

where *true* and *false* are defined as above. These reductions, and the corresponding equations, are easily verified for all t and u:
$$fst(pair\ t\ u) \Rightarrow^* t$$
$$snd(pair\ t\ u) \Rightarrow^* u$$

The natural numbers. Of the several known encodings of the natural numbers, Church's is the most elegant. Let underlined numbers $\underline{0}, \underline{1}, \ldots$, denote the **Church numerals**:
$$\underline{0} \equiv \lambda f\ x.x$$
$$\underline{1} \equiv \lambda f\ x.f\ x$$
$$\underline{2} \equiv \lambda f\ x.f(f\ x)$$
$$\vdots$$
$$\underline{n} \equiv \lambda f\ x.f^n(x)$$
Here $f^n(x)$ abbreviates $\underbrace{f(\cdots(f\ x)\cdots)}_{n\ \text{times}}$.

The function *suc* computes the successor of a number, while *iszero* tests whether a number equals zero:
$$suc \equiv \lambda n\ f\ x.n\ f\ (f\ x)$$
$$iszero \equiv \lambda n.n(\lambda x.false)true$$

It is not difficult to verify the following reductions, where $\underline{n}$ is an arbitrary Church numeral:

$$suc\ \underline{n} \Rightarrow^* \underline{n+1}$$
$$iszero\ \underline{0} \Rightarrow^* true$$
$$iszero(suc\ \underline{n}) \Rightarrow^* false$$

Church numerals allow wonderfully succinct definitions of addition, multiplication and exponentiation:

$$add \equiv \lambda m\ n\ f\ x.m\ f(n\ f\ x)$$
$$mult \equiv \lambda m\ n\ f.m(n\ f)$$
$$expt \equiv \lambda m\ n\ f\ x.n\ m\ f\ x$$

These can be formally verified by induction, and their underlying intuitions are simple. Each Church numeral $\underline{n}$ is an operator to apply a function n times. Note that

$$add\ \underline{m}\ \underline{n}\ f\ x = f^m(f^n(x)) = f^{m+n}(x);$$

the others are understood similarly.

An encoding of the natural numbers must also specify a predecessor function *pre* such that

$$pre(suc\ \underline{n}) = \underline{n}$$

for all numbers $\underline{n}$. With Church numerals, computing $\underline{n}$ from $\underline{n+1}$ is complex (and slow!); given f and x, we must compute $f^n(x)$ from $g^{n+1}(y)$ for some g and y. A suitable g is a function on pairs such that $g(z, z') = (f(z), z)$ for all (z, z'); then

$$g^{n+1}(x, x) = (f^{n+1}(x), f^n(x))$$

and we take the second component. To formalize this, define *prefn* to construct g. Then define the predecessor function *pre* and the subtraction function *sub*:

$$prefn \equiv \lambda f\ p.pair(f(fst\ p))\ (fst\ p)$$
$$pre \equiv \lambda n\ f\ x.snd(n(prefn\ f)(pair\ x\ x))$$
$$sub \equiv \lambda m\ n.n\ pre\ m$$

For subtraction, $sub\ \underline{m}\ \underline{n} = pre^n(\underline{m})$; this computes the nth predecessor of $\underline{m}$.

Lists. Lists are encoded using pairing and the booleans. A non-empty list with head x and tail y is coded by the pair of pairs $(false, (x, y))$. The empty list *nil* could be coded as $(true, true)$, but a simpler definition happens to work:

$$nil \equiv \lambda z.z$$
$$cons \equiv \lambda x \ y.pair \ false \ (pair \ x \ y)$$
$$null \equiv fst$$
$$hd \equiv \lambda z.fst(snd \ z)$$
$$tl \equiv \lambda z.snd(snd \ z)$$

The essential properties are easy to check for all t and u:

$$null \ nil \Rightarrow^* true$$
$$null(cons \ t \ u) \Rightarrow^* false$$
$$hd(cons \ t \ u) \Rightarrow^* t$$
$$tl(cons \ t \ u) \Rightarrow^* u$$

A call-by-name evaluation reduces $hd(cons \ t \ u)$ to t without evaluating u, and can process infinite lists.

Exercise 9.21   Define an encoding of ordered pairs in terms of an arbitrary encoding of the booleans. Demonstrate it by encoding the booleans with $true = \lambda x \ y.y$ and $false = \lambda x \ y.x$.

Exercise 9.22   Verify, for all Church numerals $\underline{m}$ and $\underline{n}$:

$$iszero(suc \ \underline{n}) = false$$
$$add \ \underline{m} \ \underline{n} = \underline{m + n}$$
$$mult \ \underline{m} \ \underline{n} = \underline{m \times n}$$
$$expt \ \underline{m} \ \underline{n} = \underline{m^n}$$

Exercise 9.23   Define an encoding of the natural numbers that has a simple predecessor function.

Exercise 9.24   Define an encoding of labelled binary trees.

Exercise 9.25   Write an ML function *numeral* of type $int \rightarrow term$ such that *numeral n* constructs the Church numeral $\underline{n}$, for all $n \geq 0$.

9.12   *Recursive definitions in the λ-calculus*

There is a λ-term *fact* that computes factorials of Church numerals by the recursion

$$fact \ n = if \ (iszero \ n) \ \underline{1} \ (mult \ n \ (fact(pre \ n))).$$

There is a λ-term *append* that joins two lists by the recursion

$$append \ z \ w = if \ (null \ z) \ w \ (cons(hd \ z)(append(tl \ z)w)).$$

There even is a λ-term *inflist* satisfying the recursion

$$inflist = cons\ MORE\ inflist,$$

encoding the infinite list $[MORE, MORE, \ldots]$.

Recursive definitions are encoded with the help of the λ-term Y:

$$Y \equiv \lambda f.(\lambda x.f(x\ x))(\lambda x.f(x\ x))$$

Although the intuition behind Y is obscure, a simple calculation verifies that Y satisfies the **fixed point property**

$$Y f = f(Y\ f)$$

for all λ-terms f. We can exploit this property to expand the body of a recursive object repeatedly. Define

$$fact \equiv Y(\lambda g\ n.if\ (iszero\ n)\ \underline{1}\ (mult\ n\ (g(pre\ n))))$$
$$append \equiv Y(\lambda g\ z\ w.if\ (null\ z)\ w\ (cons(hd\ z)(g(tl\ z)w)))$$
$$inflist \equiv Y(\lambda g.cons\ MORE\ g)$$

In each definition, the recursive occurrence is replaced by the bound variable g in $Y(\lambda g\ldots)$. Let us verify the recursion equation for *inflist*; the others are similar. The first and third lines hold by definition, while the second line uses the fixed point property:

$$inflist \equiv Y(\lambda g.cons\ MORE\ g)$$
$$= (\lambda g.cons\ MORE\ g)(Y(\lambda g.cons\ MORE\ g)))$$
$$\equiv (\lambda g.cons\ MORE\ g)inflist$$
$$\Rightarrow cons\ MORE\ inflist$$

Recursive functions coded using Y execute correctly under call-by-name reduction. In order to use call-by-value reduction, recursive functions must be coded using a different fixed point operator (discussed below); otherwise execution will not terminate.

9.13 *The evaluation of λ-terms*

The functor *ReduceFUN* (Figure 9.8) implements the call-by-value and call-by-name reduction strategies. Its result has signature *REDUCE*:

```
signature REDUCE =
  sig
  type term
  val eval    : term -> term
  val byvalue : term -> term
  val headnf  : term -> term
  val byname  : term -> term
  end;
```

Figure 9.8 *Reduction of λ-terms*

```
functor ReduceFUN (Lambda: LAMBDA_NAMELESS) : REDUCE =
  struct
  local open Lambda  in
  type term = term;

  fun eval (Apply(t1,t2)) =
        (case eval t1 of
             Abs(a,u) => eval(subst 0 (eval t2) u)
           | u1 => Apply(u1, eval t2))
    | eval t = t;

  fun byvalue t = normbodies (eval t)
  and normbodies (Abs(a,t)) = Abs(a, byvalue t)
    | normbodies (Apply(t1,t2)) = Apply(normbodies t1, normbodies t2)
    | normbodies t = t;

  fun headnf (Abs(a,t)) = Abs(a, headnf t)
    | headnf (Apply(t1,t2)) =
        (case headnf t1 of
             Abs(a,t) => headnf(subst 0 t2 t)
           | u1 => Apply(u1, t2))
    | headnf t = t;

  fun byname t = normargs (headnf t)
  and normargs (Abs(a,t)) = Abs(a, normargs t)
    | normargs (Apply(t1,t2)) = Apply(normargs t1, byname t2)
    | normargs t = t;
  end
end;
```

As usual, type *term* is included for completeness. The signature's other components are evaluation functions:

> *eval* evaluates a term using a call-by-value strategy resembling ML's. Its result need not be in normal form.
>
> *byvalue* normalizes a term using call-by-value.
>
> *headnf* reduces a term to **head normal form**, which is discussed below.
>
> *byname* normalizes a term using call-by-name.

Call-by-value. In ML, evaluating the abstraction **fn** x => E does not evaluate E, for there is no general way to evaluate E without having a value for x. We have often exploited ML's treatment of abstractions, writing `fn () => E` to delay the evaluation of E. This allows a kind of lazy evaluation.

The situation in the λ-calculus is different.   The abstraction $\lambda x.(\lambda y.a\,y)x$ reduces to the normal form $\lambda x.a\,x$ with no question of whether x has a value. Even so, it is advantageous not to reduce the bodies of abstractions. This permits the delaying of evaluation, like in ML. It is essential for handling recursion.

The function *eval*, given the application $t_1\,t_2$, evaluates t_1 to u_1 and t_2 to u_2. (Assume these evaluations terminate.) If u_1 is the abstraction $\lambda x.u$ then *eval* calls itself on $u[u_2/x]$, substituting the value of the argument into the body; if u_1 is anything else then *eval* returns $u_1\,u_2$. Given an abstraction or variable, *eval* returns its argument unchanged. Although *eval* performs most of the work of reduction, its result may contain abstractions not in normal form.

The function *byvalue* uses *eval* to reduce a term to normal form. It calls *eval* on its argument, then recursively scans the result to normalize the abstractions in it.

Suppose that t equals *true*. When *eval* is given *if* $t\ u_1\ u_2$, it evaluates both u_1 and u_2 although only u_1 is required. If this is the body of a recursive function then it will run forever, as discussed in Chapter 2. We should insert abstractions to delay evaluation. Choose any variable x and code the conditional expression as

$$(\textit{if } t\ (\lambda x.u_1)\ (\lambda x.u_2))\ x.$$

Given this term, *eval* will return $\lambda x.u_1$ as the result of the *if* and then apply it to x. Thus it will evaluate u_1 but not u_2. If t equals *false* then only u_2 will be evaluated. Conditional expressions must be coded this way under call-by-value.

Recursive definitions encoded using Y fail under call-by-value because the evaluation of $Y\,f$ never terminates. Abstractions may be inserted into Y to delay evaluation. The operator

$$YV \equiv \lambda f.(\lambda x.f(\lambda y.x\,x\,y))(\lambda x.f(\lambda y.x\,x\,y))$$

enjoys the fixed point property and can express recursive functions for evaluation using *byvalue*.

Call-by-name. A λ-term is in **head normal form** if, for $m \geq 0$ and $n \geq 0$, it can be viewed as follows:

$$\lambda x_1 \ldots x_m.x\ t_1 \ldots t_n.$$

The variable x may either be free or bound (one of $x_1, \ldots, x_m$).

Observe that the term's normal form (if it exists) must be

$$\lambda x_1 \ldots x_m.x \; u_1 \ldots u_n,$$

where u_i is the normal form of t_i for $i = 1, \ldots, n$. Head normal form describes a term's outer structure, which cannot be affected by reductions. We can normalize a term by computing its head normal form, then recursively normalizing the subterms $t_1, \ldots, t_n$. This procedure will reach the normal form if one exists, because every term that has a normal form also has a head normal form.

For example, the term $\lambda x.a((\lambda z.z)x)$ is in head normal form and its normal form is $\lambda x.a \; x$. A term not in head normal form can be viewed as

$$\lambda x_1 \ldots x_m.(\lambda x.t) \; t_1 \ldots t_n,$$

where $n > 0$. It admits a reduction in the leftmost part of the body. For instance, $(\lambda x \; y.y \; x)t$ reduces to the head normal form $\lambda y.y \; t$, for any term t. Many terms without a normal form have a head normal form; consider

$$Y = \lambda f.f(Y \; f).$$

A few terms, such as $(\lambda x.x \; x)(\lambda x.x \; x)$, lack even a head normal form. Such terms can be regarded as undefined.

The function *headnf* computes the head normal form of $t_1 \; t_2$ by recursively computing *headnf* t_1 and then, if an abstraction results, performing a β-conversion. The argument t_2 is not reduced before substitution; this is call-by-name.*

Function *byname* normalizes a term by computing its *headnf* and then normalizing the arguments of the outermost application. This achieves call-by-name reduction with reasonable efficiency.

Exercise 9.26 Show that $YV \; f = f(\lambda y. YV \; f \; y)$.

Exercise 9.27 Derive a head normal form of $Y \; Y$, or demonstrate that none exists.

Exercise 9.28 Derive a head normal form of *inflist*, or demonstrate that none exists.

Exercise 9.29 Describe how *byvalue* and *byname* would compute the normal form of *fst*(*pair t u*), for arbitrary λ-terms t and u.

---

* *headnf* exploits Proposition 8.3.13 of Barendregt (1984): if $t \, u$ has a head normal form then so does t.

9.14   *Demonstrating the evaluators*

Let us apply the functors to create the structures for the
λ-calculus, assuming the previous declarations of structures *Basic*,
Parse and *Pretty*. Again, note that the functors taking one argument employ the primitive syntax for functor application:

```
structure Lambda    = LambdaFUN(Basic);
structure ParseLam = ParseLamFUN
       (structure Parse=Parse and Lambda=Lambda);
structure DispLam   = DispLamFUN
       (structure Basic=Basic and Pretty=Pretty
    and          Lambda=Lambda);
structure Reduce    = ReduceFUN(Lambda);
open Basic;  open Lambda;
```

Next, we create an environment *stdenv* consisting of (*string, term*)
pairs. It defines the λ-calculus encodings of the booleans, ordered
pairs and so forth (Figure 9.9).

Function *stdread* reads a term and instantiates it using *stdenv*,
expanding the definitions. Note that "2" expands to something
large, derived from *suc*(*suc* 0):

```
fun stdread a = inst stdenv (ParseLam.read a);
> val stdread = fn : string -> term
DispLam.pr (stdread "2");
> (%n f x. n f (f x))
> ((%n f x. n f (f x)) (%f x. x))
```

This term could do with normalization. We define a function *try*
such that *try evfn* reads a term, applies *evfn* to it, and displays the
result. Using call-by-value, we reduce "2" to a Church numeral:

```
fun try evfn = DispLam.pr o evfn o stdread;
> val try = fn : (term -> term) -> string -> unit
try Reduce.byvalue "2";
> %f x. f (f x)
```

Call-by-value can perform simple arithmetic on Church numerals:
$2 + 3 = 5$, $2 \times 3 = 6$, $2^3 = 8$:

```
try Reduce.byvalue "add 2 3";
> %f x. f (f (f (f (f x))))
try Reduce.byvalue "mult 2 3";
> %f x. f (f (f (f (f (f x)))))
try Reduce.byvalue "expt 2 3";
> %f x. f (f (f (f (f (f (f (f x)))))))
```

The environment defines *factV*, which encodes a recursive factorial
function using *YV* and with abstractions to delay evaluation of

Figure 9.9 *Constructing the standard environment*

```
fun addpair (a,b) = (a, ParseLam.read b);

val stdenv = map addpair
[     (*booleans*)
 ("true", "%x y.x"),              ("false",  "%x y.y"),
 ("if", "%p x y. p x y"),
     (*ordered pairs*)
 ("pair", "%x y f.f x y"),
 ("fst", "%p.p true"),            ("snd", "%p.p false"),
     (*natural numbers*)
 ("suc", "%n f x. n f (f x)"),
 ("iszero", "%n. n (%x.false) true"),
 ("0", "%f x. x"),               ("1", "suc 0"),
 ("2", "suc 1"),                 ("3", "suc 2"),
 ("4", "suc 3"),                 ("5", "suc 4"),
 ("6", "suc 5"),                 ("7", "suc 6"),
 ("8", "suc 7"),                 ("9", "suc 8"),
 ("add",  "%m n f x. m f (n f x)"),
 ("mult", "%m n f. m (n f)"),
 ("expt", "%m n f x. n m f x"),
 ("prefn", "%f p. pair (f (fst p)) (fst p)"),
 ("pre",  "%n f x. snd (n (prefn f) (pair x x))"),
 ("sub",  "%m n. n pre m"),
     (*lists*)
 ("nil",  "%z.z"),
 ("cons", "%x y. pair false (pair x y)"),
 ("null", "fst"),
 ("hd", "%z. fst(snd z)"),       ("tl", "%z. snd(snd z)"),
   (*recursion for call-by-name*)
 ("Y", "%f. (%x.f(x x))(%x.f(x x))"),
 ("fact", "Y(%g n. if (iszero n) 1 (mult n (g (pre n))))"),
 ("append", "Y(%g z w.if (null z) w (cons (hd z) (g(tl z) w)))"),
 ("inflist", "Y(%z. cons MORE z)"),
     (*recursion for call-by-value*)
 ("YV", "%f. (%x.f(%y.x x y)) (%x.f(%y.x x y))"),
 ("factV",
  "YV (%g n.(if (iszero n) (%y.1) (%y.mult n (g (pre n))))y)")
];
```

the arguments of the *if*. It works under call-by-value reduction, computing 3! = 6:

```
try Reduce.byvalue "factV 3";
> %f x. f (f (f (f (f (f x)))))
```

Call-by-name reduction can perform the same computations as call-by-value, and more. It handles recursive definitions involving *Y* and *if*, without needing any tricks to delay evaluation. Here, we *append* the lists [*FARE, THEE*] and [*WELL*]:

```
try Reduce.byname
   "append (cons FARE (cons THEE nil)) (cons WELL nil)";
> %f. f (%x y. y)
>      (%f. f FARE
>          (%f. f (%x y. y)
>              (%f. f THEE
>                  (%f. f (%x y. y)
>                      (%f. f WELL (%z. z))))))
```

Let us take the head of the infinite list [*MORE, MORE,* ...]:

```
try Reduce.byname "hd inflist";
> MORE
```

Execution is extremely slow, especially with call-by-name. Computing *fact* 3 takes several seconds, and *fact* 4, several minutes. This should hardly be surprising, when arithmetic employs unary notation and recursion works by repeated copying. Even so, we have all the elements of functional programming.

With a little more effort, we can obtain a real functional language. Rather than encoding data structures in the pure λ-calculus, we can take numbers, arithmetic operations and ordered pairs as primitive. Rather than interpreting the λ-terms, we can compile them for execution on an abstract machine. For call-by-value reduction, the SECD machine is suitable. For call-by-name reduction we can compile λ-terms into combinators and execute them by graph reduction. Field & Harrison (1988) describe these techniques. The design and implementation of a simple functional language makes a challenging project.

Exercise 9.30 What results when *try Reduce.byname* is applied to these strings?

```
"hd (tl (Y (%z. append (cons MORE (cons AND nil)) z)))"
"hd (tl (tl (Y (%g n. cons n (g (suc n))) 0)))"
```

Summary of main points

Top-down parsers can be expressed in a natural way using higher-order functions.

The λ-calculus is a theoretical model of computation with close similarities to functional programming.

De Bruijn's name-free representation of variable binding is easily implemented on the computer.

Data structures such as numbers and lists, with their operations, can be encoded as λ-terms.

The λ-term Y encodes recursion by repeated copying.

There exist call-by-value and call-by-name evaluation strategies for the λ-calculus.

10

A Tactical Theorem Prover

ML was originally designed to serve as the programming language for a theorem prover, Edinburgh LCF. So it is fitting that a book on ML should conclude by describing a theorem prover, called Hal, inspired by LCF.* Hal constructs a proof by refinement steps, working backwards from a goal. At its simplest, this is proof checking: at each step, an inference rule is matched to a goal, reducing it to certain subgoals. If we are ever to prove anything significant, we shall require more automation. Hal provides **tactics** and **tacticals**, which constitute a high-level language for expressing search procedures. A few primitive tactics, applied using a tactical for depth-first search, implement a general tactic that can prove many theorems automatically, such as

$$\neg(\exists x \,.\, \forall y \,.\, \phi(x, y) \leftrightarrow \neg\phi(y, y))$$
$$\exists xy \,.\, \phi(x, y) \rightarrow \forall xy \,.\, \phi(x, y)$$
$$\exists x \,.\, \forall yz \,.\, (\phi(y) \rightarrow \chi(z)) \rightarrow (\phi(x) \rightarrow \chi(x))$$

For raw power Hal cannot compete with theorem provers based on the resolution principle (Wos et al., 1984). What Hal lacks in power is compensated by its flexibility. Resolution theorem provers typically support pure classical logic with equality; they cannot employ induction and do not allow the underlying logic to be modified. Tactical theorem provers allow a mixture of automatic and interactive working, and support a variety of logics:

> LCF supports a logic of domain theory (Gordon, Milner & Wadsworth 1977; Paulson, 1987).

* Hal is named after King Henry V, who was a master tactician.

The HOL system is a version of LCF modified to support Church's higher-order logic (Gordon, 1988a).

Nuprl supports a variant of Martin-Löf's Type Theory (Constable et al., 1986).

Isabelle is a generic theorem prover, supporting several different logics (Paulson, 1990). It is related to LCF but works by different principles.

Hal works in classical logic for familiarity's sake, but it can easily be extended to include induction principles, modal operators, a set theory, or whatever. Its tactics must be changed to reflect the new inference rules; the tacticals remain the same, ready to express search procedures for the new logic.

Chapter outline

The chapter contains the following sections:

A sequent calculus for first-order logic. The semantics of first-order logic is sketched and the sequent calculus is described. Quantifier reasoning involves parameters and meta-variables.

Processing terms and formulae in ML. Hal's representation of first-order logic borrows techniques from previous chapters. A major new technique is unification.

Tactics and the proof state. The LCF and Isabelle representations of logic are compared. Hal implements the sequent calculus as a set of transformations upon an abstract type of proof states. Each inference rule is provided as a tactic.

Searching for proofs. A crude user interface allows the tactics to be demonstrated. Tacticals add control structures to tactics, and are used to code an automatic tactic for first-order logic.

A sequent calculus for first-order logic

We begin with a quick overview of first-order logic; see Gallier (1986) or Reeves & Clarke (1990) for a fuller introduction. The syntax of first-order logic has been presented in Chapter 6. **Propositional logic** concerns formulae built by the connectives $\wedge$, $\vee$, $\neg$, $\rightarrow$ and $\leftrightarrow$. First-order logic introduces the quantifiers $\forall$ and $\exists$, with variables and terms. A **first-order language** augments the logical symbols with certain constants a, b, ..., function symbols f,

g, ... and predicate symbols P, Q, ... Let ϕ, ψ, χ, ... stand for arbitrary formulae.

The **universe** is a non-empty set containing the possible values of terms. Constants denote elements of the universe; function symbols denote functions over the universe; predicate symbols denote relations over the universe. A **structure** defines the semantics of a first-order language by specifying a universe and giving the interpretations of the constants, function symbols and predicate symbols. An ML structure is analogous to a logical structure.

The meaning of a formula depends on the values of its free variables. An **assignment** is a mapping from free variables to elements of the universe. Given a structure and an assignment, every formula is either true or false. The formula $\forall x \,.\, \phi$ is true if and only if ϕ is true for every possible value that could be assigned to x (leaving the other variables unchanged). The connectives are defined by truth tables; for instance, $\phi \wedge \psi$ is true if and only if ϕ is true and ψ is true.

A **valid** formula is one that is true in all structures and assignments. Since there are infinitely many structures, exhaustive testing can never show that a formula is valid. Instead, we can attempt to show that a formula is valid by formal proof using inference rules, each of which is justified by the semantics of the logic. Each rule accepts zero or more premises and yields a conclusion; a sound rule must yield a valid conclusion provided its premises are valid. A set of inference rules for a logic is called a **proof system** or a **formalization**.

Of the many different proof systems for classical first-order logic, the **sequent calculus** is the easiest to automate. Hal employs a sequent calculus similar to that of Gallier (1986, page 187). The tableau method, which is sometimes used to automate first-order logic (Oppacher & Suen, 1988), is a compact notation for the sequent calculus.

10.1 *The sequent calculus for propositional logic*

To keep matters simple, let us temporarily restrict attention to propositional logic. A **sequent** has the form

$$\phi_1, \ldots, \phi_m \vdash \psi_1, \ldots, \psi_n$$

where $\phi_1, \ldots, \phi_m$ and $\psi_1, \ldots, \psi_n$ are **multisets** of formulae. As discussed in Chapter 6, a multiset is a collection of elements whose order is insignificant. Traditionally a sequent contains lists of formulae, and the logic includes rules for exchanging adjacent formulae; multisets make such rules unnecessary.

Given a structure and an assignment, the sequent above is true if and only if some of the formulae $\phi_1, \ldots, \phi_m$ are false or some of the formulae $\psi_1, \ldots, \psi_n$ are true. In other words, the sequent has the same meaning as the formula

$$\phi_1 \wedge \cdots \wedge \phi_m \rightarrow \psi_1 \vee \cdots \vee \psi_n.$$

As a special case, $\vdash \psi$ has the same meaning as ψ. A sequent is not a formula, however; the $\vdash$ symbol (the 'turnstile') is not a logical connective.

For convenience in writing the rules, Γ and Δ will stand for multisets of formulae. The comma will denote multiset union; thus Γ, Δ stands for the union of Γ and Δ. A formula appearing where a multiset is expected (like ϕ in $\Gamma \vdash \phi$) will stand for a singleton multiset. Thus Γ, ϕ is a multiset containing an occurrence of ϕ, where Γ denotes its other elements.

Validity and basic sequents. A **valid** sequent is one that is true under every structure and assignment. The theorems of our sequent calculus will be precisely the valid sequents.

A sequent is called **basic** if both sides share a common formula ϕ. This can be formalized as the axiom

$$\phi, \Gamma \vdash \Delta, \phi.$$

In the notation just described, ϕ, Γ and Δ, ϕ are multisets containing ϕ. Such sequents are clearly valid.

The other formulae, those contained in Γ and Δ, play no part in the inference. The sequent calculus is sometimes formulated such that a basic sequent must have the form $\phi \vdash \phi$. Then sequents of the form $\phi, \Gamma \vdash \Delta, \phi$ can be derived with the help of 'weakening' rules, which insert arbitrary formulae into a sequent.

Sequent rules for the connectives. The rules of the sequent calculus come in pairs, to introduce each connective on the left or right of the $\vdash$ symbol. For example, the rule $\wedge$:left introduces a conjunction on the left, while $\wedge$:right introduces a conjunction on the right. Here is the latter rule in the usual notation, with its premises above the

Figure 10.1 *Sequent rules for the propositional connectives*

:left	:right
$\dfrac{\phi, \psi, \Gamma \vdash \Delta}{\phi \wedge \psi, \Gamma \vdash \Delta}$	$\dfrac{\Gamma \vdash \Delta, \phi \quad \Gamma \vdash \Delta, \psi}{\Gamma \vdash \Delta, \phi \wedge \psi}$
$\dfrac{\phi, \Gamma \vdash \Delta \quad \psi, \Gamma \vdash \Delta}{\phi \vee \psi, \Gamma \vdash \Delta}$	$\dfrac{\Gamma \vdash \Delta, \phi, \psi}{\Gamma \vdash \Delta, \phi \vee \psi}$
$\dfrac{\Gamma \vdash \Delta, \phi \quad \psi, \Gamma \vdash \Delta}{\phi \rightarrow \psi, \Gamma \vdash \Delta}$	$\dfrac{\phi, \Gamma \vdash \Delta, \psi}{\Gamma \vdash \Delta, \phi \rightarrow \psi}$
$\dfrac{\phi, \psi, \Gamma \vdash \Delta \quad \Gamma \vdash \Delta, \phi, \psi}{\phi \leftrightarrow \psi, \Gamma \vdash \Delta}$	$\dfrac{\phi, \Gamma \vdash \Delta, \psi \quad \psi, \Gamma \vdash \Delta, \phi}{\Gamma \vdash \Delta, \phi \leftrightarrow \psi}$
$\dfrac{\Gamma \vdash \Delta, \phi}{\neg \phi, \Gamma \vdash \Delta}$	$\dfrac{\phi, \Gamma \vdash \Delta}{\Gamma \vdash \Delta, \neg \phi}$

line and its conclusion below:

$$\frac{\Gamma \vdash \Delta, \phi \quad \Gamma \vdash \Delta, \psi}{\Gamma \vdash \Delta, \phi \wedge \psi} \wedge\text{:right}$$

To show that $\wedge$:right is a sound rule, let us assume that its premises are valid and demonstrate that its conclusion is valid. Suppose that, under some structure and assignment, every formula in Γ is true; we must demonstrate that some formula in $\Delta, \phi \wedge \psi$ is true. If no formula in Δ is true, then both ϕ and ψ are true by the premises. Therefore $\phi \wedge \psi$ is true.

Now let us justify the rule $\wedge$:left.

$$\frac{\phi, \psi, \Gamma \vdash \Delta}{\phi \wedge \psi, \Gamma \vdash \Delta} \wedge\text{:left}$$

To show that this rule is sound, we proceed as above. Suppose that every formula in $\Gamma, \phi \wedge \psi$ is true. Then both ϕ and ψ are true. Assuming that the premise is valid, some formula of Δ must be true, and this establishes the conclusion.

Figure 10.1 presents the rules for the propositional connectives $\wedge$, $\vee$, $\rightarrow$, $\leftrightarrow$ and $\neg$. All the rules are justified similarly.

Exercise 10.1   Which formula is equivalent to $\phi_1, \ldots, \phi_m \vdash$, a sequent whose right side is empty?

Exercise 10.2   Justify the rules $\vee$:left and $\vee$:right.

Exercise 10.3   Justify the rules $\leftrightarrow$:left and $\leftrightarrow$:right.

10.2   *Proving theorems in the sequent calculus*
        Inference rules are often viewed in a forwards direction, from premises to conclusion. Thus, $\wedge$:right accepts premises $\Gamma \vdash \Delta, \phi$ and $\Gamma \vdash \Delta, \psi$, yielding the conclusion $\Gamma \vdash \Delta, \phi \wedge \psi$. Applying another rule to this sequent yields another conclusion, and so forth. A formal proof is a tree constructed by applying inference rules. Here is a proof of the sequent $\phi \wedge \psi \vdash \psi \wedge \phi$:

$$\frac{\dfrac{\phi, \psi \vdash \psi \qquad \phi, \psi \vdash \phi}{\phi, \psi \vdash \psi \wedge \phi} \quad \wedge\text{:right}}{\phi \wedge \psi \vdash \psi \wedge \phi} \quad \wedge\text{:left} \qquad (*)$$

Viewed in the forwards direction, two basic sequents are combined by $\wedge$:right and the result transformed by $\wedge$:left. However, the forwards reading does not help us find a proof of a given sequent.

For the purpose of finding proofs, rules should be viewed in the backwards direction, from a goal to subgoals. Thus, $\wedge$:right accepts the goal $\Gamma \vdash \Delta, \phi \wedge \psi$ and returns the subgoals $\Gamma \vdash \Delta, \phi$ and $\Gamma \vdash \Delta, \psi$. If these subgoals can be proved as theorems, then so can the goal. The subgoals are refined by further rule applications until all the remaining subgoals are basic sequents, which are immediately valid. The proof tree is constructed from the root upwards; the process is called **refinement** or **backwards proof**.

Viewed in the backwards direction, the proof $(*)$ begins with the sequent to be proved, namely $\phi \wedge \psi \vdash \psi \wedge \phi$. This goal is refined by $\wedge$:left to $\phi, \psi \vdash \psi \wedge \phi$; this subgoal is refined by $\wedge$:right to $\phi, \psi \vdash \psi$ and $\phi, \psi \vdash \phi$. These two subgoals are basic sequents, so the proof is finished.

Under the backwards reading, each sequent calculus rule attacks a formula in the goal. Applying $\wedge$:left breaks down a conjunction on the left side, while $\wedge$:right breaks down a conjunction on the right. If all the resulting subgoals are basic sequents, then the initial goal has been proved. For propositional logic, this procedure must terminate.

A sequent may have several different proofs, depending on which formulae are broken down first. The proof $(*)$ first breaks down the conjunction on the left in $\phi \wedge \psi \vdash \psi \wedge \phi$. For a different proof, begin by breaking down the conjunction on the right:

$$\frac{\dfrac{\phi, \psi \vdash \psi}{\phi \wedge \psi \vdash \psi} \wedge\text{:left} \qquad \dfrac{\dfrac{\phi, \psi \vdash \phi}{\phi \wedge \psi \vdash \phi} \wedge\text{:left}}{}}{\phi \wedge \psi \vdash \psi \wedge \phi} \wedge\text{:right}$$

This is larger than the proof $(*)$ in that $\wedge$:left is applied twice. Applying $\wedge$:right to the initial goal produced two subgoals, each with a conjunction on the left. Shorter proofs usually result if the rule that produces the fewest subgoals is chosen at each step.

To summarize, we have the following proof procedure:

> Take the sequent to be proved as the initial goal. The root of the proof tree, and its only leaf, is this goal.
>
> Select some subgoal that is a leaf of the proof tree and apply a rule to it, turning the leaf into a branch node with one or more leaves.
>
> Stop whenever all the leaves are basic sequents (success), or when no rules can be applied to a leaf (failure).

This procedure is surprisingly effective, though its search is undirected. Both $\vee$:left and $\wedge$:right may be applied to the subgoal $p \vee q, r \vdash r \wedge r$. The former rule performs case analysis on the irrelevant formula $p \vee q$; the latter rule yields two basic subgoals, succeeding immediately.

Exercise 10.4 Construct proofs of the sequents $\phi \vee \psi \vdash \psi \vee \phi$ and $\phi_1 \wedge (\phi_2 \wedge \phi_3) \vdash (\phi_1 \wedge \phi_2) \wedge \phi_3$.

Exercise 10.5 Construct a proof of the sequent

$$\vdash (\phi_1 \wedge \phi_2) \vee \psi \leftrightarrow (\phi_1 \vee \psi) \wedge (\phi_2 \vee \psi).$$

Exercise 10.6 Show that any sequent containing both ϕ and $\neg\phi$ to the left of the $\vdash$ symbol is provable.

10.3   *Sequent rules for the quantifiers*

Propositional logic is decidable; our proof procedure can determine, in finite time, whether any formula is a theorem. With quantifiers, no such decision procedure exists. Quantifiers, moreover, introduce many syntactic complications — most of which we have already encountered with the λ-calculus (Chapter 9).

Each quantifier binds a variable; thus x and y occur bound and z occurs free in $\forall x . \exists y . R(x, y, z)$. Renaming the bound variables does not affect the meaning of a formula; the previous example is equivalent to $\forall y . \exists w . R(y, w, z)$. Some of the inference rules involve substitution, and $\phi[t/x]$ will stand for the result of substituting t for every free occurrence of x in ϕ. Less formally, $\phi(x)$ stands for a formula involving x and $\phi(t)$ stands for the result of substituting t for free occurrences of x.

The universal quantifier has these two sequent rules:

$$\frac{\phi[t/x], \forall x . \phi, \Gamma \vdash \Delta}{\forall x . \phi, \Gamma \vdash \Delta} \ \forall\text{:left} \qquad\qquad \frac{\Gamma \vdash \Delta, \phi}{\Gamma \vdash \Delta, \forall x . \phi} \ \forall\text{:right}$$

proviso: x must not occur
free in the conclusion

The rule $\forall$:left is easy to justify; if $\forall x . \phi$ is true then so is $\phi[t/x]$, where t is any term.

To justify $\forall$:right, which is the more complicated rule, let us assume that its premise is valid and demonstrate that its conclusion is valid. Given some structure and assignment, suppose that every formula in Γ is true and that no formula in Δ is true; then we must show that $\forall x . \phi$ is true. It suffices to show that ϕ is true for every possible assignment to x that leaves the other variables unchanged. By the proviso of $\forall$:right, changing the value of x does not affect the truth of any formula of Γ or Δ; since the premise is valid, ϕ must be true.

Ignoring the proviso can yield unsound inferences:

$$\frac{P(x) \vdash P(x)}{P(x) \vdash \forall x . P(x)} \ \forall\text{:right} \ \text{???}$$

The conclusion is false if $P(x)$ stands for the predicate $x = 0$ over the integers and x is assigned the value 0.

The existential quantifier has these two sequent rules:

$$\frac{\phi, \Gamma \vdash \Delta}{\exists x \,.\, \phi, \Gamma \vdash \Delta} \ \exists\text{:left} \qquad \frac{\Gamma \vdash \Delta, \exists x \,.\, \phi, \phi[t/x]}{\Gamma \vdash \Delta, \exists x \,.\, \phi} \ \exists\text{:right}$$

proviso: x must not occur
free in the conclusion

They are dual to the rules for the universal quantifier and can be justified similarly. Note that $\exists x \,.\, \phi$ is equivalent to $\neg\forall x \,.\, \neg\phi$.

The rules $\forall$:left and $\exists$:right have one feature that is not present in any of the other rules: in backwards proof, they do not remove any formulae from the goal. They expand a quantified formula, substituting a term into its body; and they retain the formula to allow repeated expansion. It is impossible to determine in advance how many expansions of a quantified formula are required for a proof. Because of this, our proof procedure can fail to terminate; first-order logic is undecidable.

Exercise 10.7 If the premise of $\forall$:right is ignored, can a proof involving this rule reach an inconsistent conclusion? (This means a sequent $\vdash \phi$ such that $\neg\phi$ is a valid formula.)

10.4 *Theorem proving with quantifiers*

Our backwards proof procedure is reasonably effective with quantifiers, at least for tackling simple problems that do not require a more discriminating search. Let us begin with an easy proof involving universal quantification:

$$\frac{\dfrac{\dfrac{\dfrac{\phi(x), \forall x \,.\, \phi(x) \vdash \phi(x), \psi(x)}{\forall x \,.\, \phi(x) \vdash \phi(x), \psi(x)} \ \forall\text{:left}}{\forall x \,.\, \phi(x) \vdash \phi(x) \vee \psi(x)} \ \forall\text{:right}}{\forall x \,.\, \phi(x) \vdash \forall x \,.\, \phi(x) \vee \psi(x)}}{} \ \forall\text{:right}$$

The proviso of $\forall$:right holds; x is not free in the conclusion. In a backwards proof, this conclusion is the initial goal.

If we first applied $\forall$:left, inserting the formula $\phi(x)$, then x would be free in the resulting subgoal. Then $\forall$:right could not be applied without renaming the quantified variable:

$$\frac{\dfrac{\dfrac{\dfrac{\phi(x), \forall x \,.\, \phi(x) \vdash \phi(y), \psi(y)}{\phi(x), \forall x \,.\, \phi(x) \vdash \phi(y) \vee \psi(y)} \ \forall\text{:right}}{\phi(x), \forall x \,.\, \phi(x) \vdash \forall x \,.\, \phi(x) \vee \psi(x)} \ \forall\text{:right}}{\forall x \,.\, \phi(x) \vdash \forall x \,.\, \phi(x) \vee \psi(x)}}{} \ \forall\text{:left}$$

The topmost sequent is not basic; to finish the proof we must again apply ∀:left. The first application of this rule has accomplished nothing. We have a general heuristic: never apply ∀:left or ∃:right to a goal if a different rule can usefully be applied.

The following proof illustrates some of the difficulties that occur with quantifiers:

$$
\cfrac{
\cfrac{
\cfrac{
\cfrac{
\cfrac{
\phi(x),\ \phi(z) \vdash \exists z.\phi(z) \to \forall x.\phi(x),\ \phi(x),\ \forall x.\phi(x)
}{\phi(z) \vdash \exists z.\phi(z) \to \forall x.\phi(x),\ \phi(x),\ \phi(x) \to \forall x.\phi(x)}
}{\phi(z) \vdash \exists z.\phi(z) \to \forall x.\phi(x),\ \phi(x)}
}{\phi(z) \vdash \exists z.\phi(z) \to \forall x.\phi(x),\ \forall x.\phi(x)}
}{\vdash \exists z.\phi(z) \to \forall x.\phi(x),\ \phi(z) \to \forall x.\phi(x)}
}{\vdash \exists z.\phi(z) \to \forall x.\phi(x)}
\begin{array}{l}
\to\text{:right} \\[4pt]
\exists\text{:right} \\[4pt]
\forall\text{:right} \\[4pt]
\to\text{:right} \\[4pt]
\exists\text{:right}
\end{array}
$$

Working upwards from the goal, ∃:right is applied, introducing z as a free variable. Although the existential formula remains in the subgoal, it remains dormant until we again reach a goal where no other rule is applicable. The next inference, →:right, moves $\phi(z)$ to the left. Since x is not free in the subgoal, ∀:right can be applied, replacing $\forall x.\phi(x)$ by $\phi(x)$. In the resulting subgoal, ∃:right is again applied (there is no alternative), substituting x for z. The final subgoal after →:right is a basic sequent containing $\phi(x)$ on both sides.

Observe that $\exists z.\phi(z) \to \forall x.\phi(x)$ is expanded twice by ∃:right. The sequent cannot be proved otherwise. Sequents requiring n expansions of a quantifier, for any given n, are not hard to devise.

Unification. When reasoning about quantifiers, we have a serious difficulty: how do we choose the term t in the rules ∃:right and ∀:left? This amounts to predicting which term will ultimately generate basic subgoals and a successful proof. In the proof above, choosing z in the first ∃:right was arbitrary; any term would have worked. Choosing x in the second ∃:right was crucial — but perhaps not obvious.

We can postpone choosing the term in ∃:right and ∀:left. Introduce **meta-variables** $?a$, $?b$, ... as placeholders for terms. When a goal can be solved by substituting appropriate terms for its meta-variables, perform this substitution — throughout the proof. For instance, the subgoal $P(?a), \Gamma \vdash \Delta, P(f(?b))$ becomes basic if we replace $?a$ by $f(?b)$; observe that $?a$ has still not been fully determined, only its outer form $f(\cdots)$. We thereby solve for unknowns incrementally. **Unification**, the process of determining the appropriate substitutions, is the key to automated reasoning about quantifiers.

The rule $\forall$:left now takes the following form, where $?a$ stands for any meta-variable:

$$\frac{\phi[?a/x], \forall x . \phi, \Gamma \vdash \Delta}{\forall x . \phi, \Gamma \vdash \Delta} \ \forall\text{:left}$$

Enforcing provisos. Meta-variables cause difficulties of their own. Recall that $\forall$:right and $\exists$:left have the proviso 'x not free in conclusion'. What shall we do when the conclusion contains meta-variables, which could be replaced by any terms? Our approach is to label each free variable with a list of forbidden meta-variables. The free variable $b_{?a_1,\ldots,?a_k}$ must never be contained in a term substituted for the meta-variables $?a_1, \ldots, ?a_k$. The unification algorithm can enforce this.

Let us simplify the terminology. Labelled free variables will be called **parameters**. Meta-variables will be called **variables**.

Using parameters, the rule $\forall$:right becomes

$$\frac{\Gamma \vdash \Delta, \phi[b_{?a_1,\ldots,?a_k}/x]}{\Gamma \vdash \Delta, \forall x . \phi} \ \forall\text{:right}$$

proviso: b must not occur in the conclusion and $?a_1, \ldots, ?a_k$ must be all the variables in the conclusion.

The first part of the proviso ensures that the parameter b is not already in use, while the second part ensures that b is not slipped in later by a substitution. The treatment of $\exists$:left is the same.

Parameters ensure correct quantifier reasoning. For example, $\forall x . \phi(x, x)$ does not, in general, imply $\exists y . \forall x . \phi(x, y)$. Consider an attempted proof of the corresponding sequent:

$$\frac{\dfrac{\dfrac{\phi(?c, ?c), \forall x.\phi(x, x) \vdash \exists y.\forall x.\phi(x, y), \phi(b_{?a}, ?a)}{\forall x.\phi(x, x) \vdash \exists y.\forall x.\phi(x, y), \phi(b_{?a}, ?a)} \ \forall\text{:left}}{\forall x.\phi(x, x) \vdash \exists y.\forall x.\phi(x, y), \forall x.\phi(x, ?a)} \ \forall\text{:right}}{\forall x.\phi(x, x) \vdash \exists y.\forall x.\phi(x, y)} \ \exists\text{:right}$$

The topmost sequent cannot be made basic. To make $\phi(?c, ?c)$ and $\phi(b_{?a}, ?a)$ identical, a substitution would have to replace both $?c$ and $?a$ by $b_{?a}$. However, the parameter $b_{?a}$ is forbidden from occurring in a term substituted for $?a$. The attempted proof may continue to grow upwards through applications of ∀:right and ∃:left, but no basic sequent will ever be generated.

For a contrasting example, let us prove that $\forall x \, . \, \phi(x, x)$ indeed implies $\forall x \, . \, \exists y \, . \, \phi(x, y)$:

$$\frac{\dfrac{\phi(?c, ?c), \; \forall x.\phi(x, x) \vdash \exists y.\phi(a, y), \; \phi(a, ?b)}{\dfrac{\forall x.\phi(x, x) \vdash \exists y.\phi(a, y), \; \phi(a, ?b)}{\dfrac{\forall x.\phi(x, x) \vdash \exists y.\phi(a, y)}{\forall x.\phi(x, x) \vdash \forall x.\exists y.\phi(x, y)} \; \forall\text{:right}} \; \exists\text{:right}}}{} \; \forall\text{:left}$$

Replacing $?b$ and $?c$ by a transforms both $\phi(?c, ?c)$ and $\phi(a, ?b)$ into $\phi(a, a)$, completing the proof. The parameter a is not labelled with any variables because there are none in the goal supplied to ∀:right.

Exercise 10.8   Reconstruct the first three quantifier proofs above, this time using (meta) variables and parameters.

Exercise 10.9   Falsify the sequent $\forall x \, . \, P(x, x) \vdash \exists y \, . \, \forall x \, . \, P(x, y)$ by letting P denote a suitable relation in a structure.

Exercise 10.10   Demonstrate that, no matter how the attempted proof of $\forall x \, . \, \phi(x, x) \vdash \exists y \, . \, \forall x \, . \, \phi(x, y)$ is continued, parameters will never allow it to succeed.

Exercise 10.11   Demonstrate that $\vdash \exists z \, . \, \phi(z) \rightarrow \forall x \, . \, \phi(x)$ has no proof that applies ∃:right only once.

Exercise 10.12   For each of the following, construct a proof or demonstrate that no proof exists (a and b are constants):

$$\vdash \exists z \, . \, \phi(z) \rightarrow \phi(a) \wedge \phi(b)$$
$$\forall x \, . \, \exists y \, . \, \phi(x, y) \vdash \exists y \, . \, \forall x \, . \, \phi(x, y)$$
$$\exists y \, . \, \forall x \, . \, \phi(x, y) \vdash \forall x \, . \, \exists y \, . \, \phi(x, y)$$

Processing terms and formulae in ML

Let us code an infrastructure for theorem proving. Terms and formulae must be represented; abstraction, substitution, parsing and pretty printing must be implemented. Thanks to the methods we have accumulated in recent chapters, none of this programming is especially difficult.

10.5 *Representing terms and formulae*

The techniques we have developed for the λ-calculus, such as the nameless representation of bound variables, work for first-order logic. In some respects, first-order logic is simpler. An inference can affect only the outermost variable binding; there is nothing corresponding to a reduction within a λ-term. The following signature defines the representation of first-order terms and formulae:

```
signature FOL =
sig
datatype term = Var     of string
              |  Param   of string * string list
              |  Bound   of int
              |  Fun     of string * term list
datatype form = Pred     of string * term list
              |  Conn    of string * form list
              |  Quant   of string * string * form
val prec_of   : string -> int
val abstract  : int -> term -> form -> form
val subst     : int -> term -> form -> form
val termvars  : term * string list -> string list
val goalvars  : (form list * form list)*string list -> string list
val termparams: term * (string * string list) list
                  -> (string * string list) list
val goalparams : (form list * form list)*(string * string list) list
                  -> (string * string list) list
end;
```

Type *term* realizes the methods described in the previous section. A variable (constructor *Var*) has a name. A *Bound* variable has an index. A *Fun* application has a function's name and argument list; a function taking no arguments is simply a constant. A parameter (*Param*) has a name and a list of forbidden variables.

Type *form* is elementary. An atomic formula (*Pred*) has a predicate's name and argument list. A connective application (*Conn*) has a connective and a list of formulae, typically "~", "&", "|", "-->", or "<->" paired with one or two formulae. A *Quant* formula has a quantifier (either "ALL" or "EX"), a bound variable name and a formula for the body.

The function *prec_of* defines the precedences of the connectives, as required for parsing and printing.

Functions *abstract* and *subst* resemble their namesakes of the previous chapter, but operate on formulae. Calling *abstract i t p* replaces each occurrence of t in p by the index i (which is increased within quantifications); typically $i = 0$ and t is an atomic term. Calling *subst i t p* replaces the index i (increased within quantifications) by t in the formula p.

The function *termvars* collects the list of variables in a term (without repetitions); *termvars*(t, bs) inserts all the variables of t into the list bs. The argument bs may appear to be a needless complication, but it eliminates costly list appends while allowing *termvars* to be extended to formulae and goals. This will become clear when we examine the function definitions.

The function *goalvars*, which also takes two arguments, collects the list of variables in a goal. A goal in Hal is a sequent. Although sequents are represented in ML using formula lists, not multisets, we shall be able to implement the style of proof discussed above.

The functions *termparams* and *goalparams* collect the list of parameters in a term or goal, respectively. Each parameter consists of its name paired with a list of variable names.

The functor *FolFUN*, presented in Figure 10.2, implements signature *FOL*. The figure omits the `datatype` declarations of *term* and *form* in order to save space; they are identical to those in the signature. The functor declares several functions not specified in the signature.

Calling *replace* $(u1, u2)\, t$ replaces the term $u1$ by $u2$ throughout the term t. This function is called by *abstract* and *subst*.

Functionals *accumform* and *accumgoal* demonstrate higher-order programming. First, recall how *foldright* can be used. Suppose that f has type *term* $\times\ \alpha \to \alpha$, for some type α, where $f(t, x)$ accumulates some information about t in x. (For instance, f could be *termvars*, which accumulates the list of free variables in a term.) Then *foldright* f extends f to lists of terms; it takes $([t_1, \ldots, t_n],\ x)$ to $f(t_1, \ldots, f(t_n, x) \ldots)$ and has type *term list* $\times\ \alpha \to \alpha$.

The function *accumform* f has type *form* $\times\ \alpha \to \alpha$, extending f to operate on formulae. It lets *foldright* f handle the arguments of a predicate $P(t_1, \ldots, t_n)$; it recursively lets *foldright* $(accumform\ f)$ handle the formula lists of connectives. The functional *accumgoal* calls *foldright* twice, extending a function of type *form* $\times\ \alpha \to \alpha$ to one of type $(form\ list \times form\ list) \times\ \alpha \to \alpha$. It extends a function involving formulae to one involving goals.

Figure 10.2 *First-order logic: representing terms and formulae*

```
functor FolFUN (Basic: BASIC) : FOL =
  struct
  local open Basic in
  datatype term = ...;  datatype form = ...;

  fun replace (u1,u2) t =
      if t=u1 then u2 else
      case t of Fun(a,ts) => Fun(a, map (replace(u1,u2)) ts)
           | _            => t;

  fun abstract i t (Pred(a,ts)) = Pred(a, map (replace(t,Bound i)) ts)
    | abstract i t (Conn(b,ps)) = Conn(b, map (abstract i t) ps)
    | abstract i t (Quant(qnt,b,p)) = Quant(qnt, b, abstract(i+1)t p);

  fun subst i t (Pred(a,ts)) = Pred(a, map (replace (Bound i, t)) ts)
    | subst i t (Conn(b,ps)) = Conn(b, map (subst i t) ps)
    | subst i t (Quant(qnt,b,p)) = Quant(qnt, b, subst (i+1) t p);

  fun prec_of "~"   = 4
    | prec_of "&"   = 3
    | prec_of "|"   = 2
    | prec_of "<->" = 1
    | prec_of "-->" = 1
    | prec_of _     = ~1    (*means not an infix*);

  fun accumform f (Pred(_,ts), xs) = foldright f (ts, xs)
    | accumform f (Conn(_,ps), xs) = foldright(accumform f)(ps,xs)
    | accumform f (Quant(_,_,p), xs) = accumform f (p,xs);

  fun accumgoal f ((ps,qs), xs) = foldright f (ps, foldright f (qs,xs));

  fun termvars (Var a, bs) = newmem(a,bs)
    | termvars (Fun(_,ts), bs) = foldright termvars (ts,bs)
    | termvars (_, bs) = bs;
  val goalvars = accumgoal (accumform termvars);

  fun termparams (Param(a,bs), pairs) = newmem((a,bs), pairs)
    | termparams (Fun(_,ts), pairs) = foldright termparams (ts,pairs)
    | termparams (_, pairs) = pairs;
  val goalparams = accumgoal (accumform termparams);
  end;
  end;
```

Functionals *accumform* and *accumgoal* provide a uniform means of traversing formulae and goals. They define the functions *goalvars* and *goalparams* and could have many similar applications. Moreover, they are efficient: they create no lists or other data structures.

The functions *termvars* and *termparams* are defined by recursion, scanning a term to accumulate its variables or parameters. They let *foldright* traverse argument lists and let *newmem* build a list without repetitions. Note that *termvars* does not regard the parameter $b_{?a_1,\ldots,?a_k}$ as containing $?a_1, \ldots, ?a_k$; these forbidden variables are not logically part of the term and perhaps ought to be stored in a separate table.

Exercise 10.13   Sketch how *FOL* and *FolFUN* can be modified to adopt a new representation of terms. Bound variables are identified by name, but are syntactically distinct from parameters and meta-variables. Would this representation work for the λ-calculus?

Exercise 10.14   Change the declaration of type *form*, replacing *Conn* by separate constructors for each connective, say *Neg*, *Conj*, *Disj*, *Imp*, *Iff*. Modify *FOL* and *FolFUN* appropriately.

Exercise 10.15   The function *accumgoal* is actually more polymorphic than was suggested above. What is its most general type?

10.6   *Parsing and displaying formulae*
      Our parser and pretty printer (from Chapters 9 and 8, respectively) can implement the syntax of first-order logic. We employ the following grammar for terms (*Term*), optional argument lists (*Termpack*), and non-empty term lists (*Termlist*):

$$Termlist \;=\; Term\,\{,\; Term\}*$$

$$Termpack \;=\; (\; Termlist \;)$$
$$|\; Empty$$

$$Term \;=\; Id\; Termpack$$
$$|\; ?\; Id$$

Formulae (*Form*) are defined in mutual recursion with primaries, which are atomic formulae and their negations:

$$Form = \texttt{ALL} \;\; Id \;\; . \;\; Form$$
$$| \;\; \texttt{EX} \;\;\; Id \;\; . \;\; Form$$
$$| \;\; Form \;\; Conn \;\; Form$$
$$| \;\; Primary$$

$$Primary = \texttt{\textasciitilde} \; Primary$$
$$| \;\; (\;\; Form \;\;)$$
$$| \;\; Id \;\; Termpack$$

The quantifiers are rendered into ASCII characters as **ALL** and **EX**; the following table gives the treatment of the connectives:

Usual symbol:	¬	∧	∨	→	↔
ASCII *version*:	~	&	|	-->	<->

The formula $\exists z . \phi(z) \rightarrow \forall x . \phi(x)$ might be rendered as

```
EX z. P(z) --> (ALL x. P(x))
```

since ASCII lacks Greek letters. Hal requires a quantified formula to be enclosed in parentheses if it is the operand of a connective.

Parsing. The signature for parsing is as small as possible. It contains the type *form*, which is necessary for completeness, and a function *read*, for converting strings to formulae:

```
signature PARSEFOL =
  sig
  type form
  val read: string -> form
  end;
```

Figure 10.3 presents the corresponding functor. It is fairly simple, but a few points are worth noting.

The functions *list* and *pack* express the grammar phrases *Termlist* and *Termpack*. These functions are general enough to define 'lists' and 'packs' of arbitrary phrases.

The parser cannot distinguish constants from parameters, or even check that functions have the right number of arguments, since it keeps no information about the functions and predicates of the first-order language. It regards any free-standing identifier as a constant, representing x by *Fun*("x", []). When parsing the quantification $\forall x . \phi(x)$, it abstracts the body $\phi(x)$ over its occurrences of the 'constant' x.

Figure 10.3 *Parsing for first-order logic*

```
functor ParseFolFUN (structure Parse: PARSE
                     and       Fol: FOL) : PARSEFOL =
  struct
  local open Parse   open Fol
    (*One or more phrases separated by commas*)
    fun list ph =   ph -- repeat ($"," -- ph >> #2) >> (op::);

    (*Either (ph,...,ph) or empty. *)
    fun pack ph =  $"(" -- list ph -- $")" >> (#2 o #1)
                   || empty;

    fun term toks =
      (   id    -- pack term     >> Fun
       || $"?" -- id             >> (Var o #2)  ) toks;

    fun makeQuant (((qnt,b),_),p) =
        Quant(qnt, b, abstract 0 (Fun(b,[])) p);

    fun makeConn a p q = Conn(a, [p,q]);
    fun makeNeg (_,p) = Conn("~", [p]);

    fun form toks =
      (   $"ALL" -- id -- $"." -- form  >> makeQuant
       || $"EX"  -- id -- $"." -- form  >> makeQuant
       || infixes (primary,prec_of,makeConn)  ) toks
    and primary toks =
      (   $"~" -- primary                   >> makeNeg
       || $"(" -- form -- $")"              >> (#2 o #1)
       || id -- pack term                   >> Pred    )  toks;
  in
    type form = Fol.form
    val read = reader form
  end
  end;
```

As discussed in the previous chapter, our parser cannot accept left-recursive grammar rules such as

> *Form = Form Conn Form.*

Instead, it relies on the precedences of the connectives. It invokes the parsing function *infixes* with three arguments:

> *primary* parses the operands of connectives.
> *prec_of* defines the precedences of the connectives.

makeConn applies a connective to two formulae.

Most of the functor body is made private by a **local** declaration. At the bottom it defines the only visible identifiers, *form* and *read*. We could easily declare a reading function for terms if necessary.

Displaying. Hal can display formulae and goals (sequents). The signature *DISPFOL* specifies the following items:

```
signature DISPFOL =
  sig
  type form
  val pr_form: form -> unit
  val pr_goal: int -> form list * form list -> unit
  end;
```

Calling *pr_form p* pretty prints the formula p. Calling *pr_goal i g* pretty prints the goal g with its goal number i. It is employed to display proof states, which may have several goals.

Functor *DispFolFUN* (Figure 10.4), which is largely straightforward, implements this signature. Our pretty printer must be supplied with symbolic expressions that describe the formatting. Function *enclose* wraps an expression in parentheses, while *list* inserts commas between the elements of a list of expressions. Together, they format argument lists as $(t_1, \ldots, t_n)$.

A parameter's name is printed, but not its list of forbidden variables. Another part of the program will display that information as a table.

The precedences of the connectives govern the inclusion of parentheses. Calling *form k p* formats the formula p — enclosing it in parentheses, if necessary, to protect it from an adjacent connective of precedence k. In producing q & (p | r), it encloses p | r in parentheses because the adjacent connective (&) has precedence 3 while | has precedence 2.

In *pr_goal*, the function *makestring* converts the goal number to a string. Although not officially part of Standard ML, many compilers provide *makestring* for displaying values of standard types.

Exercise 10.16 Explain the workings of each of the functions supplied to >> in *ParseFolFUN*.

Exercise 10.17 Modify the parser to accept, for example, the input q --> ALL x. p as correct syntax for $q \to (\forall x \,.\, p)$; it should no longer demand parentheses around quantified formulae.

Figure 10.4 *Pretty printing for first-order logic*

```
functor DispFolFUN (structure Basic: BASIC
                and Pretty: PRETTY and Fol: FOL) : DISPFOL =
  struct
  local open Basic  open Pretty  open Fol
  fun enclose sexp = blo(1, [str"(", sexp, str")"]);

  fun commas [] = []
    | commas(sexp::sexps) = str"," :: brk 1 :: sexp :: commas sexps;

  fun list (sexp::sexps) = blo(0, sexp :: commas sexps);

  fun term (Param(a,_)) = str a
    | term (Var a) = str ("?"^a)
    | term (Bound i) = str "??UNMATCHED INDEX??"
    | term (Fun (a,ts)) =  blo(0, [str a, args ts])
  and args [] = str""
    | args ts = enclose (list (map term ts));

  fun form k (Pred (a,ts)) = blo(0, [str a, args ts])
    | form k (Conn("~", [p])) = blo(0, [str"~", form(prec_of"~")p])
    | form k (Conn(C, [p,q])) =
          let val pf = form (maxl[prec_of C, k])
              val sexp = blo(0, [pf p, str(" "^C), brk 1, pf q])
          in  if (prec_of C <= k) then (enclose sexp) else sexp
          end
    | form k (Quant(qnt,b,p)) =
          let val q = subst 0 (Fun(b,[])) p
              val sexp = blo(2,
                       [str(qnt ^ " " ^ b ^ "."), brk 1,  form 0 q])
          in  if k>0  then  (enclose sexp)  else sexp  end
    | form k _ = str"??UNKNOWN FORMULA??";

  fun formlist [] = str"empty"
    | formlist ps = list (map (form 0) ps);
  in
    type form = Fol.form;

    fun pr_form p = pr (std_out, form 0 p, 50);

    fun pr_goal (n:int) (ps,qs) =
        pr (std_out,
             blo (4, [str(" "  ^ makestring n  ^  ". "),
                        formlist ps,  brk 2, str"|-  ", formlist qs]),
             50);
  end;
  end;
```

Exercise 10.18 The output of the pretty printer may sometimes contain needless parentheses. For example, the inner pair of parentheses in q & (p1 --> (p2 | r)) is redundant because | has greater precedence than -->. Suggest modifications to the function *form* that would suppress needless parentheses.

Exercise 10.19 Explain how quantified formulae are displayed.

10.7 *Unification*

Hal attempts to unify atomic formulae in goals. Its basic unification algorithm takes terms containing no bound variables. Given a pair of terms, it computes a set of (variable, term) replacements to make them identical, or reports that the terms cannot be unified. The task can be considered under the following cases:

Function applications. Two function applications can be unified only if they apply the same function; obviously no substitution can transform $f(?a)$ and $g(b, ?c)$ into identical terms. To unify $g(t_1, t_2)$ with $g(u_1, u_2)$ involves unifying t_1 with u_1 and t_2 with u_2 **simultaneously** — thus $g(?a, ?a)$ cannot be unified with $g(b, c)$ because a variable $(?a)$ cannot be replaced by two different constants (b and c).

The unification of $f(t_1, \ldots, t_n)$ with $f(u_1, \ldots, u_n)$ begins by unifying t_1 with u_1, then applies the resulting replacements to the remaining terms. The next step is unifying t_2 with u_2 and applying the new replacements to the remaining terms, and so forth. If any unifications fail then the function applications are not unifiable. The corresponding arguments can be chosen for unification in any order without significantly affecting the outcome.

Parameters. Two parameters can be unified only if they have the same name. A parameter cannot be unified with a function application.

Variables. The remaining and most interesting case is unifying a variable $?a$ with a term t (distinct from $?a$). If $?a$ does not occur in t then unification succeeds, yielding the replacement $(?a, t)$. If $?a$ does occur in t then unification fails — for possibly two different reasons:

> If $?a$ occurs in a parameter of t, then $?a$ is a 'forbidden variable' for that parameter and for the term. Replacing $?a$ by t would violate the proviso of some quantifier rule.
>
> If t properly contains $?a$ then the terms cannot be unified because no term can contain itself. For example, no replacement can transform $f(?a)$ and $?a$ into identical terms.

This is the famous **occurs check**, which most Prolog interpreters omit because of its cost. For theorem proving, soundness must have priority over efficiency; the occurs check must be performed.

Examples. To unify $g(?a, f(?c))$ with $g(f(?b), ?a)$, we begin by unifying $?a$ with $f(?b)$, which is trivial. After replacing $?a$ by $f(?b)$ in the remaining arguments, we must unify $f(?c)$ with $f(?b)$. This replaces $?c$ by $?b$. The outcome can be given as the list of pairs $[(?a, f(?b)), (?c, ?b)]$. The unified formula is $g(f(?b), f(?b))$.

Here is another example. To unify $g(?a, f(?a))$ with $g(f(?b), ?b)$, the first step again replaces $?a$ by $f(?b)$. The next task is unifying $f(f(?b))$ with $?b$ — which is impossible because $f(f(?b))$ contains $?b$. Unification fails.

Substitution in parameters. Recall that each parameter carries a list of forbidden variables; $b_{?a}$ must never be part of a term t substituted for $?a$. When a legal replacement is performed, the occurrence of $?a$ in $b_{?a}$ is replaced by the variables contained in t, not by t itself. For instance, replacing $?a$ by $g(?c, f(?d))$ transforms $b_{?a}$ into $b_{?c, ?d}$. Any substitution for $?c$ or $?d$ is effectively a substitution for $?a$, and therefore $?c$ and $?d$ are forbidden to the parameter.

For example, to unify $g(?a, f(b_{?a}))$ with $g(h(?c, ?d), ?c)$, the first step is to replace $?a$ by $h(?c, ?d)$. The second arguments of g become $f(b_{?c, ?d})$ and $?c$; these terms are not unifiable because $?c$ is forbidden to the parameter $b_{?c, ?d}$.

Parameters are not widely used in theorem proving; more traditional are **Skolem functions**. The rules $\forall$:left and $\exists$:right, instead of creating the parameter $b_{?a_1, \ldots, ?a_k}$, could introduce the term $b(?a_1, \ldots, ?a_k)$. Here, b is a function symbol not appearing elsewhere in the proof. The term behaves like a parameter; the occurs check prevents unification from violating the rules' provisos. However, parameters remain compact while the arguments of Skolem functions can grow large.

The ML code. The signature for unification contains the types *term* and *form* and an exception *Fail* for reporting non-unifiable terms. The function *atoms* attempts to unify two atomic formulae, while *instterm*, *instform* and *instgoal* apply replacements to terms, formulae and goals, respectively:

```
signature UNIFY =
  sig
  type term and form
  exception Fail
  val atoms    : form * form -> (string*term)list
  val instterm : (string*term)list -> term -> term
  val instform : (string*term)list -> form -> form
  val instgoal : (string*term)list -> (form list * form list) ->
                 (form list * form list)
  end;
```

The type $(string \times term)list$ represents a set of replacements. The pairs are cumulative rather than simultaneous, in that

$$[(?b, g(c)), (?a, f(?b))]$$

replaces $?a$ by $f(g(c))$. Compare with the definition environments of the λ-calculus interpreter, in Chapter 9. **Instantiation** means performing the replacements.

An atomic formula consists of a predicate applied to an argument list, such as $P(t_1, \ldots, t_n)$. Unifying two atomic formulae is essentially the same as unifying two function applications; the predicates must be the same and the corresponding argument pairs must be simultaneously unifiable.

Functor *UnifyFUN* (Figure 10.5) implements unification. The key functions are declared within *unifylists* in order to have access to *env*, the environment of replacements. Collecting the replacements in *env* is more efficient than applying each replacement as it is generated. Here are some remarks about the functions:

> *chase t* replaces the term t, if it is a variable, by its assignment in *env*. Nonvariable terms are returned without change; at each stage, unification is concerned only with a term's outer form.
>
> *occurs a t* tests whether the variable $?a$ occurs within term t; like *chase*, it looks up variables in the environment.
>
> *occsl a ts* tests whether the variable $?a$ occurs within the list of terms ts.

unify(*t*, *u*) creates a new environment from *env* by unifying *t*
with *u*, if possible, otherwise raising exception *Fail*. If *t*
and *u* are variables then they must have no assignment
in *env*; violating this condition could result in a variable
having two assignments!

unifyl(*ts*, *us*) simultaneously unifies the corresponding members of the lists *ts* and *us*, raising *Fail* if their lengths
differ. (If two terms are not unifiable, the exception will
arise in *unify*, not *unifyl*.)

The implementation is purely functional. Representing variables
by references might be more efficient — updating a variable would
perform a replacement, with no need for environments — but is
incompatible with tactical theorem proving. Applying a tactic to a
proof state should create a new state, leaving the original state unchanged so that other tactics can be tried. A unification algorithm
could employ imperative techniques provided they were invisible
outside.

The algorithm presented here can take exponential time in exceptional cases. Some efficient unification algorithms are strictly of
theoretical interest; Ružička & Prívara (1988) suggest a practical
and efficient algorithm using imperative data structures.

The unification function raises exception *Fail* when two terms
cannot be unified. As in parsing, the failure may be detected in
deeply nested recursive calls; the exception propagates upwards.
This is a typical case where exceptions work well.

Exercise 10.20   Explain the workings of the function *instterm*.
Could it be made more efficient?

Exercise 10.21   What could happen if the following line were
omitted from *unify*?

```
if t = Var a  then   env  else
```

Figure 10.5 *Unification*

```
functor UnifyFUN (structure Basic: BASIC and Fol: FOL): UNIFY =
  struct
  local open Basic   open Fol    in
  type term = Fol.term and form = Fol.form
  exception Fail;

  fun unifylists env =
    let fun chase (Var a) =
                (chase (lookup (env, a))) handle Lookup => Var a)
          | chase t = t
        fun occurs a (Fun(_,ts)) = occsl a ts
          | occurs a (Param(_,bs)) = occsl a (map Var bs)
          | occurs a (Var b) =  (a=b) orelse
                (occurs a (lookup(env,b))  handle Lookup => false)
          | occurs a _ = false
        and occsl a = exists (occurs a)
        and unify (Var a, t) =
                if t = Var a  then   env   else
                if occurs a t then  raise Fail  else   (a,t)::env
          | unify (t, Var a) = unify (Var a, t)
          | unify (Param(a,_), Param(b,_)) =
                if a=b then env  else  raise Fail
          | unify (Fun(a,ts), Fun(b,us)) =
                if a=b then unifyl(ts,us) else raise Fail
          | unify _ =  raise Fail
        and unifyl ([],[]) = env
          | unifyl (t::ts, u::us) =
                unifylists (unify (chase t, chase u)) (ts,us)
          | unifyl _ = raise Fail
    in  unifyl  end

  fun atoms (Pred(a,ts), Pred(b,us)) =
        if a=b then unifylists [] (ts,us)   else   raise Fail
    | atoms _ =  raise Fail;

  fun instterm env (Fun(a,ts)) = Fun(a, map (instterm env) ts)
    | instterm env (Param(a,bs)) =
        Param(a, foldright termvars (map(instterm env o Var)bs, []))
    | instterm env (Var a) = (instterm env (lookup(env,a))
                                handle Lookup => Var a)
    | instterm env t = t;

  fun instform env (Pred(a,ts))   = Pred(a, map (instterm env) ts)
    | instform env (Conn(b,ps))   = Conn(b, map (instform env) ps)
    | instform env (Quant(qnt,b,p)) = Quant(qnt, b, instform env p);

  fun instgoal env (ps,qs) =
        (map (instform env) ps, map (instform env) qs);
  end
  end;
```

Tactics and the proof state

Our proof procedure for the sequent calculus operates by successive refinements, working backwards from a goal. The proof tree grows up from the root. Coding the procedure in ML requires a data structure for **proof states**, which are partially constructed proofs. Inference rules will be implemented as functions, called **tactics**, on proof states.

10.8   *The proof state*

A formal proof is a tree whose every node carries a sequent. Branch nodes also carry the name of an inference rule, with branches leading to its premises. The ML datatype corresponding to such trees is, however, unsuitable for our purposes. Backwards proof requires access to the leaves, not to the root. Extending the proof turns a leaf into a branch node, and would require copying part of the tree. The intermediate nodes would play no useful role in the search for a proof.

Hal omits the intermediate nodes altogether. A partial proof tree contains just two parts of the proof. The root, or **main goal**, is the formula we first set out to prove. The leaves, or **current subgoals**, are the sequents that remain to be proved.

A goal ϕ paired with the singleton subgoal list $[\vdash \phi]$ represents the initial state of a proof of ϕ; no rules have yet been applied. A goal ϕ paired with the empty subgoal list is a final state, and represents a finished proof.

If the full proof tree is not stored, how can we be certain that a Hal proof is correct? The answer is to hide the representation of proof states using an abstract type *state*, providing a limited set of operations — to create an initial state, to examine the contents of a state, to test for a final state, and to transform a state into a new state by some rule of inference.

If greater security is required, the proof can be saved in some form, and checked by a separate program. Bear in mind that proofs of real theorems can be extremely large, and that no amount of machine checking can provide absolute security. Our programs and proof systems could be fallible, especially when we apply them to imprecise 'real world' tasks.

The LCF approach. LCF's type *thm* denotes the set of theorems of the logic. Functions with result type *thm* implement the axioms and inference rules.

Implementing the inference rules as functions from theorems to theorems supports forwards proof, which is LCF's primitive style of reasoning. To support backwards proof, LCF provides tactics. LCF tactics represent a partial proof by a function of type *thm list* → *thm*. This function proves the main goal, using inference rules, when supplied with theorems for each of the subgoals. A finished proof can be supplied with the empty list to prove the main goal. My book on LCF presents the details (Paulson, 1987).

Robin Milner conceived the idea of defining an inference system as an abstract type. He designed ML's type system to support this application (Gordon, Milner & Wadsworth 1977).

The Hal approach. Hal differs from LCF in implementing the inference rules as functions on proof states, not on theorems. These functions are themselves tactics and support backwards proof as the primitive style. The approach supports unification; tactics may update meta-variables in the proof state.

10.9   *The ML signature*

The abstract type *state*, with its operations, is expressed by the signature *PROOF* (Figure 10.6). It contains the following items:

Structure *Seq* implements sequences, or lazy lists; each tactic will return a sequence of proof states. Signature *SEQUENCE* was declared in Chapter 8.

Type *form* must be specified for the signature to be complete, while *state* is the new abstract type of proof states. Each value of type *state* contains a formula (the main goal) and a list of sequents (the subgoals). Although we cannot tell from the signature, each *state* contains additional information for internal use.

The function *initial* creates initial states containing a given formula as the main goal and the only subgoal. The predicate *final* tests whether a proof state is final, containing no subgoals.

The other functions in the signature have names ending in _tac to emphasize that they are tactics. These are the primitive tactics, which define the inference rules of the sequent calculus. Later, we shall introduce **tacticals** for combining tactics. Strictly speaking,

Figure 10.6 *The signature* PROOF

```
signature PROOF =
  sig
  structure Seq: SEQUENCE
  type state and form
  val maingoal      : state -> form
  and subgoals      : state -> (form list * form list) list
  val initial       : form -> state
  and final         : state -> bool
  val unify_tac     : int -> state -> state Seq.T
  and conj_left_tac : int -> state -> state Seq.T
  and conj_right_tac : int -> state -> state Seq.T
  and disj_left_tac : int -> state -> state Seq.T
  and disj_right_tac : int -> state -> state Seq.T
  and imp_left_tac  : int -> state -> state Seq.T
  and imp_right_tac : int -> state -> state Seq.T
  and neg_left_tac  : int -> state -> state Seq.T
  and neg_right_tac : int -> state -> state Seq.T
  and iff_left_tac  : int -> state -> state Seq.T
  and iff_right_tac : int -> state -> state Seq.T
  and all_left_tac  : int -> state -> state Seq.T
  and all_right_tac : int -> state -> state Seq.T
  and ex_left_tac   : int -> state -> state Seq.T
  and ex_right_tac  : int -> state -> state Seq.T
  end;
```

---

a tactic is a function of type

$$state \rightarrow state\ Seq.T$$

and maps a state to a sequence of states. The primitive tactics
generate finite sequences, typically of length zero or one; a complex
tactic, say for depth-first search, could generate an infinite sequence
of next states.

The subgoals of a proof state are numbered starting from 1. Each
primitive tactic, given an integer argument i and a state, applies
some rule of the sequent calculus to subgoal i, creating a new state.
For instance, calling

$$conj\_left\_tac\ 3\ st$$

applies $\wedge$:left to subgoal 3 of state st. If this subgoal has the form
$\phi \wedge \psi, \Gamma \vdash \Delta$ then subgoal 3 of the next state will be $\phi, \psi, \Gamma \vdash \Delta$.

Otherwise, ∧:left is not applicable to the subgoal and there can be no next state; *conj_left_tac* will return the empty sequence.

If subgoal 5 of *st* is $\Gamma \vdash \Delta, \phi \wedge \psi$, then

$\qquad$ *conj_right_tac* 5 *st*

will make a new state whose subgoal 5 is $\Gamma \vdash \Delta, \phi$ and whose subgoal 6 is $\Gamma \vdash \Delta, \psi$. Subgoals numbered greater than 5 in *st* are shifted up.

Calling *unify_tac i st* attempts to solve subgoal *i* of state *st* by converting it into a basic sequent. If it can unify a formula on the left with a formula on the right then it deletes subgoal *i* and applies the unifying substitution to the rest of the proof state. There may be several different pairs of unifiable formulae; applying *unify_tac* to the subgoal

$$P(?a), P(?b) \vdash P(f(c)), P(c)$$

generates a sequence of four next states. Only the first of these is computed, with the others available upon demand, since sequences are lazy.

10.10 *The functor heading*

$\qquad$ Functor *ProofFUN* creates a structure having the signature *PROOF*. This functor is large and is presented in parts. The first part specifies the argument structures and defines the representation of type *state*:

```
functor ProofFUN (structure Basic: BASIC and Fol: FOL
                    and Unify: UNIFY and Seq: SEQUENCE
          sharing type Fol.form=Unify.form) : PROOF =
     struct
     local open Basic  open Fol   in
     structure Seq = Seq;

     type form = Fol.form
     and goal  = form list * form list;

     datatype state = State of goal list * form * int;

     fun maingoal (State(gs,p,_)) = p
     and subgoals (State(gs,p,_))  = gs;

     fun initial p = State([ ([],[p]) ], p, 0);

     fun final (State([],p,_)) = true
       | final (State(_,p,_))  = false;
```

The sharing constraint ensures that the structures *Fol* and *Unify* share the same type *form*. If signature *UNIFY* specified *Fol* as a substructure, in place of types *term* and *form*, then *ProofFUN* would not require *Fol* as an argument and the sharing constraint would disappear. That approach has some merits, but it is hardly modular for *UNIFY* to presuppose the whole of *FOL*.

The **datatype** declaration introduces type *state* with its constructor *State*. Inside the functor body, the constructor gives access to the representation of proof states; outside, the representation is hidden. Functions *maingoal* and *subgoals* return the corresponding parts of a state.

The third component of a proof state is an integer. It is needed to generate unique names for variables and parameters in quantifier reasoning. Its value is initially 0 and is increased as necessary when the next state is created. If this name counter were kept in a reference cell and updated by assignment, much of the code would be simpler — especially where the counter plays no role. However, applying a quantifier rule to a state would affect all states sharing that reference. Resetting the counter to 0, while producing shorter names, could also lead to re-use of names and faulty reasoning. It is safest to ensure that all tactics are purely functional.

Calling *initial p* creates a state containing the sequent $\vdash p$ as its only subgoal, with p as its main goal and 0 for its variable counter. Predicate *final* tests for an empty subgoal list by pattern-matching.

Exercise 10.22 Suppose that *Proof* is an instance of the signature *PROOF*, created by applying *ProofFUN*. Is there any sense in which *Proof.state* is not an abstract type?

10.11 *The definition of* unify_tac

The next part (Figure 10.7) of functor *ProofFUN* defines the tactic *unify_tac*. It begins with *splicegoals*, a function to replace subgoal i by a new list of subgoals in a state; observe how *take* and *drop* extract the subgoals before and after i, so that the new subgoals can be spliced into the correct place.

The function *unifiable* takes lists ps and qs of atomic formulae. It returns the sequence of all environments obtained by unifying some p of ps with some q of qs. The function *find* handles the 'inner loop', searching in qs for something to unify with p. It

Figure 10.7 *Part of* ProofFUN — *the unification tactic*

```
fun splicegoals gs newgs i = take(i-1,gs) @ newgs @ drop(i,gs);
fun unifiable ([], _) = Seq.empty
  | unifiable (p::ps, qs) =
        let fun find [] = unifiable (ps,qs)
              | find (q::qs) =
                    Seq.cons(Unify.atoms(p,q),  fn() => find qs)
                    handle Unify.Fail => find qs
        in  find qs  end;
fun atomic (Pred _) = true
  | atomic _ = false;
fun inst [] st = st          (*no copying if environment is empty*)
  | inst env (State(gs,p,n)) =
        State (map (Unify.instgoal env) gs,  Unify.instform env p, n);
fun unify_tac i (State(gs,p,n)) =
  let val (ps,qs) = nth(gs,i-1)
        fun next env = inst env (State(splicegoals gs [] i, p, n))
  in Seq.map next (unifiable(filter atomic ps, filter atomic qs)) end
  handle Nth => Seq.empty;
```

generates a sequence whose head is an environment and whose tail is generated by the recursive call *find qs*, but if *Unify.atoms* raises an exception then the result is simply *find qs*.

The predicate *atomic* tests whether a formula consists of a predicate application. By considering only atomic formulae, the unification function does not have to handle bound variables. Atomic formulae tend to be small and few in number.

The function *inst* instantiates the subgoals and main goal of a proof state, creating a new state. When given an empty environment, it immediately returns the input state to avoid copying it.

The definition of *unify_tac* illustrates the processing of proof states. To select subgoal i it uses $nth(gs, i-1)$ because *nth* numbers a list's elements from 0 rather than 1. If exception *Nth* is raised then there is no subgoal i; the tactic fails by returning the empty sequence of states. Function *next*, given an environment *env*, creates a next state from the input state; it creates a new subgoal list using *splicegoals* and instantiates the state with *env*. Observe the use of the functionals *filter* and *Seq.map*.

! *Look out for other goals.* When *unify_tac* solves a subgoal, it may update the state so that some other subgoal becomes unprovable. Success of this tactic does not guarantee that it is the right way to find a proof; in some cases, a different tactic should be used instead.

Exercise 10.23   Give an example to justify the warning above. Suggest modifications to *unify_tac* that address this problem.

10.12   *The propositional tactics*

The next part of *ProofFUN* implements the rules for ∧, ∨, ¬, → and ↔. Since each connective has a 'left' rule and a 'right' rule, there are ten tactics altogether. Some of them appear in Figure 10.8.

The tactics employ the same basic mechanism. Search for a suitable formula on the given side, left or right; detach the connective; generate new subgoals from its operands. Each tactic returns a single next state if it succeeds. A tactic fails, returning an empty state sequence, if it cannot find a suitable formula. The functions *splitconn* and *SUBGOAL* express the tactics succinctly.

An example will demonstrate the workings of *splitconn*. Applied to the string "&" and a formula list *qs*, it finds the first element that matches *Conn*("&", *ps*), raising exception *TacticFailed* if none exists. It also makes a copy of *qs*, omitting the matching element. It returns *ps* paired with the shortened *qs*. Note that *ps* contains the operands of the selected formula.

A higher-order function, *SUBGOAL* creates a tactic from a function *goalf* of type *goal* → *goal list*. Applied to an integer *i* and a state, it supplies subgoal *i* to *goalf* and splices in the resulting subgoals; it returns the new state as a singleton sequence. If any exception is raised — such as *Nth* or *TacticFailed* — then the empty sequence results.

The tactics are given by **val** declarations, since they have no explicit arguments. Each tactic consists of a call to *SUBGOAL*, passing a function in **fn** notation. Each function takes the subgoal (*ps*, *qs*) and returns one or two subgoals. Thus *conj_left_tac* searches for a conjunction in the left part (*ps*) and inserts the two conjuncts into the new subgoal, while *conj_right_tac* searches for a conjunction in the right part (*qs*) and makes two subgoals.

Exercise 10.24   Define the tactics that are missing from Figure 10.8: *neg_left_tac*, *neg_right_tac*, *iff_left_tac* and *iff_right_tac*.

Figure 10.8 *Part of* ProoffUN — *the propositional tactics*

```
exception TacticFailed;     (* the tactic cannot be applied *)

fun splitconn a qs =
  let fun get [] = raise TacticFailed
        | get (Conn(b,ps) :: qs) = if a=b then ps else get qs
        | get (q::qs) = get qs;
      fun del [] = []
        | del ((q as Conn(b,_)) :: qs) =
                 if a=b then qs else q :: del qs
        | del (q::qs) = q :: del qs
  in (get qs, del qs)  end;

fun SUBGOAL goalf i (State(gs,p,n)) =
    let val gs2 = splicegoals gs (goalf (nth(gs,i-1))) i
    in  Seq.cons (State(gs2, p, n),  fn()=>Seq.empty)   end
    handle _ => Seq.empty;

val conj_left_tac = SUBGOAL (fn (ps,qs) =>
    let val ([p1,p2], ps') = splitconn "&" ps
    in  [ (p1::p2::ps', qs) ]  end);

val conj_right_tac = SUBGOAL (fn (ps,qs) =>
    let val ([q1,q2], qs') = splitconn "&" qs
    in  [ (ps, q1::qs'),    (ps, q2::qs') ]  end);

val disj_left_tac = SUBGOAL (fn (ps,qs) =>
    let val ([p1,p2], ps') = splitconn "|" ps
    in  [ (p1::ps', qs),    (p2::ps', qs)]  end);

val disj_right_tac = SUBGOAL (fn (ps,qs) =>
    let val ([q1,q2], qs') = splitconn "|" qs
    in  [ (ps, q1::q2::qs') ]  end);

val imp_left_tac = SUBGOAL (fn (ps,qs) =>
    let val ([p1,p2], ps') = splitconn "-->" ps
    in  [ (p2::ps', qs),    (ps', p1::qs)]  end);

val imp_right_tac = SUBGOAL (fn (ps,qs) =>
    let val ([q1,q2], qs') = splitconn "-->" qs
    in  [ (q1::ps, q2::qs') ]  end);
```

10.13   *The quantifier tactics*

The mechanism presented above is easily modified to express the quantifier tactics. There are a few differences from the propositional case. The code appears in Figure 10.9, which completes the presentation of functor *ProofFUN*.

The function *splitquant* closely resembles *splitconn*. It finds the first formula having a particular quantifier, "ALL" or "EX". It returns the entire formula (rather than its operands) because certain quantifier tactics retain it in the subgoal.

Although our sequent calculus is defined using multisets, it is implemented using lists. The formulae in a sequent are ordered; if the list contains two suitable formulae, the leftmost one will be found. To respect the concept of multisets, Hal provides no way of reordering the formulae. The quantifier tactics ensure that no formula is permanently excluded from consideration.

The tactics require a source of fresh names for variables and parameters. Calling *letter n*, for $0 \leq n \leq 25$, returns a one-character string from "a" to "z". (Recall that *ord* converts a character to its ASCII code, while *chr* is the inverse function.) The function *gensym* — whose name dates from Lisp antiquity — generates a string from a natural number. Its result contains a base 26 numeral whose 'digits' are lower-case letters; the prefix "_" prevents clashes with names supplied from outside.

The higher-order function *SUBGOAL_SYM* creates a tactic from a function *goalf*. It supplies both a subgoal and a fresh name to *goalf*, which accordingly has type *goal × string → goal list*. When constructing the next state, it increases the variable counter by 1. Otherwise, *SUBGOAL_SYM* is identical to *SUBGOAL*.

Each tactic is expressed, using *SUBGOAL_SYM*, in terms of a function in **fn** notation. This function takes the subgoal (ps, qs) and the fresh name b; it returns one subgoal.

Tactics *all_left_tac* and *exists_right_tac* expand a quantified formula. They substitute a variable with the name b into its body. They include the quantified formula (bound to *qntform* using **as**) in the subgoal. The formula is placed last in the list; thus, other quantified formulae can be selected when the tactic is next applied.

Tactics *all_right_tac* and *exists_left_tac* select a quantified formula and substitute a parameter into its body. The parameter has the name b and carries, as forbidden variables, all the variables in

Figure 10.9 *Final part of* ProofFUN — *the quantifier tactics*

```
fun splitquant qnt qs =
  let fun get [] = raise TacticFailed
        | get ((q as Quant(qnt2,_,p)) :: qs) =
              if  qnt=qnt2 then  q  else  get qs
        | get (q::qs) = get qs;
      fun del [] = []
        | del ((q as Quant(qnt2,_,p)) :: qs) =
              if  qnt=qnt2 then  qs  else q :: del qs
        | del (q::qs) = q :: del qs
  in (get qs, del qs)  end;

fun letter n = chr(ord("a")+n);

fun gensym n =
    if n<26 then "_" ^ letter n
    else gensym(n div 26) ^ letter(n mod 26);

fun SUBGOAL_SYM goalf i (State(gs,p,n)) =
      let val gs2 = splicegoals gs (goalf (nth(gs,i-1), gensym n)) i
      in  Seq.cons (State(gs2, p, n+1),  fn()=>Seq.empty)  end
      handle _ => Seq.empty;


val all_left_tac = SUBGOAL_SYM (fn ((ps,qs), b) =>
      let val (qntform as Quant(_,_,p), ps') = splitquant "ALL" ps
          val px = subst 0 (Var b) p
      in  [ (px :: ps' @ [qntform], qs) ]  end);

val all_right_tac = SUBGOAL_SYM (fn ((ps,qs), b) =>
      let val (Quant(_,_,q), qs') = splitquant "ALL" qs
          val vars = goalvars ((ps,qs), [])
          val qx = subst 0 (Param(b, vars)) q
      in  [ (ps, qx::qs') ]  end);

val ex_left_tac = SUBGOAL_SYM (fn ((ps,qs), b) =>
      let val (Quant(_,_,p), ps') = splitquant "EX" ps
          val vars = goalvars ((ps,qs), [])
          val px = subst 0 (Param(b, vars)) p
      in  [ (px::ps', qs) ]  end);

val ex_right_tac = SUBGOAL_SYM (fn ((ps,qs), b) =>
      let val (qntform as Quant(_,_,q), qs') = splitquant "EX" qs
          val qx = subst 0 (Var b) q
      in  [ (ps, qx :: qs' @ [qntform]) ]  end);

end
end;
```

the subgoal.

As we reach the end of *ProofFUN*, we should remember that the tactics declared in it are the only means of creating values of type *state*. All proof procedures — even if they demonstrate validity using sophisticated data structures — must ultimately apply these tactics, constructing a formal proof. If the code given above is correct, and the ML system is correct, then Hal proofs are guaranteed to be sound. No coding errors after this point can yield faulty proofs. This security comes from defining *state* as an abstract type.

Exercise 10.25   Suggest a representation of type *state* that would store the entire proof tree. Best would be an encoding that uses little space while allowing the proof tree to be reconstructed. Sketch the modifications to *PROOF* and *ProofFUN*.

Exercise 10.26   Our set of tactics provides no way of using a previously proved theorem in a proof. A tactic based on the rule

$$\frac{\vdash \phi \quad \phi, \Gamma \vdash \Delta}{\Gamma \vdash \Delta}$$

could insert the theorem $\vdash \phi$ as a lemma into a goal.* Describe how such a tactic could be implemented.

Exercise 10.27   'Functor *ProofFUN* does not involve signatures *PARSEFOL* or *DISPFOL*; therefore, faults in parsing and display cannot result in the construction of faulty proofs.' Comment on this statement.

Searching for proofs

Most of the programming is now behind us. We are nearly ready to attempt proofs on the machine. We shall implement a package of commands for applying tactics to a goal. This will demonstrate the treatment of proof states, but will also reveal the tedium of rule-by-rule proof checking. Tacticals, by providing control structures for tactics, will allow us to express an automatic theorem prover in 15 lines of code.

---

* This rule is a special case of 'cut'; its first premise could be $\Gamma \vdash \Delta, \phi$.

10.14 *Commands for transforming proof states*

The user interface does not read from the terminal, but consists of a set of commands to be invoked from the ML top level. This is typical of tactical theorem provers. The most important command is 'apply a tactic', and the tactic could be given by an arbitrary ML expression; therefore, the command language is ML itself. Remember that ML stands for Meta Language.

Hal's interface is crude. It merely provides commands for setting, updating and inspecting a stored proof state. Practical theorem proving requires additional facilities, such as an *undo* command for reverting to a previous state. Because a tactic can return several next states, applying tactics defines a search tree rooted in the initial state. A fancy user interface would provide means for exploring this tree. To keep the code simple, such facilities are left as exercises. The design and construction of a powerful interface is no easy undertaking.

Signature *COMMAND* specifies the user interface:

```
signature COMMAND =
  sig
  structure Seq: SEQUENCE
  type state
  val goal : string -> unit
  val by   : (state -> state Seq.T) -> unit
  val pr   : state -> unit
  val state : unit -> state
  end;
```

Structure *Seq* and type *state* are present for completeness. The interface consists of the following items, which (except *pr*) act upon a stored proof state:

> The *goal* command accepts a formula ϕ, given as a string; it sets the stored proof state to the initial state for ϕ.

> The *by* command applies a tactic to the current state. If the resulting sequence of next states is non-empty, its head is taken to update the stored proof state. Otherwise, the tactic has failed; an error message is displayed.

> The *pr* command prints its argument, a proof state, on the terminal.

> The function *state* returns the stored proof state.

Functor *CommandFUN*, which implements these items, appears

in Figure 10.10. Note its sharing constraint, which ensures that
the structures *Fol*, *ParseFol*, *DispFol* and *Proof* share the same
type *form*. Sharing constraints should be expected when a functor
takes five arguments.

The current state is stored in a reference cell, initialized with the
fictitious goal `"No goal yet!"`.

Recall that a parameter, such as $b_{?c,?d}$, is displayed simply as b.
The interface displays a table of each parameter, with its forbidden
variables. Function *printpar* prints the line

> `b not in ?c ?d`

for $b_{?c,?d}$; it prints nothing at all for a parameter that has no forbidden variables. Function *printgoals* prints a list of numbered
subgoals. With the help of these functions, *pr* prints a state: its
main goal, its subgoal list, and its table of parameters.

Exercise 10.28   Design and implement an *undo* command that
cancels the effect of the most recent *by* command. Repeated *undo*
commands should revert to earlier and earlier states.

Exercise 10.29   There are many ways of managing the search
tree of states. The interface could explore a single path through
the tree. Each node would store a sequence of possible next states,
marking one as the active branch. Changing the active branch at
any node would select a different path. Develop this idea.

10.15   *Two sample proofs using tactics*

To demonstrate the tactics and the user interface, let us do
some proofs on the machine. First, Hal must be linked together. We
begin by applying functors defined in previous chapters. Structure
FolKey defines the lexical syntax of first-order logic:

```
structure Basic   = BasicFUN();
structure FolKey =
    struct val alphas   = ["ALL","EX"]
          and symbols = ["(", ")", ".", ",", "?", "~",
                         "&", "|", "<->", "-->", "|-"]
    end;
structure Lex     = LexicalFUN
          (structure Basic=Basic and Keyword=FolKey);
structure Parse   = ParseFUN(Lex);
structure Pretty  = PrettyFUN();
structure Seq     = ImpSeqFUN();
```

Figure 10.10 *User interface commands*

```
functor CommandFUN (structure Basic: BASIC and Fol: FOL
                and ParseFol: PARSEFOL and DispFol: DISPFOL
                and Proof: PROOF
    sharing type Fol.form = ParseFol.form =
                DispFol.form = Proof.form): COMMAND =
struct
local open Basic  in
structure Seq = Proof.Seq;
type state = Proof.state;

val curr_state = ref (Proof.initial (Fol.Pred("No goal yet!",[])));

fun question s = " ?" ^ s;
fun printpar (a,[]) = ()    (*print a line of parameter table*)
  | printpar (a,ts) =
        output(std_out, a ^ " not in " ^
                    implode (map question ts) ^ "\n");

fun printgoals (_, []) = ()
  | printgoals (n, g::gs) =
        (DispFol.pr_goal n g;   printgoals (n+1,gs));

fun pr st =   (*print a proof state*)
    let val p = Proof.maingoal st  and  gs = Proof.subgoals st
    in  DispFol.pr_form p;
        if Proof.final st then output(std_out,"No subgoals left!\n")
        else (printgoals (1,gs);
                map printpar (foldright Fol.goalparams (gs, []));  ())
    end;

(*print new state, then set it*)
fun setstate state = (pr state;   curr_state := state);

fun goal aform = setstate (Proof.initial (ParseFol.read aform));

fun by tac = setstate (Seq.hd (tac (!curr_state)))
        handle Seq.E => output(std_out, "** Tactic FAILED! **\n")

fun state() = !curr_state;
end
end;
```

Next, we apply the functors defined in this chapter.

```
structure Fol        = FolFUN (Basic);
structure ParseFol   = ParseFolFUN
         (structure Parse=Parse and Fol=Fol);
structure DispFol    = DispFolFUN
         (structure Basic=Basic and Pretty=Pretty and Fol=Fol);
structure Unify      = UnifyFUN
         (structure Basic=Basic and Fol=Fol);
structure Proof      = ProofFUN
         (structure Basic=Basic
           and Unify=Unify and Seq=Seq and Fol=Fol);
structure Command = CommandFUN
         (structure Basic=Basic
           and Fol=Fol and ParseFol=ParseFol
           and DispFol=DispFol and Proof=Proof);
```

For convenience in referring to tactics and commands, we open the corresponding modules:

```
open Proof;
open Command;
```

Now we can perform proofs. The first example is brief, a proof of $\phi \wedge \psi \rightarrow \psi \wedge \phi$. The *goal* command gives this formula to Hal.

```
goal "P & Q  -->  Q & P";
> P & Q --> Q & P
> 1. empty  |-  P & Q --> Q & P
```

Now $\phi \wedge \psi \rightarrow \psi \wedge \phi$ is the main goal and the only subgoal. We must apply $\rightarrow$:right to subgoal 1; no other step is possible:

```
by (imp_right_tac 1);
> P & Q --> Q & P
> 1. P & Q  |-  Q & P
```

Subgoal 1 becomes $\phi \wedge \psi \vdash \psi \wedge \phi$, which we have proved on paper. Although $\wedge$:right could be applied to this goal, $\wedge$:left leads to a shorter proof because it makes only one subgoal.

```
by (conj_left_tac 1);
> P & Q --> Q & P
> 1. P, Q  |-  Q & P
```

Again we have no choice. We must apply $\wedge$:right to subgoal 1. Here is what happens if we try a different tactic:

```
by (disj_right_tac 1);
> ** Tactic FAILED! **
```

This time, apply ∧:right. It makes two subgoals.

```
by (conj_right_tac 1);
> P & Q --> Q & P
> 1. P, Q |- Q
> 2. P, Q |- P
```

Tactics are usually applied to subgoal 1; let us tackle subgoal 2 for variety. It is a basic sequent, so it falls to *unify_tac*.

```
by (unify_tac 2);
> P & Q --> Q & P
> 1. P, Q |- Q
```

Subgoal 1 is also a basic sequent. Solving it terminates the proof.

```
by (unify_tac 1);
> P & Q --> Q & P
> No subgoals left!
```

Most theorem provers provide some means of storing theorems once proved, but this is not possible in Hal. We go on to the next example, $\exists z \,.\, \phi(z) \rightarrow \forall x \,.\, \phi(x)$, which was discussed earlier.

```
goal "EX z. P(z) --> (ALL x. P(x))";
> EX z. P(z) --> (ALL x. P(x))
> 1. empty |- EX z. P(z) --> (ALL x. P(x))
```

The only possible step is to apply ∃:right to subgoal 1. The tactic generates a variable called ?_a.

```
by (ex_right_tac 1);
> EX z. P(z) --> (ALL x. P(x))
> 1. empty
>     |- P(?_a) --> (ALL x. P(x)),
>        EX z. P(z) --> (ALL x. P(x))
```

We could apply ∃:right again, but it seems sensible to analyse the other formula in subgoal 1. So we apply →:right.

```
by (imp_right_tac 1);
> EX z. P(z) --> (ALL x. P(x))
> 1. P(?_a) |- ALL x. P(x), EX z. P(z) --> (ALL x. P(x))
```

Continuing to work on the first formula, we apply ∀:right. The tactic generates a parameter called _b, with ?_a as its forbidden variable. A table of parameters is now displayed.

```
by (all_right_tac 1);
> EX z. P(z) --> (ALL x. P(x))
> 1. P(?_a) |- P(_b), EX z. P(z) --> (ALL x. P(x))
> _b not in  ?_a
```

Since the subgoal contains P(?_a) on the left and P(_b) on the right, we could try unifying these formulae. However, the forbidden variable of _b prevents this unification. Replacing ?_a by _b would violate the proviso of ∀:right.

```
by (unify_tac 1);
> ** Tactic FAILED! **
```

The situation is like it was at the start of the proof, except that the subgoal contains two new atomic formulae. Since they are not unifiable, we have no choice but to expand the quantifier again, using ∃:right. The variable ?_c is created.

```
by (ex_right_tac 1);
> EX z. P(z) --> (ALL x. P(x))
>  1. P(?_a)
>       |-  P(?_c) --> (ALL x. P(x)), P(_b),
>              EX z. P(z) --> (ALL x. P(x))
> _b not in   ?_a
```

The proof continues as it did before, with the two atomic formulae carried along. We avoid applying ∃:right a third time and instead apply →:right.

```
by (imp_right_tac 1);
> EX z. P(z) --> (ALL x. P(x))
>  1. P(?_c), P(?_a)
>       |-  ALL x. P(x), P(_b), EX z. P(z) --> (ALL x. P(x))
> _b not in   ?_a
```

The subgoal has a new formula on the left, namely P(?_c), and ?_c is not a forbidden variable of _b. Therefore P(?_c) and P(_b) are unifiable.

```
by (unify_tac 1);
> EX z. P(z) --> (ALL x. P(x))
> No subgoals left!
```

Although the first attempt with *unify_tac* failed, a successful proof was finally found. This demonstrates how parameters and variables behave in practice.

10.16 *Tacticals*

The sample proofs of the previous section are unusually short. The proof of even a simple formula can require many steps. To convince yourself of this, try proving

$$((\phi \leftrightarrow \psi) \leftrightarrow \chi) \leftrightarrow (\phi \leftrightarrow (\psi \leftrightarrow \chi)).$$

Although proofs are long, each step is usually obvious. Often, only one or two rules can be applied to a subgoal. Moreover, the subgoals can be tackled in any order because a successful proof must prove them all. We can always work on subgoal 1. A respectable proof procedure can be expressed using tactics, with the help of a few control structures.

Operations on tactics are called **tacticals** by analogy with functions and functionals. The simplest tacticals implement the control structures of sequencing, choice and repetition, as do the parsing operators --, || and *repeat* (see Chapter 9). The tacticals of LCF implement similar control structures, which also crop up in rewriting (Paulson, 1983). Each of these applications requires different implementation techniques.

Tacticals in Hal (and in Isabelle) involve operations on sequences. Let us examine the signature:

```
signature TACTICAL =
  sig
  structure Seq: SEQUENCE
  val THEN    : ('a -> 'b Seq.T) * ('b -> '_c Seq.T)
                  -> 'a -> '_c Seq.T
  val ORELSE : ('a -> 'b Seq.T) * ('a -> 'b Seq.T)
                  -> 'a -> 'b Seq.T
  val APPEND : ('a -> '_b Seq.T) * ('a -> '_b Seq.T)
                  -> 'a -> '_b Seq.T
  val all_tac  : '_a -> '_a Seq.T
  val no_tac   : 'a -> 'b Seq.T
  val TRY     : ('_a -> '_a Seq.T) -> '_a -> '_a Seq.T
  val REPEAT : ('_a -> '_a Seq.T) -> '_a -> '_a Seq.T
  val DEPTH_FIRST: ('_a -> bool) -> ('_a -> '_a Seq.T)
                  -> '_a -> '_a Seq.T
  val ORI     : (int -> 'a -> 'b Seq.T) * (int -> 'a -> 'b Seq.T)
                  -> int -> 'a -> 'b Seq.T
  end;
```

These operations are not restricted to tactics. They are all polymorphic; type *state* appears nowhere. Each operation's type gives a hint about its implementation. Imperative type variables appear because sequences employ references, but all the operations exhibit functional behaviour. Let us describe these tacticals by their effect on arbitrary functions of suitable type, not just tactics.

The tactical *THEN* composes two functions sequentially. When the function f *THEN* g is applied to x, it computes the sequence

$f(x) = [y_1, y_2, \ldots]$ and returns the concatenation of the sequences $g(y_1)$, $g(y_2)$, ... With tactics, *THEN* applies one tactic and then another to a proof state, returning all 'next next' states that result.

The tactical *ORELSE* chooses between two functions. When the function f *ORELSE* g is applied to x, it returns $f(x)$ if this sequence is non-empty, and otherwise returns $g(y)$. With tactics, *ORELSE* applies one tactic to a proof state, and if it fails, tries another. The tactical *APPEND* provides a less committal form of choice; when f *APPEND* g is applied to x, it concatenates the sequences $f(x)$ and $g(x)$.

The tactics *all_tac* and *no_tac* can be used with tacticals to obtain effects such as repetition. For all x, *all_tac*(x) returns the singleton sequence $[x]$ while *no_tac*(x) returns the empty sequence. Thus, *all_tac* succeeds with all arguments while *no_tac* succeeds with none. Note that *all_tac* is the identity element for *THEN*:

$$all\_tac\ THEN\ f = f\ THEN\ all\_tac = f$$

Similarly, *no_tac* is the identity for *ORELSE* and *APPEND*.

The remaining tacticals are defined in terms of the above, so let us turn to the functor *TacticalFUN*. It appears in Figure 10.11 and assumes the following infix directives:

```
infix 5 THEN;
infix 0 ORELSE;
infix 0 APPEND;
infix 0 ORI;
```

The function *flatseq* concatenates a sequence of sequences, yielding a sequence. Its recursive definition considers three cases — the empty sequence, a sequence whose first element is empty, and a sequence whose first element is non-empty — in order to delay the recursive call as soon as an output element is found. (Recall the discussion of *enumerate* in Chapter 5.)

The role of *flatseq* in *THEN* is clear, but its role in *APPEND* may be obscure. What is wrong with this obvious definition?

```
fun (tac1 APPEND tac2) st = Seq.append(tac1 st, tac2 st);
```

This *APPEND* may prematurely (and wastefully) call *tac2*. Defining *APPEND* using *flatseq* ensures that *tac2* is not called until the elements produced by *tac1* have been exhausted. In a lazy language, the obvious definition of *APPEND* would behave properly.

The tactical *TRY* attempts to apply its argument.

Figure 10.11 *Tacticals*

```
functor TacticalFUN (Proof: PROOF) : TACTICAL =
  struct
  structure Seq = Proof.Seq;

  local open Seq in
  fun flatseq xqq =
    if null xqq then empty
    else if null(hd xqq) then flatseq(tl xqq)
    else cons(hd(hd xqq), fn()=> append(tl(hd xqq), flatseq(tl xqq)));
  end;

  fun (tac1 THEN tac2) st = flatseq (Seq.map tac2 (tac1 st));

  fun (tac1 ORELSE tac2) st =
      let val st1 = tac1 st
      in  if Seq.null st1  then  tac2 st  else st1  end;

  fun (tac1 APPEND tac2) st =
      flatseq(Seq.cons(tac1 st,   (*delay application of tac2!*)
                      fn()=> Seq.cons(tac2 st, fn()=> Seq.empty)));

  fun all_tac st = Seq.cons(st, fn()=> Seq.empty);

  fun no_tac st = Seq.empty;

  fun TRY tac = tac ORELSE all_tac;

  fun REPEAT tac st = (tac THEN REPEAT tac ORELSE all_tac) st;

  fun DEPTH_FIRST pred tac st =
     (if pred st   then   all_tac
      else   tac THEN DEPTH_FIRST pred tac) st;

  fun (f1 ORI f2) i = f1 i ORELSE f2 i;
  end;
```

The tactical *REPEAT* applies a function repeatedly. The result of *REPEAT* f x is a sequence of values obtained from x by repeatedly applying f, such that a further application of f would fail. The tactical is defined recursively like the parsing operator *repeat*. And like *repeat*, it must not be simplified by omitting the argument st on both sides; infinite recursion would result.

The tactical *DEPTH_FIRST* explores the search tree generated by a function. Calling *DEPTH_FIRST* *pred* f x returns a sequence of values, all satisfying the predicate *pred*, that were obtained from x by repeatedly applying f.

Finally, *ORI* is just a convenient operator for calling *ORELSE*. The primitive tactics, like *unify_tac*, have type *int* → *state* → *state Seq.T*. They can be combined using *ORI* to create new functions of that type.

In order to demonstrate the tacticals, we first must build and open the structure containing them:

```
structure Tactical = TacticalFUN (Proof);
open Tactical;
```

Now let us prove the following formula, which concerns the associative law for conjunction:

```
goal "(P & Q) & R  -->  P & (Q & R)";
> (P & Q) & R --> P & (Q & R)
>  1. empty  |-  (P & Q) & R --> P & (Q & R)
```

The only rule that can be applied is →:right. Looking ahead a bit, we can foresee two applications of ∧:left. With *REPEAT* we can apply both rules as often as necessary:

```
by (REPEAT (imp_right_tac 1 ORELSE conj_left_tac 1));
> (P & Q) & R --> P & (Q & R)
>  1. P, Q, R  |-  P & (Q & R)
```

Now ∧:right must be applied twice. We repeatly apply its tactic, along with *unify_tac*, which detects basic sequents:

```
by (REPEAT (unify_tac 1 ORELSE conj_right_tac 1));
> (P & Q) & R --> P & (Q & R)
> No subgoals left!
```

We have proved the theorem using only two *by* commands; a rule-by-rule proof would have needed eight commands. For another demonstration, let us prove a theorem using one fancy tactic. Take our old quantifier example:

```
goal "EX z. P(z) --> (ALL x. P(x))";
> EX z. P(z) --> (ALL x. P(x))
>  1. empty  |-  EX z. P(z) --> (ALL x. P(x))
```

Let us *REPEAT* the necessary tactics, choosing the order carefully. Clearly *unify_tac* should be tried first, since it might solve the goal altogether. Certainly *ex_right_tac* must be last; otherwise it will apply every time and cause an infinite loop.

```
by (REPEAT (unify_tac 1 ORELSE imp_right_tac 1 ORELSE
            all_right_tac 1 ORELSE ex_right_tac 1));
> EX z. P(z) --> (ALL x. P(x))
> No subgoals left!
```

Exercise 10.30   What does $REPEAT(f\ THEN\ f)(x)$ return?

Exercise 10.31   Does $DEPTH\_FIRST$ really perform depth-first search? Explain in detail how it works.

Exercise 10.32   Describe situations where the sequence returned by $THEN$ or $APPEND$ omits some elements that intuitively should be present. Implement new tacticals that do not have this fault. Do $THEN$ and $APPEND$ have any compensating virtues?

Exercise 10.33   Write tacticals to perform bounded depth-first search and depth-first iterative deepening. (See Chapter 5.)

10.17   *An automatic tactic for first-order logic*

Using tacticals, we shall code a simple tactic for automatic proof. Given a subgoal, *depth_tac* attempts to solve it by unification, or by breaking down some formula, or by expanding quantifiers. Quantifiers can be expanded repeatedly without limit; the tactic may run forever.

The components of *depth_tac* are themselves useful for interactive proof, especially when *depth_tac* fails. They are specified in signature *FOLTAC*:

```
signature FOLTAC =
  sig
  structure Seq: SEQUENCE
  type state
  val safe_step_tac : int -> state -> state Seq.T
  val quant_tac    : int -> state -> state Seq.T
  val step_tac     : int -> state -> state Seq.T
  val depth_tac    : state -> state Seq.T
  end;
```

The signature specifies four tactics:

  safe_step_tac i applies a 'safe' rule — any rule except ∃:right and ∀:left — to subgoal *i*.

  quant_tac i expands quantifiers in subgoal *i*. It applies both ∃:right and ∀:left, if possible.

  step_tac i attempts to solve subgoal *i* by unification, then tries a safe rule, with quantifier expansion as a last resort.

  depth_tac applies *step_tac* 1 using depth-first search to the proof state.

Functor *FolTacFUN*, given below, shows how succinctly tactics can express a proof procedure. The definition of *safe_step_tac* simply lists the necessary tactics, separated by *ORI*. Tactics that create one subgoal precede tactics that create two; apart from this consideration, their order is arbitrary. The definition of *quant_tac* can almost be read as English: try *all_left_tac*, then try *exists_right_tac*. Simpler still is *step_tac*, which *depth_tac* supplies, with the predicate *final*, to the tactical *DEPTH_FIRST*.

```
functor FolTacFUN (structure Proof: PROOF
        and Tactical: TACTICAL
        sharing Proof.Seq = Tactical.Seq) : FOLTAC  =
struct
local  open Proof  Tactical  in
structure Seq = Seq;
type state = state;

val safe_step_tac =
    (*1 subgoal*)
    conj_left_tac ORI disj_right_tac ORI imp_right_tac ORI
    neg_left_tac ORI neg_right_tac ORI
    ex_left_tac ORI all_right_tac ORI
    (*2 subgoals*)
    conj_right_tac ORI disj_left_tac ORI imp_left_tac ORI
    iff_left_tac ORI iff_right_tac;

fun quant_tac i =
    TRY (all_left_tac i) THEN TRY (ex_right_tac i);

val step_tac = unify_tac ORI safe_step_tac ORI quant_tac;

val depth_tac = DEPTH_FIRST final (step_tac 1);
end
end;
```

Let us try *depth_tac* on some of the problems of Pelletier (1986). This is problem 39:

```
goal "~ (EX x. ALL y. J(x,y) <-> ~J(y,y))";
> ~(EX x. ALL y. J(x, y) <-> ~J(y, y))
> 1. empty  |-  ~(EX x. ALL y. J(x, y) <-> ~J(y, y))
```

Applying *depth_tac* proves it:

```
by depth_tac;
> ~(EX x. ALL y. J(x, y) <-> ~J(y, y))
> No subgoals left!
```

Problem 40 is more complicated.*

```
goal "(EX y. ALL x. J(y,x) <-> ~J(x,x))            \
\        -->  ~ (ALL x. EX y. ALL z. J(z,y) <-> ~ J(z,x))";
> (EX y. ALL x. J(y, x) <-> ~J(x, x)) -->
> ~(ALL x. EX y. ALL z. J(z, y) <-> ~J(z, x))
> 1. empty
>    |-  (EX y. ALL x. J(y, x) <-> ~J(x, x)) -->
>            ~(ALL x. EX y. ALL z. J(z, y) <-> ~J(z, x))
```

This problem too is easily proved.

```
by depth_tac;
> (EX y. ALL x. J(y, x) <-> ~J(x, x)) -->
> ~(ALL x. EX y. ALL z. J(z, y) <-> ~J(z, x))
```

Problem 41 is harder still ...

```
goal "~ (EX y. ALL x. p(x,y) <-> ~ (EX z. p(x,z) & p(z,x)))";
> ~(EX y. ALL x. p(x, y) <-> ~(EX z. p(x, z) & p(z, x)))
> 1. empty
>    |-  ~(EX y.
>            ALL x. p(x, y) <-> ~(EX z. p(x, z) & p(z, x)))
```

... and *depth_tac* never returns.

```
by depth_tac;
```

It is worth reiterating that *depth_tac* is no match for an advanced resolution theorem prover. Here are some of its limitations:

1 It employs depth-first search, which is incomplete.
2 It applies *unify_tac* whenever possible, regardless of its effect on other goals.
3 The search strategy is unguided. Quantifier expansion, in particular, must be controlled using heuristics.

We can develop improved tactics fairly easily. For point 1, we could implement depth-first iterative deepening. For point 2, we could employ *APPEND* to combine *unify_tac* with the other tactics. Point 3 is more difficult because *all_left_tac* and *exists_right_tac* provide no choice of which quantifier to expand; we might have to extend the abstract type *state* with additional operations.

No tactic is likely to out-perform a resolution theorem prover. The proof, no matter how it is discovered, must be constructed by applying the tactics specified in signature *PROOF*. Tactics

---

* Since the goal formula does not fit on one line, the \...\ escape sequence divides the string over two lines.

work best when the logic has no known automatic proof procedure. Tacticals allow experimentation with different search procedures, while the abstract type *state* guards against faulty reasoning.

Exercise 10.34   Draw a diagram showing the structures, signatures and functors of Hal and their relationships.

Exercise 10.35   Implement a tactic for the rule of mathematical induction, involving the constant 0 and the successor function *suc*:

$$\frac{\Gamma \vdash \Delta, \phi[0/x] \quad \phi, \Gamma \vdash \Delta, \phi[suc(x)/x]}{\Gamma \vdash \Delta, \forall x \,.\, \phi}$$

proviso: x must not occur free in the conclusion

Can you foresee any difficulties in adding the tactic to an automatic proof procedure?

Exercise 10.36   Define a tactical *SOMEGOAL* such that, when applied to a state with n subgoals, *SOMEGOAL* f is equivalent to

$$f(n) \; ORELSE \; f(n-1) \; ORELSE \; \ldots \; ORELSE \; f(1).$$

What is the effect of *REPEAT*(*SOMEGOAL conj_right_tac*) on a proof state?

Exercise 10.37   Our proof procedure always works on subgoal 1. When might it be better to choose other subgoals?

Summary of main points

The sequent calculus is a convenient proof system for first-order logic.

Unification assists reasoning about quantifiers.

The occurs check in unification is essential for soundness.

Quantified variables can be treated like the bound variables of the λ-calculus.

Inference rules can be provided as operations on an abstract type of theorems or proofs.

The tacticals *THEN*, *ORELSE* and *REPEAT* have analogues throughout functional programming.

The tactical approach allows a mixture of automatic and interactive theorem proving.

BIBLIOGRAPHY

Annika Aasa, Sören Holmström & Christina Nilsson (1988). An efficiency comparison of some representations of purely functional arrays. *BIT*, 28:490–503.

Harold Abelson & Gerald J. Sussman (1985). *Structure and Interpretation of Computer Programs*. MIT Press.

Alfred V. Aho, Ravi Sethi & Jeffrey D. Ullman (1986). *Compilers: Principles, Techniques and Tools*. Addison-Wesley.

L. Augustsson & T. Johnsson (1989). The Chalmers Lazy-ML compiler. *Computer Journal*, 32:127–141.

John Backus (1978). Can programming be liberated from the von Neumann style? A functional style and its algebra of programs. *Communications of the ACM*, 21:613–641.

H. P. Barendregt (1984). *The Lambda Calculus: Its Syntax and Semantics*. North-Holland.

William R. Bevier, Warren A. Hunt Jr., J Strother Moore & William D. Young (1989). An approach to systems verification. *Journal of Automated Reasoning*, 5:411–428.

Richard Bird & Philip Wadler (1988). *Introduction to Functional Programming*. Prentice-Hall.

Graham Birtwistle & P. A. Subrahmanyam, editors (1988). *VLSI Specification, Verification and Synthesis*. Kluwer Academic Publishers.

Robert S. Boyer & J Strother Moore (1979). *A Computational Logic*. Academic Press.

W. H. Burge (1975). *Recursive Programming Techniques*. Addison-Wesley.

F. W. Burton (1982). An efficient functional implementation of FIFO queues. *Information Processing Letters*, 14:205–206.

Luca Cardelli & Peter Wegner (1985). On understanding types, data abstraction, and polymorphism. *Computing Surveys*, 17:471–522.

Avra Cohn (1989a). Correctness properties of the Viper block model: The second level. In Graham Birtwistle & P. A. Subrahmanyam, editors, *Current Trends in Hardware Verification and Automated Theorem Proving*, pages 1–91. Springer.

Avra Cohn (1989b). The notion of proof in hardware verification. *Journal of Automated Reasoning*, 5:127–139.

R. L. Constable et al. (1986). *Implementing Mathematics with the Nuprl Proof Development System*. Prentice-Hall.

G. Cousineau & G. Huet (1990). The CAML primer. Technical report, INRIA, Rocquencourt, France.

Luis Damas & Robin Milner (1982). Principal type-schemes for functional programs. In *Symposium on Principles of Programming Languages*, 207–212. ACM.

N. G. de Bruijn (1972). Lambda calculus notation with nameless dummies, a tool for automatic formula manipulation, with application to the Church-Rosser Theorem. *Indagationes Mathematicae*, 34:381–392.

Edsger W. Dijkstra (1976). *A Discipline of Programming*. Prentice-Hall.

Anthony J. Field & Peter G. Harrison (1988). *Functional Programming*. Addison-Wesley.

R. Frost & J. Launchbury (1989). Constructing natural language interpreters in a lazy functional language. *Computer Journal*, 32:108–121.

J. H. Gallier (1986). *Logic for Computer Science: Foundations of Automatic Theorem Proving*. Harper & Row.

Michael J. C. Gordon (1988a). HOL: A proof generating system for higher-order logic. In Graham Birtwistle & P. A. Subrahmanyam, editors, *VLSI Specification, Verification and Synthesis*, 73–128. Kluwer Academic Publishers.

Michael J. C. Gordon (1988b). *Programming Language Theory and its Implementation*. Prentice-Hall.

Michael J. C. Gordon, Robin Milner & Christopher P. Wadsworth (1979). *Edinburgh LCF: A Mechanised Logic of Computation*. Springer LNCS 78.

Matthew Halfant & Gerald Jay Sussman (1988). Abstraction in numerical methods. In *LISP and Functional Programming*, 1–7. ACM.

Robert Harper, David MacQueen & Robin Milner (1986). Standard ML. Technical Report ECS-LFCS-86-2, Department of Computer Science, University of Edinburgh.

C. A. R. Hoare (1971). Computer science. Inaugural lecture, Queen's University of Belfast. Reprinted in C. B. Jones, editor, *Essays in Computing Science*, 89–101. Prentice-Hall (1989).

C. A. R. Hoare (1987). An overview of some formal methods for program design. *Computer*, 20:85–91. Reprinted in C. B. Jones, editor, *Essays in Computing Science*, 371–387. Prentice-Hall (1989).

Paul Hudak & Philip Wadler, editors (1990). *Report on the Programming Language Haskell*. Available from Glasgow University and Yale University.

John Hughes (1989). Why functional programming matters. *Computer Journal*, 32:98–107.

R. E. Korf (1985). Depth-first iterative-deepening: an optimal admissible tree search. *Artificial Intelligence*, 27:97–109.

Imre Lakatos (1976). *Proofs and Refutations: The Logic of Mathematical Discovery*. Cambridge.

P. J. Landin (1966). The next 700 programming languages. *Communications of the ACM*, 9:157–166.

John McCarthy, Paul W. Abrahams, Daniel J. Edwards, Timothy P. Hart & Michael I. Levin (1962). *LISP 1.5 Programmer's Manual*. MIT Press.

Harlan D. Mills & Richard C. Linger (1986). Data structured programming: Program design without arrays and pointers. *IEEE Transactions on Software Engineering*, SE-12:192–197.

Robin Milner & Mads Tofte (1991). *Commentary on Standard ML*. MIT Press.

Robin Milner, Mads Tofte & Robert Harper (1990). *The Definition of Standard ML*. MIT Press.

Richard A. O'Keefe (1982). A smooth applicative merge sort. Research paper 182, Department of Artificial Intelligence, University of Edinburgh.

D. C. Oppen (1980). Pretty printing. *ACM Transactions on Programming Languages and Systems*, 2:465–483.

Stephen K. Park & Keith W. Miller (1988). Random number generators: good ones are hard to find. *Communications of the ACM*, 31:1192–1201.

Lawrence C. Paulson (1983). A higher-order implementation of rewriting. *Science of Computer Programming*, 3:119–149.

Lawrence C. Paulson (1987). *Logic and Computation: Interactive proof with Cambridge LCF*. Cambridge.

Lawrence C. Paulson (1990). Isabelle: The next 700 theorem provers. In P. Odifreddi, editor, *Logic and Computer Science*, 361–386. Academic Press.

F. J. Pelletier (1986). Seventy-five problems for testing automatic theorem provers. *Journal of Automated Reasoning*, 2:191–216. Errata, JAR 4 (1988), 236–236.

Chris Reade (1989). *Elements of Functional Programming*. Addison-Wesley.

Steve Reeves & Michael Clarke (1990). *Logic for Computer Science*. Addison-Wesley.

Elaine Rich (1983). *Artificial Intelligence*. McGraw-Hill.

Peter Ružička & Igor Prívara (1988). An almost linear Robinson unification algorithm. In M. P. Chytil, L. Janiga & V. Koubeck, editors, *Mathematical Foundations of Computer Science*, pages 501–511. Springer LNCS 324.

David A. Schmidt (1986). *Denotational Semantics: a Methodology for Language Development*. Allyn and Bacon.

Robert Sedgewick (1988). *Algorithms*. Addison-Wesley, 2nd edition.

Patrick Suppes (1972). *Axiomatic Set Theory*. Dover.

Mads Tofte (1990). Type inference for polymorphic references. *Information and Computation*, 89:1–34.

David Turner (1986). An overview of Miranda. *ACM SIGPLAN Notices*, 21:156–166.

David Turner (1979). A new implementation technique for applicative languages. *Software—Practice and Experience*, 9:31–49.

Larry Wos, Ross Overbeek, Ewing Lusk & Jim Boyle (1984). *Automated Reasoning: Introduction and Applications*. Prentice-Hall.

STANDARD ML SYNTAX CHARTS

PROGRAMS AND MODULES

Program

Top level Declaration

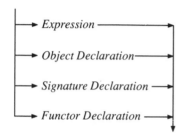

Object Declaration

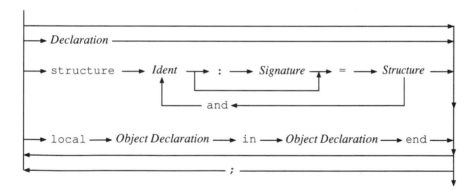

Signature Declaration

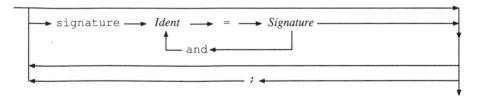

Functor Declaration

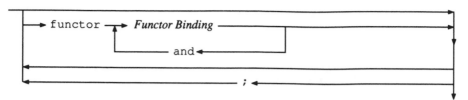

Functor Binding

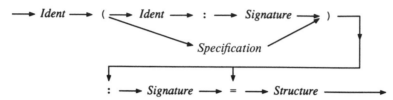

Structure

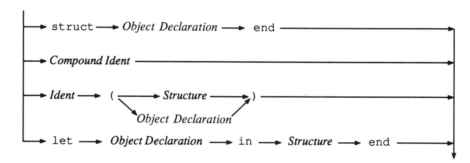

Signature

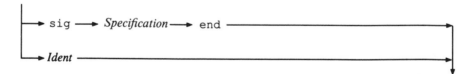

Specification

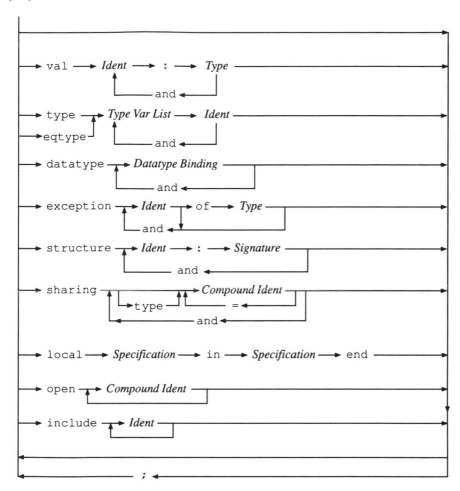

DECLARATIONS

Declaration

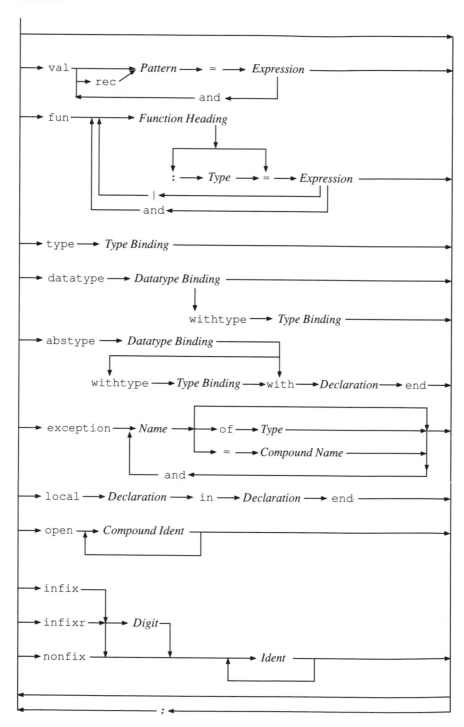

Function Heading

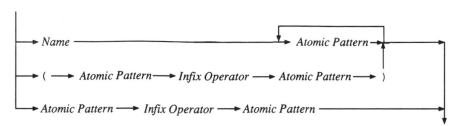

Type Binding

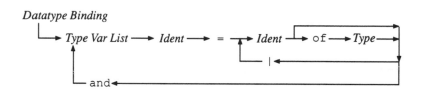

Datatype Binding

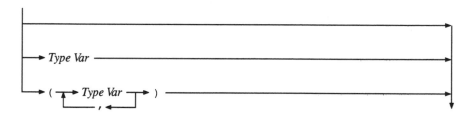

Type Var List

EXPRESSIONS

Expression

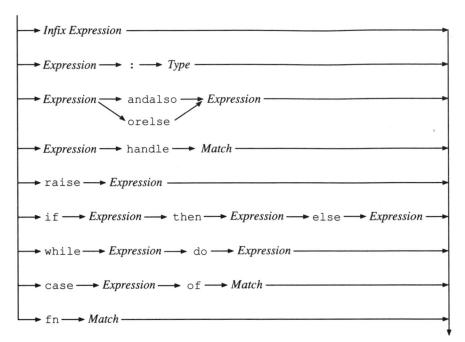

Infix Expression

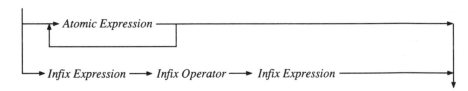

Atomic Expression

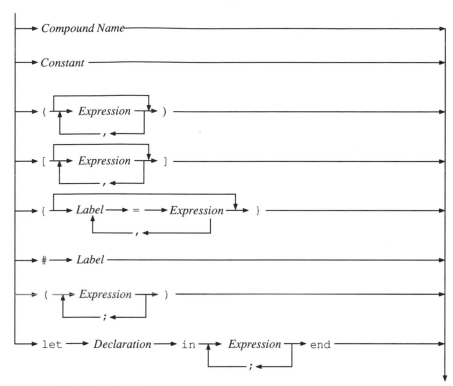

MATCHES AND PATTERNS

Match

Pattern

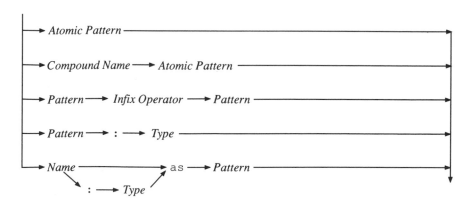

Atomic Pattern

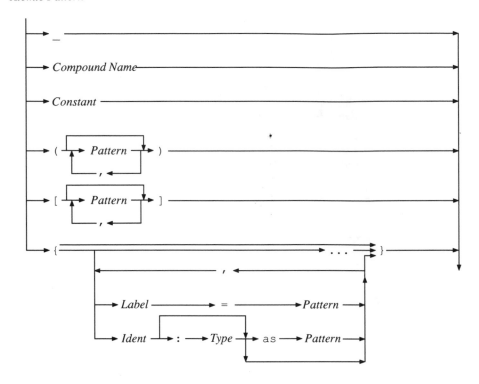

TYPES

Type

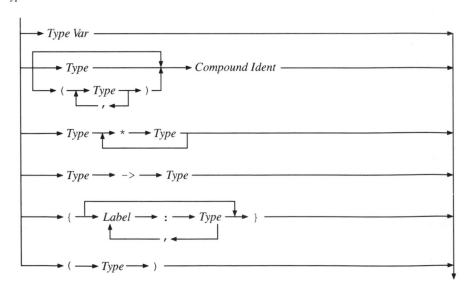

LEXICAL MATTERS: IDENTIFIERS, CONSTANTS, COMMENTS

Compound Ident

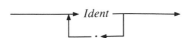

Compound Name

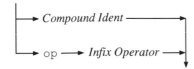

Name

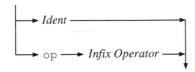

Infix Operator

any *Ident* that has been declared to be infix

Constant

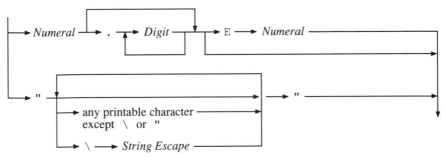

String Escape

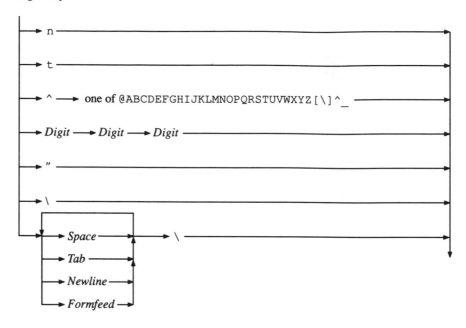

Numeral

Type Var

Ident

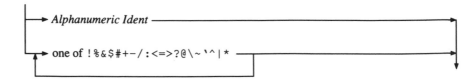

Label

Alphanumeric Ident

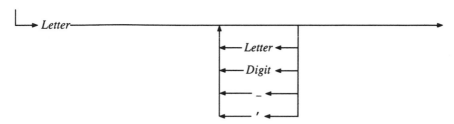

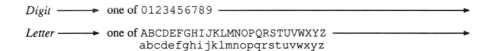

Digit ⟶ one of 0123456789

Letter ⟶ one of ABCDEFGHIJKLMNOPQRSTUVWXYZ
abcdefghijklmnopqrstuvwxyz

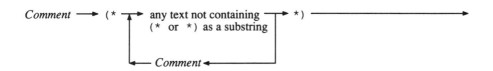

INDEX

PREDEFINED IDENTIFIERS

type *bool*		**Truth values**
true false	: *bool*	
not	: *bool -> bool*	
= <>	: *"a * "a -> bool*	equality test

type *int* **and** *real*		**Numbers**
+ - * : *int * int -> int* **or** *real * real -> real*		addition, subtraction, multiplication
~ : *int -> int* **or** *real -> real*		unary minus
abs : *int -> int* **or** *real -> real*		absolute value
/ : *real * real -> real*		real division
div mod : *int * int -> int*		integer quotient and remainder
< > <= >= : *int * int -> bool* **or**		relations
*real * real -> bool*		
floor : *real -> int*		conversion to integer
real : *int -> real*		conversion to real
sqrt : *real -> real*		square root
sin cos arctan : *real -> real*		trigonometric functions
exp ln : *real -> real*		exponential and logarithm
exception *Neg Sum Diff Prod Quot*		errors in ~ + - * /
exception *Abs Div Mod Floor*		errors in *abs div mod floor*
exception *Sqrt Exp Ln*		errors in *sqrt exp ln*

type *string*		**Character strings**
^	: *string * string -> string*	concatenation of strings
size	: *string -> int*	number of characters in string
chr	: *int -> string*	make string from ASCII code
ord	: *string -> int*	ASCII code of first character
explode	: *string -> string list*	string to list of characters
implode	: *string list -> string*	join a list of strings
exception *Ord Chr*		string conversion errors

type *'a list*		**Lists**
nil	: *'a list*	the empty list
::	: *'a * 'a list -> 'a list*	list construction
@	: *'a list * 'a list -> 'a list*	concatenation of lists
rev	: *'a list -> 'a list*	list reversal
map	: *('a -> 'b) -> 'a list -> 'b list*	apply function to all list elements
o	: *('b -> 'c) * ('a -> 'b) -> ('a -> 'c)*	composition of functions
type *unit*		**Type of empty tuple**
type *'a ref*		**References**
!	: *'a ref -> 'a*	get contents of a reference
ref	: *'_a -> '_a ref*	create a reference
:=	: *'a ref * 'a -> unit*	assignment to reference
type *instream*		**Input streams**
std_in	: *instream*	for input from the terminal
open_in	: *string -> instream*	open a file for input
close_in	: *instream -> unit*	terminate an input stream
input	: *instream * int -> string*	read characters from input
lookahead	: *instream -> string*	inspect waiting characters
end_of_stream	: *instream -> bool*	test if input has finished
type *outstream*		**Output streams**
std_out	: *outstream*	for output to the terminal
open_out	: *string -> outstream*	open a file for output
close_out	: *outstream -> unit*	terminate an output stream
output	: *outstream * string -> unit*	write characters to output
exception *Io* **of** *string*		errors during input/output
type *exn*		**Exceptions**
exception *Match*		no matching pattern
exception *Bind*		no match in **val** declaration
exception *Interrupt*		interrupt key pressed

Precedence of infixes (all but :: associate to the left)

7	/ * *div mod*
6	+ - ^
5	:: @
4	= <> < > <= >=
3	:= *o*